A COMPANION TO WILLIAM WORDSWORTH

A COMPANION TO WILLIAM WORDSWORTH

VOLUME I

Sunil Kumar Sarker

ATLANTIC

PUBLISHERS & DISTRIBUTORS (P) LTD

Published by

ATLANTIC

PUBLISHERS & DISTRIBUTORS (P) LTD

7/22, Ansari Road, Darya Ganj, New Delhi-110002
Phones : +91-11-40775252, 40775214, 23273880, 23275880
Fax: +91-11-23285873
Web: www.atlanticbooks.com
E-mail: orders@atlanticbooks.com

Printed & bound in India by Atlantic Print Services

To the very loving memory of
my dear dear father,
(late) Sudhir Chandra Sarker,
I dedicate this book.

Preface

The Romantic period of the history of English literature has always been of special interest, particularly because during this period poetry assumed some very distinctive features, the most important of these being predominance of emotion. Wordsworth and Coleridge—but, especially, Wordsworth—were instrumental, by virtue of their *Lyrical Ballads,* in the launching of the Romantic movement in English literature, and so any knowledge of the English Romantic poetry will remain incomplete without an understanding of the poetry, and of the theory of poetry, of Wordsworth. Being interested in the English Romantic poetry, I, therefore, began to read and try to understand Wordsworth's poetry, and this book is the result of my study. While I was reading Wordsworth's poetry with all attention, the revelation came to me that Wordsworth's poetry is only seemingly simple, and that underneath the simplicity, there happens to be great complexity. I say complexity, because, though garbed in very simple terms, the messages of Wordsworth's poetry cannot be so easily followed—because his poetry cannot be understood only with the help of the head, but it also needs the sympathetic cooperation of the heart: the head and the heart must go together—an *oeuvre* we are not generally used to while reading Wordsworth's poetry. Again, I was persuaded by Wordsworth to believe that poetry generates out of our passive and pure sensibilities and white-hot *esemplastic* power of imagination, and that poetry needs no special diction. Further, as I was reading, all at the same time, the opinions of a good number of critics about Wordsworth's poetry, I was taking down notes of those opinions. This book came into being from my reading of Wordsworth's poetry, as told before, as well as from my taking down those notes. I have included those notes in this book, and, certainly, I have not failed to cite credits to those critics wherever I have quoted from them.

I wanted to make this book as much comprehensive as possible, and with that end in view I have discussed about most of the distinctive aspects of Wordsworth—as a poet, as poetic theorist, a philosopher, a great lover of nature, a critic, and as a humanist. In the three appendices of this book I have included the three most important texts of Wordsworth's three critical prose works: *Preface* to *Lyrical Ballads* (1802), *Essay on Poetic Diction* (1802) and *Essay Supplementary to the Preface* (1815); and this I have done in order to make them easily available to the reader for his frequent perusals, if necessary, while reading Wordsworth's poetry, and for his considering the opinions of the critics cited. Pedantry I have consciously avoided, and so this has been a simple book.

The major portion of this book was typed by my wife Smt. Manju Sarker, and so I am thankful to her. The constant enthusiasm of my two sons—Suman and Sutanu—has given me the much-needed extra-energy to bring this book to its completion, and so they doubly deserve my affection. Lastly, I express my gratefulness to Dr. K.R. Gupta of the Atlantic Publishers and Distributors, New Delhi, without whose sympathetic attitude towards me my manuscript could not come out to show itself in the shape of a book.

SUNIL KUMAR SARKER

CONTENTS

VOLUME 1

PART 1

PART 2

PART 3

PART 4

PART 5

VOLUME 2

PART 5 (*Contd.*)

PART 6

PART 7

PART 8

PART 1

1

LIFE AND WORKS

William Wordsworth, the harbinger and high priest of the English Romantic movement, the poet who realised the mysterious presence of spirituality in Nature and worshipped Nature for the reason of that, the poet who wrote the greatest number of the most infatuating lyrics of the English language, the poet than whom no other English poet could write more voluminously, the poet whose personal life was an exemplum of his philosophical and spiritual ideals and of his poetic sensibilities and imagination, the poet who could very truly capture the spirit of his age, and the poet who has "profoundly influenced modern attitudes and sensibilities" (Ousby, 486) was born and brought up in the Lake District in the Northern part of England. William Wordsworth was born to John and Anne Wordsworth on 7th April 1770, at Cockermouth, Cumberland. John Wordsworth was attorney to Sir James Lowther (later Earl of Lonsdale). Anne was the only daughter of William Cookson, mercer of Penrith, and Dorothy (perhaps William Wordsworth's only sister Dorothy was named after this Dorothy). De Quincey writes about the birth and parentage of William Wordsworth: "William Wordsworth was born at Cockermouth, a small town of Cumberland, lying about a dozen miles to the North-West of Keswick, on the high road from that town to Whitehaven. His father was a solicitor, and acted as an agent for that Lord Lonsdale, the immediate predecessor of the present, who is not unfrequently described by those who still remember him, as 'the bad Lord Lonsdale'" (De Quincey, 111). Our Wordsworth (William Wordsworth) was the third of the five issues of his parents. Wordsworth lost his mother when he was around eight, and his father when he was around thirteen. Wordsworth affectionately recalls the memory of his mother, long afterwards, in *The Prelude* (v. 269-71):

> that He
> Who fills the mother's breast with innocent milk,
> Doth also for our nobler parts provide,....

After his father's death in 1783, Wordsworth and his brothers and sister (Dorothy) came under the guardianship of his father's brother Richard and his mother's uncle Christopher Crackanthorp, Wordsworth staying with his uncle and Dorothy spending childhood with various relatives. Wordsworth's uncle stipulated that Wordsworth would prepare himself for a career in the church. However, Wordsworth and his brothers and sister soon fell into hardship. After the death of Wordsworth's father, John Wordsworth, Sir Lowther failed to pay to Wordsworth's uncle the dues to the deceased John Wordsworth, and consequently, the five orphans (Wordsworth, his three brothers, and sister) were constrained to live very modestly. The new arrangement for the living of these five orphans at different houses of relatives led to the separation of Wordsworth from Dorothy who was younger to him by only one and a half year and who was the most loved object of his, and this caused much grief to the young Wordsworth.

In course of time Wordsworth was sent to the primary school, at Cockermouth and at Penrith, one after the other. After the completion of his primary education in 1779, Wordsworth was sent to the grammar school at Hawkshead, a village, where he remained for eight years in the lodging in the cottage of Ann Tyson, an old dame, till 1787. The living there was far from luxurious, and yet Wordsworth, along with other boys, could partake of the feast of life, with the spirit of unimpeded liberty. During his school life, Wordsworth was not as serious in the academic curriculum as expected, but rather kept himself buried in such extra-curricular great literary works as *Tom Jones, Don Quixote, Gil Blas, Gulliver's Travels, A Tale of the Tub,* etc. An usher of the school at Hawkshead, Shaw by name, taught him some Latin. What other literary pieces Wordsworth produced during his school days we do not know, but this we know that in the last year of his career at school, *i.e.,* in 1787, he wrote a sonnet, 'On Seeing Miss Helen Maria Williams Weep at a Tale of Distress,' which was published in the same year in *The European Magazine* for March. Wordsworth signed the poem as 'Axiologus' (Ousby, 1023) which is perhaps the only pseudonym of Wordsworth. But perhaps this sonnet was not his maiden publication, and he wrote some other short poems, some of which were also published. However, we have with us the following two poetic fragments, that Wordsworth wrote during his school life, a reading of which may convince us that the oak of the greatest nature-poet that Wordsworth had been was hidden in the acorn of his juvenile compositions.

FRAGMENT I

(COMPOSED: 1786. PUBLISHED: 1815)

Dear native regions, I foretell,
From what I feel at this farewell,
That, wheresoe'er my steps may tend,
And wheresoe'er my course shall end,
If in that hour a single tie
Survive of local sympathy,
My soul will cast the backward view,
The longing to look alone on you.

Thus while the Sun sinks down to rest
Far in the regions of the west,
Though to the vale no parting beam
Be given, not one memorial gleam,
A lingering light he fondly throws
On the dear hills where first he rose.

FRAGMENT II

(COMPOSED: 1786 (?). PUBLISHED IN *MORNING POST* ON 13th FEB. 1802)

Calm is all nature as a resting wheel.
The kine are couched upon the dewy grass;
The horse alone, seen dimly as I pass,
Is cropping audibly his later meal:
Dark is the ground; a slumber seems to steal
O'er vale, and mountain, and the searless sky.
Now, in this blank of things, a harmony,
Home-felt, and home-created, comes to heal
That grief for which the senses still supply
Fresh food; for only then, when memory

Is hushed, am I at rest. My friends! restrain
Those busy cares that would allay my pain;
Oh! leave me to myself, nor let me feel
The officious touch that makes me droop again.

In the school at Hawkshead, though not a very serious student, Wordsworth received a sound education. In his school days he was of irascible nature—very moody and mercurial. He would often fly into an hystrionic rage had any of his strong emotions been baulked. Once, when he was staying in the house of his maternal grandfather, at Penrith, having been slighted, he ran into the attic to kill himself, with a foil that was there. He took the foil with that intention, but his nerves failed. Wordsworth's love of nature began in his very early years. We may know more of the early life of Wordsworth from his *Autobiographical Memoranda* which he has left for us for a glimpse of his life in his school days. However, Wordsworth's uncles could correctly and early discern signs of genius in two of the five issues of their deceased brother John Wordsworth—William and Christopher—and, accordingly, sent these two nephews, for further studies, to Cambridge.

Wordsworth went to St. John's College, Cambridge, in October, 1787. Here he found an atmosphere quite defferent from that of Hawkshead. At Hawkshead he enjoyed freedom in the lap of nature, and there he found everything full of life and verve, but at Cambridge everything seemed to him mechanical. In Cambridge, he felt curriculum-burdened, and the atmosphere of Cambridge seemed to him uninspiring, because it was intellectually sophisticated. Consequently, he kept himself the more engaged in extra-curricular studies. Curiously enough, while at Cambridge, he found himself very much drawn to the study of geometry, and this interest in geometry, though he could not continue the study of it afterwards, he carried with him till very old age. He is recorded to have said that geometry is like poetry, in that like poetry it also possesses some sort of truth. At Cambridge, he found only two chances of enjoying freedom: in the summer and winter of 1790, he went on a walking tour over Germany, Switzerland and France along with his teacher, the Rev. Robert Jones, Fellow of St. John's College, Cambridge. During his walking tours, among the Alps, Wordsworth took some sketches of the natural beauties of certain regions, and basing on these sketches he composed *Descriptive Sketches* in 1791-92. Before *Descriptive Sketches,* Wordsworth wrote such poems as *An Evening Walk* (written in 1787-89; published in 1793), *Lines Written While Sailing in a Boat at Evening* (written in 1789; published in 1798), and *Remembrance of Collins* (written in 1789; published in 1798). *Descriptive Sketches* was dedicated to Wordsworth's teacher, the Rev. Robert Jones. In the Dedication, Wordsworth writes to Jones: "With still greater propriety I might have inscribed to you a description of some of the features of your native mountains, through which we have wandered together, in the same manner, with so much pleasure." In this poem also the young Wordsworth has demonstrated his fascination for, and deep love of nature. Notice, for an instance, the following few beginning lines of the poem:

> Were there, below, a spot of holy ground
> Where from distress a refuge might be found,
> And solitude prepare the soul of heaven;
> Sure, nature's God that spot to man had given
> Where falls the purple morning far and wide
> In flakes of light upon the mountain-side;
> Where with loud voice the power of water shakes
> The leafy wood, or sleeps in quiet lakes.

However, in January, 1791, Wordsworth took an ordinary B.A. degree, and left Cambridge for ever.

After Wordsworth left Cambridge, his uncles began to pressurise him to find a job, but he never had an inclination for any service and so failed to secure one. He rather chose the life of a vagrant, and first moved to London and then to France, and thus lived an itinerant life for about four years. He went to London in the spring of 1791, and there felt disgusted with the Londoners' vigorously busy life of mere accumulating and pleasure-seeking. There in the humdrum of London, he wandered lonely and aimlessly in the streets, for about four months. But his life in London was not absolutely fruitless, for there he wrote a few poems and sonnets of great worth.

London could not fetch him a job to live by, and so he sailed to France in November, 1791, with a view to learning French, to qualify himself for the job of a private tutor, either there or in London. In France, he moved to Paris, when the metropolis was seething in revolutionary fire. From Paris, he first went to Orleans and then to Blois. These two places are two bench-marks in Wordsworth's life. In Orleans he came in contact of, and struck a deep friendship with, Michel de Beaupuy, an aristrocrat and yet a staunch supporter of the French Revolution, who later became a general in the Republican army. Beaupuy infused into him the spirit of the Revolution—the spirit that he carried with him for long afterwards. Under the influence of Beaupuy, especially, Wordsworth became a supporter of the moderate Girondins. The Girondins were: "A group of deputies in the French Legislative Assembly of 1791 and subsequently in the Convention of 1792. Many of them (but not all) came from the region of the Gironde, around Bordeaux; their leaders were Brissot, Roland and his wife, Pétion, and Vergniaud. They tended to be more idealistic than their political rivals, the Jacobins (...); they who believed in a rational legal code and a predominantly middle-class state" (Palmer, 139). The Girondins fell in 1793, and almost all the prominent Girondins were soon executed. The Jacobins, the rivals of the Girondins, were: "The most radical group among the French revolutionaries 1790-94, particularly associated with Robespierre" (Palmer, 166-76). The term 'Jacobins' was derived from their club situated in the precinct where Dominican Monastery stood, and the Dominican monks were nicknamed 'Jacobins' because their original Paris home was dedicated to St. Jacques.

Blois is also an important place in the life of Wordsworth, for it was here that he, in 1791, fell in instantaneous love of Annette Vallon, the daughter of a surgeon. Annette gave birth to a daughter, Caroline, in December, 1792, and Wordsworth became an illegal father at 22. This laxity in his character—he being a staunch believer in the value of moral uprightness, from the very beginning to the very end of his life—gave Wordsworth a great cause for long pains, conscience-stricken as he was, that may be found in his poem *Vaudracour and Julia* (the poem made a part of *The Prelude* (Book IV) in its first version, but later the poet extrapolated it from *The Prelude* and published it as a separate poem):

> ...thou no longer canst be mine,
> I thine—the conscience-stricken must not woo

> The unruffled Innocent,—I see thy face,
> Behold thee, and my misery is complete!

But though the particular portion of *The Prelude* relating to Annette was taken out, *The Prelude* still bears witness to the poet's love of romantic amour in it:

> and here and there
> Slight shocks of young love-liking interspersed,
> Whose transient pleasure mounted to the head,
> And tingled through the veins.
>
> (BK IV. 316-19)

The memory of Annette Vallon may have influenced that part of Book Sixth of *The Excursion* where Wordsworth describes the utterly pathetic plight of the love-forsaken and lurched Ellen, with her child (lines 787-1052). The "rash betrayer," with whom Ellen fell in love, may be none else than the poet himself, for, really, he had neither the courage nor the qualm of conscience to "face the shame/or sorrow which his senseless guilt had caused" to Annette. It is said that Wordsworth wanted to marry Annette, but his deplorable financial condition of that time did not allow him to. However, in France he could find neither a job nor peace of mind, and so, being dejected, he returned to England in December, 1792.

The revolutionary zeal that he brought from France did not die soon. He read, and was much influenced by, the radical Thomas Paine's (1737-1809) *The Rights of Man* published in 1791-92. Paine wrote the book as a reply to Edmund Burke's *Reflection on the Revolution in France.* At this time, Wordsworth was infuriated by the Bishop of Llandaff's antirevolutionary sermon 'The Wisdom and Goodness of God in having made both Rich and Poor,' and wrote letter to the Bishop of Llandaff as a philippic reply to that sermon, but did not publish it.

The period from 1793 to 1795 was full of disappointments, disillusion and despair for Wordsworth, because, for one thing, he was suffering from extremely straitened financial condition. Secondly, he was more disillusioned when his wished-for victory of the French Revolution fizzled out and France was then seething and writhing under Jacobin terrorism and dictatorship. Thirdly, his affairs with Annette drowned him in deep moral depression. All these so much tortured his mind that at one point of time he suffered a nervous break-down. To add to his perplexity and agony, England declared war against France, against the country in which, even then, he had faith,—his beloved country which, he believed, was the only country that could show the whole of Europe the path of liberty, equality and fraternity. His national loyalty was now at stake: he wondered whether he should still remain loyal to his motherland or to France. For his political guidance, he eagerly read William Godwin's (1756-1836) *Enquiry Concerning Political Justice,* as then he could no more cleave to the political ideology of pain, but he found the dry-as-dust rationalism of *Enquiry Concerning Political Justice* too uninspiring, and so once again he found himself drowned in a perplexed gloom. Perhaps to shed off his glum, in the summer of 1793, he undertook another walking tour; this time from Salisbury to North Wales. It may be pointed out here that Wordsworth was very fond of walking, his fondness sometimes almost reaching the border of madness, and kept his habit of walking long distances till his very old age. He used to walk long distances almost everyday; and sometimes he would cover, along with a friend, such an enormous distance as forty miles in a single day. On the authority of none else but De Quincey we know that in the whole length of his long life Wordsworth walked from 175,000 to 180,000 English miles, in all (De Quincey, 100). In his 1793 tour, Wordsworth first went to Tintern Abbey. The most part of *Guilt and Sorrow* (or 'Incidents upon Salisbury Plain') was written during this tour (this portion of *Guilt and Sorrow* was later entered into *Lyrical Ballads* (of 1798) under the title *The Female Vagrant).* Wordsworth, probably, visited Paris once more in September and October, 1793, when he witnessed the guillotining of the Girondist Gorass. His revolutionary fire did not die down even at that time; rather, when he heard of the death of Robespierre, in 1794, he was wistfully expecting the coming in of the 'golden time' when, under the aegis of France, liberty, equality and fraternity would prevail all over Europe. But this hope of his soon got completely frustrated, when he, in 1798, found, to his utter bewilderment, that France herself despotically occupied Switzerland.

From 1795 to 1850 Wordsworth changed his residence four times: from 1795 to 1797 he was living at Racedown; from 1797 to 1798 at Alfoxden, from 1798 to 1799 in Germany, and from

December, 1799, till his death in 1850, he was permanently living with Dorothy in Grasmere, in the Lake District. From 1797 to 1850, Dorothy was his constant companion. When he was going through extreme financial constraint, Wordsworth thought of entering the profession of a journalist, but one, whose sensibilities and will are like those of a great poet, would not accept that profession. However, he soon came by a great windfall. Long before, Wordsworth made a close friendship with one Raisley Calvert. In January, 1795, this Calvert died leaving for Wordsworth a considerable legacy of 900 pounds, himself having no heir of his own. Helen Darbishire writes: "He [Wordsworth] seriously contemplated making a living by journalism, but he was saved from plunging into an uncongenial career by a legacy from his friend Raisley Calvert, who had had the discernment to see that this wayward, strong-willed young man with the passion for wandering, who defied his guardians and would settle to no profession, had something in him that was destined to be of benefit to mankind: he recognized in him the poet he was to become. Tributes in hard cash have a genuine ring. He left him £ 900, 'having hope',...." (Darbishire, 79). Wordsworth recalls this largesse from the large-hearted Raisley Calvert in *The Prelude.* However, with this money Wordsworth now could materialise his first dream of building a house for living with Dorothy who came back to him in 1794. But, before that Wordsworth and Dorothy took the charge of educating the little son of their widower friend Basil Montagu, and settled at Racedown in Dorset. Here Wordsworth wrote *The Ruined Cottage* and *Peter Bell: A Tale in Verse* (1798) and also his only play, in blank verse, *The Borderers: A Tragedy.*

Wordsworth and Dorothy next moved to a beautiful manor house at Alfoxden in Somerset. This change of residence was prompted by their warm and exciting friendship with S.T. Coleridge (1772-1834). Wordsworth chose Alfoxden because Coleridge had been living nearby, at Nether Stowey. Coleridge, along with his friend Robert Southey (1774-1843), and his publisher Joseph Cottle, probably first visited Wordsworth at Bristol in 1795. At their very first meeting, Coleridge struck a deep friendship with Wordsworth—the friendship that lasted till 1810. At that first meeting, Coleridge was astounded by the breadth of Wordsworth's imagination and by the sweetness of his lyricism.

At Alfoxden, Wordsworth proposed to Coleridge to jointly introduce a new genre of poetry into the history of English poetry, in which the familiar was to be translated into the unfamiliar, and the unfamiliar into the familiar. The former was the task of Wordsworth, and the latter of Coleridge. Wordsworth wrote 19 poems and Coleridge only four, and these 23 poems were published by Joseph Cottle under the title *Lyrical Ballads*. This publication was a landmark in the history of the Romantic movement in English literature.

Wordsworth's next residence, of course for a short period, was in the remote little town of Goslar, in Germany. After the publication of *Lyrical Ballads,* in 1798, the trio—William and Dorothy Wordsworths, and Coleridge—went to Germany, the Wordsworths principally for improving their knowledge of German, and Coleridge for receiving a first-hand knowledge of the German idealistic philosophies. But in February, 1799, Wordsworth wrote to Coleridge, who had been staying at a distance, that their effort of learning German was frustrated, due particularly to dearth of books, which was again due to the depletion of their burse. Consequently the Wordsworths returned home in May, 1799, leaving behind Coleridge who then went to the University of Gottingen. Though Wordsworth failed to improve his knowledge of German, while at Goslar, his journey to Germany was not all a failure, for it was at Goslar that he composed a good number of good poems, such as *Ruth, Nutting, The Poet's Epitaph,* and the 'enigmatic' (Ousby, 1024) 'Lucy' poems. But the most worthy literary work of Wordsworth, during his stay at Goslar, was his planning and part execution of *The Prelude.* However, Wordsworth and Dorothy remained in Germany from September 1798 to April 1799.

Returning to England, Wordsworth continued to stay in Grasmere, changing his residence thrice in same township, meantime marrying in 1802: from 1799 to 1808 he stayed at Dove Cottage; from 1808 to 1811 at Allan Bank; from 1811 to 1813 at Rectory; and from 1813 till death in 1850 at Rydal Mount. At Dove Cottage he found himself on the crest of his literary fame, and found a bevy of great literary persons, including Sir Walter Scott, Sir George Beaumont, and De Quincey who worshipped Wordsworth as his hero. In 1800, while at Dove Cottage, Wordsworth completed Book I of 'The Recluse.' During his Dove Cottage period, he also wrote a number of great poems that he included in the second edition of *Lyrical Ballads*, published in 1800. At Dove Cottage, he enjoyed literary fame, but his peace of mind was not all unalloyed, because during his stay at Dove Cottage he lost his sailor brother, and two of his children died in their infancy. He was also being vehemently attacked by reckless critics, for his new style and diction in poetry. Added to all these causes of his woes was his estrangement from his dearest friend Coleridge. The estrangement was completed in 1810, when Wordsworth was living at Allan Bank. A kind of reconciliation between the two friends took place in 1802, but the old and warm friendship did never return. However, here one happy event of Wordsworth's life may be noted, that of his Dove Cottage period: Wordsworth's first issue by Mary, named John, was born in 1803. But though during his Dove Cottage period he had causes for being happy, he being a famous poet, and a father, he also suffered a great mental crisis. C.M. Bowra writes: "In the spring of 1802 Wordsworth was the victim of an inner crisis. He was thirty-two years old and found that his inspiration [for writing poetry] was not what it had once been, that it did not work so readily or come in the same way as of old. That is no doubt a familiar enough experience among poets. But in Wordsworth's case the problem took a special form. He built his poetry on nature. It was the source of his creative strength and opened worlds of the imagination to him. It was, therefore, a matter of anxious concern when he realized that this source was in some ways drying up" (Bowra, 83).

In 1805, Wordsworth was perhaps the most grievously hurt: his first issue, John William, aged around two years, was drowned. F.W. Bateson writes: "John's drowning has been described by Selincourt as 'the most terrible blow either William or Dorothy had ever suffered.' For weeks their grief was uncontrollable. William cried like a baby" (Bateson, 172). Yet another great blow came to Wordsworth when, on June 5,1812, his second daughter, Catherine, died. The poignant grief of the poet at the death of catherine is obvious in his poem *Characteristics of a Child Three Years Old,* and in his sonnet *Surprised by joy—Impatient as the Wind,* about which sonnet Herbert C. Grierson and J.C. Smith write: "There is nothing in

English more poignant than the sonnet 'Surprised by joy, impatient as the wind'" (Grierson and Smith, 321).

However, after residing at Allan Bank and Rectory for five years, Wordsworth came to Rydal Mount. During those five years, he continuously poured out poems after poems, but his Rydal Mount period was not a highly literary one, compared certainly to his Dove Cottage period. And yet his Rydal Mount period was not literarily baren either. Here at Rydal Mount he published *The Excursion* in 1814, *The White Doe of Rylstone* in 1815, and *The Waggoner* and *Peter Bell* in 1819. In 1820, he published a batch of sonnets under the title *The River Duddon: A Series of Sonnets,* and in 1822 a volume of poems entitled *Memorials of a Tour on the Continent.* In 1835 Wordsworth's *Yarrow Revisited and Other Poems* was published, and in 1849-50 were published the final versions of his poems in six volumes, under the title *Poetical Works.* From all this, it should not be understood that during his Rydal Mount period Wordsworth produced no literary works, and that he only published the works he turned out earlier. In fact, he continued to write till he was physically incapable of writing anything.

In 1818 John Keats (1795-1821) came to visit Wordsworth, now a great and famous poet, with the expectation that he would see Wordsworth deeply immersed in his composition of verses. But to his utter dismay, Keats found Wordsworth busy campaigning for the Tory Lord Lonsdale in the general election. The revolutionary fervour of Wordsworth's youth, now in his well advanced age, took an about turn from 'cosmopolitan radicalism' to 'openly reactionary politics' and 'priestly patriotism' (Ousby, 1024). Though now almost an old man, Wordsworth did not lose his attraction for walking tour: in 1828, at the age of 58, he undertook an walking tour over Rhineland, with his daughter Dora, and his old friend Coleridge. In 1831, he stayed for a few days with Sir Walter Scott at Abbotsford. Wordsworth was now a most famous man (his fame came to him only in his late years, and that too very slowly), and was honoured by the University of Durham (1838) and the University of Oxford (1839). In 1843 he was made the Poet Laureate, on the death of Robert Southey, "'as a tribute of respect justly due to the first of living poets'" (Beach, 28). Wordsworth, in 1850, was an octogenerian, and in that year his health gave way, never to be restored. In April, 1850, he fell terminally ill, for a brief period, and breathed his last on 23rd April, the same year, and was buried in a churchyard at Grasmere. Long before, in 1799, Wordsworth wrote *A Poet's Epitaph.* Whether he wrote this poem for his own epitaph, we do not know; but, supposedly, he meant that. In the poem, he wishes away the statesman, the lawyer, the soldier, the moralist, and the intellectual, and invites the common man, the modest man, to his grave. Really, this is a very appropriate epitaph for Wordsworth:

> But who is He, with modest looks,
> And clad in homely russet brown?
> He murmurs near the running brooks
> A music sweeter than their own.
> ....
> —Come hither in thy hour of strength;
> Come, weak as is a breaking wave!
> Here stretch thy body at full length;
> Or build thy house upon this grave.

William Hazlitt, in his *Lectures on the English Poets and the Spirit of the Age,* writes about Wordsworth's personal features and manners: "Mr. Wordsworth, in his person, is above the middle size, with marked features, and an air somewhat stately and Quixotic. He reminds one of some of Holbain's heads, grave, saturnine, with a slight indication of sly humour, kept under by the manners of the age or by the pretensions of the person. He has a peculiar sweetness in his smile, and great depth and manliness and a rugged harmony, in the tones of his voice. His manner of reading his own poetry is particularly imposing; and in favourite passages his eye beams with preternatural lustre, and the meaning labours slowly up from his swelling breast.... His language may not be intelligible, but his manner is not to be mistaken. It is clear that he is either mad or inspired. In company, even in a téte-a-téte, Mr. Wordsworth is often silent, indolent, and reserved. If he is become verbose and oracular of late years, he was not so in his better days. He threw out a bold or an indifferent remark without either effort or pretension, and relapsed into musing again" (Hazlitt, 257-58). A.C. Bradley writes about Wordsworth's character, and about his composing verses: "He was from the beginning self-willed, and for a long time he appeared aimless.... He had a passion for wandering.... Sometimes he worked hard at his poetry, even heroically hard; but he did not work methodically, and often wrote nothing for weeks, but loafed and walked and enjoyed himself. He was not blind like Milton, but the act of writing was physically disagreeable to him, and he made his woman-kind write to his dictation. He would not conform to the rules, or attend to the dinner-bell, or go to the church (he made up for this neglect later)" (Bradley, 119-20). Bradley further writes: "If the poetic fit was on him he could attend to nothing else. He was passionately fond of his children, but, when the serious illness of one of them coincided with an onset of inspiration, it was impossible to rouse him to a sense of danger" (Bradley, 120).

The general impression about Wordsworth's nature is—and this impression is gathered from his commonest portraiture, and his poetry—that Wordsworth was of serene, suave and docile nature, and that he was generous, affable, social, and peaceful. But, Oliver Elton writes: "The tributes of his sister, and *Brougham Castle,* and many other things, show that Wordsworth was not soft, though he wrote of kittens and the little celandine, and that he was not naturally peaceful. His mother found him a 'stiff, moody, and violent' child. Carlyle judged the look of his face in old age to be 'not bland or benevolent,' but rather 'close, impregnable, and hard':

> A deep, earnest man, who had thought silently and painfully about many things...essentially cold, hard, silent, practical man, who if he had not fallen into poetry would have done effectual work of some sort in the world... 'A man of a softer mood, more sympathetic?' No, not at all, he was a man quite other than that; a man of an immense head and great jaws like a crocodile's, cast in a mould designed for prodigious work.

Of course Wordsworth was not cold, but he had a strong head and an iron programme, and he reined and bitted in his temper only too much, because he thought it his mission to be tranquil. He took public affairs, especially when they were grievous, with Miltonic intensity. In *The Recluse* he says that he is instructed by Nature to 'be mild and cleave to the gentle things,' and to do so without fear that his natural attributes,

> The longing, the contempt, the undaunted quest,

will thereby be enfeebled; they will only be transformed to finer uses. And this they really are" (Elton, 55). Oliver Elton's opinion about Wordsworth's personality agrees with De Quincey's. De Quincey writes about the poet: "I do not conceive that Wordsworth *could* have been an amiable boy; he was austere and unsocial, I have reason to think, in his habits; not generous; and not self-denying" (De Quincay, 121). Wordsworth, it is said, was wayward, but not harmfully so. A.C. Bradley writes: "Wordsworth's lawlessness was of the innocuous kind, but it is a superstition to suppose that he was a disgustingly well-regulated person" (Bradley, 120). W.L. Renwick agrees with Bradley, and says that Wordsworth was "a powerful, headstrong, unsophisticated young man, at a loose end among strangers..." (Renwick 141).

Wordsworth developed sort of inalienable morosity which had gerontological effect on his look: he seemed much older than he really was. "De Quincey tells a story of a fellow-passenger on the stage-coach appealing to the other passengers for a verdict on Wordsworth's age. 'You'll never see three-score, I'm of opinion.' And everybody agreed, De Quincey assures us, that Wordsworth was rather over than under sixty. This was in 1809, when he was really only thirty-eight or thirty-nine!" (Bateson, 171).

In his old age,Wordsworth enjoyed himself as a famous man, being proud of his greatness. Thomas Carlyle recalls his memories of Wordsworth: "During the last seven or ten years of his life, Wordsworth felt himself to be a recognized lion, in certain considerable London circles, and was in the habit of coming up to town with his wife for a month or two every season, to enjoy his quiet triumph and collect his bits of tribute *tales quales*" (Sutherland, 180). Queer enough—or, nay, this is not queer at all for a poet of nature—, Wordsworth could not bear with intense light; so much did he detested it that on particular occasions he used to carry with him candles for softer light. Thomas Carlyle writes: "The light was always afflictive to his eyes; he carried in his pocket something like a skeleton brass candle-stick, in which, setting it on the dinner-table, between him and the most afflictive or nearest of the chief lights, he touched a little spring, and there flirted out, at the top of his brass implement, a small vertical green circle which prettily enough threw his eyes into shade, and screened him from that sorrow" (Sutherland, 180). Wordsworth is said to have been used to wear quaint dresses; but, howbeit, in solemn occasions he also used to dress himself, and behave, most properly and with all dignity. Lady Chatterton Georgiana (1806-76), novelist and miscellaneous writer, recalls an occasion of her meeting with Wordsworth: "I got out of the carriage and was shown into the drawing room, where, to my surprise, I found him and dear old Wordsworth in court dresses, with swords and cocked hats dancing the *minuet de la cour.* Wordsworth said he was rehearsing his bows for the Queen's ball, and getting a lesson from Rogers about it." (Sutherland, 183), Georgiana has, indeed, given us an amusing information about Wordsworth!

Wordsworth, like most of the other great Romantic poets, was politically conscious, and believed in the three core political values: liberty, equality and fraternity. He was much influenced by the French Revolution and the political philosophy of Jean-Jacques Rousseau (1712-78) in understanding those three core political values. But before coming under the influence of Rousseau, Wordsworth held William Godwin (1756-1836), the father-in-law of Shelley, as his political *beau idéal.* Godwin's philosophy of 'rational individualism' could not continue to persuade Wordsworth for long, because, Wordsworth's frame of mind was not intellectual. So turning his back on Godwin in 1797 (he was an admirer of Godwinism from 1793 to 1797), he became a worshipper of Rousseau. Wordsworth being a lover of nature, Rousseau's *Emile* inspired him much. Rousseau published his *On the Origin of Inequality* in 1755, and his *The Social Contract* in 1762. In both the treatises, Rousseau upheld the original goodness of man in his original natural living condition, and argued that the misery of mankind was due to abusing the benefits of civilisation. Wordsworth was much attracted by such ideas, and this is evident at some places of *The Prelude.* Take, for an instance, the following lines of BK XIII of *The Prelude* (lines 87-100):

> Why this glorious creature to be found
> Only one in ten thousand? What one is,
> Why may not millions be? What bars are thrown
> By Nature in the way of such a hope?

Our animal appetites and daily wants,
Are these obstructions insurmountable?
If not, then others vanish into air.
"Inspect the basis of the social pile:
Enquire," said I, "how much of mental power
And genuine virtue they possess who live
By bodily toil, labour exceeding far
Their due proportion, under all the weight
Of that injustice which upon ourselves
Ourselves entail."

Wordsworth's natural love for man at first led him to derecognise national boundaries, and to think himself to be "a patriot of the world" (Griersin, 325), but, in actuality, he did never lose his sense of nationality; he never failed to love his motherland, England. Once he was enraged aganist England, when she sent her troops to France to help suppress the French Revolution that he thought to be rightful and humanitarian, but immediately afterwards, his love of his motherland calmed him down. True, he loved the world at large, but, to him, the centre of that world was but England. When England supplied men and arms to France, the poet felt mortally hurt "Britain put forth her freeborn strength in league,/ Oh, pity and shame! with those confederate Powers!" (*The Prelude*, X, 264-65). And yet he so gleefully writes about his happy, very happy, days in London, in BK VII of *The Prelude.* He was all praise for England, and wished that his motherland, whom he thought to be the most civilized, the most sane and rational, of all the countries of the world, teaches the whole of Europe what a nation should ideally be. In this sense, he was an extreme nationalist, but his nationalism was not autocephalic and chauvinistic. Grierson and Smith wrote: "Wordsworth's patriotism was not jingoistic, nor even imperialistic. He held that Britain, having kept herself free, should help other nations to freedom. Foreign conquest was a violation of a nation's personality, and to Wordsworth the personality of every nation was sacred. Thus he was the prophet of Nationalism, the first man to discern and comprehend the force that has moulded the destinies of Europe from that day to this. But his Nationalism, like his patriotism, was inaggressive, generous, and sane" (Grierson and Smith, 325-26).

Our knowledge of Wordsworth's belief in God is hazy. According to Helen Darbishire, Wordsworth was a 'believing Christian,' but for a brief period. Darbishire writes: "At no time of his life, except perhaps at the brief period of disillusion after his return from France in 1793, was Wordsworth other than a believing Christian" (Darbishire, 137). He was disillusioned by the atrocities and orgies let loose in France, under the eyes of God. He perhaps reasoned that in the creation of an all sympathetic God such things could not happen. But in cases of belief, reasons may change, and perhaps this happened in the case of Wordsworth's belief in God—his temporary disillusionment gave way to his belief in God. But Coleridge thought that Wordsworth was neither a believer nor a non-believer, and Coleridge may be right, for Wordsworth swung like a pendulum between theism and atheism. For instance, in 1790, in a letter to his sister, Wordsworth shows his belief in God: "'Among the awful scenes of the Alps, he writes, 'I had not a thought of man, or of a single created being: my whole soul was turned to him who produced the terrible majesty before me'" (Garrod, 50). But only two years afterwards, he was a changed soul: he could not hold his belief in God, being disillusioned by his horrific experiences in France, during the Revolution and its aftermath, and by the "panic dread of change" and injustices ("The weak were praised, rewarded, and advanced") in Britain (*The Excursion*. III, 827-28). However, H.W. Garrod writes: "After all, it was in 1796 that Coleridge spoke of Wordsworth as still 'at least a semi-atheist'" (Garrod, 51). However, Wordsworth's life, theologically considered, may be divided into two parts or phases: the atheist or sceptic phase or the phase in which he was hanging in a balance, and the phase in which he was a confirmed believer. The watershed between the two phases is the year 1818: before this year he was, so to say, a non-believer or a non-confirmed believer, but from this year on he showed a firm belief in God. H. W. Garrod writes of the year 1818: "By that data he [Wordsworth] reached a theistic position which the *Evening Voluntories,* as a whole reflect. Nature is no longer identified with God or the divine; but God is conceived in an external relation, as the creator of Nature; and our perception of Nature and its glory we owe, no longer to the senses, but to 'Grace,' 'reminds us of the light'" (Garrod, 122-22).

It may be added here that consequent upon his disillusionment with the goings-on in France and Britain, Wordsworth lost his faith in the truth of religion, and this led to his mental depression, a reference to which may be found in the third Book of *The Excursion*:

> "So, westward, tow'rd the unviolated woods
> I bent my way; and, roaming far and wide,
> Failed not to greet the merry Mocking-bird;
> And, while the melancholy Muccawis
> (The sportive bird's companion in the grove)
> Repeated o'er and o'er his plaintive cry,
> I sympathised at leisure with the sound;
> But that pure archetype of human greatness,
> I found him not."
>
> (lines 944-52)

Our confusion about Wordsworth's theology is due particularly to his deep love and adulation of nature. He sometimes behaves so respectfully with nature that it seems that to him nature was his God; sometimes, when he speaks of some sort of 'presences' in nature, it seems that to him these 'presences' were identical with God; and sometimes his poems present a pantheistic view. Again, he was so much concerned with the fallen condition and nature of man that he seems to be oblivious of the existence of God. All these are responsible for our misty view of Wordsworth's religion; but, perhaps, certain it is that since 1818 till his last, Wordsworth was a confirmed believer, though he did never air his changed view about God.

Wordsworth's doubt about, or belief in, God did never interfere in his conception and love of man and nature, or in his belief in the relation between man and nature, which was the single theme of all his poetry. But Shelley thought that Wordsworth was, principally, the poet of nature, though he also sang in praise of truth and liberty. Shelley once peeved Wordsworth for the latter's paucity of imagination, but the same Shelley, after Wordsworth's death, praised him in glorious terms, in his poem *To Wordsworth*:

> Poet of Nature, thou hast wept to know
> That things depart which never may return;
> Childhood and youth, friendship and love's first glow,

Have fled like sweet dreams, leaving thee to mourn.
These common woes I feel. One loss is mine,
Which thou too feel'st; yet I alone deplore.
Thou wert as a lone star, whose light did shine
On some frail bark in winter's midnight roar:
Thou hast like to a rock-built refuge stood
Above the blind and battling multitude:
In honoured poverty thy voice did weave
Songs consecrate to truth and liberty,—
Deserting these, thou leavest me to grieve,
Thus having been, that thou shouldst cease to be.

And, in April 1850, in his *Memorial Verses,* Matthew Arnold sings that on the death of Wordsworth, the "last poetic voice is dumb":

Goethe in Weimar sleeps, and Greece,
Long since, saw Byron's struggle cease.
But one such death remain'd to come.
The last poetic voice is dumb.

Besides Shelley and Arnold, Wordsworth has had a great number of other admirers. H.W. Garrod writes: "Emerson (also) was one of Wordsworth's earliest admirers, making two pilgrimages to Rydal Mount (in 1833 and 1848), of which he has left a brief record in *English Traits*" (Garrod, 18-19).

But, unfortunately, most of Wordsworth's own intellectual compatriots at first failed to take cognizance of Wordsworth as a great poet, and only slowly and belatedly compensated for their ignorance of him. Grierson and Smith write: "The British public took a long time to make up its mind whether the imposing appearance called Wordsworth was a mountain or a cloud: it was convinced at last that he was a mountain, the most massive in the lofty range which we call the Romantic Revival." (Grierson and Smith, 306). Today, not only Britain, but the whole world recognises Wordsworth as an imposing mountain. On the death of Wordsworth, his friend Coleridge cried for his personal loss: "O Friend! O Teacher! God's great gift to me!" and "O Friend! my Comforter! my Guide!" But Shelley, who once had derogatorily quipped at Wordsworth's boast for the immensity of the great function of the imaginative faculty by saying that he [Wordsworth] possessed the amount of imagination that could dwell on the head of a pin, and who mocked at Wordsworth's *Peter Bell* by writing his *Peter Bell the Third,* wept, on the demise of Wordsworth, not only for his personal loss, but also for the great loss to the 'blind and battling multitude.'

We read biographies of great men not to know so much about the special events of their lives, not to know so much about the nitty-gritty of their day-to-day lives, as to know as much as possible about the sorts of men that they really had been—about the quintessences of their personalities. But, then, of what sort of personality had Wordsworth been? Here, we cannot do better than quote, at some length, what A.C. George writes about Wordsworth's personality: "Externally, Wordsworth appeared to lack geniality and flexibility. His temperament was a little stiff, austere, a little pompous, and devoid of humour. From early boyhood he was self-centred and self-contained. The peculiar nature of his life and work—his isolation, his lonely introspective habits, his intense pre-occupation with his works all helped to deepen his self-absorption into an egotism. But this egotism was closely related to some of the most estimable qualities of the nature. This egotism set him apart from the rest of his contemporaries and he was not even able to appreciate the work of Scott and Southey.

But his character was strong and noble. A northern countryman to his backbone he had something of the hardness and the sterling virtues of the stock from which he sprang. His simplicity, his indifference to worldly honours and rewards, his steady devotion to art and his sense of mission are all admirable. His fortitude, self-control, the stability of his mind and his fine power of linking the ideal with the common places of everyday life are unique. Like his own sky lark he was the

> Type of the wise who soar, but never roam,
> True to the kindred points of Heaven and Home.

He set a shining example of plain living and high thinking. The same purity, lofty temper, and utter transparency of soul, are all reflected in his poetry also" (George, 165-66).

WORKS

Wordsworth was a voluminous writer, particularly in poetry, and wrote much more poetry than Coleridge or any of the other great Romantic poets. But he wrote much less prose than Coleridge did. Wordsworth wrote only one play, *The Borderers,* a tragedy in verse (composed 1795-96, published 1842). A rather exhaustive list of Wordsworth's poems, along with their dates of composition, is given by F.W. Bateson in Appendix II of his book *Wordsworth: A Re-interpretation* (Longmans, 1968).

We are giving below a short list of Wordsworth's principal poetic and prose works, following *Cassell's Encyclopaedia of Literature* (2 vols), edited by S.H. Steinberg, and published by The Standard Literature, Calcutta and London (1953), and *The New Encyclopaedia Britannica* (30 vols), 15th edition (1981).

Wordsworth's Poetical Works. *An Evening Walk and Descriptive Sketches* (1793); Lyrical Ballads *(with S.T. Coleridge, 1798); Poems* (2 vols,1807); *The Excursion* (1814); *Poems* (1815); *The White Doe of Rylstone* (1815); *Thanksgiving Ode, with Other Short Pieces* (1816); *Peter Bell* (1819); *The Waggoner, and Sonnets* (1819); *The River Duddon, Vaudracour and Julia,* etc. (1820); *Miscellaneous Poems* (4 vols, 1820); *Memorials of a Tour on the Continent,1820* (1822); *Ecclesiastical Sketches* (1822); *Yarrow Revisited and Other Poems* (1835); *The Sonnets of William Wordsworth* (1838); *Poems,* including *The Borderers* (1842); *The Prelude, or Growth of a Poet's Mind* (1850); and *The Recluse* (1st book, posthumous, 1888).

Wordsworth's Prose Works. *Preface to Lyrical Ballads* (1800); *Concerning the Relations of Great Britain, Spain and Portugal, to Each Other, and to the Common Enemy, at This Crisis, and Specifically as Affected by the Convention of Cintra* (1809)*; A Description of the Scenary of the Lakes in the North of England* (1810), written as the introduction to J. Wilkinson's *Select Views in Cumberland,* but later revised and published in 1822).

Wordsworth first published his poem, *Lines Written as a School Exercise,* in 1785, and he wrote his last poem, *Artegal and Elidura,* in 1815. During the long period of 30 years, between 1785 and 1815, he composed a very great amount of poetry, but during the long period of 35 years, since 1815 till his death in 1850, he did not write anything, perhaps because he could not.

PART 2

2

Twelve Select Poems of Wordsworth

(I) LINES COMPOSED A FEW MILES ABOVE TINTERN ABBEY, ON REVISITING THE BANKS OF THE WYE DURING A TOUR, JULY 13, 1798

According to H.W. Garrod, *Tintern Abbey* (or, *Lines Composed a Few Miles above Tintern Abbey, on Revisiting the Banks of the Wye During a Tour, July* 13, 1798) "is indeed Wordsworth's first essay in philosophic poetry" (Garrod, 107) which was followed by such other philosophic poems of his as *The Prelude, The Excursion,* etc. *Tintern Abbey* was the last poem of the 1798 edition of *Lyrical Ballads.* As we know, Wordsworth generally placed last, in a volume of poems, that poem which he valued the most, and so, from *Tintern Abbey's* being the last poem of the 1798 edition of *Lyrical Ballads,* we may deduce the conclusion that the poet valued this poem very much. But, in the 1800 edition of *Lyrical Ballads,* Wordsworth replaced *Tintern Abbey,* as the finishing poem of the volume, by *Michael,* though he retained it in that edition of *Lyrical Ballads.* About the composition of *Tintern Abbey,* Wordsworth himself wrote in July 1798: "No poem of mine was composed under circumstances more pleasant for me to remember than this. I began it upon leaving Tintern, after crossing the Wye, and concluded it just as I was entering Bristol in the evening, after a ramble of 4 or 5 days, with my sister. Not a line of it was altered, and not any part of it written down till I reached Bristol." (Wordsworth and Coleridge, 290). Not a line of the 159-line poem was altered, and not a part of the whole poem was written down for a considerably long while, but was kept in memory without cramming, and the whole poem was composed in the brief period of time that was necessary to cover the distance between Tintern and Bristol! A great feat, even for a poet, indeed! And, in all these regards, this poem may be compared with Coleridge's *Kubla Khan,* if we like. However, "De Selincourt quotes from a letter to the Rev. T.S. Howson from the Duke of Argyle written in September 1848: 'He [Wordsworth] told us he had written *Tintern Abbey* in 1798, taking four days to compose it, the last 20 lines or so being composed as he walked down the hill from Clifton to Bristol.'" (Wordsworth and Coleridge, 290).

(I) TINTERN ABBEY

Five years have past; five summers, with the length
Of five long winters! and again I hear
These waters, rolling from their mountain-springs
With a soft inland murmur.—Once again
Do I behold these steep and lofty cliffs,
That on a wild secluded scene impress
Thoughts of more deep seclusion; and connect
The landscape with the quiet of the sky.
The day is come when I again repose
Here, under this dark sycamore, and view
These plots of cottage-ground, these orchard-tufts,
Which at this season, with their unripe fruits,
Are clad in one green hue, and lose themselves
'Mid groves and copses. Once again I see
These hedge-rows, hardly hedge-rows, little lines
Of sportive wood run wild: these pastoral farms,
Green to the very door; and wreaths of smoke
Sent up, in silence, from among the trees!
With some uncertain notice, as might seem
Of vagrant dwellers in the houseless woods,
Or of some Hermit's cave, where by his fire
The Hermit sits alone.

These beauteous forms,
Through a long absence, have not been to me
As is a landscape to a blind man's eye:
But oft, in lonely rooms, and mid the din
Of towns and cities, I have owed to them,
In hours of weariness, sensations sweet,
Felt in the blood, and felt along the heart;
And passing even into my purer mind,
With tranquil restoration:— feelings too

Of unremembered pleasure: such, perhaps,
As have no slight or trivial influence
On that best portion of a good man's life,
His little, nameless, unremembered, acts
Of kindness and of love. Nor less, I trust,
To them I may have owed another gift,
Of aspect more sublime; that blessed mood,
In which the affections gently lead us on,—
Until, the breath of this corporeal frame
And even the motion of our human blood
Almost suspended, we are laid asleep
In body, and become a living soul:
While with an eye made quiet by the power
Of harmony, and the deep power of joy,
We see into the life of things.
                                        If this
Be but a vain belief, yet, oh! how oft—
In darkness and amid the many shapes
Of joyless daylight; when the fretful stir
Unprofitable, and the fever of the world,
Have hung upon the beatings of my heart—
How oft, in spirit, have I turned to thee,
O sylvan Wye! thou wanderer thro' the woods,
How often has my spirit turned to thee!

And now, with gleams of half-extinguished thought,
With many recognitions dim and faint,
And somewhat of a sad perplexity,
The picture of the mind revives again:
While here I stand, not only with the sense
Of present pleasure, but with pleasing thoughts
That in this moment there is life and food
For future years. And so I dare to hope,
Though changed, no doubt, from what I was when first
I came among these hills; when like a roe
I bounded o'er the mountains, by the sides
Of the deep rivers, and the lonely streams,
Wherever nature led: more like a man
Flying from something that he dreads than one
Who sought the thing he loved. For nature then
(The coarser pleasures of my boyish days,

And their glad animal movements all gone by)
To me was all in all.—I cannot paint
What then I was. The sounding cataract
Haunted me like a passion: the tall rock,
The mountain, and the deep and gloomy wood,
Their colours and their forms, were then to me
An appetite; a feeling and a love,
That had no need of a remoter charm,
By thought supplied, nor any interest
Unborrowed from the eye.—That time is past,
And all its aching joys are now no more,
And all its dizzy raptures. Not for this
Faint I, nor mourn nor murmur; other gifts
Have followed; for such loss, I would believe,
Abundant recompense. For I have learned
To look on nature, not as in the hour
Of thoughtless youth; but hearing oftentimes
The still, sad music of humanity,
Nor harsh nor grating, though of ample power
To chasten and subdue. And I have felt
A presence that disturbs me with the joy
Of elevated thoughts; a sense sublime
Of something far more deeply interfused,
Whose is the light of setting suns,
And the round ocean and the living air,
And the blue sky, and in the mind of man:
A motion and a spirit, that impels
All thinking things, all objects of all thought,
And rolls through all things. Therefore am I still
A lover of the meadows and the woods,
And mountains; and of all that we behold
From this green earth; of all the mighty world
Of eye, and ear,—both what they half create,
And what perceive; well pleased to recognise
In nature and the language of the sense
The anchor of my purest thoughts, the nurse,
The guide, the guardian of my heart, and soul
Of all my moral being.
                                                  Nor perchance,
If I were not thus taught, should I the more

Suffer my genial spirits to decay:
For thou art with me here upon the banks
Of this fair river; thou my dearest Friend,
My dear, dear Friend; and in thy voice I catch
The language of my former heart, and read
My former pleasures in the shooting lights
Of thy wild eyes. Oh! yet a little while
May I behold in thee what I was once,
My dear, dear Sister! and this prayer I make,
Knowing that Nature never did betray
The heart that loved her; 'tis her privilege,
Through all the years of this our life, to lead
From joy to joy: for she can so inform
The mind that is within us, so impress
With quietness and beauty, and so feed
With lofty thoughts, that neither evil tongues,
Rash judgments, nor the sneers of selfish men,
Nor greetings where no kindness is, nor all
The dreary intercourse of daily life,
Shall e'er prevail against us, or disturb
Our cheerful faith, that all which we behold
Is full of blessings. Therefore let the moon
Shine on thee in thy solitary walk;
And let the misty mountain-winds be free
To blow against thee: and, in after years,
When these wild ecstasies shall be matured
Into a sober pleasure; when thy mind
Shall be a mansion for all lovely forms,
Thy memory be as a dwelling place
For all sweet sounds and harmonies; oh! then,
If solitude, or fear, or pain, or grief,
Should be thy portion, with what healing thoughts
Of tender joy wilt thou remember me,
And these my my exhortations! Nor, perchance—
If I should be where I no more can hear
Thy voice, nor catch from thy wild eyes these gleams
Of past existence—wilt thou then forget
That on the banks of this delightful stream
We stood together; and that I, so long
A worshipper of Nature, hither came

Unwearied in that service: rather say
With warmer love—oh! with far deeper zeal
Of holier love. Nor wilt thou then forget
That after many wanderings, many years
Of absence, these steep woods and lofty cliffs,
And this green pastoral landscape, were to me
More dear, both for themselves and for thy sake!

In 1793, during a walking tour, the poet visited the Tintern Abbey and thc place, a few miles above Tintern Abbey, whose scenic beauty the poet is describing in this poem. Five years afterwards, to be precise, on 13th July, 1798, he has again come here from Bristol, along with Dorothy, and is again hearing the sound of the gushing out of the water of the mountain spring. He had been in the cacophonous city of Bristol where he felt lonely, secluded, ostracised, and therefore depressed, for there he could not find spiritual victuals for his soul. There in the 'de-natured' Bristol, he always thought about his seclusion, but now here in the wooded seclusion of the mountain, five miles above Tintern Abbey, he is being compelled by the surroundings to think more deeply about his secluded life ('more deep seclusion'). He is now meditating on the mutability and the transitoriness of the creation, and especially on his own existence, and so he is feeling the oppressive seclusion more intensely. He is thinking that he cannot eternally, perpetually, cleave to anything, and that he is an altogether separate being that must undergo mutability, and must have an end. In Bristol, he felt secluded within the narrow confine of his dwelling, but here he feels secluded within the broad surround of the mountain comprised between the rocky landscape below and the azure sky above. In the vastness of the jointure of the landscape and the sky, the poet feels himself to be a tiny speck, to be almost nullity, and this feeling compels him to philosophise upon existence, upon after-life, and upon the ontological truth of the spirituality of nature.

In the poem, the poet says that five years have passed by now, that is, five summers have gone away, and five winters, each one of them as long as the summers, have also passed, and after the lapse of these five years he has been hearing, once again, the music or sound of the waters 'rolling from their mountain-springs.' The sound of the 'rolling' waters of the spring or river is soft, and subdued, *i.e.*, the sound is confined within the conclave of the mountain ('inland'), and the sound of the waters is inarticulate ('murmur'). ('The river is not affected by the tides a few miles above Tintern.') After the lapse of five years, the poet is, once again, viewing the 'steep and lofty cliffs' of the mountain, which are compelling the poet to think over ('impress/Thoughts') 'more deep seclusion,' while he is remaining within this 'wild secluded scene' of the mountain. The 'steep and lofty cliffs' of the mountain are conjoining the landscape below and the peace or quietude of the sky above.

The poet, next, describes the beautiful green arboreal surround, while he is reclining ('repose'), on this day, as he was doing on another day five years ago ('The day is come'), against the dark-coloured or black maple or plane tree ('sycamore'). He is seeing plots of land where there are cottages ('plots of cottage-ground') and thickets of vines ('orchard-tufts') whose grapes are not yet ripe 'at this season' (in the month of July) and so the grapes are all still green ('clad in one green hue'). The profuse grapes are hanging among groves and coppices ('lose themselves/' 'mid groves and copses'). The poet is once again enjoying the sight of the sportive or swinging hedge-rows which, seen from a great distance, seem to be 'little lines'; and the rows of the hedges are swinging so much in the wind that they seem to be gone mad ('run wild'). The poet is delighted to see there the farm-houses in the pastoral surrounding—farm-houses whose yards are covered with green grass upto the very doors of the farm-houses. The poet is also delighted to see the coiling smoke rising noiselessly from the hearths that are there under huddling groves of trees. The poet does not perceive very clearly ('uncertain notice') where from the coiling smoke may be rising up, but presumes that it may be rising up from the dwelling places of some aimless itinerants ('vagrant dwellers') who have taken shelter in that wood where there are no houses. Or, says the poet, the coiling smoke may be rising from the fire, in some hermit's cave, beside which the hermit is sitting lonely.

Five years ago, the poet saw all these lovely things, *i.e.* the 'orchard-tufts', green grapes, dancing hedge-rows, coiling smoke, etc. ('beauteous forms'), but the long intervening period of five years, during which he could not see ('absence') all these things, has not been able to obliterate his memory of them, and so these things are not a nullity to him as is a painting of a landscape is to a blind man ("As is a landscape to a blind man's eye"). He would rather recall the memory of these beautiful scenarios, sitting lonely in a room, in the din and bustle 'Of towns and cities,' whenever he would feel bored ('weariness'). And recalling the memory of these beautiful scenarios or things, he would revive the pleasant sensation, that these things had given rise to, and that he actually realised, five years ago, and reviving the pleasant sensation he would feel their presence in his blood and in his heart. That pleasant sensation would travel even upto his transcendental or supra-mundane consciousness ('purer mind')—(which would have become jaded by the lowly commerce of the daily life, and by the cacophony of the towns and cities)—and would bestow upon his transcendental consciousness tranquility or peace and convalescence ('restoration') (and thus restored it to its true nature).

Along with that sweet sensation also would come to the poet feelings of other pleasures that he had enjoyed in the past but could not actually recall either the object from which he derived the pleasure or the nature of that pleasure itself (but yet could feel the pleasure) ('unremembered pleasure'). Such 'unremembered pleasure,' says the poet, has, perhaps, no 'slight or trivial influence' "On the best portion of a good man's life," but a great salutary influence on his life. Such 'unremembered pleasure' is got from past simple ('little'), forgotten ('unremembered') and indefinite or casual ('nameless') acts of kindness shown to some person, or from the love for some one. By the salutary influence of 'unremembered pleasure' on a good man's life the poet means the spiritual upliftment of a good man by 'unremembered pleasure.' And, the poet means to say that he got 'sensations sweet' and 'unremembered pleasure' from those beautiful scenarios five miles above Tintern Abbey, and so to those beautiful scenarios ('To them') he is greatly ('Nor less') indebted, and also ('I may have owed another gift') for his another benefit, that is, his spiritual upliftment which is more worthy or elevated ('sublime') than the other two benefits—'sensations sweet' and 'feelings' of 'unremembered pleasure.' And when one's soul is thus spiritually uplifted, one is in a 'blessed mood,' and in such a mood the oppressive or painfully burdensome obscurity of life ('mystery') and the greatly torturous or pounding and wearisome affairs or goings-on of human life ('the heavy and weary weight') of this abstruse ('unintelligible') world are removed or nearly removed ('lightened').

The mood, about which the poet is speaking, is calm and peaceful ('serene') and heavenly ('blessed'), and in such a mood our feelings ('affections') slowly ('gently') conduct us forward, until our stirring or living body ('the breath of this corporeal frame') becomes non-functional ('suspended'), and even the circulation of our blood ('the motion of our human blood') ceases ('suspended'), and our body becomes, as if, dead ("we are laid asleep/In body") and, contrarily, our soul becomes more active ('become a living soul'), *i.e.,* we become more spiritually inclined or elevted. And, further, in that mood, our perception or understanding becomes tranquil ('an eye made quiet') (*i.e.,* we understand things clearly) by our realisation of the prevailing harmony in nature or in the whole of the creation, and by the intense joy ('the deep power of joy') that we get in that mood. And then with our tranquil understanding and intense joy we become capable of probing into the essence or meaning of all the objects of the creation ("We see into the life of things").

The poet says that if this belief of his—that those 'sensations sweet' and 'feelings too/Of unremembered pleasure' lighten the 'burthen of the mystery' of 'this unintelligible world,' and lead him on to the uphill path of sublimity—proves false ('vain'), yet he is not frustrated, depressed. Because, whenever he had been in the spiritual vacuity ('darkness') of the city or whenever he felt a spiritual vacuity in his soul, and whenever he moved among joyless things ('shapes') in broad daylight of the city of Bristol, he frequently recalled his memory of ('I turned to thee') the 'hedge-rows,' the green 'orchard-tufts,' the 'groves and copses' in arboreal ('sylvan') surround of the river Wye, five miles above Tintern Abbey, to receive solace from the memory of them. And whenever he had been being pounded within himself ('hung upon the beatings of my heart') by the profitless or meaningless corroding or chafing ('fretful') commotion or hurry of the city life, he frequently recalled the memory of those things for consolation. The poet wonderfully recalls how frequently his soul ('spirit'), in those distressful situations, recalled the memory of Wye ('turned to thee!')—the river Wye that courses through woods.

And now, five years after his first visit to this spot, the poet has once again come to this place. The impressions of the scenarios of this place, that he took away five years ago, have become faint ('half-extinguished'), and he has now only gleams or bedimmed lights of those bright or glowing impressions in his mind. He can now recognise only dimly or faintly the objects he previously saw ('recognition's dim and faint'). And this makes him a little perplexed, because the objects now stand in the interface between recognition and non-recognition, and so he feels a little sad ("With many recognitions dim and faint,/And somewhat of a sad perplexity"). But the bedimmed memory of those delightful objects, that was there in his mind before his coming here, brightens up ('revives') once again. As the poet is standing amid those scenarios, he is being imbued not only with the pleasures of the present moment—derived from the present scenarios—but also with the thought that in these scenarios there is victuals for his body and mind (such as pleasures and thoughts for the mind and salubrious weather for the body) ('life and food') and that these thoughts will sustain him, or his body and mind, in future. And so he is courageously hoping that these things—the present pleasures from the scenarios, and his discovery that there is 'life and food' in the scenarios—will certainly sustain him in future, though he has certainly become changed (both bodily and mentally) from what he had been, five years ago, when he came to these hills. Young as he was then, he would be leaping and capering over the mountains or hills, or along the banks of ravines or 'lonely streams,' like a little deer ('roe'), wherever he would be attracted by particular beautiful objects of nature ('Wherever nature led'). He would caper or run along the bank as fast as one who rather runs away from ('Flying from') something he is afraid of ('dreads') than runs towards something he loves. Because then nature was everything or the most desirable thing ('all in all') to him, though now he is not that much interested in nature due to the fact that now the raw or unrefined ('coarser') pleasures in the sensualities of nature do not attract him, and, consequently, he does not merrily ('glad') engage himself in the pleasures of moving or running, like an animal (or like the little deer), across a waste of nature. ("The coarser pleasures of my boyish days,/ And their glad animal movements all gone by.")

The poet admits his inability to describe ('paint') what sort of person he then (five years ago) had been. Yet he knows that he was then passionately attracted by the murmuring waterfall ('sounding cataract'), the 'tall rock,' the mountain, and the deep and dark ('gloomy') forest. The colours and the forms of the trees of the forest were then very attractive ('appetite') to him. The colours and shapes or forms produced in him such a (pleasant) feeling that needed no sharpening or intensification by the addition of fancy ('remoter charm') created ('supplied') by thought—the fancy that is not perceived with interest by the eye ("interest/Unborrowed from the eye").

The poet says that those days, when he had enjoyed all these things, are now gone, and so are also gone the very intense ('aching') joys that he had had then as well as the giddy or extreme ('dizzy') delight or ecstasy ('rapture') that was produced in him by that intense joy. But the poet does not repent ('faint') for this his loss, nor does he mourn or babble ('murmur') in agony for this his loss, because he believes that he has been amply compensated for that loss ('Abundant recompense') by other enjoyable or pleasurable things ("other gifts/Have followed"). He has now learned to look at nature in a manner different from that of his young age, when he could not meditate ('thoughtless') on anything. And now he has been frequently hearing or experiencing the constant ('still') and painful ('sad') moaning ('music') of human beings, which is neither rough, cacophonous or jarring on the senses ('harsh') nor wearing or irritating ('grating'), but which has immense ('ample') power or strength to purify ('chasten') or to allay or quell his earlier animal thoughts and sensibilities. And now he has realised ('felt') the existence of some sort of spirit ('presence') in nature—spirit that agreeably excites him with joy ('disturbs me with the joy') of lofty ('elevated') thoughts. And then he is imbued with an elevated or lofty sense ('sense sublime') of something (not fully realised) which is inextricably related with nature or with the whole of the creation—the lofty sense whose symbol ('dwelling') may be thought to be the heavenly beauty of the dim and variegated light of the 'setting suns,' or the rotund ('round') (or limitless, because the brim of the vast ocean cannot be perceived) ocean, or the pure air of the upper sky ('living air'), or the vast expanse of the upper azure sky, or the pure or heavenly 'mind of man.' The poet calls that 'presence' 'A motion and a spirit' and says that it presides over and controls all conscious beings ('thinking things') as well as all objects of consciousness, and so it penetrates, and flows through, ('rolls') all the things of the world, both conscious and unconscious. True it is that the poet has now lost his former attraction toward the beauty—the sensual beauty—of nature, but yet, till now, he loves nature, not for anything else, but for the subsistence of that 'presence' (or spirit) in her. And, for this reason, *i.e.,* for the subsistence of that 'presence' in nature, he, even now, loves the meadows, the woods, the mountains, and all other things that he is at this moment perceiving from this particular spot of the verdurous ('green') earth. In short, even now he loves (for that reason) everything of the world that he can perceive with his eyes and ears, and is thereby greatly influenced ('mighty'). He loves not only what his eyes and ears perceive but also what they imagine or fancy (or, rather, what his consciousness imagines or fancies with the percepts that he receives through his eyes and ears) ("both what they half create,/and what perceive"). The poet is exulted to find or realise ('recognise') in nature as well as in his sense-perceptions ('the language of the sense') the roots or moorings of his elevated or sublime ('purest') thoughts (his lofty thoughts are grounded in his sense-perceptions of the beauty of nature). (The poet means to say that his elevated thoughts are not rootless and abstract, but they arise out of nature where the 'presence' or spirit perpetually prevails.) He says that this mooring, or this link between the sublime and the earthly, is the nourisher ('nurse'), the conductor or monitor ('guide'), the overseer or controller ('guardian') of his heart, and the central force ('soul') of his moral ideals ('moral being').

If the poet, by any chance ('perchance'), would not have learnt this new philosophy of nature ('If I were not thus taught'), his good or benevolent ('genial') spirit would have to face ('Suffer') the more tellingly ('the more') its own decaying. The poet confesses all this to his sister (Dorothy), whom he calls his 'dear Friend,' while they are remaining on the bank of the 'fair river' Wye. He tells her that, five years ago, when he visited this particular spot, he was as young as she (Dorothy) is now (in fact, Dorothy was younger to Wordsworth by only one year or two years, and so he is exaggerating the difference between their ages). However, the poet can recall and recognise what sort of passionate youth he had been five years ago ('The language of my former heart') when he hears the voice of Dorothy ('in thy voice I catch'), and can understand ('read') his 'former pleasures' in nature when he sees the darling flashes ('shooting lights') of her 'wild eyes', *i.e.*, when he sees her do merriment in nature. The poet longs ('Oh!') to have a glimpse ('a little while') of his younger self (his self five years ago) now in Dorothy (who was younger to him actually by two years). He appeals to her for this ('this prayer I make') because he knows that nature never betrays anyone who loves her (nature), *i.e.*, as nature is honest, she will produce in Dorothy the same effect that she (nature) produced in him five years ago, because Dorothy loves nature as much as he did ("Nature never did betray/The heart that loved her"). Nature has the power ('privilege') to conduct ('lead') one from joy to joy *i.e.*, nature has the power to give one joy after another continually throughout one's life. Nature can mould ('inform') our mind (or, rather re-mould our mind) by bestowing upon it ('impress') peace ('quietness') and goodness ('beauty'). Thus moulding or remoulding our mind, nature stuffs, or supplies, ('feed') our mind with elevated ('lofty') thoughts. And when our mind is so moulded, neither evil acrimony ('evil tongues'), nor impetuous and unjust comments of others ('Rash judgments'), nor cynical contempt's ('sneer') of selfish persons, nor perfunctory invitations or wishing good of men having no sympathy ('greetings where no kindness is'), nor the grey and monotonous ('dreary') daily business of the worldly life ('intercourse of daily life') will be powerful enough to control and influence us ('prevail against us'), or to change ('disturb') our happy belief ('cheerful faith') that whatever we see around us—all the objects of the creation, including nature—are full of goodness or full of the blessings of God ('blessings').

For this reason, the poet importunes the moon to shine on Dorothy ("let the moon/Shine on thee") when she will be walking lonely ('solitary walk'); and he importunes the winds over the mountain, that is full of mists, to freely blow against her (to give her pleasure, and make her happy and merry without having any anxiety about her future life), to make her ecstatically pleasant. The poet says that Dorothy, as she is young now, will ecstatically enjoy the sensuous beauty of nature, but in future ('in after years') she will mature, and then all her sensuous pleasures of nature will become mellowed, and she will then be able to enjoy the serene and quiet ('sober') pleasure of the nature ("When these wild ecstasies shall be matured/ Into a sober pleasure"). And then her mind will be a long record, or a great treasure-house, ('mansion') of all the beautiful impressions of nature ('all lovely forms'), and then her memory ('Thy memory') will be a record ('dwelling place') of 'sweet sounds and harmonies' that she will have gathered from nature.

The poet wonderfully ('oh!') and very earnestly urges ('these my exhortations') upon Dorothy to remember him, along with all the salubrious ('healing') thoughts about the mild or mellowed pleasures, associated with himself and with the particular spot of nature on which they are now remaining, if she, in future, when she will be what had been told earlier, suffers ('be thy portion') 'solitude, or fear, or pain, or grief.' The poet is aware that one day he will die, and then his soul will be transported to a certain place from where he will not be able to hear the voice of Dorothy, and will not be able to see ('catch') the bright beams of light ('gleams') in her much animated or darting ('wild') eyes—the voice and the beams which are present now to the poet, but will be gone in future, when he will die ('Of past existence'). The poet tells Dorothy that in the case of his death in future ('perchance'), she will not ('Nor') forget that one day (this present day) on the bank of this delightful rivulet Wye ('stream') they both stood together, and that the poet—who has so long been a worshipper of nature—came to this particular spot to serve nature continually, without ever being tired ('Unwearied') of serving nature, or, rather—the poet corrects himself—let her (Dorothy) know ('rather say') that he came to nature for his excessive ('warmer') love of her (nature), or, rather—the poet wonderfully once again corrects himself—he came to this spot of nature with the most enthusiastic ('far deeper zeal') and very sacred ('holier') love of nature. The poet further tells Dorothy that in the case of his death, she will also not forget ('Nor will thou then forget') the fact that, after his many aimless jauntings (in the crowded city of Bristol), and many days of his remaining away from nature ('absence'), these high-rise trees, these high-rise picks of the mountain ('lofty cliffs'), and this 'green pastoral landscape' were to him 'more dear' or more attractive because these things are intrinsically beautiful ('for themselves'), and, further because she (Dorothy) was present among these things when he was viewing them ('and for thy sake').

Tintern Abbey is one of the most important poems of Wordsworth, and, according to Graham Hough, it is "Wordsworth's greatest poetry"(Hough, 1983, 56), as *The Rime of the Ancient Mariner* and *Kubla Khan* are Coleridge's. Wordsworth himself thought it to be one of his greatest poems, at the least of all the poems of his in the 1800 edition of *Lyrical Ballads,* for, as we have earlier said, it was his peculiar habit to place the most important poem (particularly that one which carried in it the central theme or message of at the least most of the poems of a volume) at the end of a collection of poems (Garrod, 107), and *Tintern Abbey* was the last poem of the 1800 edition of *Lyrical Ballads.* In addition to allegedly bearing the central theme of *Lyrical Ballads, Tintern Abbey* contains the essential spiritual autobiography of the poet. Alan Gardiner writes: "The most intensely personal of the poems in the first *Lyrical Ballads* (the Lucy poems were in the second volume), 'Tintern Abbey' heralded a new preoccupation with the poet's inner life. It is the first major work to be explicitly autobiographical and thus begins a sequence of great poems that culminates in '*The Prelude*'. It expresses some of Wordsworth's central ideas about nature, perception, spiritual growth" (Gardiner, 53). According to H.W. Garrod, *Tintern Abbey* is "Wordsworth's first essay in philosophic poetry" (Garrod, 107). Garrod further writes about *Tintern Abbey*: "The poem is the crown and coping stone of the *Lyrical Ballads,* and it may still perhaps be regarded as containing more of the pure gospel of Wordsworth than anything else which he wrote" (Garrod, 107-8). And Helen Darbishire writes about the poem: "'This is the first poem in which Wordsworth's genius find full expression: the blank verse, low-toned and familiar, yet impassioned, moves with a sureness and inevitable ease from phase to phase of his mood. It has the quiet pulse, suggesting "central peace" which is felt under all his great poetry'" (Wordsworth and Coleridge, 291). According to Arthur

Compton Rickett, *Tintern Abbey* is a document of Wordsworth's idealistic or transcendental philosophy that the whole of the creation is spiritual in nature. Rickett writes about the poem: "The matter of the universe was for Wordsworth merely the vesture of a great spiritual power interpenetrating Nature; *a rock,* a flower, a sunset, a mountain torrent, the beauty of a girl, were for him varying manifestations of this unifying principle. This is the underlying thought of *Tintern Abbey*" (Rickett, 138).

Herbert Lindenberger calls *Tintern Abbey* a 'satellite-poem' of *The Prelude* (Williams, 143), and very rightly, because *Tintern Abbey* breathes the same spirit, the same core philosophy, and the same experience, though within a brief space, that are available there in *The Prelude.* This similitude between *Tintern Abbey* and *The Prelude is also* noticed by H.W. Garrod: "in a passage of the *Prelude,* he [Wordsworth] tells us that, even in the visionary experiences of his childhood 'an auxiliar might come from his mind' bestowing 'new splendour' on the forms of Nature (ii. 359-70). This 'auxiliar might' he calls 'creative sensibility' (ii. 360); and in *Tintern Abbey,*...he speaks of the 'mighty world' which 'eye and ear' half create and half perceive" (Garrod, 131). Again, writes Garrod: "in the sixth book of the *Prelude* (599-602), he [Wordsworth] finds the characteristic of the highest sense perception to be that, in the very act itself of seeing,

the light of sense
Goes out, but with a flash that has revealed
The invisible world.

Similarly, in the Tintern poem, he tells us that in the deeper moods of contemplation, though we use the bodily senses, yet there is *a* serene and exalted condition of sensuous apprehension wherein.

we are laid asleep
In body, and become a living soul (45-6)."

(Garrod, 110)

Geoffrey Durrant has found some distinguishing marks of *Tintern Abbey*: "These lines [*Tintern Abbey*], unlike most of the poems in the volume [*i.e., Lyrical Ballads,* 1798], present no story, and are spoken not through a narrator, but directly by the poet as the expression of his own thought and feeling. We tend to think of the mode of personal confession as characteristic of

Romantic poets, so it is as well to remember that at this stage of Wordsworth's career a poem of this kind was the exception, not the rule. Just as the ballads in the volume [*i.e., Lyrical Ballads,* 1798] are linked with an older tradition, 'Tintern Abbey' is itself a development of the continuing eighteenth-century tradition, chiefly represented by Thompson and Cowper, of the meditative observation of the countryside" (Durrant, 34).

As we have said, *Tintern Abbey* is an autobiographical poem, though it presents us with only a scant knowledge of the poet's personal life—his love of nature; his perception or realisation of the presence of spirit in nature; his animal pleasure in the lap of nature, during his young age; and his love of his sister Dorothy. But the poem is autobiographical not so much for all these as for the fact that it shows us the inner structure of the poet's mind as amply displayed. The poem gives us an estimation of the philosophical dimension of the poet's mind: it shows us how ineluctably the poet's mind is connected with nature, or, rather, with the whole of the creation, and it shows us how the spirit of nature, or, of the universe, converses with him, or how that spirit instructs him about the 'still, sad music of humanity.' R.O.C. Winkler, in his essay 'Wordsworth's Poetry,' in vol. 5 of *The Pelican Guide to English Literature,* writes in this regard: "*Tintern Abbey* forms a kind of bridge which links the purely autobiographical poems with those that concern themselves with the 'still, sad music of humanity' in a wider sense. 'Nature' is to embrace not only inanimate nature but (in the true eighteenth-century tradition) human nature also. The connection between the two he [Wordsworth] expresses in the lines that follow (...):

And I have felt
A presence that disturbs me with the joy
Of elevated thoughts; a sense sublime
Of something far more deeply interfused,
Whose dwelling is the light of setting suns,
And the round ocean and the living air,
And the blue sky, and in the mind of man:
A motion and a spirit, that impels
All thinking things, all objects of all thought,
And rolls through all things.

The dichotomy between the mental and material worlds which philosophers had increasingly taken for granted since the seventeenth century was to Wordsworth (as to Kant) wholly antipathetic and he frequently in his verse attempts a general statement of the basis of their unity. Nowhere does he so more impressively or more successfully than here [in *Tintern Abbey*]" (Ford, 168-69). David Daiches agrees with Winkler on the point that *Tintern Abbey* is spiritually autobiographical, and says that the poem is also confessional: "'Tintern Abbey' is really a different sort of poem.... There is a confessional element here, with the threads of the author's autobiography converging through his contemplation of a particular scene in the company of his sister...." (Daiches, 1996, 886).

Wordsworth is not only a philosophical poet, but also a moral poet, or, we may rather say that in his poetry he preaches a moral philosophy that, says he, we, all of us, can learn from the calm, serene and beautiful nature, once we succeed in developing within us an *Einfuhlung* (empathy) with her. Wordsworth tells us that we learn morality from nature, or, rather, that our moral sense can grow up only in the ambience of nature. However, Graham Hough writes about the moral teaching of nature, as we find in *Tintern Abbey*: "Wordsworth first [in *Tintern Abbey*] relates his moral doctrine: the memory of this beautiful scene [of *Tintern Abbey*] has been not only calming and restorative, but has aroused almost unnoticed sensations of pleasure, which have had their results in impulses of kindness and love. This seems truer and more adequate than saying that a wood in spring can teach you all about ethics" (Hough, 50).

The poetic achievement of Wordsworth, *a la* his own theory of poetry, is simply astonishing. In poetry Wordsworth wanted a 'union of deep feeling with profound thought,' and such a union requires great poetic power, and he has certainly shown his great poetic power in *Tintern Abbey*. "It is this [great poetic] power that makes the figure of the Leech-gatherer [*Resolution and Independence*] something more than a mere remembered old man, and Tintern Abbey something more than a remembered landscape. In both detached material reminiscences are made into new wholes under the pressure of a powerful impulse of feeling" (Hough, 82). The meditative mood of the poem is so deep that it may be compared with trance-like condition, or with mystic vision, in which one's rationality comes under the mercy of his profound emotion, and in which one sees beyond the bound of reality. This meditative mood of *Tintern Abbey* is the deepest in the following lines of it:

> the breathe of this corporeal frame
> And even the motion of our human blood
> Almost suspended, we are laid asleep
> In body, and become a living soul:
> While with an eye made quiet by the power
> Of harmony, and the deep power of joy,
> We see into the life of things.

Almost the same meditative mood may be found in Andrew Marvell's (1621-78) *The Garden*:

> Here at the fountain's sliding foot,
> Or at some fruit-tree's mossy root
> Casting the body's vest aside,
> My soul into the boughs does glide:
> There, like a bird, it sits and sings,
> Then whets and combs its silver wings,
> And, till prepared for longer flight,
> Waves in its plumes the various light.

The qualitatively improved meditative mood of the poet in *Tintern Abbey* is also noticed by David Daiches. Daiches further notices some other very attractive features of the poem: "'Tintern Abbey' is, of course, the star of 1798 volume [of *Lyrical Ballads*] and it shows how Wordsworth developed out of eighteenth century meditative verse a richer and more personal idiom appropriate to a poetry which linked reflection to sensation in a new and organic way. The poem is important in giving one of the most succinct of Wordsworth's accounts of the development of his attitude to nature—moving from the animal pleasure of childhood through adolescent passion for the wild and gloomy to adult awareness of the relation of our perception of the natural world—but its poetic interest lies in its brilliant combination of the lyric and the meditative, the exaltation of reminiscence into poetry through the proper handling of—to use Wordsworth's own phrase—relationship and love" (Daiches, 1996, 879).

G.W. Knight, in his *The Starlit Dome*, highly praises the

poem: "The one [*Tintern Abbey*] beautifully describes the calmness of the creative mood—(again) describing rather than using—through which a 'creative soul' is born from physical quiescence [*cf.* the Indian Yoga system]; and continues with a noble sense of underlying spirit infusing, buoying up into existence, all natural and cosmic manifestations; and concludes with 'the still sad music of humanity" (Knight, 36). On the publication of *Tintern Abbey* in *Lyrical Ballads* in 1798, Robert Southey wrote in the journal *The Critical Review* (Vol. XXIV, October, 1798) a review of *Lyrical Ballads,* in which he also highly appreciated this poem. In his review he said that such poems of *Lyrical Ballads,* as *The Foster Mother's Tale, The Dungeon, Lines upon the Yew Tree Seat,* deserved our appreciation due to various reasons. He also said that the poem *The Tale of the Female Vagrant* was 'admirable'; but, compared with this poem, *Tintern Abbey* is far superior. Southey wrote in that review about *Tintern Abbey*: "Admirable as this poem [*The Tale of the Female Vagrant*] is, the author seems to discover still superior powers in the *Lines written near Tintern Abbey.* In the whole range of English poetry, we scarcely recollect anything superior to a part of the following passage [of *Tintern Abbey*]:

> 'And so I dare to hope,
> Though changed, no doubt, from what I was when first
> I came among these hills.' etc."
>
> (*Wordsworth and Coleridge,* 314)

In the June 1799 issue of *The Monthly Review* (Vol. XXIX), Dr. Burney wrote a review of *Lyrical Ballads,* in which he critically appreciated *Tintern Abbey* and the other poems of the volume: "The reflections of no common mind; poetical, beautiful, and philosophical: but somewhat tinctured with gloomy, narrow, and unsociable ideas of seclusion from the commerce of the world: as if men were born to live in woods and wilds, unconnected with each other.... So much genius and originality are discovered in this publication that we wish to see another from the same hand, written on more elevated subjects and in a more cheerful disposition"(Wordsworth and Coleridge, 317). Among our contemporary critics, Oliver Elton appreciated the 'new scene of life,' 'new manner of language,' and the 'fresh species of poetry' that he found in *Tintern Abbey*: "the contributions of Wordsworth are signal, not only for the new scene of life he disclosed, and the new manner of language which he critically defended, but [*also*] for his invention and execution of fresh species of poetry, the 'lyrical ballad' being one, and the meditation, like *Tintern Abbey,* another" (Elton, 52). In February 1801, Wordsworth sent Charles Lamb a copy of the 2 vol. new edition of *Lyrical Ballads,* in which *Tintern Abbey* re-appeared. Lamb wrote to Wordsworth about his opinion of the volume, and Wordsworth, being irritated, if not enraged, at Lamb's opinion, wrote back a fiery letter, to which Lamb wrote another letter to Wordsworth. From the last letter, we learn that Lamb very much enjoyed *Tintern Abbey.* Lamb wrote: "'no single piece had moved me so forcibly as *Ancient Mariner, The Mad Mother,* or the *Lines at Tintern Abbey*'" (Williams, 38).

Graham Hough dubs the style of *Tintern Abbey* as 'higher style,' and praises the poem for its *ganzheit* or gestalt or wholeness, and also for the message it delivers: "In *Tintern Abbey* it is at once apparent that we have a poem written in an altogether higher style. The air of familiar anecdote is abandoned, and the embarassing playfulness that sometimes appears in Wordsworth's domestic pieces totally disappears. Reading *Tintern Abbey* in conjunction with the slighter pieces in *Lyrical Ballads* we feel that they are the data on which this great reflective poem is based, that the intellect has been used, not for meddling or dissecting, but to fuse into a whole the scattered impressions for which commonly 'in consequence of the film of familiarity and selfish solitude we have eyes, yet see not, ears that hear not, and hearts that neither feel nor understand'" (Hough, 50). Helen Darbishire, on the other hand, enjoys, especially, the blank verse used in *Tintern Abbey,* and says that this sort of blank verse is intrinsically characteristic of Wordsworth: "The instrument he used [in *Tintern Abbey*]...was a kind of blank verse, familiar yet impassioned, which could rise with a natural ease from simple personal narrative to exalted meditation. This mode of blank verse which he had preferred at one stroke in *Tintern Abbey,* with its long well-knit paragraphs and inevitable transitions, deserves to be called Wordsworthian as surely as Milton's in *Paradise Lost* to be called Miltonic" (Darbishire, 144).

R.O.C. Winkler, as we have said, is full of praise for Wordsworth's abnegation of the 'dichotomy between the mental and material worlds' in *Tintern Abbey,* but he is critical of the form of the poem: "Despite Wordsworth's obvious striving to be as specific as he can, the sonority of the verse distracts attention from the meaning rather than enforces it. Clarity of vision concentrates upon the separate fragments—'the light of setting suns,' 'the round ocean,' 'the living air,' 'the blue sky,' 'the mind of man'—rather than on what it is that unites them. Hence the various references to this latter read like a series of attempts rather than a cumulative description: 'a presence,' 'a scene,' 'something,' 'a motion,' 'a spirit;' and the two verbs predicated of this thing, 'impels' and 'rolls through,' contradict rather than reinforce each other. The attempt to convey this universality by repeating four times in two lines the word 'all' is heroic rather than successful" (Ford, 169). Winkler, however, appends a rider to the above criticism of his: "This is not to say that the passage is not impressive: only that the claim Wordsworth makes in it [*Tintern Abbey*] is not, to use his own phrase, 'carried alive into the heart by passion'" (Ford, 169). Albert S. Gerard, in his article 'Exploring *Tintern Abbey,*' ironically admits that "'Tintern Abbey' share's with Coleridge's 'The Eolian Harp' the dubious honour of being one of the most lopsidedly quoted poems in the whole corpus of English poetry. No student of Wordsworth, or, for that matter, of Romanticism in general, can refrain from squeezing all the doctrinal juice he can out of lines 34-49 and 93-111 [of *Tintern Abbey*]. Those two passages are admittedly remarkable for the loftiness of the feelings and ideas they convey, and for the eloquence with which they are conveyed. In consequence it is hard to resist the temptation of extending to the poem as a whole the triumphant impression they make on the reader" (Cowell, 58). But Gerard immediately afterwards subjoins the unpalatable announcement that to the readers of the present age (20th century), *Tintern Abbey* is *passe*. Gerard writes in the same article: "...we find F.W. Bateson confidently asserting of 'Tintern Abbey' that 'rhetorically it is superbly assured and persuasive'. This is probably the reason why it was so dear to Victorian hearts. But the present age feels only contemptuous dislike for what is 'superbly assured': hence the twentieth-century reaction against 'Tintern Abbey.' For William Empson, it [*Tinterm Abbey*] is a hopeless muddle on all planes, beginning with the grammatical" (Cowell, 58). W.L. Renwick rues the imbalance between 'the delight of external beauty and the sobriety bred of his [Wordsworth's] experience of humanity' and the poet's melancholic meditation in *Tintern Abbey*: "The balance between the delight of external beauty and the sobriety bred of his [Wordsworth's] experience of humanity—which is the theme of *Tintern Abbey*—seems disturbed by his melancholy" (Renwick, 178).

However, if we ignore these objections raised against *Tintern Abbey,* we may say that it is one of the finest poems not only of the Romantic period, but also of the English language, or, rather, even taking into account all of them, we may say so. The poem is a fine blend of deep philosophy, keen sensibility, adroit versification, and personal emotion that has been elevated to a universal one. It has a touch of mysticism, and that is why its wording, at places, fails to capture the totality of the meaning. Its theme is enormous, encompassing the spirituality of the whole of the creation as well as the mutable tiny speck—that is the soul—that dwells evanascently within that enormous spirituality. And that spirituality, which eludes total comprehension, is somehow in concordance with our sensuous delight that we immediately comprehend,—and this is the theme of the poem. Words must fail to fully express this concordance, and so any poet, who is going to deal with such a theme, is sure to proceed with trepidation, or with anxiety. Such a complex theme is not only there in *Tintern Abbey,* but also in many of Wordsworth's poems of his earlier phase. In the case of *Tintern Abbey,* this anxiety of Wordsworth is more noticeable, because the poem was composed at a time when the poet lost, or at least he thought he lost, the vigour of his poetic faculty. However, John Williams writes about this anxiety of Wordsworth as is revealed in *Tintern Abbey,* or as is at work in the poem: "Much has been made of Wordsworth's anxiety, expressed in 'Tintern Abbey' (1798), that at the very moment of discovering his poetic voice, he found himself threatened by silence because his creative powers seemed to be on the wane. This anxiety should be more properly understood as a recognition on his part that the true subject of his and every poet's art seem to lie beyond words, forever unattainable" (Williams, 16). David Daiches says that there is a tension, in *Tintern Abbey,* between the strong emotion and the control of the formal verse, and that this tension enhances the pleasure of the poem: "The tension here [in *Tintern Abbey*] between willing emotion and formal verse rhythms, with interruption and repetition worked into the fabric of the verse, is most effective"(Daiches, 1996, 887). So we may say that, inspite of his 'anxiety' Wordsworth has wrought a marvel in this poem, at least in this regard.

(II) THE THORN

This is a simple but touching poem on the theme of superstition and working of mind relating to it. The poem was composed in 1798 and was published in *Lyrical Ballads* in the same year. Wordsworth intended to write a prefatory poem for *The Thorn*, which he never wrote, but, instead, did write an introductory comment on it. Dorothy Wordsworth, in the entry of her Journal for 19th March, 1798, wrote about the origin of this poem. Forty-five years afterwards Wordsworth confirmed the truth of Dorothy's entry. Stephen Maxfield Parrish writes: "In Dorothy's Alfoxden journal the entry for March 19, 1798, opens: 'Wm. [William] and Basil [Montagu] and I walked to the hill-tops, a very cold bleak day. We were met on our return by a severe hailstorm.' The scenes of this walk were familiar, but during the storm Wordsworth's eye was caught and his poetic imagination fired by a solitary, aged tree. Dorothy marked the event by noting laconically as she closed the day's entry: 'William wrote some lines describing a stunted thorn. Forty-five years later William corroborated her account of the genesis of one of his 'lyrical ballads' [*The Thorn*]. 'The Thorn,' he told Isabella Fenwick, 'arose out of my observing, the ridge of Quantock Hill, on a stormy day, a thorn which I had often passed in calm and bright weather without noticing it. I said to myself, 'Cannot I by some invention do as much to make this Thorn permanently an impressive object as the storm has made it to my eyes at this moment?'" (Abrams, 1979, 75).

Wordsworth used to be drawn by trees, as by hills, and trees played great roles in his imagination. David McCracken writes: "Wordsworth felt the power of hills—of old Helvellyn, Place Fell, and Glaramara—and he also felt the power of trees, large or small, single or in groves. Trees grew in his imagination. In *Lyrical Ballads*, Ruth dwells alone, 'Under the greenwood tree'; a retired seaman, no Ancient Mariner, tells the strange tale of

Martha, who appears to him by the small, gnarled hawthorn that is the centre of 'The Thorn' ('some will say/ She hanged her baby on the tree'); and Simon Lee works pathetically at the root of an old tree" (McCracken, 160).

The poem is divided into 22 stanzas, each stanza containing eleven lines in the rhyme-scheme: a b c b d e f f e g g. Thorn or hawthorn is 'a small tree of the rose family, much used for hedges.'

THE THORN

I

"There is a Thorn—it looks so old,
In truth, you'd find it hard to say
How it could ever have been young,
It looks so old and grey.
Not higher than a two years' child
It stands erect, this aged Thorn;
No leaves it has, no prickly points;
It is a mass of knotted joints,
A wretched thing forlorn.
It stands erect, and like a stone
With lichens is it overgrown.

II

"Like rock or stone, it is o'ergrown,
With lichens to the very top,
And hung with heavy tufts of moss,
A melancholy crop:
Up from the earth these mosses creep,
And this poor Thorn they clasp it round
So close, you'd say that they are bent
With plain and manifest intent
To drag it to the ground;
And all have joined in one endeavour
To bury this poor Thorn for ever.

III

"High on a mountain's highest ridge,
Where oft the stormy winter gale
Cuts like a scythe, while through the clouds
It sweeps from vale to vale;

Not five yards from the mountain path,
This Thorn you on your left espy;
And to the left, three yards beyond,
You see a little muddy pond
Of water—never dry,
Though but of compass small, and bare
To thirsty suns and parching air.

IV

"And, close beside this aged Thorn,
There is a fresh and lovely sight,
A beauteous heap, a hill of moss,
Just half a foot in height.
All lovely colours there you see,
All colours that were ever seen;
And mossy network too is there,
As if by hand of lady fair
The work had woven been;
And cups, the darlings of the eye,
So deep is their vermilion dye.

V

"Ah me! what lovely tints are there
Of olive green and scarlet bright,
In spikes, in branches, and in stars,
Green, red, and pearly white!
This heap of earth o'ergrown with moss,
Which close beside the Thorn you see,
So fresh in all its beauteous dyes,
Is like an infant's grave in size,
As like as like can be:
But never, never any where,
An infant's grave was half so fair.

VI

"Now would you see this aged Thorn,
This pond, and beauteous hill of moss,
You must take care and choose your time
The mountain when to cross.
For oft there sits between the heap,
So like an infant's grave in size,
And that same pond of which I spoke,

A Woman in a scarlet cloak,
And to herself she cries,
'Oh misery! oh misery!
Oh woe is me! oh misery!'

VII

"At all times of the day and night
This wretched Woman thither goes;
And she is known to every star,
And every wind that blows;
And there, beside the Thorn, she sits
When the blue daylight's in the skies,
And when the whirlwind's on the hill,
Or frosty air is keen and still,
And to herself she cries,
'Oh misery! oh misery!
Oh woe is me! oh misery!'

VIII

"Now wherefore, thus, by day and night,
In rain, in tempest, and in snow,
Thus to the dreary mountain-top
Does this poor Woman go?
And why sits she beside the Thorn
When the blue daylight's in the sky
Or when the whirlwind's on the hill,
Or frosty air is keen and still,
And wherefore does she cry?—
O wherefore? wherefore? tell me why
Does she repeat that doleful cry?"

IX

"I cannot tell; I wish I could;
For the true reason no one knows:
But would you gladly view the spot,
The spot to which she goes;
The hillock like an infant's grave,
The pond—and Thorn, so old and grey;
Pass by her door—'tis seldom shut—
And if you see her in her hut—
Then to the spot away!

I never heard of such as dare
Approach the spot when she is there."

X

"But wherefore to the mountain-top
Can this unhappy Woman go,
Whatever star is in the skies,
Whatever wind may blow?"
"Full twenty years are past and gone
Since she (her name is Martha Ray)
Gave with a maiden's true good-will
Her company to Stephen Hill;
And she was blithe and gay,
While friends and kindred all approved
Of him whom tenderly she loved.

XI

"And they had fixed the wedding day,
The morning that must wed them both;
But Stephen to another Maid
Had sworn another oath;
And, with this other Maid, to church
Unthinking Stephen went—
Poor Martha! on that woeful day
A pang of pitiless dismay
Into her soul was sent;
A fire was kindled in her breast,
Which might not burn itself to rest.

XII

"They say, full six months after this,
While yet the summer leaves were green,
She to the mountain-top would go,
And there was often seen.
What could she seek?—or wish to hide?
Her state to any eye was plain;
She was with child, and she was mad;
Yet often was she sober sad
From her exceeding pain.
O guilty Father—would that death
Had saved him from that breach of faith!

XIII

"Sad case for such a brain to hold
Communion with a stirring child!
Sad case, as you may think, for one
Who had a brain so wild!
Last Christmas-eve we talked of this,
And grey-haired Wilfred of the glen
Held that the unborn infant wrought
About its mother's heart, and brought
Her senses back again:
And, when at last her time drew near,
Her looks were calm, her senses clear.

XIV

"More know I not, I wish I did,
And it should all be told to you;
For what became of this poor child
No mortal ever knew;
Nay—if a child to her was born
No earthly tongue could ever tell;
And if 'twas born alive or dead,
Far less could this with proof be said;
But some remember well
That Martha Ray about this time
Would up the mountain often climb.

XV

"And all that winter, when at night
The wind blew from the mountain-peak,
'Twas worth your while, though in the dark,
The churchyard path to seek:
For many a time and oft were heard
Cries coming from the mountain head:
Some plainly living voices were;
And others, I've heard many swear,
Were voices of the dead:
I cannot think, whate'er they say,
They had to do with Martha Ray.

XVI

"But that she goes to this old Thorn,
The Thorn which I described to you,

And there sits in a scarlet cloak,
I will be sworn is true.
For one day with my telescope,
To view the ocean wide and bright,
When to this country first I came,
Ere I had heard of Martha's name,
I climbed the mountain's height:—
A storm came on, and I could see
No object higher than my knee.

XVII

"twas mist and rain, and storm and rain:
No screen, no fence could I discover;
And then the wind! in sooth, it was
A wind full ten times over.
I looked around, I thought I saw
A jutting crag,—and off I ran,
Head-foremost, through the driving rain,
The shelter of the crag to gain;
And, as I am a man,
Instead of jutting crag I found
A Woman seated on the ground.

XVIII

"I did not speak—I saw her face;
Her face!—it was enough for me;
I turned about and heard her cry,
'Oh misery! oh misery!'
And there she sits, until the moon
Through half the clear blue sky will go;
And when the little breezes make
The waters of the pond to shake,
As all the country know,
She shudders, and you hear her cry,
'Oh misery! oh misery!'

XIX

"But what's the Thorn? and what the pond?
And what the hill of moss to her?
And what the creeping breeze that comes
The little pond to stir?"
"I cannot tell; but some will say

She hanged her baby on the tree;
Some say she drowned it in the pond,
Which is a little step beyond:
But all and each agree,
The little Babe was buried there,
Beneath that hill of moss so fair.

XX

"I've heard, the moss is spotted red
With drops of that poor infant's blood;
But kill a new-born infant thus,
I do not think she could!
Some say if to the pond you go,
And fix on it a steady view,
The shadow of a babe you trace,
A baby and a baby's face,
And that it looks at you;
Whene'er you look on it, 'tis plain
The baby looks at you again.

XXI

"And some had sworn an oath that she
Should be to public justice brought;
And for the little infant's bones
With spades they would have sought.
But instantly the hill of moss
Before their eyes began to stir!
And, for full fifty yards around,
The grass—it shook upon the ground!
Yet all do still aver
The little Babe lies buried there,
Beneath that hill of moss so fair.

XXII

"I cannot tell how this may be,
But plain it is the Thorn is bound
With heavy tufts of moss that strive
To drag it to the ground;
And this I know, full many a time,
When she was on the mountain high,
By day, and in the silent night,
When all the stars shone clear and bright,

That I have heard her cry,
'Oh misery! oh misery!
Oh woe is me! oh misery!'"

The narrator of the story of the poem says that there is an hawthorn or thorn which is so old and grey that one can hardly believe that it had once been young. The height of the thorn or hawthorn is greater than that of a child of two years. The thorn has no leaves and 'no prickly points,' and it seems a 'mass of knotted joints'. It looks like a forlorn and wretched thing, and yet it is standing erect. It is overcast, like a stone, with lichens "a compound plant consisting of a fungus and an alga living symbiotically, forming crusts and tufts on stones, trees and soil" (*Chambers Twentieth Century Dictionary*) (*Stanza I*). The thorn is overgrown with lichens up to the top, and 'tufts of moss' are thickly ('heavy') hanging around it, giving it a melancholic look ('A melancholy crop'). The tufts of moss are creeping up and clasping the thorn so closely that one may think that they have the 'plain and manifest' intention of dragging the thorn down to the ground. Nay, more than that: one may think that all the tufts of moss are unitedly trying to 'bury this poor Thorn for ever.' (*Stanza II*). This thorn is to be seen 'on a mountain's highest ridge' where 'stormy winter gale,' that moves ('sweeps') 'from vale to vale' 'through the clouds,' will be felt cutting you like a scythe, with its chill. One can find ('espy') the thorn on the left side, less than 'five yards from the mountain path.' And three yards to the left of that place (where the thorn is standing) is 'a little muddy pond'. The pond is small in compass, and it has no branches of trees over it ('bare'). The pond is exposed to the scorching ('thirsty') sun and hot ('parching') air, and yet it is not dry—it contains water (*Stanza III*).

Close beside this old thorn, there is the 'fresh and lovely sight' of a beautiful heap or mound ('hill') of moss that is exactly 'half a foot in height.' In that heap of moss one can see all the lovely colours that we have seen. There is a network or embroidery in the moss, which seems to be woven by a fair lady. There are also beautiful ('darlings of the eye') cup-lichens or cup-mosses (lichens or mosses with cup-shaped structures) with very bright red pigment ('So deep is their vermilion dye') in the mosses (*Stanza IV*). The narrator of the story of the poem is delighted to see the beautiful colours ('tints')—olive green, bright scarlet, green, red and pearly white—in the thorns ('spikes') and the branches of the hawthorn, conglomerated or arranged in star-like shapes ('in stars'). Near the thorn there is also a mound of earth, covered with moss, that looks very fresh with all its beautiful colours. The size of the mound is that of an infant's grave, and the mound and the grave are very much alike, or the mound seems very much to be an infant's grave ('As like as like can be'). But no infant's grave has been even half as fair as that mossy mound of earth. (*Stanza V*). The narrator tells us that whatever time we may choose to walk over ('cross') the mountain, this thorn, this pond and this beautiful heap ('hill') of moss will come to our view. 'A woman in scarlet cloak' frequently sits between the heap of moss, of the size and shape of an infant's grave, and the same pond, and cries to herself: "'Oh misery! oh misery!/Oh woe is me! oh misery!'" (*Stanza VI*). Any time, either during day or during night, this wretched woman goes to that place, and she is known to the stars and the winds. She sits there when the sun shines in the clear ('blue') sky, and when whirlwind blows over the hills, or when the air is frosty and biting ('keen') and motionless ('still'), and sitting there the wretched woman cries: "'Oh misery! oh misery!/ Oh woe is me! oh misery!'" (*Stanza VII*). The narrator asks: why does this 'poor Woman' go to the fearful ('dreary') mountain-top, by day or by night, in spite of rain, tempest or snow-fall, and sits beside that hawthorn, whether the sun shines in the clear sky, or whirlwind blows over the hill, or the air is frosty, biting and motionless, and repeat that mournful cry? (*Stanza VIII*).

The narrator (in answer to the foregoing question of his) says that he does not know the reason (why the wretched woman goes to the mountain-top and cries), and that nobody else knows the reason, and that he wishes he knew. He says that everyone would be glad to see the particular spot where she goes—the spot, which is a small hill ('hillock'), and which is of the size of an infant's grave, where there are that pond and that 'old and grey' hawthorn. He asks us to pass by the woman's door which infrequently ('seldom') remains closed, and, if we see her in her hut, to go speedily ('away!') to that particular spot. The narrator says that he has never heard that anybody dared to go near ('Approach') 'the spot when she is there' (*Stanza IX*).

The narrator asks why this unhappy woman goes to that spot, whether the stars in the heaven ('skies') are bright or no, or whether the wind that blows over there is breezy or violent ("Whatever star is in the skies,/Whatever wind may blow?"). The narrator says that full twenty years ago, this woman, whose name is Martha Ray, was a maiden, and at that time she gave her marriage-vow to Stephen Hill, along with her honest good will ("Gave with a maiden's true good-will/ Her company to Stephen Hill"). Then Martha was spritely ('blithe') and happy; and then all the friends and fellows ('kindred') of Stephen approved of his proposed marriage with Martha whom he affectionately loved (*Stanza X*). Martha and Stephen ('they') appointed the day in the morning of which they were to get married to each other. But Stephen had (earlier) given his marriage vow to another maid ('sworn another oath') with whom the senseless ('Unthinking') Stephen went to a church to get married. Consequently, 'on that woeful day,' Martha felt a pang in her soul, due to the 'pitiless' conduct of Stephen, and was dismayed. And a passion ('fire') was enkindled in her breast, that would not burn itself out, or would not be extinguished ("Which might not burn itself to rest") (*Stanza XI*).

People ('they') say that after this, for 'full six months' during summer, when the leaves of trees were still green, Martha would go to that spot, and she would often be seen to be there on 'the mountain-top'. The narrator asks what Martha ('she') then might be seeing or hiding there on the mountain-top. He says that any man ('eye') could easily ('plain') understand her plight or mental condition. He says that Martha was carrying a child and that she was violent or mad. And, yet, sometimes she was sober and sad, due to her excruciating pain. The narrator here condemns Stephen, the would-be father of the unborn child of Martha ('O guilty Father'). The narrator wonders if, in case Martha gives delivery to a still-born baby ('that death'), Stephen would be absolved ('saved') of the guilt of breach of marriage vow ('faith') (*Stanza XII*). The narrator exclaims that it was very sad for the perplexed Martha to think ('brain') about, or feel, any interaction with the child stirring in her womb ("Sad case for such a brain to hold/ Communion with a stirring child!"). The narrator says that it was an all the more sad case—as we may think it to be ('as you may think')—because Martha was then mad ('a brain so wild'). In the last Christmas evening, the narrator was conversing with Wilfred, an old man who lives in a wooded valley ('glen'), and Wilfred told him that the unborn baby (of Martha) generated affection ('wrought'), for itself, in the heart of its mother, and thereby brought her to her good senses ('Her senses back again'). And, at last, when the time of child-birth came near, Martha really became calm, and she really came to her senses—she became rational ('her senses clear') (*Stanza XIII*).

The narrator does not know (about Martha) more than this, but he wishes he knew more than this, and had he known more than this, he would tell us about all that. But no one knew what happened to the luckless ('poor') child of Martha. Not only this ('Nay'), no man ('No earthly tongue') could tell if a child was actually born to Martha, or, if a child was at all born, whether it was born alive or dead. And if any one of all these possible events could be narrated, it could hardly be supported with proofs ("Far less could this with proof be said"). But some persons well remember that during that time Martha would climb up the mountain (*Stanza XIV*). However, during the whole winter, "when at night/ The wind blew from the mountain-peak," it was worth one's while to pass through the path along the churchyard, though he had to move through darkness. If one would walk in that path, often and for many years, he could hear "Cries coming from the mountain head." The cries were 'plainly living voices' (voices or cries of some living person, presumably of Martha). But, says the narrator, he heard some persons swear that those voices or cries were of somebody else who had been dead. But the narrator ('I') cannot understand or believe ('think') that whatsoever these people say refers to Martha Ray (*Stanza XV*). The narrator can swear that ("I will be sworn is true") Martha goes to that old hawthorn which he described to us earlier, and that she sits there 'in a scarlet cloak.' He is confirmed about this because of the following fact ('For'). When he came to this country for the first time, before he came to hear Martha's name, one day he went up to the peak of that mountain with his telescope to 'view the ocean wide and bright.' Then a storm blew, and he could see no object more high than his knee. (*Stanza XVI*).

The narrator says that the day was misty, stormy and rainy,

and that for that reason he could see no shelter to defend him against danger ('a shield against danger'). Then a wind, that was ten times stronger than normal, really blew. The narrator looked around and thought that he found a protruding 'rough steep rock,' and fast ran ('Head-foremost') through 'the driving rain' to take shelter under that 'rough steep rock.' But he found that the 'rough steep rock' was not really a crag but "A woman seated on the ground;" and he says that this is as true as the fact that he is a real man ('as I am a man') (*Stanza XVII*).

Then the narrator did not speak with Martha (that woman who seemed a rock) but saw, and wondered at, her face, and was affected by it ("Her face;—it was enough for me"). He 'turned about and heard her cry'. She cried: "Oh misery! oh misery!" The narrator says that she sits there regularly till the moon passes through half the 'clear blue sky,' *i.e.*, till it is midnight. And when mild ('little') breezes create ripples in the water of that pond ("when the little breezes make/ The waters of the pond shake"), then ('As') all the people of the country know that Martha is writhing ('shudders') and crying: "Oh misery! oh misery!'" (*Stanza XVIII*). But what are the meanings of that hawthorn, the pond, the 'hill of moss,' and the slow-moving ('creeping') breeze that stirs the water of the pond, to Martha? The narrator cannot answer the question, exactly. But he says that some people say that she 'hanged her baby on the tree,' and some say that 'she drowned it in the pond' which is at a little distance ('a little step beyond'). But everybody agrees that the little baby was buried under the beautiful hill of moss (*Stanza XIX*). The narrator has heard that the mound of moss is 'spotted red' "With drops of that poor infant's blood." But he does not think that Martha could kill that 'new-born infant.' The narrator tells us that some say that if one goes to the pond and fixes his 'steady view' on it, then he can descry ('trace') in the water a shadow of that baby, or the baby itself, with its face turned toward him. Whenever one will look on the water of the pond, that baby will clearly ('plain') look at him, once again (*Stanza XX*).

Some people (supposedly, being enraged by the immoral act of Martha, of killing the baby) pledged that she would ('should') be brought to 'public justice,' and (for this purpose) they would exhume ('brought') 'the little infant's bones' with the help of spades. But (as they went there to dig at the mound of moss) within a moment they saw that the mound of moss was stirring before their eyes, and that the grass, spread over 'full fifty yards' of land ('ground'), also vibrated (perhaps in fear or in disgust). The narrator says that till to-day ('Yet') everyone spurns away ('aver') the notion that the little baby lies buried under the beautiful hill of moss (*Stanza XXI*). The narrator does not understand why ('how this may be') the hawthorn or thorn is overgrown ('bound') with thick pads ('heavy tufts') of moss which are, as if, trying to drag the hawthorn down to the grown. But he knows that many a time Martha was on the top of that mountain, either in day time, or in silent nights, when "all the stars shone clear and bright," and he has heard Martha cry: "Oh misery! oh misery!/ Oh woe is me! oh misery!'" (*Stanza XXII*).

In the 'Advertisement' of the 1798 edition of *Lyrical Ballads,* Wordsworth wrote a note for *The Thorn,* and this note was considerably expanded in the 'Advertisement' of the 1800 edition of *Lyrical Ballads.* This expanded note may help us understand the poem better. This expanded note runs thus: "'This poem ought to have been preceded by an introductory poem, which I have been prevented from writing by never having felt myself in a mood when it was probable that I should write it well.—The character which I have here introduced speaking is sufficiently common. The Reader will perhaps have a general notion of it, if he has ever known a man, a Captain of a small trading vessel for example, who being past the middle age of life, had retired upon an annuity or small independent income to some village or county town of which he was not a native, or in which he had not been accustomed to live. Such men having little to do become credulous and talkative from indolence; and from the same cause, and other disposing causes by which it is probable that such men may have been affected, they are prone to superstition. On which account it appeared to me proper to select a character like this to exhibit some of the general laws by which superstition acts upon the mind. Superstitious men are almost always men of slow faculties and deep feelings; their minds are not loose, but adhesive; they have a reasonable share of imagination, by which word I mean the faculty which produces impressive effects out of simple elements; but they are utterly destitute of fancy, the power by which pleasure and surprise are excited by sudden varieties of situation and by accumulated imagery.

"'It was my wish in this poem to show the manner in which such men cleave to the same ideas; and to follow the turns of passion, always different, yet not palpably different, by which their conversation is swayed. I had two objects to attain; first, to represent a picture which should not be unimpressive yet consistent with the character that should describe it, secondly, while I adhered to the style in which such persons describe, to take care that words, which in their minds are impregnated with passion, should likewise convey passion to Readers who are not accustomed to sympathise with men feeling in that manner or using such language. It seemed to me that this might be done by calling in the assistance of Lyrical and rapid Metre. It was necessary that the Poem, to be natural, should in reality move slowly; yet I hoped, that, by the aid of the metre, to those who should at all enter into the spirit of the Poem, it would appear to move quickly. The Reader will have the kindness to excuse this note as I am sensible that an introductory Poem is necessary to give this poem its full effect'" (Wordsworth and Coleridge, 282).

Regarding its subject-matter, at least, *The Thorn* is a difficult poem, indeed. Wordsworth thought about writing an introductory poem for *The Thorn* perhaps because he himself could feel the difficulty of understanding this poem without any introduction to it. But that introductory poem had never been written; and, moreover, Wordsworth's note for this poem does not throw, as we have seen, sufficient light on the subject-matter of this poem. It is for this reason that commentators are generally at variance with each other as to the real subject-matter of the poem. Stephen Maxfield Parrish writes: "Of the dozens of critics who have commented on 'The Thorn,' hardly one appears to have discerned who the central character is and what the poem is about" (Abrams, 75). In the poem, the poet is, supposedly, absent, and in it there are two characters—the narrator from whose mouth we hear the story of the poem; and Martha Ray, the abandoned mother of a dead child. But who the central character is we do not know, because we do not, in fact, clearly understand the meaning of the poem. Perhaps Wordsworth deliberately kept the poem misty, as he did *Resolution and Independence*, at least to some extent. About *The Thorn,* Wordsworth felt that his imaginative experience in the poem "exists beyond language;..., exists beyond knowing" (Williams, 12-13).

Stephen Maxfield Parrish writes that according to De Selincourt, the majority opinion of critics about *The Thorn* is that the poem is "'the extreme example of W.'s [Wordsworth's] experiment "to ascertain how far the language of conversation in the middle and lower classes of society is adapted to the purpose of poetic pleasure'" (Abrams, 75). But this cannot be the only object of Wordsworth in the poem, for he had this same object in some other poems as well. Further, "As Wordsworth conceived it, 'The Thorn' is a portrayal of the superstitious imagination." (Abrams, 76). Perhaps, we may trust Wordsworth and understand the poem as a study in superstition, or, if not, we may take the poem as "a haunting and powerful study in social morality" (Abrams, 76). But, what sort of study in superstition is the poem? Stephen Maxfield Parrish answers: "More literally than any other poem, it [*The Thorn*] carries out the principal object of *Lyrical Ballads*: to trace in situations of common life 'the primary laws of our nature,' chiefly 'as regards the manner in which we associate ideas in a state of excitement.' For the manner in which the narrator associates ideas is precisely what 'The Thorn' is about. The ideas themselves—that is, the 'events' of the poem—are unimportant except as they reflect the working of the narrator's imagination. In fact, the point of the poem may very well be that its central 'event' *has* no existence outside the narrator's imagination—that there is no Martha Ray sitting in a scarlet cloak behind a crag on the mountain top, that the narrator has neither seen her nor heard her, that what he has seen is a gnarled old tree in a blinding storm, that what he has heard (besides the creaking of the branches, or the whistling of the mountain wind) is village superstition about a woman years ago" (Abrams, 76-77).

Now, if we accept this explanation of the meaning or subject-matter of the poem—and perhaps we may—then we may say that Wordsworth should have given indications of the superstition of the narrator in the poem itself; and, indeed, should he have done that, he would not feel that he should have written an introductory poem for *The Thorn,* which, as it exists, seems to be a truncated poem. The lack of such an indication certainly betrays a great fault of the poem. However, it may be pointed out here that the 'laws of association' on which, on his own admission, Wordsworth has built this poem, belongs to David Hartley's psychology. Hartley, an English philosopher, physician and psychologist, in his *Observations on Man, His Frame, His Duty and His Expectations* (1749), said that sensations and ideas may be connected with each other if they are contiguous in time or space, in such a way that, once such connection is established, if one of them is roused, the connected other will also be automatically aroused. In *The Thorn*, the narrator (Wordsworth tells us that the narrator is an old and retired navigator, a captain of ships) heard the sad story that some Martha Ray used to cry 'Oh misery! oh misery!' in the wilderness beside the hawthorn, for her dead child and for her fate. As he heard the story, the two images—one of Martha, and another of the hawthorn—because of their being contaguous to one another in the story, were psychologically connected to each other, in his imagination (as per Hartley's psychology). And now, when the narrator, in the poem, perceives, in his imagination, the bare hawthorn, the whole myth or superstition about Martha, or the story of her sufferance, comes to his head, so vividly that, as if, he perceives Martha and all other things associated with her story.

The Thorn is obviously an experimental poem, appropos of Wordsworth's announcement, in his note for this poem, in *Lyrical Ballads*. Wordsworth wanted to write 'new sorts of poem' and *The Thorn*, like *Ruth*, is a perfect instance of these 'new sorts of poem.' Oliver Elton writes: "Whatever *The Thorn* and *Ruth* may be called, they are a new kind of poem. The old names do not fit them, neither does that of 'lyrical ballad'" (Elton, 63). W.L. Renwick says that Wordsworth "tried the common story-teller's trick of the imaginary narrator in *The Thorn*" (Renwick, 165). This trick has certainly saved Wordsworth from the stock charge against him that he is too prone to depicting details, because in the poem it is the narrator, and not he himself, who is giving us the details, in excess, about Martha and about her surroundings. Wordsworth has also resorted to a ploy, here, to justify the excess details. He tells us that the narrator is old and listless, and so, as usually happens, he is 'credulous and talkative from indolence,' and is 'prone to superstition.'

However, almost immediately after the publication of *The Thorn* in *Lyrical Ballads,* in 1798, Robert Southey wrote a comment on the volume, and published it in *The Critical Review,* vol. XXIV, October, 1798. In his comment, Southey scathingly criticised *The Thorn*: "'With that which is entitled *The Thorn,* we were altogether displeased. The advertisement [of *Lyrical Ballads*] says, it is not told in the person of the author, but in that of some loquacious narrator. The author should have recollected that he who personates tiresome loquacity, becomes tiresome himself. The story of a man who suffers the personal pain of cold, because an old woman prayed that he might never be warm, is perhaps a good story for a ballad, because it is a well-known tale: but is the author certain that it is 'well authenticated'? And does not such an assertion promote the popular superstition of witchcraft?'" (Wordsworth and Coleridge, 313). But we cannot quite agree with Southey. Because, firstly, the story, or rather the poem, is not tiresome; it may be slow-moving, but not tiresome, as it is interesting; the details are also necessary for producing an effectively superstitious story, which is the subject-matter of the poem. Secondly, Wordsworth cannot be accused of promoting witchcraft through this poem, because poets are not supposed to be aware of the effects of such a poem on the society, and also because we should not read the poem as an instance of (let alone proof of) superstition, but simply as a fine poem. We should not forget that poets, *per se,* are not supposed to be necessarily social activists whose object is to ameliorate the condition of society; to eradicate, for instance, some superstitions; of course they are also not supposed to whip them up, and Wordsworth is not doing that—he is simply showing us, as he said, how superstition works, and that is that. Further, Wordsworth tells us that the superstitious story of Martha Ray had been in vogue in that part of England, and that he is just narrating it. Where then does his fault lie? However, though *The Thorn* could not satisfy Southey, it could do that another (anonymous) commentator, who published his review of *Lyrical Ballads* in *The Analytical Review,* vol. XXVIII, December, 1798. In his review, the commentator writes: "'Among the poems which particularly pleased us from their character either of simplicity or tenderness, or both, are,..., *The Thorn, The Mad Mother, The Idiot Boy,* and *The tale of Goody Blake and Harry Gill*'" (Wordsworth and Coleridge, 314-315).

In the poem, Wordsworth has invited an elderly loquacious narrator to tell the sad story of Martha Ray. But why does not the poet himself tell the tale? And, if a narrator is at all required, why does the poet bring in an elderly suffering man? Presumably, Wordsworth thought that an elderly suffering person would better feel the bottomless suffering of Martha. But such a presupposition is wrong, for a suffering person feels less the suffering of others than one who does not suffer. In any case, Oliver Elton, like S.T. Coleridge, is not happy with the introduction of the elderly and suffering seaman for the function of the narrator. Elton writes: "Most of *The Thorn* is out of keeping, as Coleridge observed, with the elderly seafaring man who is supposed to relate it" (Elton, 66). Elton further says that, in the poem, Wordsworth fails to depict human miseries, or those of Martha Ray, with appropriate nuances of darkness, let alone with poetical overtones, because his poetical skill was of a different ilk. The story of Martha Ray, Elton supposes, Wordsworth could better write not in verse but in prose: "It has been written that 'Wordsworth's eyes avert their ken from half of human fate.' Rather, he watches that half through a glass as though from a kind of observatory. He does not say like Miss Austen, 'Let other pens write of guilt and misery.' He is a man of very hard grain, and he does write of them, and that with stubborn veracity. And for some time he positively traffics in them, and fails to make them more than half poetical; as in *The Borderers,* and even in *The Thorn* which might well have been left for prose and told in the way of Edgar Allan Poe" (Elton, 68). A.C. Swinburne (1837-1909) also could not stand *The Thorn,* as he also could not *The Idiot Boy.* According to him, the two poems are "'doleful examples of eccentricity in dullness'" (Bradley, 104). And, yet, we cannot ignore the touching story of the deeply suffering Martha, narrated in very simple terms and in a familiarly conversational tone in the poem, the story that leaves an indelible impression upon our mind, and continues to remain there, even after we may have forgotten the poem itself.

(III) A NIGHT-PIECE

Wordsworth ofcourse delighted to see the still beauty of nature; but he was also enamoured of the changing, shifting beauty of her, perhaps because, to him, the changes and the movements of nature enhanced her vitality, and thereby added to her beauty. Wordsworth was not only that sort of painter whose model stands still before him, but he was also a painter of that sort whose model dances to inspire him. *A Night-Piece* shows Wordsworth's mastery in painting a changing, moving, shifting scenario, or his great skill in presenting the kaleidoscopic aspects or *facades* of nature. *A Night-Piece* was composed on 25 January, 1798, and was first published in 1815. The poem is included in the group of poems generally known as 'Poems of the Imagination.' It was included in Francis Turner Palgrave's *The Golden Treasury* in 1861.

A NIGHT-PIECE

— The sky is overcast
With a continuous cloud of texture close,
Heavy and wan, all whitened by the Moon,
Which through that veil is indistinctly seen,
A dull, contracted circle, yielding light
So feebly spread that not a shadow falls,
Chequering the ground—from rock, plant, tree, or tower.
At length a pleasant instantaneous gleam
Startles the pensive traveller while he treads
His lonesome path, with unobserving eye
Bent earthwards; he looks up—the clouds are split
Asunder,—and above his head he sees
The clear Moon, and the glory of the heavens.
There in a black-blue vault she sails along,
Followed by multitudes of stars, that, small
And sharp, and bright, along the dark abyss
Drive as she drives: how fast they wheel away,
Yet vanish not!—the wind is in the tree,
But they are silent;—still they roll along
Immeasurably distant; and the vault,
Built round by those white clouds, enormous clouds,
Still deepens its unfathomable depth.
At length the Vision closes; and the mind,
Not undisturbed by the delight it feels,
Which slowly settles into peaceful calm,
Is left to muse upon the solemn scene.

The sky is covered with the blanket of closely woven ('texture') and huddling or unbroken ('continuous') stretches of clouds that are thick ('Heavy') and that have lost their colour (of black, because of the moon-shine). The clouds are blanched by the light of the moon which is vaguely ('indistinctly') seen through the (pores or holes of the) blanket of clouds ('veil'). The dull moon seems to be a circle whose circumference has been reduced ('contracted'), *i.e.*, the moon has a diminutive circumference, and the moon is giving a light that is so dimly spread below that the objects of the earth—be it a rock, a plant, a trcc, or a tower—produce no shadows of themselves, that may affect the earth ('Conquering the ground'). At last, a delightful and sudden ('instantaneous') gloss of the moon-shine surprises the thoughtful ('pensive') traveller who is walking on a deserted way, always keeping himself bent towards the way, but seeing nothing whatsoever ('unobserving eye'). As the lone walker is startled by the sudden flare of moon-shine, he looks up at the sky, and observes that the clouds are (now) split into fragments, and he sees the 'clear Moon,' and the 'glory of the heavens' in the sky ('above his head'). The walker sees in the sky ('There') that the moon ('she') is gliding ('sails') along in the raised space ('vault') of the sky of blackish blue colour, being followed by a train of innumerable stars. Those innumerable stars ('that') are small, sharp, and bright, and they are moving after the gliding moon ('Drive as she drives') along the dark and vast hollowness ('abyss') of the sky. The poet wonders that the stars are running ('wheel') at a great speed, and yet they are not becoming invisible ('vanish not!'). The wind (that is driving the moon and the stars) is blowing against the trees, and yet they are neither moving or swinging nor making any sound with their leaves ('silent'), *i.e.*, the wind is breezy. Now, the moon and the stars ('they') have gone a long way, and yet ('still') they are running or gliding ('roll') along inconceivably long ('Immeasurably distant') path. And the open and high-rise space ('vault'), that is created around the white enormous clouds, is yet ('still') widening ('deepens') to create an immeasurably deep space or abyss ('unfathomable depth'). The poet has seen all these in a vision. At last ('At length') his vision has vanished ('the Vision closes'), and then his mind, which was stirred ('Not undisturbed') by delight that he felt while he was having his vision, slowly becomes peaceful and calm, and now the poet begins to meditate upon that serene and sombre ('solemn') vision ('scene').

A Night-Piece is a beautiful description of a particular windy night, in which the 'sky is overcast' with black clouds and the moon is wan. In such a night, a lonesome and pensive traveller is pulling himself forward along his way, keeping his 'unobserving eye' turned downwards. There are two sorts of things in the scenario of the eerie but attractive night: the fast moving things—the clouds, the wind, and the multitude of stars; and the stationary and slow-moving things—the 'silent' trees (stationary), the moon, and the 'pensive traveller'. There are also two colours in the scenario: the stars are bright, but the moon is dim, wan. There is, again, a sudden change in the scenario: when the dark clouds burst, the abyssmal darkness is split asunder, and 'the glory of the heavens' shows itself to the traveller as a vision that fills the mind of the traveller with delight and blissful calm.

A Night-Piece may be compared with lines 621-640 of Book VI of *The Prelude,* which were published as a separate poem, with the title *The Simplon Pass,* in 1803. In both the poems, the scenarios are dreary, and both the poems are visionary—both of them show the calm, sympathetic and lovely, but incomprehensible, face of the heavens. In *A Night-Piece,* the black clouds split, and the lonely traveller perceives the "clear Moon, and the glory of the heavens," and, in *The Simplon Pass,* violent scenario shows "Characters of the great Apocalypse,/The types and symbols of Eternity."

The first seven lines of *A Night-Piece* may remind us of the second passage of Shelley's *Ode to the West Wind,* where Shelley depicts the dreary and superciliously windy sky:

> Thou on whose stream, 'mid the steep sky's commotion,
> Loose clouds like earth's decaying leaves are shed,
> Shook from the tangled boughs of Heaven and Earth.

In *A Night-Piece,* the pensive traveller sees in a vision the heavenly glimpse of hope ('clear Moon'), and in *Ode to the West Wind* Shelley hears in the West Wind the 'trumpet of a prophecy.'

A Night-Piece is undoubtedly one of the beautiful lyrics of Wordsworth. Its imagery is as unforgettable as the alternating chiaroscuro of the scenario that spans the unimaginably vast space from the vault of the sky above to the dreamy path of the traveller below. The 'pensive traveller' of the poem may be understood as a symbol of the suffering humanity, and the traveller's 'Vision' may be construed as an intimation of the ontological existence of the sympathetic and succouring divinity.

Lastly, in the begining lines of *A Night-Piece,* Wordsworth has described a fearful and eerie night-sky, and this may correct our general wrong impression that Wordsworth's nature is always soothing and sympathetic. The truth of this is corroborated by another poem of his: *Elegiac Stanzas: Suggested by...George Beaumont.*

(IV) THE SIMPLON PASS

The Simplon Pass is a 'poem of the imagination' like *A Night-Piece, She was a Phantom of Delight, Three Years She Grew in Sun and Shower, The Reverie of Poor Susan, Resolution and Independence, The Thorn, To a Skylark,* etc. The Simplon Pass is in Italy. In the summer of 1790, Wordsworth, along with his friend Jones, went to Italy, when they walked through that Pass, and this occasioned this poem. We do not know the exact date of the composition of this poem; it was composed probably in 1799, but in no case after 1803. Long after its composition, the poem was first published in 1845. After this, the poem was included in Book VI ('Cambridge and the Alps') of *The Prelude* (lines 621-640).

As *A Night-Piece* is a beautiful description of a particular night-sky—of a particular aspect or appearance of nature—, so also *The Simplon Pass* is an exquisite description of a particular hilly path—again, a description of another aspect or appearance of nature. Both the aspects of nature, in the two poems, are both fearsome and attractive, all at the same time, and so the two poems may be taken to be two exempla of the Romantic perception of beauty, or of Romantic beauty. In both the poems, the poet speaks of his experiences of visions. In these two poems, Wordsworth describes the fearful but attractive aspects of nature, but from this we should not assume that he failed to notice the soothing and attractive aspect of nature. In Book VI of *The Prelude* (lines 528-547), Wordsworth describes the beautiful and soothing aspect of nature that he came across at Chamouny. In that particular place also Wordsworth had had a vision. And in all the three cases, nature, as if revealed herself to the poet.

(IV) THE SIMPLON PASS

—Brook and road
Were fellow-travellers in this gloomy Pass,
And with them did we journey several hours
At a slow step. The immeasurable height
Of woods decaying, never to be decayed,
The stationary blasts of waterfalls,
And in the narrow rent, at every turn,
Winds thwarting winds bewildered and forlorn,
The torrents shooting from the clear blue sky,
The rocks that muttered close upon our ears,
Black drizzling crags that spake by the wayside
As if a voice were in them, the sick sight
And giddy prospect of the raving stream,
The unfettered clouds and region of the heavens,
Tumult and peace, the darkness and the light—
Were all like workings of one mind, the features
Of the same face, blossoms upon one tree,
Characters of the great Apocalypse,
The types and symbols of Eternity,
Of first, and last, and midst, and without end.

The poet and his friend were walking through the dark ('gloomy') Simplon Pass along which a small stream or rivulet ('Brook') and a road ran in such a manner that they (*i.e.* the stream and the road) seemed to be fellow travellers of the poet and his friend. The poet and his friend walked for several hours, as if, along with that small stream and that road ('with them'), at a slow pace. The trees, that stood along their path, were of great ('immeasurable') height. When the poet and his friend were climbing up, the height of the tallest trees, behind them, seemed to be gradually getting reduced in height ('decayed'); but, on the other hand, the other tallest trees, that were before them, looked as having the same very great height ('The immeasurable height/ Of woods decaying, never to be decayed').

There were constant loud noises or boisterous sounds ('stationary blasts') of water-falls, and clashes ('thwarting') between unidirectional winds and directionless or straying ('bewildered and forlorn') winds, in the narrow fissures ('rent') of the hill, at every turning point of their way. And torrential rain was pouring down ('shooting') 'from the clear blue sky.' The rocks that lay 'by the wayside'—the black, steep and pointed rocks ('crags')—were dropping rainwater, and thus were making a muttering sound near the poet's and his friend's ears in such a manner that it seemed that the rocks were, as if, speaking ('a voice were in them') to the poet and his friend. The mad ('raving') stream or rivulet was coursing forward ('prospect') at a speed that will make one dizzy or unsteady ('giddy'), and the sight of this peremptory rivulet was sickening ('the sick sight').

In the sky above, clouds were at large, and were moving at will ('unfettered'). There, in the sky, was a region which was so beautiful that it symbolised the heavens, and there were both wild noise and peaceful silence, and there, moreover, were darkness and light. The poet says that all these things were, as if ('like'), wrought by ('workings') one (supreme) spiritual being or consciousness ('one mind'), and that all these (all that the poet saw there at that particular moment) were the different aspects ('features') of the same unitary supreme consciousness or mind, or the different flowers ('blossoms') of the same tree that is that unitary supreme consciousness or mind. The poet says that all these aspects of nature were, as if, the letters ('Characters') of the great Apocalypse or the last book of the New Testament (Apocalypse reveals the future or the last events of the creation), and that all these were the modes or signs ('types and symbols') of the Eternity—the ultimate ontological timeless being—that existed before the creation ('first'), will exist till the end of the creation ('last'), and will never cease to be ('without end').

The most striking element of this poem is its timelessness: it does nowhere indicate the time when the poet accosts the particular dreary, fearful, but unforgetably beautiful and attractive scenario—it does not begin, for instance, like *Nutting* with an indication of the time:

—It seems a day
(I speak of one from many singled out)
One of those heavenly days that cannot die;....

This is so because in *The Simplon Pass* the poet is so much engrossed in the countenance of the spot of nature that he is quite oblivious of the time. The fearfully attractive scenario impinged upon his consciousness and occupied the whole of it, and he had no residual consciousness with which he could pay attention to the passage of time. In his Rede Lecture for 1951, on *Inspiration and Poetry,* Sir Maurice Bowra said: "'The all-absorbing activity which comes with inspiration means that the poet not only forgets anything outside the immediate object of his vision but looses his sense of time. Past and future no longer exist for him, and he enjoys a timeless condition. Nor is this condition negative, a mere state of omissions and absences. It is strikingly positive. In the poem, the poet feels that his whole being is enlarged and that he is able to enjoy in an unprecedented completeness what in his ordinary life he enjoys only in fragments with afterthoughts and misgivings and distractions. This experience receives its fullest treatment from the Romantics, who use for it the word "eternity" and through this seek to convey its absolute, all-absorbing character. For Blake the man who exerts his imagination "lives in Eternity's sunrise." For Wordsworth the elements of natural scenary in the Simplon Pass are:

> The types and symbols of Eternity,
> Of first, and last, and midst, and without end.'"

(Skelton, 78)

Oliver Elton has found another important element in *The Simplon Pass.* Elton says that, in the poem, the poet is absolutely lonely, unlike in most of his other poems, where he is not absolutely alone, but alone with nature, or with the universe. In most of his poems, though Wordsworth may not be conversing with nature, yet he feels the spirit of nature present beside him—understanding nature, sympathetic nature. But, in *The Simplon Pass,* the poet is isolated even from nature—there is no correspondence between him and nature: he is only a distant observer. Elton writes: "Wordsworth often speaks as if he were not only alone with the universe but alone in it. This is the impression left by two of the loftiest passages of *The Prelude*; once, when, in a college vacation, he comes out from a gay festivity into the night, and a vow from unknown sources, undefined but irresistible, descends upon him, and he knows that he will be 'a dedicated spirit'; and once in the verses on the Simplon Pass, which he crossed in the summer of 1790. Rain and wind, snow and vapour, all the works of the Lord, are then:

> like workings of one mind, the features
> Of the same face, blossoms upon one tree,

Characters of the great Apocalypse,
The types and symbols of Eternity,
Of first, and last, and midst, and without end.

This is the feeling that is otherwise expressed in the more than Virgilian Pantheism of *Tintern Abbey*" (Elton, 59).

Yet another point to notice in *The Simplon Pass* is Wordsworth's pantheism. The objects that the poet saw in the Simplon Pass are not separate entities, existing independently, and having separate ontological beings, but they subsist in the 'one mind' of which they are but expressions—signs and symbols, or, as the poet says, 'types and symbols.' And, lastly, as we have already said, the poem is revelatory. In the poem, the poet explicitly says that what he perceived in the Simplon Pass was apocalyptic, revelatory ('Characters of the great Apocalypse')—the Eternity had presented itself before the eyes of the poet. What the poet saw was not simply a vision; it had a religious tone; and so Elton is quite right in calling Wordsworth, at least so far as this present poem goes, a '*vates sacer* of Pantheism' (Elton, 59)—a prophet of religion or a religious prophet. Such revelation we again find in Book IV of *The Prelude* (lines 323-337), as just now pointed out by Elton. Here, the poet, during his college summer vacation, came out of a night-long gaiety, and suddenly accosted a heavenly scenario in the early morning sun. The beautiful scenario 'drenched in empyrean light' filled the heart of the poet, to the brim. The scenario was revelatory to the poet because it appeared to him that the scenario was the phenomenal expression of some spiritual being (the 'one mind') that demanded his willing subservience to it:

I made no vows, but vows
Were then made for me; bond unknown to me
Was given, that I should be, else sinning greatly,
A dedicated Spirit.

(V) MICHAEL

(*A Pastoral Poem*)

As we know, Wordsworth preferred to put his choicest poem at the end of a volume of poems. He therefore placed *Tintern Abbey* at the end of the 1798 edition of *Lyrical Ballads,* but he replaced *Tintern Abbey* by *Michael,* as the finishing poem of the 1800 edition of it. From this, we may guess that according to Wordsworth *Michael* is the most important of all the poems of the 1800 edition of *Lyrical Ballads,* and, with a stretch of logic, further, that he thought that *Michael* bears more desired purport of his than *Tintern Abbey* that was left out in the 1800 edition of *Lyrical Ballads. Michael* is indeed a great poem of stoic fortitude, and, in this regard, the poem can be compared with such other great poems of Wordsworth as *Ode: Intimations of Immortality, Ode to Duty, Resolution and Independence* and *Eliziac Stanzas...on Peele Castle.*

This is a narrative poem, but Wordsworth has himself also described the poem as a pastoral, and both as a narrative poem and a pastoral poem, *Michael* is almost unparalleled. Geoffrey Durrant writes that "Wordsworth wrote a number of narrative poems, in styles varying from the bald and homely language of 'Simon Lee' to the classical decorum and the Virgilian cadences of 'Laodamia'" (Durrant, 76). And *Michael* may be compared with *Simon Lee,* regarding the style and language of the two poems. Though *Michael* is a pastoral poem, it is so with a distinction. Geoffrey Durrant again writes: "'The poem [*Michael*] is described by Wordsworth as a 'pastoral.' This should be noticed, because it seems intended to remind us that the humble life of Michael is not to be taken as the kind of realism that we find, for example, in the poetry of Crabbe. On the contrary, the poem deals with the condition of human life, of which Michael is a representative, chosen because in his isolation as a shepherd and among the hills he has an elemental dignity" (Durrant, 76).

As Wordsworth continued to mature in years, he more and more enquired into simple and elemental emotions, rather than into compounded emotions, such as are to be found with the village folks. In *The Idiot Boy, The Old Cumberland Beggar, Michael,* etc., Wordsworth has dexterously presented some simple and elemental emotions. In Michael, the elemental and simple emotions are two—but the two are not compounded, because one follows the other. The first emotion arises out the love of a father (Michael) for his only son (Luke)—the filial love of a 84 years old father for his 18 years old son; and the second emotion arises out of the father's grief when the filial love is interfered with hopelessness. In the story of the poem, Luke leaves behind his old father and mother, with the honest objective of saving the hereditary habitation and small property from a deceptive aggression. David Mecracken writes: "The story of Luke's leaving his parents to try to redeem their estate was based on a story that Wordsworth heard from Ann Tyson during his school days. She had lived and worked at Rydal and knew much about the neighbourhood; Wordsworth no doubt had it from her that Luke's family lived in what is now Dove Cottage. 'The character and circumstances of Luke,' Wordsworth said, 'were taken from a family to whom it had belonged, many years before, the house we lived in at Town-End, along with some fields and woodlands on the eastern shore of Grasmere'" (McCracken, 38-39). McCracken further writes about the origin of the story of *Michael*: "Long before he [Wordsworth] moved to Grasmere, Helvellyn [a high-rise hill] had been a presence in Wordsworth's life. In one of his earliest prose fragments, an Ossianic bard proclaims, 'Spirit of these Mountains I see thee throned on Helvellyn, but thy feet and head are wrapped in mist. "His [Wordsworth's] old dame at Hawkshead, Ann Tyson, had lived near Helvellyn and told him stories of it, one of them about a shepherd and his son who ranged the mountains looking for a lost sheep" (McCracken, 55).

The story of the "shepherd and his son who ranged the mountains looking for a lost sheep"was used by Wordsworth for a passage of verses, which he intended to include in *Michael,* but ultimately included the passage in *The Prelude* as it stood in 1805. Yet another passage of verses was written by Wordsworth, for inclusion in Michael, but was never utilised anywhere. David McCracken writes: "This passage [the first passage], and the entire tale of the lost sheep, was originally written for the poem 'Michael' but was not used until the 1805 *Prelude.* Another passage, written for 'Michael' but not used in any published poem, tells of the old shepherd and his son on top of Helvellyn." (McCracken, 56). However, the poem *Michael,* as we read it today, was written between 11 October and 9 December, 1800, and was published in the same year.

MICHAEL

(*A Pastoral Poem*)

If from the public way you turn your steps
Up the tumultuous brook of Green-head Ghyll,
You will suppose that with an upright path
Your feet must struggle; in such bold ascent

The pastoral mountains front you, face to face.
But, courage! for around that boisterous brook
The mountains have all opened out themselves.
And made a hidden valley of their own.
No habitation can be seen; but they
Who journey thither find themselves alone
With a few sheep, with rocks and stones, and kites
That overhead are sailing in the sky.
It is in truth an utter solitude;
Nor should I have made mention of this Dell
But for one object which you might pass by,
Might see and notice not. Beside the brook
Appears a straggling heap of unhewn stones!
And to that simple object appertains
A story—unenriched with strange events,
Yet not unfit, I deem, for the fireside,
Or for the summer shade. It was the first
Of those domestic tales that spake to me
Of Shepherds, dwellers in the valleys, men
Whom I already loved;—not verily
For their own sakes, but for the fields and hills
Where was their occupation and abode.
And hence this Tale, while I was yet a Boy
Careless of books, yet having felt the power
Of Nature, by the gentle agency
Of natural objects, led me on to feel
For passions that were not my own, and think
(At random and imperfectly indeed)
On man, the heart of man, and human life.
Therefore, although it be a history
Homely and rude, I will relate the same
For the delight of a few natural hearts;
And, with yet fonder feeling, for the sake
Of youthful Poets, who among these hills
Will be my second self when I am gone.

Upon the forest-side in Grasmere Vale
There dwelt a Shepherd, Michael was his name;
An old man, stout of heart, and strong of limb.
His bodily frame had been from youth to age
Of an unusual strength: his mind was keen,

Intense, and frugal, apt for all affairs,
And in his shepherd's calling he was prompt
And watchful more than ordinary men.
Hence had he learned the meaning of all winds,
Of blasts of every tone; and oftentimes,
When others heeded not, He heard the South
Make subterraneous music, like the noise
Of bagpipers on distant Highland hills.
The Shepherd, at such warning, of his flock
Bethought him, and he to himself would say,
"The winds are now devising work for me!"
And, truly, at all times, the storm, that drives
The traveller to a shelter, summoned him
Up to the mountains: he had been alone
Amind the heart of many thousand mists,
That came to him, and left him, on the heights.
So lived he till his eightieth year was past.
And grossly that man errs, who should suppose
That the green valleys, and the streams and rocks,
Were things indifferent to the Shepherd's thoughts.
Fields, where with cheerful spirits he had breathed
The common air; hills, which with vigorous step
He had so often chimed; which had impressed
So many incidents upon his mind
Of hardship, skill or courage, joy or fear:
Which, like a book, preserved the memory
Of the dumb animals, whom he had saved,
Had fed or sheltered, linking to such acts
The certainty or honourable gain;
Those fields, those hills—what could they less? had laid
Strong hold on his affections, were to him
A pleasurable feeling of blind love,
The pleasure which there is in life itself.

His days had not been passed in singleness.

His Helpmate was a comely matron, old—
Though younger than himself full twenty years.
She was a woman of a stirring life,
Whose heart was in her house: two wheels she had
Of antique form; this large, for spinning wool:
That small, for flax: and, if one wheel had rest,

It was because the other was at work.
The Pair had but one inmate in their house,
An only Child, who had been born to them
When Michael, telling o'er his years, began
To deem that he was old,—in shepherd's phrase,
With one foot in the grave. This only Son,
With two brave sheep-dogs tried in many a storm,
The one of an inestimable worth,
Made all their household. I may truly say,
That they were as a proverb in the vale
For endless industry. When day was gone,
And from their occupations out of doors
The Son and Father were come home, even then,
Their labour did not cease; unless when all
Turned to the cleanly supper-board, and there,
Each with a mess of pottage and skimmed milk,
Sat round the basket piled with oaten cakes,
And their plain home-made cheese. Yet when the meal
Was ended, Luke (for so the Son was named)
And his old Father both betook themselves
To such convenient works might employ
Their hands by the fire-side; perhaps to card
Wool for the Housewife's spindle, or repair
Some injury done to sickle, flail, or scythe,
Or other implement of house or field.
Down from the ceiling, by the chimney's edge,
That in our ancient uncouth country style
With huge and black projection over-browed
Large space beneath, as duly as the light
Of day grew dim the Housewife hung a lamp;
An aged utensil, which had performed
Service beyond all others of its kind.
Early at evening did it burn—and late,
Surviving comrade of uncounted hours,
Which, going by from year to year, had found,
And left, the couple neither gay perhaps
Nor cheeful, yet with objects and with hopes,
Living a life of eager industry.
And now, when Luke had reached his eighteenth year,
There by the light of this old lamp they sate,

Father and Son, while far into the night
The Housewife plied her own peculiar work,
Making the cottage through the silent hours
Murmur as with the sound of summer flies.
This light was famous in its neighbourhood,
And was a public symbol of the life
That thrifty Pair had lived. For, as it chanced,
Their cottage on a plot of rising ground
Stood single, with large prospect, north and south,
High into Easedale, up to Dunmail-Raise,
And westward to the village near the lake;
And from this constant light, so regular,
And so far seen, the House itself, by all
Who dwelt within the limits of the vale,
Both old and young, was named The Evening Star.

Thus living on through such a length of years,
The Shepherd, if he loved himself, must needs
Have loved his Helpmate; but to Michael's heart
This son of his old age was yet more dear—
Less from instinctive tenderness, the same
Fond spirit that blindly works in the blood of all—
Than that a child, more than all other gifts
That earth can offer to declining man,
Brings hope with it, and forward-looking thoughts,
And stirrings of inquietude, when they
By tendency of nature needs must a fail.
Exceeding was the love he bore to him,
His heart and his heart's joy! For oftentimes
Old Michael, while he was a babe in arms,
Had done him female service, not alone
For pastime and delight, as is the use
Of fathers, but with patient mind enforced
To acts of tenderness; and he had rocked
His cradle, as with a woman's gentle hand.

And in a later time, ere yet the Boy
Had put on boy's attire, did Michael love,
Albeit of a stern unbending mind,
To have the Young-one in his sight, when he
Wrought in the field, or on his shepherd's stool

State with a fettered sheep before him stretched
Under the large old oak, that near his door
Stood single, and, from matchless depth of shade,
Chosen for the Shearer's covert from the sun,
Thence in our rustic dialect was called
The Clipping Tree a name which yet it bears.
There, while they two were sitting in the shade,
With others round them, earnest all and blithe,
Would Michael exercise his heart with looks
Of fond correction and reproof bestowed
Upon the Child, if he disturbed the sheep
By catching at their legs, or with his shouts
Scared them, while they lay still beneath the shears.

And when by Heaven's good grace the boy grew up
A healthy Lad, and carried in his cheek
Two steady roses that were five years old;
Then Michael from a winter coppice cut
With his own hand a sapling, which he hooped
With iron, making it throughout in all
Due requisites a perfect shepherd's staff,
And gave it to the Boy; wherewith equipt
He as a watchman oftentimes was placed
At gate or gap, to stem or turn the flock;
And, to his office prematurely called,
There stood the urchin, as you will divine,
Something between a hindrance and a help;
And for this cause not always, I believe,
Receiving from his Father hire of praise;
Though nought was left undone which staff, or voice,
Or looks, or threatening gestures, could perform.

But soon as Luke, full ten years old, could stand
Against the mountain blasts and to the heights,
Not fearing toil, nor length of weary ways,
He with his Father daily went, and they
Were as companions, why should I relate
That objects which the Shepherd loved before
Were dearer now? that from the Boy there came
Feelings and emanations—things which were

Light to the sun and music to the wind;
And that the old Man's heart seemed born again?

Thus in his Father's sight the Boy grew up;
And now, when he had reached his eighteenth year,
He was his comfort and his daily hope.
While in this sort the simple household lived
From day to day, to Miachel's ear there came
Distressful tidings. Long before the time
Of which I speak, the Shepherd had been bound
In surety for his brother's son, a man
Of an industrious life, and ample means;
But unforeseen misfortunes suddenly
Had prest upon him; and old Miachel now
Was summoned to discharge the forfeiture,
A grievious penalty, but little less
Than half his substance. This unlooked for claim,
At the first hearing, for a moment took
More hope out of his life than he supposed
That any old man ever could have lost.
As soon as he had armed himself with strength
To look his trouble in the face, it seemed
The Shepherd's sole resource to sell at once
A portion of his patrimonial fields.
Such was his first resolve; he thought again,
And his heart failed him. "Isabel," said he,
Two evenings after he had heard the news,
"I have been toiling more than seventy years,
And in the open sunshine of God's love
Have we all lived; yet, if these fields of ours
Should pass into a stranger's hand, I think
That I could not lie quiet in my grave.
Our lot is a hard lot; the sun himself
Has scarcely been more diligent than I;
And I have lieved to be a fool at last
To my own family. An evil man
That was, and made an evil choice, if he
Were false to us; and, if he were not false,
There are ten thousand to whom loss like this
Had been no sorrow. I forgive him;—but
'Twere better to be dumb than to talk thus.

When I began, my purpose was to speak
Of remedies and of a cheerful hope,
Our Luke shall leave us, Isabel; the land
Shall not go from us, and it shall be free;
He shall possess it, free as is the wind
That passes over it. We have, thou know'st,
Another kinsman—he will be our friend
In this distress. He is a prosperous man,
Thriving in trade—and Luke to him shall go,
And with his kinsman's help and his own thrift
He may return to us. If here he stay,
What can be done? Where every one is poor.
What can be gained?"

At this the old Man paused,
And Isabel sat silent, for her mind
Was busy, looking back into past times.
There's Richard Bateman, thought she to herself,
He was a parish boy—at the church-door
They made a gathering for him, shillings, pence,
And halfpennies, wherewith the neighbours bought
A basket, which they filled with pedlar's wares;
And, with this basket on his arm, the lad
Went up to London, found a master there,
Who, out of many, chose the trusty boy
To go and overlook his merchandise
Beyond the seas; where he grew wondrous rich,
And left estates and monies to the poor,
And, at his birth-place, built a chapel floored
With marble, which he sent from foreign lands.
These thoughts, and many others of like sort,
Passed quickly through the mind of Isabel,
And her face brightened. The old Man was glad,
And thus resumed:—"Well, Isabel! this scheme
These two days has been meat and drink to me.
For more than we have lost is left us yet.
We have enough—I wish indeed that I
Were younger;—but this hope is a good hope.
Make ready Luke's best garments, of the best
Buy for him more, and let us send him forth

To-morrow, or the next day, or to-night:
If he could go, the Boy should go to-night."

Here Michael ceased, and to the fields went forth
With a light heart. The Housewife for five days
Was restless morn and night, and all day long
Wrought on with her best fingers to prepare
Things needful for the journey of her son.
But Isabel was glad when Sunday came
To stop her in her work: for, when she lay
By Michael's side, she through the last two nights
Heard him, how he was troubled in his sleep:
And when they rose at morning she could see
That all his hopes were gone. That day at noon
She said to Luke, while they two by themselves
Were sitting at the door, "Thou must not go:
We have no other Child but thee to lose,
None to remember—do not go away,
For if thou leave thy Father he will die."
The Youth made answer with a jocund voice;
And Isabel, when she had told her fears,
Recovered heart. That evening her best fare
Did she bring forth, and all together sat
Like happy people round a Christmas fire.

With daylight Isabel resumed her work;
And all the ensuing week the house appeared
As cheerful as a grove in Spring: at length
The expected letter from their kinsman came,
With kind assurances that he would do
His utmost for the welfare of the Boy;
To which, requests were added, that forthwith
He might be sent to him. Ten times or more
The letter was read over; Isabel
Went forth to show it to the neighbours round;
Nor was there at that time on English land
A prouder heart than Luke's, when Isabel
Had to her house returned, the old Man said,
"He shall depart to-morrow." To this word
The Housewife answered, talking much of things
Which, if at such short notice he should go,

Would surely be forgotten. But at length
She gave consent, and Michael was at ease.

Near the tumultous brook of Green-head Ghyll,

In that deep valley, Michael had designed
To build a Sheep-fold; and, before he heard
The tidings of his melancholy loss,
For this same purpose he had gathered up
A heep of stones, which by the streamlet's edge
Lay thrown together, ready for the work.
With Luke that evening thitherward he walked:
And soon as they had reached the place he stopped,
And thus the old Man spake to him:—"My son,
To-morrow thou wilt leave me; with full heart
I look upon thee, for thou art the same
That wert a promise to me ere thy birth,
And all thy life hast been my daily joy.
I will relate to thee some little part
Of our two histories; 'twill do thee good
When thou art from me, even if I should touch
On things thou canst not know of.—After thou
First cam'st into the world—as oft befalls
To new-born infants—thou didst sleep away
Two days, and blessings from thy Father's tongue
Then fell upon thee. Day by day passed on,
And still I loved thee with increasing love.
Never to living ear came sweeter sounds
Than when I heard thee by our own fire-side
First uttering, without words, a natural tune;
While thou, a feeding babe, didst in thy joy
Sing at thy Mother's breast. Month followed month,
And in the open fields my life was passed
And on the mountains; else I think that thou
Hadst been brought up upon thy Father's knees.
But we were playmates, Luke: among these hills,
As well thou knowest, in us the old and young
Have played together, nor with me didst thou
Lack any pleasure which a boy can know."
Luke had a manly heart; but at these words
He sobbed aloud. The old Man grasped his hand,
And said, "Nay, do not take it so—I see

That these are things of which I need not speak.
—Even to the utmost I have been to thee
A kind and a good Father: and herein
I but repay a gift which I myself
Received at others' hands; for, though now old
Beyond the common life of man, I still
Remember them who loved me in my youth.
Both of them sleep together: here they lived,
As all their Forefathers had done; and, when
At length their time was come, they were not loth
To give their bodies to the family mould.
I wished that thou shouldst live the life they lived,
But 'tis a long time to look back, my Son,
And see so little gain from threescore years.
These fields were burthened when they came to me;
Till I was forty years of age, not more
Than half of my inheritance was mine.
I tolled and toiled; God blessed me in my work,
And till these three weeks past the land was free.
—It looks as if it never could endure
Another Master. Heaven forgive me, Luke.
If I judge ill for thee, but it seems good
That thou shouldst go."

At this the old Man paused;

Then, pointing to the stones near which they stood,
Thus, after a short silence, he resumed:
"This was work for us; and now, my Son,
It is a work for me. But, lay one stone—
Here lay it for me, Luke, with thine own hands,
Nay, Boy, be of good hope;—we both may live
To see a better day. At eighty-four
I still am strong and hale;—do thou thy part;
I will do mine.—I will begin again
With many tasks that were resigned to thee:
Up to the heights, and in among the storms,
Will I without thee go again, and do
All works which I was wont to do alone,
Before I knew thy face,—Heaven bless thee, Boy!
Thy heart these two weeks has been beating fast
With many hopes; it should be so—yes—yes—

I knew that thou couldst never have a wish
To leave me, Luke: thou hast been bound to me
Only by links of love: When thou art gone,
What will be left to us!—But I forget
My purpose. Lay now the corner stone,
As I requested; and hereafter, Luke,
When thou art gone away, should evil men
Be thy companions, think of me, my Son,
And of this moment; hither turn thy thoughts,
And God will strenghten thee: amid all fear
And all temptation, Luke, I pray that thou
May'st bear in mind the life thy Fathers lived,
Who, being innocent, did for that cause
Bestir them in good deeds. Now, fare thee well—
When thou return'st, thou in this place wilt see
A work which is not here: a covenant
'it will be between us; but, whatever fate
Befall thee, I shall love thee to the last,
And bear thy memory with me to the grave."

The Shepherd ended here; and Luke stooped down,
And, as his Father had requested, laid
The first stone of the Sheep-fold. At the sight
The old Man's grief broke from him; to his heart
He pressed his Son, he kissed him and wept;
And to the house together they returned.
—Hushed was that House in peace, or seeming peace,
Ere the night fell:—with morrow's dawn the Boy
Began his journey, and, when he had reached
The public way, he put on a bold face;
And all the neighbours, as he passed their doors,
Came forth with wishes and with farewell prayers,
That followed him till he was out of sight.
A good report did from their Kinsman come,
Of Luke and his well-doing: and the Boy
Wrote loving letters full of wondrous news,
Which, as the Housewife phrased it, were throughout
"The prettiest letters that were ever seen."
Both parents read them with rejoicing hearts.
So, many months passed on: and once again
The Shepherd went about his daily work

With confident and cheerful thoughts; and now
Sometimes when he could find a leisure hour
He to that valley took his way, and there
Wrought at the Sheep-fold. Meantime Luke began
To slacken in his duty; and, at length,
He in the dissolute city gave himself
To evil courses: ignominy and shame
Fell on him, so that he was driven at last
To seek a hiding-place beyond the seas.

There is a comfort in the strength of love;
'twill make a thing endurable, which else
Would overset the brain, or break the heart:
I have conversed with more than one who well
Remember the old Man, and what he was
Years after he had heard this heavy news.
His bodily frame had been from youth to age
Of an unusual strength. Among the rocks
He went, and still looked up to sum and cloud,
And listened to the wind; and, as before,
Performed all kinds of labour for his sheep,
And for the land, his small inheritance.
And to that hollow dell from time to time
Did he repair, to build the Fold of which
His flock had need. 'tis not forgotten yet
The pity which was then in every heart
For the old Man—and 'tis believed by all
That many and many a day he thither went,
And never lifted up a single stone.

There, by the Sheep-fold, sometimes was he seen
Sitting alone, or with his faithful Dog.
Then old, beside him, lying at his feet.
The length of full seven years, from time to time.
He at the building of this Sheep-fold wrought,
And left the work unfinished when he died.
Three years, or little more, did Isabel
Survive her Husband: at her death the estate
Was sold, and went into a stranger's hand.
The Cottage which was named the Evening Star
Is gone—the ploughshare has been through the ground
On which it stood; great changes have been wrought

In all the neighbourhood;—yet the oak is left
That grew beside their door; and the remains
Of the unfinished Sheep-fold may be seen
Beside the boisterous brook of Green-head Ghyll.

The poet tells the reader, who is supposed to be a traveller ('You'), that if he abandons the path that men generally use, and walks upwards over the hill, along the fiercely noisy ('boisterous') ravine ('brook') of Green-head Ghyll (Ghyll or gill is a small ravine or rivulet, or wooded glen), then he will feel ('suppose') that he has struggled to walk upwards. Here the path is sharply rising upwards, and here he will confront ('front') 'face to face' the pastures over the mountains. The poet asks the reader (or the traveller) to courageously move forward to find there an open space around and over the mountains, and also a 'hidden valley'. In the valley, there is no dwelling house, and those shepherds who go ('journey') there, with a few sheep, find themselves lonely, and can see only rocks and stones, and kites (a kind of birds) flying ('sailing') across the sky. Really, there prevails absolute silence (in the valley over the mountains). The poet would not otherwise mention the valley ('Dell'), but for the reason that the reader may have passed by it (in future), or may have already seen the valley, though not with attention ('notice not'). The poet tells the reader that beside that ravine, a sprawling and untidy heap of natural or uncut ('unhewn') boulders will show itself ('Appears'), and that around that heap of simple stones ('simple object') a story hangs ('appertains'). The story is embellished with 'strange events,' but, yet, thinks the poet ('I deem'), it is worth listening to, sitting by fireside in winter, or sitting under a shade in summer. The particular story (that the poet is going to relate) is one of those stories that the poet heard ('spoke to me') while they were being narrated in the family circle, or is one of those stories that refer to familial events ('domestic tales') of those shepherds who dwell in those valleys—the shepherds whom the poet loved. The poet loved those shepherds not indeed ('not verily') for themselves, but for the fields and hills where they worked and lived ("Where was their occupation and abode"), and because of this ('hence'), when he was a boy, who was disinterested in books but who could feel the attraction ('power') of nature, he was fascinated or allured ('led me') by that story's ('this Tale') description of the gentleness of the natural objects, such as woods and valleys ('by the gentle agency/Of natural objects'). And when he listened to this story (the story of *Michael*), he was made to realise the passions of another person, *i.e.*, of Michael ('to feel/For passions that were not my own'), empathetically. And then he thought—of course aimlessly or disorderly or illogically ('At random') and incorrectly ('imperfectly')—about man, and his emotions ('the heart of man'), and about human life. And so he (the poet) will narrate the life-story ('history') of Michael, the shepherd—the life-story, or simply the story, that is familial ('Homely') and pathetic ('rude'), for the enjoyment of the few people whose hearts have sensibility and emotions ('natural hearts'). He (the poet) will tell the story with more than normal eagerness ('with yet fonder feeling') for young poets who will be present among those hills which are around the Green-head Ghyll, after his (the present poet's, or Wordsworth's) death ('when I am gone') (*Lines 1-38*).

The story is this. In the forest of Grasmere valley, there lived a shepherd whose name was Michael. He was old, but was strong in body and heart. From Youth to old age, he was an uncommonly strong man, with a mind that was sharp, strong and alert ('frugal'), *i.e.*, the mind did not require much effort to understand, or to make one understand, something. The mind was capable of doing all sorts of things ('apt for all affairs'). In his vocation ('calling') as a shepherd, he was uncommonly ('more than ordinary men') prompt and watchful. For this reason, he learned the different effects of all sorts of storms ('winds') and thunders ('blasts') of all sorts of sounds. Frequently, he heard, when others heeded not to hear, the subterranean or underground ('subterraneous') sweet sound ('music') that seemed to be the music or sound ('noise') of 'bagpipers' playing on their musical instruments, on the distant hills. Whenever the shepherd would hear such a sound of warning, he would think about it, and would say to himself that the storm was asking him to do the work of bringing his sheep back to the fold or enclosure for keeping sheep ('devising work for me'). And, really, as it always happens that storms urge upon travellers to seek shelter, the said storms, as if, called the shepherd to go over to the upper part of the mountain for shelter. The shepherd went there and began to live alone there, remaining enveloped by many layers of screens of mists, and continued to live there till he was eighteen. The poet says that one will be very much wrong ('grossly that man errs') if he supposes that the wooded valleys, the brooks, and the rocks that surrounded him, did not influence ('indifferent to') the thought-processes of the shepherd. The fields, where he delightfully ('with cheerful spirits') breathed the general air, and the hills, whose massive ('vigorous') steps he climbed had imprinted many things or events upon his mind which was fully of 'hardship, skill or courage, joy or fear,' *i.e.*, upon the mind which was industrious, skilled, and full of courage, joy, and fear. And the mind of that shepherd retained the memory of the speechless sheep ('animal') whom he protected, fed, and provided with shelter. By doing all these things for the sheep, the shepherd was certain that he would get some profit through a rightful means ('honourable gain'), to live by. And the fields and the hills provided him with nothing less ('what could they less?') than affecting his feelings very much ('had laid/Strong hold'), and the fields and hills were to him objects of pleasurable feeling of instinctual ('blind') love, and those fields and hills gave him the pleasures that life can provide one with (*Lines 39-77*).

The shepherd did not live there lonely, as a bachelor ('singleness'), as his beautiful wife ('comely matron') was his helpmate. She was old, but she was younger than the shepherd by twenty complete ('full') years. She was a burstling woman ('woman of a stirring life') who devoted herself to the household affairs. She had two very old ('antique') spinning wheels ('wheels'): one of them for spinning woolen thread, and the other for spinning 'the fibres of the plant linum' (for weaving linen cloth) ('flax'). She used to remain incessantly engaged either at the one spinning wheel or at the other ('if one wheel had rest,/It was because the other was at work'). The shepherd and his wife ('Pair') had only one loving or close ('intimate') object—their only child (Luke) who was born when the shepherd (Michael), who was then feeling the burden of his years and was getting to know that he was old, or, to express the same thing in his own words, he was beginning to realise that he had one foot in the grave. In their house, besides the shepherd and his wife, there were their only son(Luke), and two sheep-dogs with which their son managed ('tried') the sheep in many a storm.

One of the sheep-dogs was very worthy or efficient. The poet verily says that the shepherd, his wife, and their son were so industrious that their industry or hard labour became proverbial. When it was night ('day was gone'), the father and the son used to leave their work ('occupation') outside the household, and come home; but then even in the household they used to be working ('Their labour did not cease') until they used to sit for dinner around a clean dining table ('unless when all/Turned to the clearly supper-board'). On the dining table there would be pots of edibles, disorderly laid ('mess of pottage'); and skimmed milk; and a basket, full of cakes made of oat and 'plain home-made cheese.' Even after they would have finished those things of the meal pots ('meal/Was ended'), Luke and his father used to go ('betook themselves') to the fire-side and engage themselves in some less strenuous or easy ('convenient') works, such as combing ('card') wool for the housewife's (Michael's wife's) spindle, or repairing some broken part ('injury') of the sickle, or of flail, or of scythe, or repairing other tools, either of the household or of the field (*Lines 78-109*).

When night would, as usual or regularly ('duly'), begin to fall, or as the light of the sun would begin to become dim ('as the light/ Of day grew dim'), the housewife would suspend a lamp, made in a mode or design or fashion ('style') that was very old and simple and belonged to the villages, from the ceiling, beside the chimney. The lamp had a very long and black upward ('overbrowed') projection, and its bottom had a large space. This old lamp ('utensil') served longer than such other lamps. Early in the evening the Lamp would begin to give light and continued to burn till late in the night, and thus the lamp gave light for more hours than other lamps did ('comrades'), and thus survived them. This lamp saw ('found') the shepherd and his wife neither full of gaity nor full of cheerfulness, and yet it found them possessing their necessary objects, having hopes, and leading their lives being prone ('eager') to hard works ('industry'). When Luke was eighteen years of age, he and his father sometimes used to idle away their time sitting around the lamp, while his mother would silently engage herself in her particular ('peculiar') works, for hours together in the night, and when she worked on this wise, a murmuring sound ('singing in a very low pith'), like that of summer flies, would fill the cottage. The light of that lamp was famous in that region, and it was a symbol of that husband (Michael) and his wife who lived there economically ('thrift'), to the people of that region ('public'). The light of that lamp was a symbol (of the fact that if one is industrious, he must prosper), because ('For') it happened ('as it chanced') that the highly pictorial scene ('large prospect') of the cottage of the family stood lonely ('single') 'on a plot of rising ground' and extended towards the north and the south and rose upwards ('High') through ('into') Easedale, and upto Dunmail-Raise, and also toward the west upto the village that was situated near the lake. All those, who lived within the periphery of the valley, both young and old, saw the unflickering ('constant') and regular (because the light appeared each and every night, without fail) light of that lamp, from a great distance ('so far seen'). And it was due to the light of this lamp that ('And from this') the cottage ('House') itself was called The Evening Star (*Lines 110-139*).

However, on this wise the shepherd lived for a great number of years, and he certainly ('needs') loved his wife as much as he loved himself ('if he loved himself, must needs/ Have loved his Helpmate'). But to him, his son, who was born to him in his old age, was more dear than his wife. He loved his son so much ('less') not due to the tender spirit of his parental instinct—which lovely spirit ('Fond spirit') works in all human beings—as due to the fact that a son brings hope, optimistic ('forward-looking') thoughts, and the burstlings of life's restlessness or activities ('stirrings of inquietude') to an aging ('declining') man whose hope, optimism and liveliness must naturally ('By tendency of nature') give way. No other gifts (other than those from a son) that the world may provide an aging man with can bring for that aging man so many things (hope, optimism, etc.) and so much of them. The shepherd loved his son inordinately ("Exceeding was the love he bore to him") and the son was a joy to the shepherd. The poet says this because ('For'), frequently, the old shepherd Michael, when Luke, his son, was a baby and would be nursed in his (Michael's) arms, would behave with that baby as tenderly as a woman does ('Had done him female service'). The old shepherd did so not only ('alone') because he delighted in doing so, as fathers delight in doing so, but also because his patient mind (as that of a woman) compelled him to behave with that baby tenderly. And with such tenderness he would undulate ('rocked') the cradle of the baby, as tenderly as a woman does (*Lines 140-158*).

Afterwards ('in a later time'), but before the baby grew up into a boy ('put on boy's attire'), Michael was pleased to keep the young Luke within his sight, inspite of ('Albeit') of the fact that Michael had a severe and unmollifiable mind, with which he wanted to govern him (Luke) ('stern unbending mind'). When the child (Luke) would remain within the sight of him, Michael would either work ('Wrought') in the field, or sit ('Sate') on his stool with a tethered sheep before him—the sheep, the while, resting, extending its limbs ('stretched') under the big and old oak that stood lonely near Michael's cottage ('door'). The shade of the oak was exceptionally deep, and it was meant ('chosen') as an umbrella ('covert') for reapers of corn ('Shearers') to protect them from the sun. For this reason ('Thence'), the oak, in the language of the village ('in our rustic dialect') was called Clipping Tree (the word 'clipping,' in the dialect of Northern England, means 'reaping' or 'shearing'), and the tree till now bears that name of Clipping Tree. Michael and Luke would sit under the shade of that oak, gathering some other persons around them, and all of them would be full of eagerness (to sit there) and cheerfulness ('blithe'). There, sometimes, Michael would lovingly correct ('fond correction') the wrongs of Luke ('Child') or admonish him ('reproof bestowed') with his (Michael's) affectionate looks ('exercise his heart with looks'). Michael would correct Luke's behaviour by admonishing him if Luke would annoy the sheep by catching hold of their legs, or would scare them by shouting at them, while the sheep would even then ('still') be lying under the sheaves ('shears') *(Lines 159-176)*.

In course of time, by the grace of God, the boy (Luke) grew up into a youth ('Lad'), and then his two cheeks seemed like two fresh ('steady') roses that resemble the two cheeks of a boy of five years. Then Michael himself cut a sapling of coppice that grew in the winter, and fitted an iron ring ('hopped') on one end of the stave, and thus converted the stave into a perfect shepherd's staff, having all the necessary features ('Due requisites') of a shepherd's staff, and then Michael gave it to the boy (Luke). And armed ('equiped') with this staff, Luke would frequently remain posted, as a watchman, at the gate of their cottage, or in the cleft or notch or pass in a mountain-ridge ('gap'), to restrain ('stem') the sheep from straying, or to bring them back ('turn'). The boy Luke was called upon to take up his profession or vocation of the shepherd ('to his office') early in his life, *i.e.*, before he matured or came of age ('prematurely'), and the uncouth or rustic boy ('urchin')—that Luke was—joined his vocation ('There stood'). The poet tells us that we are to understand ('divine') that Luke was then something between an obstruction and a helper to Michael, *i.e.* sometimes Luke would create troubles to the smooth functioning of Michael, but at other times he would be of help to his father. For this reason, the poet believes that Luke did not always receive praises ('hire of praise') from his father, although he did everything ('nought was left undone') which he could do with the help of his staff, or voice, or threatening looks or gestures (*Lines 177-193*).

Soon Luke became ten years old, and could withstand the onslaughts of storms belowing over the hills. Everyday, Luke and his father used to climb up to the picks ('heights') of the hills, without being daunted ('Nor fearing') by their labour in walking up, and by the long and wearisome (hilly or upward) paths that they were to cover by walking, to reach the picks. And while walking up they were as companions. The poet says that he is not going to tell about ('relate') the objects (on the hills) which Michael had loved and which have now became more loveable ('dearer') to him (because of the presence of his son near him). The poet is also not going to tell that there grew in Luke feelings and emotions ('emanations') which, as if, were the sources of the sun's light, and of the wind's music ('light to the sun and music to the wind'). Further, he is not going to tell us that now Michael's ('old Man's) heart seemed to be rejuvinated ('seemed born again') (*Lines 194-203*).

However, in this way, Luke grew up under the supervision of his father ('in his father's sight'), and now became eighteen years of age. He was now his father's ('his') happiness ('comfort') and his continual ('daily') hope. And while on this wise ('sort') the members of the poor ('simple') family were living from day to day, Michael heard ('to Michael's ear these came') a depressing news ('Distressful tidings'). Long before the time about which the poet is telling us, Michael became a guarantor ('had been bound/ In security') of his nephew who was an industrious and rich ('ample means') man. But some unforeseen misfortune fell upon that nephew who became depressed by that misfortune ('Had prest upon him'). Then Michael was requested ('summoned') by his nephew to pay the forfeiture ('that to which right is lost' due to a crime committed, or otherwise) that the nephcw himself was to pay. The amount of the forfeiture or penalty was so great('grievous') that it was not worth even a bit less than half the property of Michael ('Than half his substance'). When Michael first heard this news (of the forfeiture of his nephew), he was, for a while, full of more hope or courage (to repay the forfeiture of his nephew), gathered with all effort, than, he thought, any old man may ever lose ("took/ More hope out of his life than he supported/ that any old man ever could have lost"). But when he gathered strength and tried directly to challenge or drive away his anxiety ('trouble') of paying the requisite amount of money for the forfeiture, it was found ('it seemed') that his (Michael's) only source of money was selling, at once, a portion of his landed property ('field') that he got from his forefathers ('patrimonial fields'). And he decided to sell that portion of his landed property. But as he thought about selling that portion, he became frustrated ('his heart failed him').

Two days ('Two evenings') after he got the news of his nephew's forfeiture, Michael told his wife Isabel, that he had been labouring for more than seventy years then, and that so far they (Himself, Luke and Isabel) had lived with the unstinted or abundant joy of God's love (open sunshine of God's love). Nevertheless, if he sold the land, and consequently somebody else possessed it, he supposed, he would not be happy even after his death ('I could not lie quiet in grave'). He said that they were not fortunate, and that he had been more industrious than the sun ("the sun himself/Has scarcely been more diligent than I"), and that, nevertheless, he had been taken, at the end, by his family to be a fool. Michael told his wife that if his nephew, in future, proves to be false (by not repaying the money advanced to him by Michael), then his nephew would be counted as an evil person ('An evil man') who requested him (Michael) with a criminal intention ('made an evil choice'). But if his nephew proved to be an honest person ('if he were not false') (but could not repay the money given him by Michael, due to inability), then his loss would not be counted as a great loss (to mourn), for the fact that there were thousands of people to whom such a loss was no cause of sorrow (and so he also would not sorrow). And, further, (for the same reason) he would forgive or exonerate his nephew for his breach of contract, or dishonesty. Telling his wife Isabel this far, Michael thought it better to remain silent ('dumb') than talking about the matter of paying his nephew a sum of money ('thus').

When Michael again began to talk, he was talking about how he could prevent the loss of money to be advanced to his nephew, or how he could make good the loss of money ('remedies'), and finding a means of making good the loss, he said, they would be cheerfully hopeful of really making good that loss. Michael suggested that Luke would go abroad, or to a far region, leaving them (Michael and Isabel) behind (to work there and amass money). Michael told Isabel that their landed property would not be forfeited (because it would be taken back, paying the money Luke would bring from the far region), and that it will remain free from all claims. He said that Luke would be the proprietor ('shall possess it') as independently as the wind that blows over their plot of land. He said that they had another relative who now might act as a friend in their sufferings ('distress'). He said that Luke would go to this relative who was a rich man, and who was doing well ('Thriving') in business. With the help of this relative, Luke might get a job, and thus earn money, and save the money living thriftily, and with the money saved Luke would make good ('repair') their loss (the loss of half his property that would be sold for his nephew), and only after that Luke might return home. On the other hand, said Michael, if instead of going to that relative and living in a distant land, Luke stayed there at home, he (Luke) could do nothing—he would not get any profitable job ('What can be gained?'), because there, in the region where Michael and his family lived, everyone was poor (*Lines 204-255*).

Saying all these things, Michael stopped, but Isabel did not say anything. She kept silent because she was recapitulating the things of the past. She was thinking that one Richard Bateman had been a boy in the village church ('parish-boy'). The church-going people ('at the Church-door/ They') collected money for that boy ("made a gathering for him, shillings, pence,/ And half-pennies"), and with this money the neighbouring people bought a basket and filled it with those wares which a huckster ('pedlar') sells. According to the biddings of those neighbours, the boy, Richard Bateman, went to London for selling those wares. There a merchant ('master') chose this trustworthy boy, from among many boys, and took him in his (the merchant's) service, and asked him to go abroad and supervise his merchandise. Abroad, the boy Bateman became very ('wonderous') rich, and from the foreign country sent materials and money ('left estates and moneis') for his poor neighbours, and at his birth place built a chapel whose floor was covered with marbel. This thought and other cognate thoughts quickly passed across the screen of Isabel's memory, and, consequently she became delighted with hope ('her face brightened'). Michael, supposedly seeing the gladness of Isabel, was also glad. He told her that this plan of his ('this scheme') (of sending Luke to a far-away country) he had been very much enjoying for those two days ("this scheme/ These two days has been meat and drink to me"). He said he thought that they (though Michael had already advanced the money to his nephew) yet possessed much more property than they had lost (by advancing the money to that nephew), and that they had yet enough resources. Michael told Isabel that he wished he were young, and that the hope that she had generated in him by innuendoing (to the story of the success of Bateman) was a good one. He asked her to make the best clothes or garment for Luke ready, and also to buy some more garments of the best quality for him (Luke), and let him be sent abroad the next day, or the day after the next day, or, if possible, that very night (*Lines 255-282*).

Michael said this much, and then went to the field with a light heart. For five days since then, Isabel herself very carefully ('with her best fingers') prepared the things for the journey of Luke. But on Sunday she was happy and did no work. This was due to the following reason. For the last two nights (before that Sunday) Isabel slept beside Michael, and heard from him that he could not sleep well ('troubled in his sleep') (because he was afraid of, or he had forebodings about Luke's going abroad).

When she and her husband rose in the next morning, she could realise that all of his (Michael's) hopes were gone (because his hopes were pinned on Luke who was going away). Now, on that Sunday Isabel told Luke, while the two were sitting at the door, not to go away, because he was their only child, and in case he went away, they might lose him ("We have no other Child but thee to lose"). She told Luke that if they (She and Michael) lost him, there would be no one else to remember them. So she asked him not to go away, for, in case he left, his father would die. (Isabel was glad on that Sunday, because she thought Luke would obey her persuading of not going away.) Luke answered his mother's persuasion in a jovial mood ('jocund voice'). When, earlier, she told Luke about her fears (about Luke's going away), her heavy heart became light. In the evening of that day, Isabel brought in her best prepared food ('best fare'), and all of the family sat for dinner, like the happy people who gather 'round a Christmas fire' (*Lines 283-303*).

Early in the morning ('With daylight'), Isabel used to begin her work, and the following ('ensuing') week the Cottege remained gay, as if it were a gathering of jocund people in a forest grove in spring time. At last ('at length') a letter from that kinsman, which all the member of the family of Michael expected, arrived. In the letter, the kinsman assured all of the family that he would do his best for the good of Luke, and requested Micahel and Isabel to send Luke to him immediately. The letter was read ten times or more than that. Isabel went out to show the letter to neighbours all around. At that time, Luke was so proud (because he was going abroad) that an equally proud person was not to be found in England. When, after showing the letter to the neighbours, Isabel returned home, Michael told her that Luke would leave home the next day, to go to the Kinsman. Hearing this, Isabel said many things which, if Luke went very promptly ('at such short notice'), would certainly be forgotten. However, at last she consented to Luke's going abroad, and so Michael was happy ('at ease') (*Lines 304-321*).

In that deep valley, near that noisy rivulet called Green-head Ghyll, Michael planned to build an enclosure for his sheep. During this time Michael faced his great loss (due to Luke's going abroad) for which reason he became full of sorrow ('melancholic loss'), but before that he had gathered up a heap of stones, putting one stone close by another ('Lay thrown together'), on the bank of that rivulet, for the purpose of building an enclosure('ready for the work'). That evening, Michael walked, along with Luke, toward the place where the enclosure was to be built up ('thitherward'), and reaching the place of the proposed enclosure, he told Luke that he (Luke) was leaving them(Michael and Isabel) the next day. He told Luke that he was looking up to him with his heart full of hope ('with full heart'), because he was a promise to him (Michael), and (Luke) was the same child who, before he was born, through his life, he (Luke) had been his constant ('daily') enjoyment. Michael told Luke that he would tell him a little about Luke's as well as his own biographies ('our two histories'). Michael further told Luke that when Luke would be staying away from him, his telling about the two biographies would be of benefit to him (Luke), even if he (Michael) would tell about ('touch') some things of the two biographies that Luke did not know or did not understand ('canst not know of').

Michael told Luke that after he (Luke) was born—as it frequently ('oft') happened to new-born babies—he (Luke) slept continually for two days, and after that he (Michael) blessed him ('blessings from thy Father's tongue/Then fell upon thee'). With the passage of time, Michael loved Luke more and more ('increasing'). There was no sound, that human beings heard ('to living ear'), more sweet than the sound that he (Michael) heard, sitting by the fire—the sound that Luke uttered with a baby's natural tune, but without forming a word, while sucking at his (Luke's) mother's breast ('feeding babe'), the sound of Luke seeming to be that of singing in joy. Month after month went by while Michael ('I') passed his days ('life') working in the open fields or over the hills. Barring the time that Michael passed working in the fields or over the hills, he (Michael) nursed Luke all the while, keeping him (Luke) on his lap ('knees'), so that he (Michael) thought that Luke had been brought up on his (Michael's) lap ("else I think that thou/Had been brought up upon thy Father's knees"). However ('But'), they (Michael and Luke) used to play among those hills, and this Luke knew. Michael told Luke that he was an old man and he (Luke) was a young man; and, nevertheless, Luke did not lack in the pleasure that a boy got from playing with another boy ('which a boy can know').

Luke was courageous ('had a manly heart'); and yet, when he heard Michael tell all that, he cried loudly. Then Michael held him by the hand, and asked him (Luke) not to take what he (Michael) told him as something full of sorrow ('do not take it so'). Michael told him that he then understood that he (Michael) needed not speak about the things he had already spoken about. Michael said that he had been an extremely ('Even to the utmost') kind and good father. He told Luke that by telling him all that ('herein') he was paying him (Luke) the love that he (Michael) received from his own father and mother ("repay a gift which I myself/Received at others' hands"). Michael said that though he was then an old man, and though he had lived for more years than a man generally lives, he till then recalled the love that he received, in his youth, from them (from his father and mother). His father and mother ('Both of them') were there in their graves, put side by side ('together'). They lived there in that place, as all their forefathers did, and when at last they were to die ('their time was come'), they did not hate, or were not unwilling ('were not loth') to get entombed in the family grave-yard ('mould'). Michael said that it was his wish that Luke would live like his forefathers, but to think of them was to go back to long past ('long time to look back'), because they (Michael's father and mother) died sixty years ago, and so now Luke could gain very little if he thought about them, or if he knew about them. Michael told Luke that the plots of land that he inherited from his father ('when they came to me') were mortgaged ('burthened'), and when he was forty years of age, not more than half his inheritance belonged to him (probably he sold some plots to release the others from mortgage). Michael said that he laboured very hard ('toiled and toiled'), and God blessed him in his work, and so, just three weeks ago all his landed property was free from mortgage ('the land was free'). Now it seemed that his land could not, in future, remain under the possession of any proprietor other than himself ("it never could endure/ Another Master"). Michael prayed to God to forgive him if his decision (regarding Luke's going abroad) was bad, but he told Luke that he thought that it was good for Luke to go a way (*Lines-322-382*).

Saying so far, Michael stopped, and then he drew Luke's notice to the heap of stones beside which they stood, and after a brief period of silence, again began to speak to Luke. He told Luke that the building or enclosure for the sheep-fold ('It') was to be constructed by himself (in the absence of Luke) ('work for me'). Yet he requested Luke to lay a stone (in the on-going construction) with his (Luke's) own hand for his (Michael's) sake. He asked Luke to be hopeful that they two would live to 'see a better day' (in future). Michael told him that even at eighty-four years of age, he was still strong and healthy ('hale'). He told Luke to do his own duty or task (of going abroad), and said that he (Michael) himself would again begin to do the works that were assigned ('resigned') to him (Luke). Michael told Luke that he would go over to the mountains or hills ('heights'), without him (Luke), and do all the works that he (Michael) was habituated ('wont') to do alone, before he (Luke) was born ('Before I knew thy face') in the fierce winds ('storms') blowing over there. Michael prayed to God to bless him (Luke). He told Luke that, for the past two weeks, his (Luke's) heart was full of exultation ('beating fast') because it was full of hopes, and that the heart of a young man like Luke should be so full of exultation and hopes ('it should be so—yes—Yes'). Nevertheless, said Michael, he knew that Luke could not harbour in his heart any desire to leave him (Michael) behind, because Luke was bound with him by the bond ('link') of love. Michael said that it would be despairing when Luke would leave them behind, because in the case of his leaving actually nothing would be left for them. (Retrieving himself from his digression) Michael said that he was forgetting what he was telling Luke ('My purpose'). He asked Luke to lay the principal stone of the foundation ('corner-stone') of the would-be sheep-fold, as he asked him earlier to do; and if evil people followed him with evil motives ('Be thy companions'), after he (Luke) would have gone away from there, to remember him (Michael) and that happy moment (in which they had then been). Michael advised him to think about, or recall, all those things ('hither turn thy thoughts'), and told him that God would give him strength in all his (Luke's) fears and temptations. He requested him (Luke) to keep ('bear') in mind the examples of the lives of his (Luke's) forefathers, who were honest and who engaged themselves in ('Bestir them') good works to make their lives exemplary ('for that cause'). He told Luke that he was then bidding farewell to him, and told him that when he (Luke) would come back home, he would find there a structure (sheep-fold) which was not visible ('which is not here') at that moment. Michael told him that structure or building would be, as if, an agreement ('covenant') between them two (*i.e.* that structure would be a symbol of bond between Michael and Luke). Michael further told Luke that whatever sort of luck might be his (Luke's), he (Michael) would continue to love him till his (Michael's) death ('last'), and would continue to remember him (Luke) till the time of his (Michael's) entering into grave (*Lines 382-417*).

Michael stopped here, and Luke (in order to raise a stone) stooped low, and according to his father's request, laid 'The first stone of the Sheep-fold.' As Michael, the old man, saw Luke laying the stone ('At the sight'), he cried out in joy ('grief broke from him'), and embraced and kissed Luke, and then shed tears ('wept'). Thereafter, the father and the son together went to the cottage. There prevailed silence ('Hushed') in the cottage, and the cottage was peaceful, or seemed to be so, till midnight. The next morning came, and Luke began his journey. When Luke reached the thoroughfare or highway ('public way') he became courageous ('bold face'). As he was passing by neighbouring houses, neighbours came out of their houses, and wished Luke well, and then said their prayers to God for the welfare of Luke ('farewell prayers'), and their prayers continued till Luke could no more be seen (*Lines 418-430*).

Good news about Luke's doings abroad came from that relative of the family of Michael ('their'), and Luke ('Boy') himself wrote to the family letters expressing his love for his father and mother, and bearing astonishing news about his achievements. Isabel said that those letters were the most beautiful or lovely ones that were ever read ('seen'). Both Michael and Isabel read those letters with pleasure in their hearts ('rejoicing hearts'). In this way, many months went by, and once again (after a depressive and sorrowful period that was due to Luke's absence, Michael resumed ('went about') his daily work with a confident and cheerful mind ('thoughts'). And then whenever Michael could find some moments for leisure, he would go ('look his way') to that valley and work ('Wrought) at the sheep-fold. In the meantime, Luke began to neglect ('slacken') his duty, and at last he mingled himself ('gave himself') with the unlawful or bad things ('evil courses') of life in that immoral ('dissolute') city. And, consequently, he became a notorious and disgraceful person ("ignominy and shame/Fell on him"), as a result of which he was forced ('driven') at last to seak a refuge ('hiding-place') in another country, beyond the seas (*Lines 431-447*).

The poet says that there is comfort or happiness in the bond ('strength') of love, and that the bond of love will make human beings and the relations among them ('a thing') live longer ('endurable'). He says that where love is absent ('which else'), the thought process or rationality ('brain') of human beings becomes ineffectual or upset ('overset'), and the hearts of human beings break down. The poet says that he has talked with some persons ('more than one') who could remember Michael and his condition ('what he was') many years after he got the news of Luke's disgrace and shame. Michael's physical strength was inordinately great, from his youth till his old age. He would go over the hills ('rocks') (even after he heard the unfortunate news of Luke), and would look at the sun and the clouds and do all kinds of works as before for his sheep and for his plots of land that he got through inheritance. Sometimes he would also go ('Did he repair') to the valley ('dell') to build the sheep-fold which his sheep required. But the pity that everybody felt in his heart ('every heart') for Michael was not yet gone. And everybody believed that on numerous days Michael went to that place where he intended to build a sheep-fold ('thither'), but he did never lift up a stone to build that sheep-fold (*Lines 448-466*).

Beside that (improvised) sheep-fold, Michael would sometimes remain lonely or sometimes he would remain there with his faithful dog beside him—the dog which was then old, and used to be lying at his feet. For well seven years, Michael would, at times, work ('wrought') for the structure of the sheep-fold ('building'), but left that structure unfinished at the time of his death. For three years, or a little over that period, after the death of her husband, Isabel was alive, and when she was about to die ('at her death'), her property ('estate') was sold, as a result of which that property belonged to an unknows person ('went into a stranger's hand'). The cottage of Michael and his family, which was known as 'Evening Star', was gone, and the ploughshare of Michael remained inserted into the ground, erect and still, ("has been through the ground/On which it stood") *i.e.* the ploughshare remained unused. Meanwhile, many changes have been done all over the neighbouring area (of the cottage of Michael), and, nevertheless ('yet'), that oak, which stood ('grew') beside the cottage of Michael, remained untouched ('left'). And, one may see even today the debris ('remains') of the unfinished sheep-fold of Michael beside the noisy stream or rivulet of Green-head Ghyll.

As the sub-title of the poem ('A Pastoral Poem') announces, and as we have already said, *Michael* is a pastoral poem, but the poem may also be classified as an eclogue, because in modern times there is very little difference between the pastoral and the eclogue, though in ancient times the eclogue, and not the pastoral, comprised songs of two contesting shepherds. Michael is a pastoral in the sense in which Milton's *Lycidas,* Shelley's *Adonais,* and Arnold's *Thyrsis* are pastorals. *Michael,* as an eclogue, may also be compared with *Virgil's Bucolics.* However, Graham Hough writes about the pastoral nature of *Michael*: "*Michael* is described as a pastoral poem; and it is indeed a poem about shepherds; but the label seems puzzling if we think of earlier senses of 'pastoral'; for though Dr. Johnson might quite likely have found *Michael* 'easy, vulgar and therefore disgusting,' it would certainly have been so in a very different sense from *Lycidas.* It is completely without the consicious literary artifice that we associate with pastoral poetry, and free from the trick of using rural simplicities to light up some sophisticated situation. But its has the essential quality of pastoral—the imaginative sympathy for a life of unself conscious simplicity from which the poet, merely by being a poet, is detached" (Hough, 44). Alan Gardiner says that "The traditional pastoral presented a nostalgic vision of the life of shepherds, portraying a peaceful, carefree existence in idyllic surroundings" (Gardiner, 50). At least in this sense of the pastoral, we certainly say that *Michael* is a pastoral poem.

The story of *Michael* is built up on two 'present' characters, Michael and Isabel, and one 'absent,' character, Luke. Regarding the source-materials of the poem, Wordsworth, in a note to this poem, had written in October-December 1800: "'The sheep-fold, on which so much of the poem turns, remains, or rather the ruins of it. The character and circumstances of Luke were taken from a family to whom had belonged, many years before, the house we lived in at Town-End, along with some fields and woodlands on the eastern shore of Grasmere. The name of the Evening Star was not in fact given to this house but to another on the same side of the valley more to the north.'" (Wordsworth and Coleridge, 302). The gentle and suffering woman, Isabel, of the poem *Michael,* resembles Margaret of lines 502-590 of BkI of *The Excursion,* which lines were written before 1795 (Hough, 88), that is, well before *Michael* (which was written in 1800). The character of Margaret again appears in *Afflictions of Margaret* (Wordsworth dated this poem 1804, but, in all probability, it was written before 1801). Wordsworth had, perhaps, a fascination for the name of Margaret as well as for such a character as that of Margaret or Isabel—a very gentle woman, almost mute, having infinite power of bearing pounding griefs. And Michael, in some respects, resembles the Wanderer of *The Excursion* and the leech-gatherer of *Resolution and Independence,* while all the three characters, taken together, may function as Wordsworth's ideal stoic model.

Wordsworth wrote *Michael* with certain explicit purpose, and this is clear from a letter of his written to Charles James Fox, whom he wanted "to interest in the plight of small farmers in the Lake District." A part of that letter of Wordsorth reads thus: "'In the two Poems, 'The Brothers' and 'Michael,' I have attempted to draw a picture of the domestic affections, as I know they exist amongst a class of men who are now almost confined to the North of England. They are small, independent *proprietors* of land here called statesmen, men of respectable education who daily labour on their own little properties. The domestic affections will always be strong amongst men who live in a country not crowded with population, if these men are placed above poverty. But if they are proprietors of small estates, which have descended to them from their ancestors, the power which these affections will acquire amongst such men is inconceivable to those who have only an opportunity of observing hired labourers, and the manufacturing Poor. Their little tract of land serves as a kind of permanent rallying point for their domestic feelings, as a tablet upon which they are written which makes them objects of memory in a thousand instances when they would otherwise be forgotten'" (Williams, 93-94).

Wordsworth, like most of the other Romantic poets, rose against the mindless spurt of industrialisation of England, that divorced man from his natural surroundings and traditions, thus growing in him a sense of isolation and frustration. The rapid industrialisation was the result of a series of scientific discoveries. Men reverentially submitted themselves to the will of science, being wondered at the immediate gains from it; and, consequently, the fixed anchors of their consciousness into the traditional values were suddenly hauled up, leaving them in a valueless vacuum. This was the reason why Wordsworth also protested against science. The Renaissance and the Reformation, that went before, and also along with, industrialisation, strove for *éclaircissement,* and thus marginalised the medieval supernaturalism. But the new-come industrialism was, to Wordsworth, also a sort of 'supernaturalism' in so far as it clouded human consciousness with a new mode of thought-process that was strange to the natural man's 'naturalism.' Wordsworth vehemently protested against this new 'supernaturalism' initiated by the *éclat* for industrialisation—the new 'supernaturalism' which conceived of man not as a natural being, not as a part of nature, not, at the least, as something living in harmony with nature, but as a machine, as a switch board that responds whenever a button is pressed. Geoffrey Hartman writes about Wordsworth's protest against such de-naturalisation of the country: "Industrialisation is causing great changes, changes affecting also the minds of men; and Wordsworth, writing toward the beginning of this epoch, is not less than prophetic. The industrial revolution, in his eyes, is divorcing man from the earth as effectively as a debased supernaturalism. He sees that what is happening is indeed a revolution, cutting men off from their past, and their imagination from its normal food" (Williams, 35). *Michael* is a remonstrating poem that protests against the uprooting of the natural man from his moorings in the past and in his imagination by the credo of industrialisation. Luke is allured by the scientifically advanced world, by the city where his relative (or Michael's relative) works, and he goes there, and he destroys himself as well as his family. Ofcourse the poem does not explicitly pronounce its protest against the evil of industrialisation, yet it certainly does this by insinuation, by minimal imaginative suggestions. And, as Geoffrey Hartman informs us, "A truely great, unblunted imagination, Henry James said, is better served by the minimum of valid suggestion than by the maximum" (Williams, 35).

Wordsworth did not agree with his contemporary interpretation of the concept of (societal) progress that involves uplifting of man's natural and traditional moorings—man's moorings in his love of nature, and in his value system—and amassing of scientific implements merely for his hedonistic benefits. Science, the mother of all material and hadonistic benefits, Wordsworth did not regard so greatly. He said that science merely procures for us "props for our infirmity" (*The Prelude*). Roger Sales writes about Wordsworth's view of progress, as is covertly presented in *Michael*: "'Michael' appears to be concerned with refuge. It is necessary to leave 'the public way' in order to reach the 'straggling heap of unhewn stones,' which, like the bones of a dead sheep, are strewn over a particular part of the landscape. This 'public way' represents orthodox interpretations of historical progress. Wordsworth establishes [in *Michael* and some such other pastorals] a contrast between such official, linear versions of history and a more private version [of his]. Michael's, in other words, with what historians classify as important events. It is 'a history' or a story, rather than history. Wordsworth is not, however, just taking refuge in early eighteenth-century rural society. He is trying to suggest that the lessons which may be drawn from this simple story of farming folk might offer a more acceptable social foundation. He draws out these lessons or worthy purposes by reflecting on the relative merits of past and present. His emphasis is rather reflective rather than purely descriptive. He implies that the virtues of thrift, frugality, patience and perseverance, all of which he claims to have found in this early eighteenth-century society, could put the country back on the right road. Reflection has led to thoughts of rescue. His initial suggestion is that such rescue will be on a fairly limited scale:

> Therefore, although it be a history
> Homely and rude, I will relate the same
> For the delight of a few natural hearts,
> And with yet fonder feeling, for the sake
> Of youthful Poets, who among these Hills
> Will be my second self when I am gone."
>
> (Williams, 94-95)

These are some of the meanings or interpretations, of the poem *Michael,* as produced by some commentators; but let us now see what the poet himself wanted to say in the poem. In October-December, 1800, Wordsworth wrote some notes for this poem, for the 1800 edition of *Lyrical Ballads.* One of these notes is the following: "I have attempted to give a picture of a man, of strong mind and lively sensibility, agitated by two of the most powerful affections of the human heart; the parental affection, and the love of property, *landed* property, including the feeling of inheritance, home, and personal and family independence" (Wordsworth and Coleridge, 302). However, G.W. Knight has found in *Michael* a contrast, a wrangle, between the life of the village and that of the city, and has opined that this contention between the two sorts of life-styles and value-systems is the corner-stone of Wordsworth's philosophy, and the materials of his poetic productions, and also that this contrast distinguishes Wordsworth's poetry from Coleridge's, very fundamentally. "[*Michael*] shows a typical old shepherd of rock-like strength and grave morality whose loved son has been ruined by the vicious encroachments of city-life, eternally, and alone, climbing a hill to build with grey stones the sheepfold planned in happier days: and this terrible, and lonely determination to build from a rock-like and impregnable simplicity and bleakness symbolizes Wordsworth's life-work. A contrast of that sheepfold with Coleridge's flashing dome in *Kubla Khan* almost distinguishes the two poets" (Knight, 36-37). In his interpretation of the poem, G.W. Knight has perhaps overlooked a vital element of the rural scenario—the soothing ambience of it. *Michael* is not only a lession on the stoic 'sturdiness of character' (that of Michael) and on the contrast between the rural simplicity and the urban complexity, but it is also a portrait that shows the soothing and healing ambience of the pastoral scenario that sustains the sturdiness of the character of Michael: "*Michael,* a study in simple sturdiness of character and the healing power of nature, is a moving poem in spite of its oversimplified and tractish contrast between the innocent country and the wicked city" (Brown, 486).

Michael betrays some distinguishing features. In it, to start with, there is no garrulousness in the narrator, as there is, for an instance, in *The Brothers,* and in this sense *Michael* is a better poem not only than *The Brothers,* but also than most of Wordsworth's other narrative poems. Secondly, according to R.O.C. Winkler, Wordsworth, in *Michael,* keeps himself at a distance from the created emotion of the poem. Thirdly, in this poem, the protagonist Michael is actually not a personality of high resolution, but is a being that is almost quite merged with nature; and it is for this reason that there is no suggestion in the poem to Michael's seeking after consolation in nature in his fathomless grief. Winkler writes in this regard: "In *Michael* Michael is part of natural world himself, and the strength of his body and mind, the birth, growth and bereavement of his love for Luke, are all enforced in terms of his work among the things of nature; so that the old man's feelings are shown as working themselves out with the power and simplicity appropriate to the forces of nature. Because of this identification of Michael's feelings with the natural world around him, there is no scope for turning to nature for consolation" (Ford, 183).

Geoffrey Hartman has found that the theme of *Michael* may be interpreted phenomenologically, particularly following the phenomenological systems of Edmund Husserl and Martin Heidegger. Phenomonology is a discipline that seeks to understand the essence (and not the existence or connotations or designations) of phenomena. Hartman says that in *Michael* Wordsworth presents the phenomenological essence of nature which is the humanizing power that is "both transcedental and 'real.'" Heidegger, on the other hand, emphasizes the organic relationship between human beings and nature, and such organic relation may be found in *Michael* (Williams, 21). *Michael* may also, perhaps, be interpreted in the line of Marxian philosophy, or in the line of Marx's view of historicity. We have cited above an extract from Wordsworth's letter to Fox, where we have found the poet's concern about the small farmers and their loss of 'domestic affections' due to the rapid industrialisation of

England. In his 'Preface' to *Lyrical Ballads* also Wordsworth has expressed his disparagement with the dehumanizing effects of the exploiting city life. It is, among other things, for these reasons that John Williams writes that "'Michael' is (therefore) a poem to be read inextricably 'based' not in nature, but in the changing processes of history" (Williams, 24).

But all these are, perhaps, going too far from the basic and intended meaning of the poem. We say this because Wordsworth was neither a phenomenologist nor a social thinker of the Marxist type. Further, in the original manuscript of the poem, there occurred four additional lines which were dropped when the poem was published, and if we take into consideration these four lines along with the extant 482 lines of the poem, the meaning and purport of the poem will be clearer, and the poem will show itself to be concerned only, or principally, with the disparaging human condition, and the consequent human suffering. The dropped out four lines are:

> There is a shapeless crowd of unhewn stones
> That lie together, some in heaps, and some
> In lines, that seem to keep themselves alive
> In the last dotage of a dying form.
>
> (Durrant, 77)

Now, taking into account also these four dropped out lines, Geoffrey Durrant interprets the poem thus: "In this manuscript version Wordsworth makes clear what is only strongly hinted at the poem—that the 'straggling heap of unhewn stones'—all that remains of the sheepfold Michael is building in the poem—are themselves a representation of man's life. The 'dotage of a dying form' links the process by which the forces of wind, sun, and gravity cause the collapse of the wall with the more eleaborate but equally inexorable forces which reduce man himself to dotage and finally to death. What this poem is concerned with, then, is the process of dissolution, and the reducing of man's achievement and his very life to shapelessness and disintegration. It is a story of man's struggle to maintain himself and his values in a hostile universe" (Durrant, 77). In our opinion, this interpretation of the poem is more acceptable than the others we have discussed.

However, the poetic qualities of *Michael* are simply excellent.

Edgar Allan Poe, in his essay 'The Poetic Principle' writes: "While this Principle itself is, strictly and simply, the Human Aspiration for Supernal Beauty, the manifestation of the Principle is always found in *an elevating excutement of the Soul*—quite independent of that passion which is the intoxication of the Heart—or that Truth which is the satisfaction of the Reason" (Poe, 904). *Michael* does not imbue us with its passion, nor does it clarify any truth of reason, but we are certainly and somehow elevated by the impinging condition of its protagonist Michael: after reading the poem we are not what we had been before; and after reading the poem we exist in a mysterious plane that is not mundane. Here lies the authenticity of *Michael.* And, in spite of having this great quality, the poem is astonishingly simple, regarding both its language and its narrative thread. David Daiches writes about the quality of the poem: "*Michael* has simplicity. The opening lines have 'persuasive colloquial movement that Wordsworth often aims at but does not often succeed so fully in attaining" (Daiches, 1996, 884). Daiches further writes about the affability of the poem's blank verse, its simple narration, and its special kind of poignant emotion: "The rhythms of the blank verse here serve to give a simple gravity to the utterance, and the alteration between reflection, reminiscence and quietly controlled narrative of simple events helps to provide the poem's special kind of emotion" (Daiches, 1996, 885). Daiches also highly appreciates the serene and sacred tone of *Michael*: "As the story of the elderly rustic couple and their only child develops, the tone [of the poem] becomes more and more elemental and biblical" (Daiches, 1996, 885).

Oliver Elton is appreciative of the blank verse of the poem: "The blank verse of *Michael* lasts longer, moving forward incessantly but with dignity, like the old shepherd climbing the cairn" (Elton, 65). Geoffrey Durrant says that *Michael* "is one of the most successful [poems of Wordsworth], uniting purity of language and directness of style with a decorum and firmness which may properly be called classical" (Durrant, 76). Alan Gardiner deems *Michael* to be "the finest of the rustic poems in the *Lyrical Ballads*" (Gardiner, 49). *Michael* has received much of appreciation not only in our contemporary times, but it had also received much of it during the life time of the poet. When it was first published in *Lyrical Ballads* in 1800, Mary Moorman wrote about the poem, in October-December, 1800, in her book *William Wordsworth: A Biography. Vol. I. The Early Years. 1770-1803*: "'The poem itself has always been one of the best loved of all Wordsworth's writings, not only because of the pathos of the story, but because of the profound yet extraordinarily simple statements of thought and feeling, arising from the power of Wordsworth's ethical discovery that suffering, when illuminated, by love, creates its own nobility of heart" (Wordsworth and Coleridge, 302).

(VI) RESOLUTION AND INDEPENDENCE

This is a simple poem, as most of Wordsworth's poems are, but is very grave in bearing, again as most of his poems are. In no other poem of his, but in this one, has Wordsworth so plainly but clearly related his conception of the relation between man and nature—his theory that man and nature are in complete harmony, and that when this harmony is disturbed, man must needs suffer. This poem is not only about nature, as many of Wordsworth's poems are, but also about the relation between nature and man, and so this poem is, in a sense, more important than even *Tintern Abbey*, the more widely appreciated nature poem of Wordsworth. The two poems, *Resolution and Independence* and *Tintern Abbey*, may be treated as companion or mutually complementary poems.

The poem, *Resolution and Independence*, was composed in May, 1802 (*Tintern Abbey* was written in 1798). The title of the present poem perhaps needs clarification. The poet is mentally wearied and depressed so much so that he has become melancholic; and physically he is suffering from pain, cold and exhaustion. He now can hardly bear with the cares of the world, of the ways of life, and has become bent under the weight of morbidity and sadness. He has lost the firmness of will to live by, and is feeling imprisoned in the world. But when, in the wilderness, he sees the old leech-gatherer, who is quite insouciant of the passage of time and of the changes and the cares of the world, he regains his resolution to live independently—to live without caring for the cares of the world. Hence, the title of the poem is very apt, and is justly approved of by Matthew Arnold.

Resolution and Independence was first drafted in May, 1802, and was revised before publication, in 1807, in *Poems in Two Volumes*. Further changes were made in the poem in subsequent editings.

RESOLUTION AND INDEPENDENCE

I

There was a roaring in the wind all night;
The rain came heavily and fell in floods;
But now the sun is rising calm and bright;
The birds are singing in the distant woods;
Over his own sweet voice the Stock-dove broods;
The Jay makes answer as the Magpie chatters;
And all the air is filled with pleasant noise of waters.

II

All things that love the sun are out of doors;
The sky rejoices in the morning's birth;
The grass is bright with rain-drops; -on the moors
The hare is running races in her mirth;
And with her feet she from the plashy earth
Raises a mist; that, glittering in the sun,
Runs with her all the way, wherever she doth run.

III

I was a Traveller then upon the moor;
I saw the hare that raced about with joy;
I heard the woods and distant waters roar;
Or heard them not, as happy as a boy:
The pleasant season did my heart employ:
My old remembrances went from me wholly;
And all the ways of men, so vain and melancholy.

IV

But, as it sometimes chanceth, from the might
Of joy in minds that can no further go,
As high as we have mounted in delight
In our dejection do we sink as low;
To me that morning did it happen so;
And fears and fancies thick upon me came;
Dim sadness—and blind thoughts, I knew not, nor could name.

V

I heard the sky-lark warbling in the sky;
And I bethought me of the playful hare:
Even such a happy Child of earth am I;
Even as these blissful creatures do I fare;
Par from the world I walk, and from all care;
But there may come another day to me—
Solitude, pain of heart, distress, and poverty.

VI

My whole life I have lived in pleasant thought,
As if life's business were a summer mood;
As if all needful things would come unsought
To genial faith, still rich in genial good;
But how can He expect that others should
Build for him, sow for him, and at his call
Love him, who for himself will take no heed at all?

VII

I thought of Chatterton, the marvellous Boy,
The sleepless Soul that perished in his pride;
Of Him who walked in glory and in joy
Following his plough, along the mountain-side:
By our own spirits are we deified:
We Poets in our youth begin in gladness;
But thereof come in the end despondency and madness.

VIII

Now, whether it were by peculiar grace,
A leading from above, a something given,
Yet it befell that, in this lonely place,
When I with these untoward thoughts had striven,
Beside a pool bare to the eye of heaven
I saw a Man before me unawares:
The oldest man he seemed that ever wore grey hairs.

IX

As a huge stone is sometimes seen to lie
Couched on the bald top of an eminence;
Wonder to all who do the same espy,
By what means it could thither come, and whence;
So that it seems a thing endued with sense:

Like a sea-beast crawled forth, that on a shelf
Of rock or sand reposeth, there to sun itself;

X

Such seemed this Man, not all alive nor dead,
Nor all asleep— in his extreme old age:
His body was bent double, feet and head
Coming together in life's pilgrimage;
As if some dire constraint of pain, or rage
Of sickness felt by him in times long past,
A more than human weight upon his frame had cast.

XI

Himself he propped, limbs, body, and pale face,
Upon a long grey staff of shaven wood:
And, still as I drew near with gentle pace,
Upon the margin of that moorish flood
Motionless as a cloud the old Man stood,
That hearth not the loud winds when they call;
And moveth all together, if it move at all.

XII

At length, himself unsettling, he the pond
Stirred with his staff, and fixedly did look
Upon the muddy water, which he conned,
As if he had been reading in a book:
And now a stranger's privilege I took;
And, drawing to his side, to him did say,
"This morning gives us promise of a glorious day."

XIII

A gentle answer did the old man make,
In courteous speech which forth he slowly drew:
And him with further words I thus bespake,
"What occupation do you there pursue?
This is a lonesome place for one like you."
Ere he replied, a flash of mild surprise
Broke from the sable orbs of his yet-vivid eyes.

XIV

His words came feebly, from a feeble chest,
But each in solemn order followed each,

With something of a lofty utterance drest—
Choice word and measured phrase, above the reach
Of ordinary men; a stately speech;
Such as grave Livers do in Scotland use,
Religious men, who give to God and man their dues.

XV

He told, that to these waters he had come
To gather leeches, being old and poor:
Employment hazardous and wearisome!
And he had many hardships to endure:
From pond to pond he roamed, from moor to moor;
Housing, with God's good help, by choice or chance;
And in this way he gained an honest maintenance.

XVI

The old Man still stood talking by my side;
But now his voice to me was like a stream
Scarce heard; nor word from word could I divide;
And the whole body of the Man did seem
Like one whom I had met with in a dream;
Or like a man from some far region sent,
To give me human strength, by apt admonishment.

XVII

My former thoughts returned: the fear that kills;
And hope that is unwilling to be fed;
Cold, pain, and labour, and all fleshly ills;
And mighty Poets in their misery dead.
— Perplexed, and longing to be comforted,
Ply question eagerly did I renew,
"How is it that you live, and what is it you do?"

XVIII

He with a smile did then his words repeat;
And said that, gathering leeches, far and wide
He travelled; stirring thus about his feet
The waters of the pools where they abide.
"Once I could meet with them on every side;
But they have dwindled long by slow decay;
Yet still I persevere, and find them where I may."

XIX

While he was talking thus, the lonely place,
The old Man's shape, and speech—all troubled me:
In my mind's eye I seemed to see him pace
About the weary moors continually,
Wandering about alone and silently.
While I these thoughts within myself pursued,
He, having made a pause, the same discourse renewed.

XX

And soon with this he other matter blended,
Cheerfully uttered, with demeanour kind,
But stately in the main; and, when he ended,
I could have laughed myself to scorn to find
In that decrepit Man so firm a mind.
"God," said I, "be my help and stay secure;
I'll think of the Leech-gatherer on the lonely moor!"

The poem is divided into twenty Spenserian stanzas. In the first stanza, the poet draws a contrast between the weather of the previous night and that of the present moment. In the previous night the wind was violent, and it was raining heavily, and the rain-water inundated all around. By contrast, now, in the next morning, 'the sun is rising calm and bright.' In the far away woods, birds are chirping and singing, and the stock-dove is musing on its 'own sweet voice,' and the popinjay ('Jay') and the magpie are, as if, conversing between themselves. The air is filled with the pleasant sound of the cascades ('noise of waters'). Stanza II of the poem expatiates on the pleasantness of the present moment, or of the morning that has followed the previous dampening night. Everything is enjoying the sun-light in the open air ('out of doors') and the sky seems happy because the sun has risen, and the rain-drenched grass is looking shiny. In the bush ('moors') a female hare is running fast ('races'), while her feet are casting upwards the muddy ('plashy') earth, so that it seems that a mist (of earth) is accompanying her wherever she is running to.

In the third stanza, the poet presents himself in the bush, and describes his mental state. He says that he was walking ('a Traveller') through the bush where, he saw, a hare was running in joy. He heard the sound of the woods, and of the waters at a distance (and was full of joy); or, may be, he did not hear those sounds, and yet he was as happy as a boy ('Or heard them not, as happy as a boy'). The present pleasant moment ('season') of that wild place imbued his heart with so much of joy ('did my heart employ) that all his memories of the meaningless ('vain') and melancholic manners (or deportments and thoughts) of the men of the world completely escaped his mind ('My old remembrances went from me wholly;/And all the ways of men, so vain and melancholy.')

In stanza IV, the poet says that sometimes it happens ('chanceth') that once we become extremely joyful, and with the strongest ('that can no further go') force of our joy we rise up to the highest point of delight ('As high as we have mounted in delight'), but, in the next moment, sink deepest in dejection. He says that that morning the same thing happened to him. When his poignant delight left him, fanciful or irrational fears ('fears and fancies') came to him in shoals ('thickly'), and bedimmed and saddened him. Along with the fanciful fears came to him such dark or irrational ('blind') thoughts as he could not identify ('I knew not, nor could name'). In stanza V, the poet writes in the same vein as in the just preceding stanza. Ha says that he heard the warbling of the sky-lark in the sky, and was thinking ('bethought me') of the 'playful hare.' He thought that he was as happy as that hare ('such a happy Child of earth am I'), and was as blessed as such creatures as that hare ('Even as these blissful creatures do I fare'), and he was then passing his time without being disturbed by the concerns or responsibilities ('care') of the world, because he was then roaming away from the noisy and hurried milieu of the city ('Far from the world I walk, and from all care'). But he was afraid or apprehensive that, though then he was a happy being, in near future he might have to suffer 'Solitude, pain of heart, distress, and poverty.'

In stanza VI, the poet recalls that he had been living with only pleasant thoughts in his mind, and that his life had been a life only of genial thoughts, as if, to him, life was ('life's business') as pleasant as the summer season ('summer's mood'), and, as if, everything that was necessary to reinforce his good ('genial') faith and goodness (*i.e.* to reinforce the value of his life) would come to him without his seeking for them (As if needful things would come unsought/ To genial faith, still rich in genial good'). But, then, the poet had realised that nobody was really going to build houses, and sowing crops, for him, and that nobody was going to love him at his bidding, while he himself would remain insouciant to those things ('take no heed at all').

In stanza VII, the poet recalled the fates of the two tragic poets: Thomas Chatterton (1752-70) and Robert Burns (1759-96). Chatterton was a good young poet ('marvellous Boy') (who he had an untimely and tragic death), and Burns, the 'ploughman poet, was a farmer ('Following his plough'), and he ploughed the hilly lands ('along the mountain-side'). Burns suffered much humiliation at the hands of the public, and, consequently, he died at an early age (like Chatterton). (It may be mentioned here that, unlike Wordsworth who was a conservative, Burns was an egalitarian, and once Burns vehemently attacked the Calvinists, for which he had to bear with utter humiliation.) The poet says that Burns always thought ('The Sleepless Soul') about the means and ways of changing the society, and that Burns was proud of his verses ('pride') composed with the aim of attacking the (conservative) Calvinists, for which reason he was denounced severely, as a result of which he died ('perished'). These two instances of the lives or fates of Chatterton and Burns have convinced the poet (Wordsworth) that poets are not really exalted ('deified') by the people, but by the poets' own spirits, *i.e.*, poets are noble beings not because they are praised by the people, but because they possess nobler or higher spirits. The poet had realised that (like Chatterton and Burns) poets begin their (poetic) lives with happiness, but they and their (poetic) lives end in 'despondency and madness'.

In stanza VIII, the poet introduces the peculiarly interesting story of the happy and carefree leech-gatherer whom he met in that wood, due either to some 'peculiar grace', or to a guidance, of God ('whether it were by a peculiar grace,/ A leading from above, a something given'). It occurred that, in the wood, when the poet was meditating on the distressful and painful incidents of the lives of Chatterton and Burns ('When I with these untoward thoughts had striven'), sitting or standing by the pool of water that was there in the open air ('bare to the eye of heaven'), he saw a man, of whom he was not aware before ('unawares'), present before him. The man, with grey hair on his head, was the second oldest man that the poet saw in his life.

In stanzas IX and X, the poet produces an extended simile between the figure or stature of that old man (the leech-gatherer), sitting still, as a huge and secured stone on a prominence. He tells us that sometimes we see a huge stone remaining securedly ('Couched') on a treeless and shrubless ('bald') mound ('eminence'), and seeing ('espy') it wonder at it. We ask ourselves: Wherefrom and how did it (the huge bald stone) reach there? We sometimes even wonder that it might have been a living creature, endowed ('endued') with sense-organs, and think that, like some creatures of the sea, it had crawled or slouched up to that place, to bask in the sunshine, while resting on a shelf of rock or on sand. The man, 'in his extreme old age,' seemed to be such a huge stone, and he was so still and stolid that one could not say if he was alive or dead, or if he was sleeping profoundly. His stature stooped so low that it seemed that it was folded ('bent double'), and his feet and head were tucked inwards, as he was proceeding towards the end of his life's course ('pilgrimage'). From the physical condition of the man it seemed ('As if') that a chronic ('in times long past') writhing or debilitating pain ('constraint of pain'), or a desperation ('rage'), grown out of his long sufferance due to illness, descended upon his body like a heavy weight.

In stanza XI, the poet tells us that the man (the leech-gatherer) sat at that spot, his whole body, including his limbs and pale face, remaining butressed by a 'long grey staff of shaven wood.' The man sat motionless on the bank ('margin') of that pool of water in the wilderness ('moorish flood'), till the poet approached him, walking gently. The man was almost stone-deaf, and so could not hear even the noise or sound of the fierce wind when it blew ('heareth not the loud winds when they call'); and he moved about gawkishly, swinging the whole body ('all together') and he moved very rarely ('if it move at all'). So long we have seen (as the poet has told us) the old man to be still and motionless, but in stanza XII we know that he began to stir. The poet talls us that after a long while the old man bestirred himself, no longer remaining settled or stationed there ('himself unsettling'). Then he made a commotion in that pool ('pond'), as a result of which the water of the pool became muddy; and, like a reader of a book, the old man was, as if, reading or understanding ('conned') the muddy water very intently ('fixedly did look'). Just at that moment ('now'), the poet took the advantage ('privilege') of being a stranger (to the old man), and going to that old man ('drawing to his side'), wished that that particular morning might promise for them both 'a glorious day.'

In stanza XIII, the old man for the first time communicates with the poet. In answer to the wishing of the poet, the old man immediately ('forth') said something ('speech') gently and in polite and obliging ('courteous') language, slowly and with some effort ('drew'). Then the poet engaged the old man in further conversation. He asked the old man what he had been ferreting out or searching for in that lonesome place. Before the old man made a reply, a flare or lightning gloss of surprise shone in the black circles ('sable orbs') of his eyes which were still lively ('vivid') in spite of his old age.

The question of the poet , put before the old man, in stanza XIII, will be answered by the old man, in stanza XV. Meanwhile, in stanza XIV, the poet describes the manner of the pronouncement of the answer of the old man, and the quality of the old man's language. The poet says that the old man spoke feebly, because his heart was weak ('feeble chest'), but his words were sombre and fiducial ('solemn'), having the quality of elegance ('With something of a lofty utterance drest'). The old man used select and elegant words, and succinct ('measured') phrases, which were beyond common parlance ('above the reach/ Of ordinary men'). The old man's language was courteous like that of the Scot Presbyterians who are religious and who pay their dues (homage, love, help, sympathy, etc.) to God and mankind. Now, in stanza XV, the poet tells us what the answer of the old man was. The old man told the poet that he had come to that place (*i.e.* to the woods, or, rather, near the pool) to collect leeches (to sell them to medical practitioners), because he was poor, and because he was too old to find any other job. The old man said that leech-gathering was a troublesome and tiresome vocation ('Employment'). It was a hard job, because to collect leeches, he had to travel 'From pond to pond' and 'from moor to moor,' and so he had to put up or live at any place whatsoever he could find ('Housing') 'with God's help, or choice or chance.' The old man told the poet that in that way he eked out a living, honestly ('an honest maintenance').

In stanza XVI, we hear that the old man was still talking and standing beside the post. But presently the voice of the old man became almost inaudible ('Scarce heard'), like the sound of a silent stream or narrow river; and his words became indistinct, the words overlapping one with the other ('nor word from word could I divide'). To the poet, the whole body of the old man seemed shadowy and unreal—the poet, as if, was seeing the body of the old man in a dream. Or, it seemed to the poet that the body of the old man (or the old man himself) was sent to him 'from some far region', from a transcendental sphere, with a view to give him (the poet) 'human strength' (*i.e.* to give him courage to live by, in his resignation or mental depression), and to appropriately ('apt') rebuke ('admonishment') the poet for his lack of courage or resolution to live his life without yielding to the cares of the world and thus to live independently.

At this moment, says the poet in stanza XVII, his former fearful and depressing killer thoughts returned to him. His hope also, of course, came back to him, but his hope would not get enkindled ('unwilling to be fed')—the hope was gradually getting dampened. Then such thoughts or images came to him as those of the indifference of the world (or of the people of the world for one another) ('cold'), or of the pains of the people (both mental and physical pains), or of the hardships ('labour') of the people, or of the carnal immoralities ('fleshly ills') of the people. Thoughts or images also came to him (the poet) of the great poets (perhaps including Chatterton and Burns) who succumbed to death in their misery, having no courage or resolution to live by, as the old leech-gatherer did have. At this moment, the poet became non-plused, bewildered, because he could not understand why so many great poets succumbed to their misery, while the old leech-gatherer, with all the weight of his miseries, well continued to live, with resolution or determination to live, and with freedom. The poet wanted to get out of this his perplexed state and become comforted, and with this objective, he, once again ('renew'), eagerly asked the leech-gatherer to tell him (the poet) how he (the leech-gatherer) could continue to live, and what he did to sustain his life ('How is it that you live, and what is it you do?').

We have seen that the leech-gatherer previously answered (in stanza XV) almost the same question (which, of course bore a slightly different meaning) of the poet (in stanza XIII). But, as the poet repeated his question (in stanza XVII), the leech-gatherer similarly repeated his answer. The leech-gatherer said that he lived by gathering leeches. For gathering leeches, he travelled 'far and wide,' and wherever there were ('abide') pools, that he came by, he stirred the water thereof, as he was then stirring the water of the pool thus (the leech-gatherer demonstrated by swinging his feet in that pool), to gather leeches. The old leech-gatherer further told the poet that the pools, from which he used to gather leeches for long, were then hardly having ('dwindled') leeches, and, nevertheless, he continued to gather leeches, with perseverance, from wherever he found them.

In stanza XIX, the poet says that when the old leech-gatherer was telling him all this, he (the poet) was disturbed and perplexed ('all troubled me') by that lonely place, and by the decrepidity of the old leech-gatherer ('old Man's shape') and by his talk ('speech') about his resolution to go on living (in spite of all his adversities) in independence (*i.e.* without seeking help of anybody). And in his imagination the poet saw ('In my mind's eye'), as if in a movie picture, that the old leech-gatherer was wandering wearily through ('About') the moors, lonely and silently, while the poet himself was meditating upon the image of the continually wandering old leech-gatherer ('I these thoughts within myself pursued'). And while the poet was doing this, the leech-gatherer kept silent and ceased wandering for a while ('made a pause'), and then repeated what he said earlier ('the same discourse repeated')—*i.e.*, he once again said that he was living on a small number of leeches that he could gather with hard toil and perseverance. In the last stanza, the poet tells us that then the old leech-gatherer not only repeated what he told him (the poet) earlier but also told him something more ('other matter blended'), gladly ('cheerfully uttered') and modestly ('with demeanour kind'), but with all dignity ('stately in the main'). The poet says that when the old man ceased, he (the poet) could laugh to admonish himself, because he found in that old leech-gatherer enough firmness of will ('so firm a mind')—(which the poet lacked in)—to continue to live, in spite of all the hazards. And then the poet prayed to God so that God might help him (the poet) and keep him securely ('slay secure') in this world, and, in his prayer, he told God that he would continue to remember the old leech-gatherer whom he met 'on the lonely moor.'

In this poem, the poet is not the only speaker, but there is another speaker in it—the old leech-gatherer, whom the poet describes as 'credulous and talkative from indolence,' and as 'prone to superstition.' The poet tells about his experiences, and the old leech-gatherer—the narrator—narrates the story of his life. The poem is built out of a real experience of the poet. Allan Gardiner writes about this real experience of the poet: "We know from Dorothy Wordsworth's Journal that 'Resolution and Independence' is based upon an incident which took place on 3 October 1800. William and Dorothy met an 'old man almost double,' who told them that he had formerly been a leech-gatherer but owing to the increasing scarcity of leeches had abandoned this occupation and was now a beggar" (Gardiner, 58). In the poem, two changes have been made of the actual incident: first, Dorothy is not present in the poem; and second, the old man actually left his vocation as a leech-gatherer, but in the poem he is still a leech-gatherer. Wordsworth also may have altered the character or disposition of the leech-gatherer. In the poem, the leech-gatherer is a model stoic character: he encounters all the rough and windy events of his life with all mental fortitude, and without fear, like the ancient Greek philosopher Zeno (d.c. 261 B.C.). The old leech-gatherer has robust endurance to fearlessly encounter all sufferings and adversities, which the poet very much lacks in.

The title of the poem is extraordinarily significant, and it needs clarification. The word 'Resolution' implies, by contrast, irresolution or perplexity. The poet, before witnessing the stoicism of the old and decrepit leech-gatherer, was perplexed by the way-ward, rough and adverse events and pains of his life or of the world. His mind was being tossed by the windy events all around him, and so his feelings and emotions were battered by the rough events of the world. This means that his mind was passive, in the sense that the various states of his mind were dependent on the alterations of the events of the world. The poet earnestly wanted to get rid of his irresolution and of his dependence on the events of the world. But he failed pitifully in his effort to resolve and be independent. He was incessantly being crushed, pounded, under the heavy weight of the world, of life itself. In such a condition, he met the poor and old leech-gatherer, and was imbued with the leech-gatherer's astonishing fortitude, or resolution and independence, and rebuked, and laughed at, his irresolute and dependent mind or self:

> I could have laughed myself to scorn to find
> In that decrepit Man so firm a mind.
> 'God,' said I, 'be my help and stay secure;
> I'll think of the Leech-gatherer on the lonely moor!'

In the first three stanzas of the poem, we find that the nature is full of gaiety, as the poet's mind is: there is a mutuality, a correspondence, a harmony, between the nature and the consciousness of the poet, which is a significant feature of Wordsworth's poetry. In the fourth stanza, this mutuality breaks down, and the consciousness (or the previously genial mood) of the poet becomes overcast with dejection, fears and fancies:

> And fears and fancies thick upon me came;
> Dim sadness—and blind thoughts, I knew not, nor could name.

In the fifth, sixth and seventh stanzas, the dejection of the poet is aggravated. The poet perceives dejection not only within himself, but also in others: in the poets Chatterton and Burns. In stanzas VIII-XI, the poet describes the old and decrepit man (the leech-gatherer); and in stanzas XII-XVI, he converses with the old leech-gatherer who seems, to him, to be "a man from some far region sent,/To give me human strength, by apt astonishment." In stanzas XVII-XIX, the poet asks the old leech-gatherer about the way of his life, and the leech-gatherer narrates the story of his life—he says that he has been quite insouciantly moving through all the troubles. This discourse of the leech-gatherer teaches the poet about 'human strength,' and the poet is stoically transformed by the discourse of the leech-gatherer. And in the last stanza of the poem (stanza XX), the poet resolves to live on stoically since now, like the leech-gatherer, and so feels independent, feels free.

The subject-matter and the style of the poem are in keeping with Wordsworth's theory of poetry: the subject-matter, the encounter of the poet with the poor and old leach-gatherer, is a common phenomenon; and this subject-matter is dealt with in the natural language of the common man; and the treatment of the subject-matter is unceremonious and unelaborate. And yet it is a marvellous poem, because, among other things, though the poem is built upon a trifling thing, it edifies us tremendously in the ideal philosophy of life. Geoffrey Durrant writes about this poem: "This is a poem which shows Wordsworth's audacity in taking a most unpromising subject and making it the occasion for one of his profoundest comments on human life, and in particular on the life of the poet. The central figure of the poem is a leech-gatherer Wordsworth and his sister met with on one of their walks. This deliberate choice of a most unpoetic occupation, and of a most unheroic hero, shows Wordsworth's challenging contemporary ideas of decorum and poetic elevation" (Durrant, 89). Apparently, the subject of the poem is the curious life-style and mentality of the old and poor leech-gatherer, but, in actuality, it is the poet's own concern about his encounter with the windy and unsympathetic world. Geoffrey Durrant writes in this regard: "Just as the daffodils themselves are not the real subject of 'I wandered lonely as a cloud,' so the real subject of 'Resolution and Independence' is not the leech-gatherer himself, but the poet and his fate" (Durrant, 89).

David Daiches, agreeing with Geoffrey Durrant, says that the theme of the poem is actually the general life of all human beings and its problems, and also the problem of encountering it. Daiches says that the central image or concept of the poem is the phrase 'life's pilgrimage' that occurs at line 67. The blunted meaning of the clichè 'life's pilgrimage' is, here in this poem, given a new keenness and efficacy by Wordsworth, by juxtaposing the poet's dull and perplexed dejection and the leech-gatherer's unfezzed and stolid optimism grown out of, and reinforced by, his (the leech-gatherer's) robust perseverance. David Daiches writes: "The clichè 'life's pilgrimage' is given a new, almost literal meaning.... The significance of the old man's [the old leech-gatherer's] appearance to the poet at that particular time and place, the paradoxical mood of the optimistic trust which the old man's life inspired in the poet, and the sense of the old man's lack of the true significance of what he was telling, are conveyed by a deliberate juxtaposition of factual remarks and imaginative speculation, and the sheer deliberateness with which Wordsworth sets these side by side prevents the effect from becoming ludicrous..." (Daiches, 1996, 886). David Daiches is quite right in presuming that the poem might have become ludicrous, due to the blatantly unpoetical subject-matter of it. And here lies Wordsworth's great skill as a poet: he has transformed, or rather elevated the near ludicrous to the level of the grave and serious, with the help of his high imaginative faculty. Geoffrey Durrant writes in this regard: "Like many of Wordsworth's poems, 'Resolution and Independence' is at once an account of the working of the imagination, and an exercise of it. The leech-gatherer, we are given to understand, will be a talisman for the poet, who when in dejection will always have in the leech-gatherer a useful reminder of his own ability to transform the most intractable material, and invest it with 'the consecration, and the poet's dream'" (Durrant, 98). But the poem may be a talisman not only to any other poet, but also to all of us, the common men, for, from the poem, we may learn, like Wordsworth, the philosophical and mystic truth and praxis of life. And so the meanness of the subject-matter, or the flatness of the style, of the poem have not been any barrier in its becoming a great poem. Geoffrey Durrant is very just when he writes about the poem: "Wordsworth (then) has achieved, in spite of what seemed to be handicaps of subject-matter and style, a poem that remains impressive and deeply moving, in spite of all the ridicule that can be brought against it" (Durrant, 97).

In most of the poems of Wordsworth, there is a correspondence, or mutuality of influences, between human beings and nature: between the conscious man and the unconscious nature, or between man and his outer world. Wordsworth sometimes transforms nature or the outer world in such a way that it is vested with sort of consciousness, having wisdom and morality, and the so-transformed nature or the outer world modifies the consciousness, or wisdom and morality, of human beings. This is noticeable particularly in such poems as *Margaret, Michael* and *Resolution and Independence.* In the last one, the whole of the nature is not transformed and vested with consciousness, but a part of it—the leech-gatherer. Though the leech-gatherer is, of course, a human being, he behaves not like a normal person, but like a thing, like an object—like a speck or part of nature. At first the leech-gatherer seemed to the poet to be nothing else than a things:

> it seemed a thing endued with sense:
> Like a sea-beast crawled forth, that on a shelf
> Of rock or sand reposeth, there to sun itself.

The poet could not recognise the leech-gatherer to be a human being, but as an object, as a stationary cloud: "Motionless as a cloud the old Man stood." To the poet, therefore, the leech-gatherer was only a part of the unconscious nature, or of the outer world. But soon the poet invested the leech-gatherer with consciousness, and with wisdom withal, and after that there ensued a communication between the poet and the leech-gatherer—a communication through which the poet was influenced and modified by the leech-gatherer, but not the other way round. Thus, Wordsworth, in *Resolution and Independence*, had humanised a part of nature and invested it with profound wisdom by which he himself had been benefited. R.O.C. Winkler, in his essay 'Wordsworth's Poetry,' writes: "In *Resolution and Independence* Wordsworth meets on a moor an old leech-gatherer who is not only himself a natural object, so closely is he assimilated to his surroundings, but at the same time mediates between the natural world and Wordsworth in such a way as to bring home to him the qualities of mind and character which are the fruit of the influence of natural objects, and which, in the immediacy of his personal melancholy, he has temporarily lost sight of" (Ford, 169).

R.O.C. Winkler has found a moral precept in the poem, as Geoffrey Durrant has noticed Wordsworth's concern about human fate in it. But G.W. Knight, in his *The Starlit Dome*, says that the emphasis of the poem is not so much on the moral issue of 'human strength' as Winkler supposes, or on man's fate as Durrant understands, but on eternity, although, of course, both the moral of 'human strength' and the issue of fate are intimately related to eternity. Knight understands that in *Resolution and Independence* the solitary leech-gatherer is a symbol of eternity, as the mountains too, in Wordsworth's poems are: "Just as those eternity-structures, his [Wordsworth's] mountains, become almost personal, so his favourite, usually solitary, persons become likewise symbols of eternity" (Knight,

12). Knight says that the poem does not so much teach us fortitude in adversities as it betrays before us the tragic destiny of human beings against the backdrop of eternity. Knight further writes about Resolution and Independence: "The poem penetrates far deeper than its title and superficial didacticism indicate. A mood of 'dim sadness' and 'blind thoughts,' with meditation on the tragic destiny of man and especially of 'mighty poets in their misery dead,' frames the advent of a lonely, aged, figure:

> The old man he seemed that ever wore grey hairs.

He is compared to a 'huge stone' on 'the bald top of an eminence' whose position makes it seem a 'thing endued with sense,' like some 'sea-beast crawled forth' 'to sun itself.' He appears neither all alive, nor dead, nor asleep, standing 'motionless as a cloud.' You see how nature's enigmatic and awful appearances are identified with a human figure of this lonely, enduring, unemotional, type. The poem is more than a eulogy of endurance. It attempts a reference of the deeps of human personality to man's natural setting and tragic destiny. These are all, more over, self-exploitations; for Wordsworth too is solitary, monastic, and prophetic in cast of mind, bearing as best he may some awful yet mystically placid, yet again disturbing, revelation. His simple heroic persons, he takes care to tell you, are not literary poets; and neither, in his main direction, is he. He is rather a lonely prophet of the eternal" (Knight, 12).

Knight's contention is attested by Geoffrey Durrant: "The effect of the description of the old man as praeternaturally linked with the universe, as infinitely old, and as bearing an unequalled burden of suffering, gives to the leech-gatherer's stirring of the waters, and looking into them as though 'reading a book,' the suggestion of a diviner, a seer, or a prophet" (Durrant, 94). David Daiches, on the other hand, says that the message of the poem pertains to the moral instruction that mental fortitude and stoic attitude towards the predicaments of life should be the basis of our existence.

However, David Daiches says that Wordsworth's use of the rhyme royal stanza ('a stanza of seven decasyllabic lines rhyming a b a b b c c') in the poem has been very appropriate. Daiches writes: "Here the use of the rhyme royal stanza enables Wordsworth to give a special shape to each significant movement in the development of the moral situation" (Daiches, 1996, 885-86). R.O.C. Winkler says that in the whole of stanza IX and in the beginning two lines of stanza X (*i.e.* lines 57-65), there is a rare Wordsworthian simile that is very skilfully and enjoyably drawn. Winkler writes: "This is one of Wordsworth's comparatively rare similes, and he develops it at length so that it takes on a life of its own in which the original subject is submerged. Its independent force is, indeed, considerable enough to make possible an internal simile: 'Like a sea-beast....' The slow, almost laboured, building up of the image gives an effect of timelessness and permanence which contrasts with the feverish state of the poet's mind. 'Eminence' and 'wonder' suggest the impact made on that mind. The internal simile serves to reinforce the permanence of inanimate objects with the strength of beasts: of the sort of beasts that might belong to another element as old and permanent as rock—the sea" (Ford, 170).

But, Daiches says that though, in this poem, Wordsworth has very masterfully juxtaposed 'factual remarks and imaginative speculation,' for heightened effect, at least in one place (at the end of stanza XIX) such a juxtaposition has become ludicrous, because here while the poet was imaginatively perceiving the old Man (the leech-gatherer) wandering about in the wilderness, we hear that, or the poet tells us that, the old Man 'the same discourse renewed' (Daiches, 1996, 886). Salvador de Madariaga, writing in 1920, accuses Wordsworth of distorting a fact in favour of his preconceived plan of this poem. Madariaga writes: "It should be noticed (moreover) that in this poem [*Resolution and Independence*] Wordsworth distorts reality in order to adjust it to his preconceived plan. We know through Dorothy Wordsworth's Journal that the meeting with the old man took place on the road to Grasmere, not 'on the lonely moor" (Cowell, 29). Madariaga has two other objections to this poem. Firstly, says Madariaga, though Wordsworth seems to be engrossed in meditation on the leech-gatherer, in reality he is not so; he has rather a scant regard for the poor and old leech-gatherer: "Our poet has *his* own world to put in order, his own house to build, his own axe to grind. He has not a single thought for the old man as he really is, and therefore not one single feeling for him. He immediately starts thinking about himself with such self-centered distraction that, as he says:

> The old man still stood talking by my side;
> But now his voice to me was like a stream
> Scarce heard; nor word from word could I divide,

and *giving* him nothing, not even the courtesy of listening, he *takes* from him comfort for his fit of depression—his depression which was a mere surfeit of joy" (Cowell, 28).

Secondly, Madariaga says that Wordsworth's resolution and independence, at the end of the poem, is fake. Madariaga writes: "Far from being 'true enough' the poem differs from the facts in one essential respect, namely that the 'resolution and independence' of which Wordsworth made the substance of the poem only existed in his imagination. The leech-gatherer of the poem says that leeches have become scarce,

> Yet still I persevere and find them where I may.

But let us turn to Dorothy Wordsworth who had no poem to write and no lesson to teach: 'His [the old leech-gatherer of the poem] trade was to gather leeches, but now leeches were scarce, and he had not strength for it. He lived by begging, and was making his way to Carlisle where he should buy a few godly books to sell.' Begging is not independence, and 'not having strength for it' is not resolution. It will be seen therefore that Wordsworth 'made up' not merely the scenery but the very substance of his poem. No one would find fault with this, where he engaged in a purely aesthetic task. But that is not the case. 'Resolution and Independence' was written in order to justify optimism by means of feelings supposed to be taken from nature" (Cowell, 29).

However, A.C. Bradley, in his *Oxford Lectures on Poetry*, has very rightly said that *Resolution and Independence* is "the most Wordsworthian of Wordsworth's poem, and the best test of ability to understand him" (Bateson, 4).

(VII) ODE: INTIMATIONS OF IMMORTALITY FROM RECOLLECTIONS OF EARLY CHILDHOOD

To many critics, this poem is the acme of Wordsworth's poetic achievement, and is an intimate record of his personal philosophy, and of his love of nature. Wordsworth had a vague belief in his own amorphous notion of the Platonic philosophy of immortality, transmigration and rebirth of the soul. He believed in the unity of all: man, nature, and God. He was in love with nature, and detested his contemporary 'palsied Age' of 'endless imitation' (Mathew Arnold: 1822-88). In describing his own age as 'palsied,' Wordsworth foreshadowed Arnold's perception of his contemporary life and this may be found in this poem. The poem is also a panegyric of childhood, and this may remind one of Henry Vaughan's (1622-95) eulogy of childhood in *The Retreat.*

The poem was written during the period from 1803 (or 1802) to 1806. Wordsworth wrote the first four stanzas of the poem in March 1803 (or 1802) (about that time, Coleridge was writing his *Dejection: An Ode*) and the rest of the poem was composed in 1806. According to H.W. Garrod, the first four stanzas of this poem may be treated as a complete poem (Garrod, 113). The poem was first published in 1807. At first Wordsworth did not give any title to this poem, and called it simply *Ode,* but later on, on the suggestion of Henry Crabb Robinson (1775-1867: diarist, journalist, letter-writer), gave it a long and full title: *Ode. Intimations of Immoratality from Recollections of Early Childhood.*

The poem consists of 207 lines, which are divided into 11 stanzas, and it is generally capped with a head-piece of three lines taken from the poet's unentitled poem 'My heart leaps up when I behold' (composed in 1802, and published in 1807):

> The Child is father of the Man;
> And I could wish my days to be
> Bound each to each by natural piety.

And, perhaps, these three lines express the essence of the 207 lines of the poem *Ode. Intimations of Immortality from Recollections of Early Childhood,* or, simply, *Immortality Ode.*

Ode. Intimations of Immortality from Recollections of Early Childhood

> *The Child is father of the Man,*
> *And I could with my days to be*
> *Bound each to each by natural piety.*

I

There was a time when meadow, grove, and steam,
The earth, and every common sight,
To me did seem
Apparelled in celestial light,
The glory and the freshness of a dream.
It is not now as it hath been of yore;-
Turn wheresoe'er I may,
By night or day,
The things which I have seen I now can see no more.

II

The Rainbow comes and goes,
And lovely is the Rose,
The Moon doth with delight
Look round her when the heavens are bare,
Waters on a starry night
Are beautiful and fair;
The sunshine is a glorious birth;
But yet I know, where'er I go,
That there hath past away a glory from the earth.

III

Now, while the birds thus sing a joyous song,
And while the young lambs bound
As to the tabor's sound,
To me alone there came a thought of grief:
A timely utterance gave that thought relieve,
And I again am strong:
The cataracts blow their trumpets from the steep;
No more shall grief of mine the season wrong;
I hear the Echoes through the mountains throng,
The Winds come to me from the fields of sleep,
And all the earth is gay;
Land and sea
Give themselves up to jollity,
And with the heart of May
Doth every Beast keep holiday;
Thou Child of Joy,
Shout round me, let me hear thy shouts, thou happy
Shepherd-boy!

IV

Ye blessed Creatures, I have heard the call
Ye to each other make; I see
The heavens laugh with you in your jubilee;
My heart is at your festival,
My head hath its coronal,
The fullness of your bliss, I feel—I feel it all.
Oh evil day! if I were sullen
While earth herself is adorning,
This sweet Many-morning,
And the Children are culling
On every side,
In a thousand valleys far and wide,
Fresh flowers; while the sun shines warm,
And the Babe leaps up on his Mother's arm:
I hear, I hear, with joy I hear!
But there's a Tree, many, one,
A single Field which I have looked upon,
Both of them speak of something that is gone:
The Pansy at my feet
Doth the same tale repeat:
Whither is fled the visionary gleam?
Where is it now, the glory and the dream?

V

Our birth is but a sleep and a forgetting:
The Soul that rises with us, our life's Star,
Hath had elsewhere its setting,
And cometh from afar!
Not in entire forgetfulness,
And not in utter nakedness,
But trailing clouds of glory do we come
From God, who is our home:
Heaven lies about us in our infancy!
Shades of the prison-house begin to close
Upon the growing Boy.
But He beholds the light, and whence it flows,
He sees it in his joy;
The Youth, who daily farther from the east
Must travel, still is Nature's Priest,
And by the vision splendid

Is on his way attended;
At length the Man perceives it die away,
And fade into the light of common day.

VI

Earth fills her lap with pleasures of her own;
Yearnings she hath in her own natural kind,
And, even with something of a Mother's mind,
And no unworthy aim,
The homely Nurse doth all she can
To make her Foster-child, her Inmate Man,
Forget the glories he hath known,
And that imperial palace whence he came.

VII

Behold the Child among his new-born blisses,
A six years' Darling of a pigmy size!
See, where 'mid work of his own hand he lies,
Fretted by sallies of his mother's kisses,
With light upon him from his father's eyes!
See, at his feet, some little plan or chart,
Some fragment from his dream of human life,
Shaped by himself with newly-learned art;
A wedding or a festival,
A mouring or a funeral;
And this hath now his heart,
And unto this he frames his song:
Then will he fit his tongue
To dialogues of business, love, or strife;
But it will not be long
Ere this be thrown aside,
And with new joy and pride
The little Actor cons another part;
Filling from time to time his "humorous stage"
With all the Persons, down to palsied Age,
That Life brings with her in her equipage;
As if his whole vocation
Were endless imitation.

VIII

Thou, whose exterior semblance doth belie
Thy Soul's immensity;

Thou best Philosopher, who yet dost keep
Thy heritage, thou Eve among the blind,
That, deaf and silent, read'st the eternal deep.
Haunted for ever by the eternal mind,-
Mighty Prophet! Seer blest
On whom those truths do rest,
Which we are toiling all our lives to find,
In darkness lost, the darkness of the grave;
Thou, over whom thy Immortality
Broods like the Day, a Master o'er a Slave,
A Presence which is not to be put by;
To whom the grave
Is but a lonely bed without the sense or sight
Of day or the warm light,
A place of thought where we in waiting lie;
Thou little Child, yet glorious in the might
Of heaven-born freedom on thy being's height,
Why with such earnest pains dost thou provoke
The years to bring the inevitable yoke,
Thus blindly with thy blessedness at strife?
Full soon thy Soul shall have her earthly freight,
And custom lie upon thee with a weight,
Heavy as frost, and deep almost as life!

IX

0 joy! that in our embers
Is something that doth live,
That nature yet remembers
What was so fugitive!
The thought of our past years in me doth breed
Perpetual benediction: not indeed
For that which is most worthy to be blest;
Delight and liberty, the simple creed
Of Childhood, whether busy or at rest,
With new-fledged hope still fluttering in his breast:
Not for these I raise
The song of thanks and praise;
But for those obstinate questionings
Of sense and outward things,
Fallings from us, vanishings;
Blank misgivings of a Creature

Moving about in worlds not realised,
High instincts before which our mortal Nature
Did tremble like a guilty Thing surprised:
But for those first affections,
Those shadowy recollections,
Which, be they what they may,
Are yet the fountain-light of all our day,
Are yet a master-light of all our seeing;
Uphold us, cherish, and have power to make
Our noisy years seem moments in the being
Of the eternal Silence: truths that wake,
To perish never:
Which neither listlessness, nor mad endeavour,
Nor Man nor Boy,
Nor all that is at enmity with joy,
Can utterly abolish or destroy!
Hence in a season of calm weather
Though inland far we be,
Our Souls have sight of that immortal sea
Which brought us hither,
Can in a moment travel thither,
And see the Children sport upon the shore,
And hear the mighty waters rolling evermore.

X

Then sing, ye Birds, sing, sing a joyous song!
And let the young Lambs bound
As to the tabor's sound!
We in thought will join your throng,
Ye that pipe and ye that play,
Ye that through your hearts to-day
Feel the gladness of the May!
What though the radiance which was once so bright
Be now for ever taken from my sight,
Though nothing can bring back the hour
Of splendour in the grass, of glory in the flower;
We will grieve not, rather find
Strength in what remains behind;
In the primal sympathy
Which having been must ever be;
In the soothing thoughts that spring

Out of human suffering;
In the faith that looks through death,
In years that bring the philosophic mind.

XI

And O, ye Fountains, Meadows, Hills, and Groves,
Forebode not any severing of our loves!
Yet in my heart of hearts I feel your might;
I only have relinquished one delight
To live beneath your more habitual sway.
I love the Brooks which down their channels fret,
Even more than when I tripped lightly as they;
The innocent brightness of a new-born Day
Is lovely yet;
The Clouds that gather round the setting sun
Do take a sober colouring from an eye
That hath kept watch o'er man's mortality;
Another race hath been, and other palms are won.
Thanks to the human heart by which we live,
Thanks to its tenderness, its joys, and fears,
To me the meanest flower that blows can give
Thoughts that do often lie too deep for tears.

The first stanza of the poem may remind one of the line of thought that is there in *Tintern Abbey* which was written about five years before the present poem was composed. In *Tentern Abbey,* the poet said that the intermission of five years between his first experience of the beautiful natural scenario near the rivulet Wye, five miles above Tintern Abbey, and his second experience of it, five years afterwards, had greatly changed his earlier feeling and emotion and thought process. In *Tintern Abbey,* the poet said that five years ago he found in that natural scenario sensuous pleasure, and only that, but after five years the sensuous pleasure was replaced by his sense of the presence of some spirit or spiritual being not only in that particular scenario but in the whole of the creation—the spiritual being that teaches us, among other things, moral sense. In *Tintern Abbey,* the two experiences of the poet greatly differed from one another, and yet the two experiences were equally pleasant to him. But in *Immortality Ode,* the poet speaks of two quite different feelings or emotions: one pleasant, and the other mournful or depressing. The poet begins the first stanza of

Immortality Ode by telling us that there was a time when meadows, groves, streams, and the whole earth, in general,—in short, every commonplace thing of the earth—seamed to him to be covered or enriched with ('Apparelled') 'celestial light' and with the freshness of a dream. But now all things have become different from what they had been ('hath been of yore') by losing their 'celestial light' or heavenliness, and their fancifulness or unearthliness. It does make no difference whether the poet looks at all the things of the world during day or during night, or whether he looks ('Turn') at this object or at that object ('wheresoe'er'), but, thinks the poet, all the things have become different from what they had earlier been. And so he now cannot see the things (things with their heavenly lustre) that he saw earlier: "The things which I have seen I now can see no more."

In the second stanza, the poet says that what he has said so far should not be construed as meaning that now he does not find either beauty or pleasure in the things of the world, to wit, in nature. He says that even now he enjoys the appearing and dissolving of the rainbow, and even to-day he becomes exulted when the moon rises lively in the cloudless and clear sky ('heavens are bare'). He says that even now waters are 'beautiful and fair' in starry nights, and that when the sun rises, it seems that something glorious is born ('sunshine is a glorious birth'). Nevertheless, the poet feels that the glory of the earth (that he could earlier see) has departed from every part of it.

In the second stanza, the poet said that the world had become changed; that though it had not lost its beauty, it had certainly lost its glory; but there he did not say what this change in the world had done to his heart. At the beginning of the third stanza, the poet says that the change has affected his heart: he says that now no pleasures of the world make him pleased; on the contrary, he becomes stricken by grief at the pleasures of the world. Now, when birds sing joyful songs, or young lambs, as if, dance to the sound of a tabour, he becomes full of thoughts of grief. But, just at this moment ('timely'), *i.e.* when he is stricken by grief, a 'voice' ('utterance') drives away his thoughts of grief, and he is relieved of that grief ("A timely utterance gave that thought relief"), and he sheds off his former weakness—weakness, which was due to his grief—and he becomes mentally strong again, due to the reassuring 'voice'. That 'voice' which seems to tell him something and thus give him a short assurance, comes from the commanding and trumpet-like sound of the cataracts flowing down the high mountains ('steep'), and then his grief cannot mar ('wrong') his enjoyment of the beautiful season (of May). That 'voice' is heard in the repeated echoes ('throng') of the mountains, and when he hears those echoes, he feels the genial wind that comes to him from the field which seems to be sleeping, and then the earth also seems to be full of gaiety. Then, it seams to the poet that the land and the sea are full of jollity, and creatures are merry-making ('keep holiday'), with cheerful hearts appropriate for the jolly season, in the month of May. The poet calls that 'voice' 'Child of Joy' and 'Shepherd-boy,' and bids it to repeatedly cry aloud, so that he can hear the shouting around himself frequently.

In the second stanza and at the beginning of the third stanza, we found the poet half-glad and half-gloomy—half-glad, because nature is still full of jollity; and half-gloomy, because the 'glory' of the earth has departed ('there hath past away a glory from the earth'). The same argument is repeated in the fourth stanza. In it the poet says that he has understood the significance of the sonic communications among the blessed sub-human creatures (the fauna) ("I have heard the call/Ye to each other make"), and that he sees the heavens laughing gladly as the creatures do merry-making in congregation ('jublee'). He tells the creatures that he is participating in their celebration ('My heart is at your festival'), and that he therefore feels like a king, *i.e.*, he is as proud as a king ("My head hath its coronal"), and also that he can realise ('feel') their perfect blessedness ('The fulness of your bliss, I feel'). In this sweet May morning, says the poet, the earth is decorating ('adorning') herself (with herbs and flowers); and children are collecting fresh flowers in many ('a thousand') wide valleys in the distance, while the sun is shining brightly; and babies are, as if, dancing ('leap up') in joy, in their mothers' arms. The poet says that if he remains mournful on this jubilant day, he will thereby make it an 'evil day' for himself. He repeats that he is joyfully hearing the sonic communications among the sub-human creatures he which interprets as a call to him to participate in their jubilation, or to be gleeful ("I hear, I hear, with joy I hear!").

But, yet, the poet cannot be happy and merry, because he remembers the Tree of Life ('there's a Tree'), the outstanding Tree among many trees ('of many!' one'), and the Garden of Eden ('A single Field') that he saw in his former life ('I looked upon'), and his remembrance of the Tree of Life and the Garden of Eden ('Both of them') makes him aware ('speak of') of the fact that he has lost the heavenliness or godliness ('something') of his previous life, or the heavenliness or godliness of the earth has vanished ('is gone'). The poet says that even the little flower, violet ('Pansy'), that lies under his feet, tells him the same thing ('the same tale repeat'), *i.e.*, the violet tells him that he has lost the heavenliness of his previous life, or that the heavenliness has departed from the face of the earth. He uses different epithets for that heavenliness: 'visionary gleam,' 'glory,' and 'dream.' And he raises the question: where has that heavenliness escaped into, where it is now?

In stanzas I-IV, the poet has said that something is absent from the earth, that the heavenliness has departed from the face of the earth. But why is that heavenliness—the 'something'—absent on the earth? In the fifth stanza, the poet answers the question, perhaps following the philosopher Plato's and the philosopher Plotinus' theory of transmigration and re-birth of the soul. He says that our soul, which is the precious centre of our life ('life's Star'), dwells (in waking condition) somewhere (in heaven) away from this earth ('elsewhere its setting'), and comes (for temporary residence) to this earth from that place ('cometh from afar'). Here, by the words 'somewhere' and 'afar,' the poet perhaps means heaven or some other transcendental place. The soul climbs down from, or arises out of ('rises'), from that place, and then comes to this earth, and, in the transit, it forgets all about its experiences while existing or dwelling in heaven or some other transcendental region, like we forget everything of our waking state while we are asleep ('a sleep and a forgetting'). The poet is here comparing our birth, *i.e.*, our transportation from heaven to this earth, with a phase of our sleeping. However, the poet, next, demystifies the words 'somewhere' and 'afar,' and says that the two words refer to God, and that God is our home or the dwelling place of our soul, and that we come to this earth from

Him. We come along wearily ('trail') from God to this earth, through the scattered resplendences of God ('clouds of glory'). Though, while coming to this earth, we leave behind our memory of that celestial sphere and of God, we do not totally forget our memory, but partially remember it, *i.e.*, we partially remember the celestial sphere or God ('Not in entire forgetfulness'), and we do not shed all the former heavenly hallow around us ('not in utter nakedness'). The poet wonders that only till we remain infants, we remain surrounded ('about us') by our former heavenly bliss ('Heaven') ("Heaven lies about us in our infancy!").

The poet says that as we begin to grow up from our infancy ('growing Boy'), the darkness of the material world ('prison house') gradually covers or envelops us. Even though the infant begins to grow to a youth, he can perceive the heavenly glory ('light') and also the source of that glory ('whence it flows'), *i.e.*, God, in all his joys. And when the infant has become a youth, and then day by day advances towards manhood, like the sun that of necessity ('Must') more and more advances from the eastern sky towards the western sky, even then the infant, now turned a youth, admires the heavenly glory that is there in nature ('still is Nature's Priest'). And even then he can percieve the heavenly light in a vision (not directly) ('vision splendid') in his course to attaining manhood ("Is on his way attended"). But when the youth has already attained manhood, the heavenly glory or light completely fades away ('die away'), and that heavenly light or glory is then replaced by the light of the material world ('the light of common day'), *i.e.*, unsteady of perceiving the heavenly light, he perceives the common things of this material world in the ordinary light of the sun.

In stanza VI, the poet describes the state of the grown-up man. He says that the earth enriches her treasure ('fills her lap') only with her chosen objects of sensual pleasure—objects which she feverishly desires ('yearnings'), and naturally desires ('in her own natural kind'), *i.e.*, desires according to her own manner or choice. The earth acts like the family nurse or governess ('homely Nurse') to the infant and the youth, with the affection and parental care of a mother ('with something of a Mother's mind'), and does everything within her capacity ('all she can')—and, says the poet, this is a good objective or end of the earth ('no unworthy aim')—to help the infant or the youth, who is her foster-child (the infant or the youth is actually the Child of God), now grown up into a worldly man ('Intimate Man') and intimate man, because the man is now anchored with the world. And when the youth, on this wise, grows up into a man, he quite forgets his former heavenly glories ('the glories he hath known') and his earlier heavenly abode ('imperial palace') from where he has come to this earth.

In stanza VII, Wordsworth compares the blissful state of the child with the 'humourless stage' of the grown-up man—the man which the child one day will become. The poet wonders at, and asks us to look at, the little ('pigmy size') lovely child of six years ('six years' Darling'), who is surrounded by his newly brought things of his choice ('new-born blisses'). The poet means to tell us that such a child is an object of delight. The child, in such a state, remains engrossed in his fanciful plans with his play-things, and is delightfully irritated ('Fretted') by the repeated kisses of his mother, while the eyes of his father delightfully shine on him. The poet asks us to see that while the child thus sits among his play-things, he has, under his view or notice ('at his feet') some small or playful plans or schedule to execute with those play-things. Those plans of the child are parts ('fragments') of his vision ('dream') of human life, so far as he has been able to realise human life. And those plans are drawn ('Shaped') by him according to the degree of skill ('art') that he has acquired recently ('newly-learned'). What are some of his plans (of his future life)? They are a marriage, a festival, a mourning, and a funeral (relating to his dolls, or to his own future life). And all these events are now his objects of devotion ('hath now his heart'), and all these events he now loves the most, and to these events he engages his whole being ('unto this he frames his song'), *i.e.*, he begins, as if, to compose songs appropriate for the particular events—marriage, festival, mourning, and funeral. After this, the child will learn the wordly and corrupt language ('fit the tongue') of communication ('dialogues') relating to business, love, and quarrel ('strife').

Before long the child will further grow up, and then he will cast away all the aforementioned things; and will enjoy the pleasure of, and will be proud of, his new role of life ('new joy and pride'). Attaining manhood, the child will consider himself to be an actor (cf. "Life's but a walking shadow, a poor player" in *Macbeth*), *i.e.* he will think that he has to play a part in the affairs of the world; and to perform that part or role in the affairs of the world, he will learn ('con') new manners of action or behaviour ('part'); and learning that new manners, he will continue to actually behave like his new learning, as occasions will demand or allow in this ludicrous world ("Filling from time to time his 'humorous stage'" (cf. "That struts and frets his hour upon the stage" in *Macbeth*). The grown-up child, *i.e.*, the man, will act along with other men ('Persons') in this lifeless or insipid or humourless ('palsied') age (cf. "this strange disease of modern life, /With its sick hurry, its divided aims, /Its heads o'ertax'd, its palsied hearts" in Matthew Arnold's *The Scholar Gipsy*). And this insipid age has been brought in by the perpetual course of human life ('That Life brings'), as human life's decoration or accessory things ('equipage'). And in such an age, the actor-man will live in the world in such a way that it will seem that the actor-man's only profession or action ('his whole vocation') is to continually imitate the in-things of the world, or to continually accustom or adjust himself with the go of the world.

The poet begins stanza VIII by chastising the child ('Thou'). He says that the child's soul is great or immense in might, knowledge and godliness, but his overt behaviour ('exterior') does not reflect or show ('belie') the greatness of his soul. He says that the child possesses the supreme knowledge of the ultimate reality ('Thou best Philosopher'); and that the child possesses within himself his divine origination ("dost keep/Thy heritage"); and that the child is like an eye among the ignorant or irrational people ('thou Eye among the blind'), *i.e.*, among the philosophically ignorant people, and that it is only the child that can see the truth. It is (only) the child ('that') who, not being perturbed or affected by the cacophonous (and irrational and non-spiritual) world ('deaf'), remains silently ('silent') engrossed in the musing about the eternal mystery ('deep'), perpetually pervaded or frequented by the 'eternal mind.'

The poet calls the child a prophet (because he can say what we should do or be in future) and a blessed seer (because he can see what is going to occur in future), and says that the truths lie with the child, or that the child knows the (ultimate) truths.

But we, who are grown-ups, though we are striving to find out those truths all our lives, fail to find those out till we enter into the darkness of our graves ("In darkness lost, the darkness of the grave"); *i.e.* we remain ignorant about the ultimate truths of life since we begin to grow up till our death. (Those truths are that our essential beings are in continual exisistence from our birth or childhood till our death, and that our childhood feelings and emotions and our childhood spirituality are immortal, *i.e.*, all these remain with us, in unmanifested mode, in our adult life, till we die.) The poet says that the heavenliness or spirituality ('Immorality') remains inalienably ('Broods') with the child, and shines on him as the sun shines over us from above ('Broods like the Day'), and that heavenliness or spirituality ('Master') exerts control over the feelings, emotions, perceptions and thoughts of the child ('Slave'), as a master monitors or controls the activities of the slave ('a Master o'er a Slave'). The poet calls that the spirituality ('Immortality') 'Presence' (perhaps for want of a better or more explicit term) (cf. "And I have felt/ A presence that disturbs me with the joy/ Of elevated thoughts" in *Tintern Abbey*). This 'presence' the child cannot alienate himself from, or the child cannot put off this 'presence' like he does his garment ('which is not to be put by').

There is a parenthesis of four lines here. This parenthesis was there in the 1807 and 1815 editions of the poem, but it was extrapolated in the 1820 and subsequent editions. In the parenthesis, the poet says that to the child the grave is a lonely place ('bed') where one cannot feel anything ('without the sense') or see anything as he can see in daytime ("sight/Of day"), and also there is the 'warm light' of the sun. In such a place we, the grown-up people, have to lie, after our death; and lying there, we think about our past activities and or about the ultimate truth, and wait for our souls to be uplifted to heaven or again to be endowed with new bodies.

However, the poet tells the little child that he is till now (so long he will remain a child) enjoying the glory of possessing the powerful or absolute freedom that is available only in heaven, and so he is an elevated being ("yet glorious in the might/ Of heaven-born freedom on thy being's height"). And if so, the poet asks the child, why should he (the child) earnestly desire to grow up into manhood ("with such earnest pains dost thou provoke"), and thereby to be put under the ineluctable and pounding weight ('yoke') of the common life of the material world ("Thus years to bring the inevitable yoke"). The poet asks why should he so desire without any rationale or reason behind his so desiring, and knowing that his growing up will be in contrariety ('at strife') with his present blessedness. But, whether the child is willing to grow up or not, he will very soon ('Full soon') grow up into a man, and will bear the heaviness ('freight') of the earthly life or the common man's life, and will also bear the burden of the compulsive customs of the society (such as manners, tradition, convention, etc.) ("And custom lie upon thee with a weight"). The customs are compulsive, and therefore they are heavy; and the customs are irrational and illogical, and so these are opaque like frost; and both these customs are penetrative and inescapable ('deep') nearly like the course of life ("Heavy as frost, and deep almost as life!").

In stanza IX, the poet compares the grown-up man with embers or smouldering pieces of charcoal or wood, and the soul with fire, and says that he is delighted ('0 joy!) to think that even in our grown-up state, which is like ember, there exists the 'something' which is like fire; and to think that even in our grown-up state, our soul or mind ('nature'; to Wordsworth nature includes both mind or soul and matter) recalls the spirituality that was once (in Childhood) its property, i.e. though in our grown-up state we remain engrossed in the material world, yet our soul can recall that it is but an exile ('fugitive') from heaven and has only taken refuge in the body of ours. Here, perhaps, the poet is not alluding to the Platonic theory of the transmigration of the soul, but is only saying that in our infancy or childhood, we have the power of imagination ('something'), but as we grow old this faculty of imagination escapes us ('fugitive'). Here, at this place of the poem, the poet is delighted to think that even in our grown-up state that faculty of imagination is there in us, though faintly. When the poet thinks that his past experiences (heavenly experiences) are still there in him ('our past years in me'), this thought of his brings ('breed') for him eternal bliss ('Perpetual benediction'). The poet is delighted not so much, or not really, ('not indeed') for his thinking that in his childhood he had the most worthy and blessed things ("For that which is most worthy to be blest"), but he is delighted to think or recall, that in his childhood he possessed two sacred ('creed') but simple things—delight and liberty, or enjoyment and freedom—along with newly born ('new-fledged') hope that was till then very lively or stirring ('fluttering') 'in his breast,' whether he had been busy in his childish activities, or had been at rest.

The poet is now loudly ('raise') singing in praise of God, and for thanking God ('I raise/The song of thanks and praise'), not because of all these, *i.e.*, not because in his childhood he enjoyed pleasure and freedom, or because even in his grown-up stage he possesses some amount of his childhood imagination. He says that, on the contrary ('But'), he is singing in praise of God, because he is feeling or realising within himself some forceful and nagging queries ('obstinate questionings') about the underlying truth of the sensations that he is receiving, and about the underlying truth of the things of the external world ("Of sense and outward things")—things that are gradually moving away from us, or vanishing from us (as we are gradually advancing in age) ("Falling from us, vanishings"), *i.e.*, things to which we are day by day becoming less and less attracted. He says that he is a poor being ('a Creature') who is living and walking about ('Moving about') in various places or spheres of the earth ('worlds') which he does not understand, and so he is disbelieving or mistrusting ('misgivings') outright ('Blank') the places or spheres of the earth ("Blank misgivings of a Creature/Moving about in worlds not realised"). When he was young, he had powerful or mighty instincts ('High instincts') with which he could realise the divinity or spirituality that is pervading over the whole creation, and before that powerful instincts (divine or heavenly instincts) our worldly or lower instincts ('mortal Nature') felt guilty or accused, and so trembled, as if attacked by something, to be destroyed ('surprised') ("High instincts before which our mortal Nature/ Did tremble like a guilty thing surprised"). However, the poet is not singing in praise of God for those things—the powerful instincts that he possessed in his childhood.

But he is singing in praise of God for the fact that, even in his advanced age, he can faintly remember or recall ('shadowy recollections') the (divine) feelings which he had in his childhood ('first affections'). What those feelings were, or of what nature the faint recollections of his childhood feelings are he is not interested in knowing ("Which, be they what they may"). He knows that those faint recollections of his childhood feelings are till now ('Yet'), in his manhood, the leading light, or sustaining happiness ('fountain-light') with which we are capable of running the course of our daily life, and which is the controlling or guiding force or light ('master-light') which controls our perception of the things of the world ('of all our seeing'), *i.e.* the affections or feelings of our childhood colours the things of the world, and bestows values upon the neutral things, or 'value-less' things, of the world. The poet says that the faint recollections of the childhood feelings keep us buoyant and entertain ('cherish') us. They have the power to make our busy and cacophonous life ('noisy years') seem a period ('moments') in the 'eternal Silence'—the blissful eternity, or the encompassing divinity, that works without making any noise—and then we realise the revelation of the truths ('truths that wake')—the truths of the fact that we are immortal, in the sense that our childhood feelings and our childhood divinity never completely leave us ("To perish never"). These truths which neither our idleness (' listlessness') nor our demented or irrational activities ('mad endeavour') can absolutely nullify ("Can utterly abolish or destroy!"). Neither grown-up people ('Man') nor children ('Boy') nor anything that is at war with our pleasure can absolutely nullify or obliterate those truths. Therefore ('Hence') when we are in a quiet and tranquil mood ('in a season of calm weather'), though we are well inside the mainland and so far from the sea—*i.e.*, we are far away from the sea of the eternity or the divinity ("Though inland far we be" and 'immortal sea'), —our souls can see that sea of eternity from which we have come here on this earth ("Which brought us hither"). Not only this, we can, in a short while ('in a moment'), even go near that sea of eternity ('travel thither'), if we will, and see the blessed souls ('Children') playing on the shore of that sea, and also hear the sound of the high-rise ('mighty') waves of the waters of that sea that are billowing eternally ('rolling eternally').

This reassuring thought delights the poet, and so he asks the birds to sing merry songs, and the young lambs to caper ('bound'), in frolic, to the sound of a tabor. He assures the birds and the young lambs that he, along with others ('We'), will imaginatively (or empathetically) ('in thought') join their band or gathering ('throng')—the band of the birds and lambs, who are now singing in piping tune ('pipe') and are playing, and who are, on this day, feeling in their hearts the gladness of the month of May. The poet's exultation is not dampened by his awareness of the fact that the keen radiating pleasure ('radiance') that was within his heart in his childhood has been lost, or has gone away for ever ("What though the radiance which was once so bright/ Be now forever taken away from my sight"), due to his grown-up age, or by his awareness of the fact that nothing can bring back to him the moments of his childhood when he enjoyed the sparkling pastoral beauty of the surround ('splendour in the grass'), including the beauty ('glory') of the flowers. But the poet (and also those who will understand like himself) ('We') will not mourn for those things of childhood that he has already lost, rather he will try to find more hope ('strength') in those things (or thoughts) that are still remaining with him ('what remains behind'). He will seek for hope or strength in his natural or fundamental ('primal') *Einfuhlung* or empathy with all the objects of the creation ('primal sympathy')—the fundamental empathy that has so long remained with him, and that will of necessity (because it is fundamental) remain with him in future ("Which having been must ever be"). He will seek for hope or strength in the appeasing or comforting or tranquillising ('soothing') thoughts that arise ('spring') in our minds whenever we think of human sufferings ("In the soothing thoughts that spring/ Out of human suffering"). And he will seek for hope or strength in the faith in the existence of our being even after our (physical) death ('that looks through death')—the faith that, when we become old ('In years,'), makes us inclined towards philosophical speculations ('that bring the philosophic mind').

In stanza XI, *i.e.*, at the end of the poem, the poet urges upon nature, that comprises, among other things, 'Fountains, Meadows, Hills, and Groves' ('ye'), not to make the unpalatable or evil prediction ('Forebode') that the tie of love between himself and nature will be snapped ('severing of our loves'). The poet feels in the centre of his heart ('heart of hearts') the strong attraction ('might') with which nature draws him towards herself. He has parted with ('relinquished') only one pleasure—

the pleasure of living in the ambience of the splendour and celestial light of nature (as in his childhood) in order to be ever guided or governed ('sway') by the very spontaneous ('habitual') shaping skill, or the plastic force, of nature ("To live beneath your more habitual sway"). The poet says that (even to-day) he loves the streams ('Brooks') of the mountain which run downward their courses ('channels'), making noise ('fret'), and that he loves those streams more than he did when, in his childhood, he walked trippingly or liltingly as those streams run trippingly or liltingly ("Even more than when I tripped lightly as they"). He further says that even now ('yet') the clear and bright morning ('innocent brightness of a new-born Day') is attractive ('lovely') to him. Even now the clouds around the 'setting sun'—the clouds which assume mild ('sober') colours which, as if, brood or meditate over human beings' sad mortality ('hath kept watch o'er man's mortality')—are attractive to him.

The poet had run a course ('Another race hath been') in his childhood, and thereby won trophies ('palms'), *i.e.*, he had been victorious in enjoying the pleasures of the heavenly childhood, or in enjoying the spelndours of nature. And now, in his grown-up state, he is running another course and he has to win other trophies ('palms'), *i.e.*, he has to enjoy the other qualities of nature—the philosophic and serene depths of nature ('other palms'). The poet concludes by saying that it is due to ('Thanks') the humaneness or sympathy of the human heart that sustains our life ('human heart by which we live'), and it is due to ('Thanks') the compassions ('tenderness') of the human heart, and the 'joys and fears' that are there in it, that to him even commonest or lowly ('meanest') flower that blooms ('blows') can raise in his mind ('can give') such thoughts as are often concerned with the deeper meaning ('that do often lie too deep') of our life and reality—the deeper meaning of the evanescence of our life and of everything—and when he is engrossed in these thoughts, he is hurt in his heart, and, consequently, sheds tears ("Thoughts that do often lie too deep for tears").

Before entering into a discussion on this poem, it may be profitable to follow the brief analysis of the arguments of this long poem, done by H.W. Garrod: "The first four stanzas of the *Ode* put the fact: 'There hath passed away a glory from the earth;' and in the last two lines of them, ask the explanation of it. Stanzas V-VIII give the explanation in the form of the doctrine of anamnesis or reminiscence. Stanzas IX-XI are an attempt to vindicate the value of a life from which 'vision' has fled" (Garrod, 115). It may also help us to learn that during the time when *Intimations Ode* was composed, *i.e.* around 1806, or to be more accurate, during the period from 1802 to 1806, Wordsworth wrote two other poems—'My heart leaps up when I behold" (or 'Rainbow') and *To the Cuckoo,* which was written in 1802 and was published in 1807 (not the other poem of the same title which was published in 1827). H.W. Garrod says that both of these two poems inform us about the particular mental state in which *Intimations Ode* was composed. In fact, in *Intimations Ode,* the word 'rainbow' of the poem 'My heart leaps up when I behold' and the word 'Birds' (for 'cuckoo') of the poem *To the Cuckoo* recur (at lines 10 and 172). Further, Wordsworth has used the last three lines of the poem 'My heart leaps up when I behold' as the epigraph of *Intimations Ode* when it was published in 1815. From all this, we may surmise that there is some connection among the two poems and the present ode, regarding the subject matters or themes of the two poems and the present ode. To see this connection, let us quote the two poems, in full, below:

My heart leaps up when I behold

My heart leaps up when I behold
A rainbow in the sky:
So was it when my life began;
So is it now I am a man;
So be it when I shall grow old,
Or let me die!
The Child is father of the Man;
And I could wish my days to be
Bound each to each by natural piety.

To the Cuckoo

O blithe New-comer! I have heard,
I hear thee and rejoice.
O Cuckoo! shall I call thee Bird,
Or but a wandering Voice?

While I am lying on the grass
Thy twofold shout I hear;
From hill to hill it seems to pass
At once far off, and near.

Though babbling only to the Vale,
Of sunshine and of flowers,
Thou bringest unto me tale
Of visionary hours.

Thrice welcome, darling of the Spring!
Even yet thou art to me
No bird, but an invisible thing,
A voice, a mystery;
The same whom in my schoolboy days
I listened to; that Cry
Which made me look a thousand ways
In bush, and tree, and sky.

To seek thee did I often rove
Through woods and on the green;
And thou wert still a hope, a love;
Still longed for, never seen.

And I listen to thee yet;
Can lie upon the plain
And listen, till I do beget
That golden time gain.
O blessed Bird! the earth we pace
Again appears to be
An unsubstantial, faery place;
That is fit home for thee!

H.W. Garrod has first noticed the relationship of these two poems with *Intimations Ode*. Let us quote him at some length: "It is worthwhile first to reconstruct the circumstances in which the *Ode* [*Intimation Ode*] was written. It was began in the spring of 1802...on 22nd March Dorothy Wordsworth records in her journal that, on a mild morning, William 'worked at the Cuckoo poem'; and again on 25th March: 'A beautiful morning W. [William] worked at Cuckoo.' Then on the next day: 'William wrote to Annette, then worked at the Cuckoo....' in the evening 'he wrote the *Rainbow*'" (Garrod, 112). After this, Garrod first explains the meanings of the Cuckoo and the Rainbow poems, and then shows the textual and significative connections of these two poems with *Intimations Ode*. Garrod writes: "First the Cuckoo. This is the poem place second among the Poems of the Imagination. The voice of the cuckoo brings to Wordsworth 'a tale of visionary hours' [*sic*]—a tale of days of childhood when the cuckoo was 'an invisible thing, and voice, a mystery.' As he hears him now again, once more suddenly the earth 'appears to be an unsubstantial faery place that is meet home for thee' [*sic*]. He is back in the world of those visionary experiences of childhood which he regarded as the source of the deepest illumination.

"He [Wordsorth] had no sooner finished the *Cuckoo* than he began upon the *Rainbow*. The sight of the rainbow still brings to him the old 'leaping up of the heart' which he had as a boy. He prays that it may always continue to be so:

> The child is father of the man
> And I could wish my days to be
> Bound each to each by natural piety.

In the edition of 1815 these lines are prefixed as the motto to the *Ode* [*Intimations Ode*] There is the external link, that they were composed contemporaneously with it. But there is an inner connection, the significance of which has, I think, not been fully apprehended. In the first place it has, I fancy, not been pointed out that, when in lines 22-23 of the *Ode* Wordsworth says

> To me alone there came a thought of grief:
> A timely utterance gave that thought relief,

the timely utterance may very well be the *Rainbow* poem itself. Secondly, the conception of human days bound together by natural piety is the clue to the interpretation of the *Ode* in its entirety" (Garrod, 113).

Intimations Ode is a benchmark in the poetic life of Wordsworth. Firstly, because this *Ode* synchronises with the beginning of the decline of his poetic faculty. Since about the time of the composition of this ode, Wordsworth "did cease to see things" (Garrod, 119). Astonishingly, the beginnings of the loss of poetic faculty of both Wordsworth and Coleridge were almost synchronous, the time of the beginnings of their loss of poetic faculty being the dates of the composition of Wordsworth's *Intimations Ode* (began in 1802) and Coleridge's *Dejection; An*

Ode (composed April 4,1802). In *Dejection: An Ode,* Coleridge rues his loss of poetic power:

> There was a time when, though my path was rough,
> This joy within me dallied with distress,
> And all misfortunes were but as the stuff
> Whence fancy made me dream of happiness:....

And in *Intimations Ode,* Wordsworth mourns his own loss of poetic power:

> O joy! that in our embers
> Is something that doth live,
> That nature yet remembers
> What was so fugitive!

Here the two poems, *Dejection: An Ode* and *Intimations Ode,* certainly have some resemblance, but there is a great difference between them as well. David Daiches says that while *Dejection: An Ode* is a poem of lamentation, *Intimations Ode* is about how the 'shadowy recollections' of our childhood experiences colour our grown-up lives and experiences, and make us poetically inclined. David Daiches writes, in this regard, about *Intimations Ode*: "This poem is not—as in Coleridge's '*Dejection Ode,*' in some ways so similar—a lament for the decline of poetic powers: it is a record of the profit and loss of growing up. The poet is only born when the child's bliss gives way to the man's more sober but more profound sensibility, which works through 'relationship and love' rather than through mere animal sensation. The poem is thus one of Wordsworth's most central and illuminating works" (Daiches, 1996, 881).

Secondly, when the two poems were already completed by the two poets, the inchoate breach of friendship between them curiously began to widen at a fast pace, never to be bridged. However, before the breach was complete, each one of them to an extent poetically or philosophically affected by the other: Coleridge was influenced poetically, and Wordsworth philosophically. *Intimations Ode* of Wordsworth bears the impress of Coleridge's Platonic philosophy, particularly where it speaks about anamnesis or reminiscence of former life or childhood (Stanzas V-VIII):

> Our birth is but a sleep and a forgetting:
> The Soul that arises with us, our life's Star,

Hath had elsewhere its setting,
And cometh from afar:
Not in entire forgetfulness,
And not in utter nakedness,
But trailing clouds of glory do we come
From God, who is our home:....

(Stanza V, lines 58-65)

At least one instance of the fact that Wordsworth was philosophically influenced by Coleridge may be found in the above-quoted lines, and also a token of his indebtedness to Coleridge may be found in the above-quoted lines; and as a token of his indebtedness to Coleridge, Wordsworth refers, at lines 85-86 of *Intimations Ode*, to Coleridge's son Hartley Coleridge, who was, at the time of the composition of (the latter part of) this *Ode* (*i.e.* around 1806) around six years old:

Behold the Child among the new-born blisses,
A six years' Darling of a pigmy size!

H.W. Garrod says: "I cannot help thinking that the child depitcted in the *Ode* [*Intimations Ode*] is actually Hartley Coleridge" (Garrod, 116).

G. Wilson Knight, in his *The Starlit Dome*, very justifiably writes about *Intimations Ode* that "The poem is far from easy" (Knight, 38) (to understand), and this is so particularly because of the allusiveness of its expressions. Here in this poem, Wordsworth expressly glorifies childhood, under the guise of the Platonic philosophy of reincarnation of the soul, and this very much complicates the apparently simple meaning of the poem. The central meaning of the poem is situated on the notion of immortality of soul. On the surface meaning of the poem, it seems that the poet has taken cognizance of certain signals or signs of the immortality of soul. And this may lead an unweary reader to believe that the poem breathes the Platonic philosophy of immortality of soul, and transmigration and reincarnation of soul. But one should not fall into this trap of the poem's illusive Platonism. G. Wilson Knight writes about the notion of immortality as in this poem: "Our poem [*Intimations Ode*] (thus) imagines the immortality in terms of (i) the child, imagined objectively as a thing enjoying its existence perfectly; and (ii) moments of vision, themselves to be related to the experiences of childhood. The two alternate. Neither by itself is wholly satisfying to us or to the poet suffering his loss of delight. He can see the shepherd-boy in youthful happiness, but he himself is sad; he can remember his own one-time visions, yet they return but fitfully, and then in terms of themselves and vague, 'shadowy' abstractions, rather than nature, thus lacking a certain reality. The immortality will be perfectly incarnated when these two approaches are married; when the poet's own desire is fused with an object, that object or image alight with the poet's immediate vision" (Knight, 42).

The word 'Immortality' has, therefore, been invested, here in this poem, or, rather, in the title of this poem, with a different connotation which has very little connection with Plato's theory of immortality of soul. In his *Biographia Literaria,* Coleridge, therefore, warns us against the fallacy of interpreting the word 'Immortality' in its ordinary, lexicographic meaning. Coleridge, in *Biographia Literaria*, writes that *Intimations Ode* "was intended for such readers only as had been accustomed to watch the flux and reflux of their inmost nature, to venture at times into the twilight realms of consciousness, and to feel a deep interest in modes of inmost being, to which they know that the attributes of time and space are inapplicable and alien, but which can yet not be conveyed, save in symbols of time and space. For such readers the sense is sufficiently plain, and they will be as little disposed to charge Mr. Wordsworth with believing the Platonic pre-existence in the ordinary interpretation of the words, as I am to believe that Plato himself ever meant or tought it!" (Garrod, 116-17). H.W. Garrod says that Wordsworth's theory of 'Immortality' (if we take it to be his theory), as may be found in *Intimations Ode,* is quite at variance with Plato's theory of immortality: "But for Wordsworth, it should be clear, the doctrine has both a different foundation and a different significance from that which it has in Plato" (Garrod, 117). Garrod elaborates on the reason of this variance between these two notions—of Plato and Wordsworth—of 'Immortality,' and also on how to interpret the message or theme of *Intimations Ode*: "Wordsworth, (as I have said is a pure sensualist. Plato, on the other hand, is a pure intellectualist. To Plato the doctrine of reminiscence is a theory of knowledge: an explanation of how we get to know and think. The senses are the source of all error. The world of 'Ideas' alone has truth. It is only by escape from the contamination of the senses, only by getting away from eyes and ears, that we are able truly to see and hear, and to come to the truth of things. The process is a long and painful labour of obstruction. But to Wordsworth the truth of things comes in flashes, in gleams of sense-perception; and in abstraction the truth dies. Wordsworth's doctrine is, in fact, not a theory of knowledge, but a romance of sensation. The absorbing interest of Plato is in the logical meanings of things; to Wordsworth logical meanings are precisely that part of things which has no value. There is some degree of delusion, therefore, in speaking of Platonism of Wordswoth; and if we are to read the *Ode* [*Intimations Ode*] rightly we shall do well to begin by putting Plato out of our minds" (Garrod, 117-18). W.L. Renwick says, about the first four sections or stanzas of *Intimations Ode* (which were composed in 1802), that "These first sections of the *Immortality Ode* [*Intimations Ode*] have nothing to do with immortality but repeat, in a heightened lyrical style enriched by his recent reading, the statement in lines 65-85 of *Tintern Abbey*" (Renwick, 178).

But Gilbert Highet does not agree with the foregoing critics: H.W. Garrod and W.L. Renwick. Highet says that *Intimations Ode* is of course Platonic, *i.e.*, it certainly speaks of Plato's theory of soul's recollection of its previous existence in carnation, and that Wordsworth learned about this theory from 'the great Platonist' Coleridge: "His [Wordsworth's] finest poem is not Stoical: it is Platonic. This is the ode, *Intimations of Immortality from Reminiscences of Early Childhood*, written at a turning-point of his own life, and, despite its fundamental emphasis on eternal life, implying a lament for his own approaching spiritual death. The ode is a great question, and a great answer. It asks why the poet himself no longer feels the exulting beauty and joy experienced by nature and animals, and children; and it replies that children enter the world, from heaven and still remember how they lived there: heaven 'lies about them in their infancy.' Children and their joy in nature are therefore a proof that the soul is immortal. The adult sees only 'The light of common day,' and has no knowledge of eternity except the

> Obstinate questionings
> Of sense and outward things....

Those first affections,
Those shadowy recollections

which are a lasting remembrance of heaven. This is the doctrine which Plato expressed through Socrates, in the theory of Ideas known perfectly in heaven before birth, and 'recollected' under proper stimulus in the world. Plato stresses its intellectual side: Knowledge is recollection of heavenly knowledge. Wordsworth stresses its emotional and imaginative side: joy in nature is recollection of heavenly happiness. But the doctrine is the same, and no doubt it was the great Platonist, Samuel Taylor Coleridge, who imparted it to him [Wordsworth]" (Renwick, 411-12). However, Cleanth Brooks, in his *The Well Wrought Urn*, tells us that Wordsworth himself wanted that we understood the word 'Immortality' in its literal sense, but Brooks himself does not oblige the poet, though he (Brooks) admits that there is a supernatural element in the ode. Brooks writes: "We do not of course, as Wordsworth himself suggested, have to take literally the doctrine about pre-existence" (Brooks, 113) to understand the ode.

David Daiches says that the theme of *Intimation Ode* is the gradual enrichment and elevation of the child's perception, in course of its growing up into adulthood. Daiches further says that, in this regard, *Intimation Ode* almost repeats in 'greater detail,' what the poet told us in *Tintern Abbey*. He writes: "In the 'Immortality Ode' [*Intimations Ode*] Wordsworth gave his most complete account of the balance sheet of maturity as he saw it: in a poem whose very fabric is remembered perception giving way to reflection, he charts the course of the developing sensibility, much as he did in 'Tintern Abbey' though in much greater detail. The naive freshness of the child's awareness gives way to the more sober vision of the man; meditated by love, the child's perceptions in a strange world take on a meaning which, as he grows up, finally emerges as the recognition of profound human significance in nature" (Daiches, 1996, 881). But, though the child's experience is rather crude, unelevated and unexalted, his experience is the stuff out of which the adult's profound vision may be generated. This is the only sense, according to Graham Hough, in which the word 'Immortality' should be construed. Hough says that the Platonic myth of immortality or transmigration of soul or pre-existence of soul is only the guise in which Wordsworth tells about all this. Hough writes about the theme of *Intimations Ode*: "The theme is the gradual decline in keenness of imagination as we pass from childhood to maturity. Wordsworth connects it with a sort of Platonic belief in pre-existence, a belief that

> Our birth is but a sleep and a forgetting,
> The soul that rises with us, our life's star,
> Hath had elsewhere its setting
> And cometh from afar.

And this is certainly something that Wordsworth did not hold as an article of faith. But if he is here presenting his subject, as he rarely does, in an almost mythological guise, he has lost none of his power of dealing plainly with the facts of experience. The development described is as true to the movements of his own heart as the least elaborated passages of the *Prelude,* and beneath the quasi-Platonic myth is the essential truth that the deepest springs of his inspiration are in his childhood" (Hough, 55).

Geoffrey Hartman also tells us that the theme of *Intimations Ode* is 'growing up'—the growing up of man from childhood through maturity. He says that in *Intimations Ode* Wordsworth is deeply concerned about the process of growing up and its fall-out, because in the course of his growing up man loses the keenness of his sensibility, though he gains in his power of abstract thinking, for Wordsworth believed that if we lost the keenness of our sensibility, we actually lost the greater part of our soul, and the greater portion of our happiness. Hartman believes that this is the central part or point of the argument of *Intimations Ode.* Hartman writes: "The subject of the Ode [*Intimations Ode*], Lionel Trilling has said, is growing up.... The poet fears a decay of his 'genial' responses to nature, and he fears that this decay has affected his powers of renovation. Growing up is not enough. The development of abstract sympathies is not enough; these must be linked, else they cannot be actualised, to the renewal of earlier feelings, to joy in nature. It is easy to gain the world and to lose one's soul" (Williams, 45). After this, Hartman continues to explain, in detail, the central theme of the poem: "This deeper concern with renewal explains why Wordsworth is so affected by what appears to be a very little thing: a wrong echo. On this May morning, his heart responds with a thought of grief instead of equal gaiety. All other creatures have the proper harmonic echo, the immediate internal response to nature's influence. The young lambs bound 'As to the labor's sound'—there is no tabor, but Wordsworth sees their joy as a representative joy. He calls them and the other participants in nature's jubilee of 'blessed Creatures': 'And God created...every living creature that moveth...and God saw that it was good. And God blessed them, saying, Be fruitful and multiply.' God responded to them, God *recognised* them, but the poet's heart is dull. We remember the opening of 'Resolution and Independence,' where everything echoes and responds: the jay to the Magpie, the Stockdove to his own call, and even the glittering mist to the hare wherever the latter runs" (Williams, 45). Such is the state of affairs around the poet—the 'objective correlative' of the state of the mind of the poet, says Hartman, up to stanza viii (of *Intimations Ode*). But then the state of the mind of the poet changes, and there arise 'obstinate questionings' in the mind of the poet—'obstinate questionings'

> Of sense and outward things
> Falling from us, vanishings;

and, then, the poet receives intimations of immortality. Hartman says that there are two intimations of immortality in *Intimations Ode*: "There are, if we look closely, two quite different 'intimations of immortality.' Whereas one implies the mortality of nature:

> questionings....
> Of sense and outward things,
> Falling from us, vanishings;
> Blank misgivings of a Creature
> Moving about in worlds not realised...

the other implies its immortality:

> The primal sympathy
> Which having been must be."

(Williams, 46-47)

Hartman says that, according to Wordsworth, so far as it is evident in *Intimations Ode*, "A child is an 'Alien scatter'd from the Clouds,' but the strength which its imagination exhibits in going out of itself and blending with a lesser nature is the source of all further strength: it is for Wordsworth the act of re-generation" (Williams, 47). And this 're-generation' is, says Hartman, what Wordsworth calls 'Immortality.'

However, even if we follow all these interpretations of the poem *Intimations Ode*, yet we may fail to comprehend the meaning of the poem clearly, and the poem may appear to us opaque, and so let us further be enlightened by Wordsworth's own interpretation of this ode. In a letter of 1814, Wordsworth wrote about this ode: "The poem rests entirely upon two recollections of childhood, one that of a splendour in the object of sense which is passed away, and the other an indisposition to lend to the law of death as applying to our particular case. A Reader who has not a vivid recollection of these feelings having existed in his mind cannot understand the poem" (Durrant, 99). If we know the source or background of the material of the poem, we may perhaps understand the poem better, and so let us have a look at the source or background of the poem. Basing his interpretation of this ode on Wordsworth's another (not the foregoing one) comment on this ode, which Wordsworth made after 1814, Geofrey Durrant writes: "In a later comment Wordsworth tells us that at times when he was a child the world around him seemed at once intensely dream-like and vivid, both unreal and more than real; and that he felt himself to belong to another world. It is on this recollection that the poem is based; and the doctrine of which it makes use is only one of several ways of talking about an experience which many people remember from their own childhood. From this starting-point, the poem examines the whole story of human life as an exile from an earlier and more perfect state. It expresses man's sense of living in a mode of existence that in some sense is foreign to his essential being. In other words, man lives in the world of the senses, and in space and time, with a recurrent feeling that he has known, or at least is capable of knowing, a more perfect state" (Durrant, 99). In our opinion, Durrant's interpretation of the theme of this ode, *Intimations Ode*, approaches nearest to the true interpretation of the ode. And, we may say that this opinion of ours is reinforced by the similar opinion of Herbert J.C. Grierson and J.C. Smith. Grierson and Smith write about the meaning of *Intimations Ode*: "Wordsworth's private illumination had faded when he set himself to philosophise upon it in the ode on *Intimations of Immortality*, finding in the doctrine of pre-existence a notion that unified his mystical experiences with his memories of his childhood. We come from God, and our true life is a striving towards Him. As the auroral light which lay about our infancy fades, and we can no longer live by impulse, relying on the genial sense of youth, we must learn to walk by the light of duty, but the memory of that light remains, nay, in seasons of calm weather we still have glimpses of it, to remind us of 'our destiny, our nature, and our home'" (Grierson and Smith, 327). It may be mentioned here, as an *obiter dictum*, that the word 'Immortality' occurs only in the title of the poem, and only once in the body of the poem: at line 118 (stanza viii).

However, Graham Hough calls *Intimations Ode* a 'spiritual autobiography': "Like so much of the best of Wordsworth, it [*Intimations Ode*] is a piece of spiritual autobiography" (Hough, 55). And Cleanth Brooks, in his article 'Wordsworth and the Paradox of the Imagination,' agrees with Graham Hough: "Wordsworth's great 'Intimations' ode has been for so long intimately connected with Wordsworth's own autobiography, and indeed, Wordsworth's poems in general have been so consistently interpreted as documents pertaining to that autobiography, that to consider one of his longer poems as an object in itself may actually seem impertinent" (Abrams, 170). And G.M. Bowra calls *Intimations Ode* a 'personal document' (Bowra, 76). And all these are perhaps true, because throughout his life and poetic career, Wordsworth, like no other poet, had been very keenly and closely observing how the spirit of the child changes from time to time, as he grows up to adulthood and to old age, particularly how his own spirit had been changing throughout his life, from childhood to old age. In many of his poems, including *Tintern Abbey, The Prelude,* and *The Excursion.* Wordsworth consistently follows the development of, or the different changes in, the spirit of man. In this regard, we may say that *Intimations Ode* is not a unique poem of Wordsworth.

As the title of the poem announces, it is an ode. The word 'ode' derived from a Greek word which means 'song.' The ode is a relatively long poem with "elaborate stanza-structure, a marked formality and stateliness in tone and style (which makes it ceremonius), and lofty sentiments and thoughts" (Cuddon, 460). The earliest composer of odes is Sappho (fl. 600 B.C.) who was followed by Pindar (522-442 B.C.) and Horace (b. 65 or 68

B.C.). In England, Edmund Spenser (1552-1599) first showed great skill in the ode with his *Epithalamion* (1595) and *Prothalamion* (1596). Spenser was followed by Drummond (1585-1649), Samuel Daniel (1562/3-1619), Michael Drayton (1563-1631), Andrew Marvel (1621-78), Abraham Cowley (1618-1669) and others. In the Romantic period, Coleridge wrote some odes, such as *France: An Ode* and *Dejection: An Ode*; Keats wrote such odes as *On a Grecian Urn, To Autumn, On Melancholy* and *To Psyche*; and Shelley wrote his most famous *Ode to the West Wind*.

Wordsworth also wrote a number of odes, such as *Vernal Ode, Ode* (1815), *Ode* (1816), *Ode to Duty, Ode: Composed on a May Morning*. But his most famous ode is *Intimations Ode*. *Intimations Ode* is a Pindaric ode. Pindar's odes "were designed for choric song and dance. The words, the sole surviving element of the total Pindaric experience, reflect the demands of the other two arts. A strophe, a complex metrical structure whose length and pattern of irregular lines varies from ode to ode, reflects a dance pattern, which is then repeated exactly in an anti-strophe, the pattern being closed by an epode, or third section, of differing length and structure" (Preminger, 585). The Pindaric ode is more free and emotional than the Horatian ode. In modern times, the ode has undergone some changes—both the Pindaric ode and the Horatian ode. Wordsworth's *Intimations Ode* is a fine specimen of the modern Pindaric ode. Gilbart Highet writes: "The greatest modern Pindaric poem, (however,) is Wordsworth's *Ode—Intimations of Immortality from Recollections of Early Childhood*. It seems at first to be far, far from Pindar's world and Pindar's clear energy. Yet, just as the form is Pindar's adapted to the stresses of the modern poetic mind, so, turned inwards and darkened with modernity, is the spirit.... The ode [*Intimations Ode*] is not a glorification of triumph [like the odes of Pindar], but a description of a painful conflict, gradually resolved. Through a series of irregular stanzas, some dancing and lyrical, some brooding and meditative, Wordsworth moves on the final proclamation of victory, out of the suffering which (as Aeschylus wrote) teaches wisdom:

> Another race hath been, and other palms are own."
>
> (Highet, 251-252)

According to A.C. Bradley, Wordsworth could not achieve excellence in the genre of the ode, excepting only in the cases of two of his odes—*Ode to Duty* and *Ode*: *Intimations of Immortality*—and Wordsworth's sonnets were generally better poems than his *ode*s. Bradley writes: "The Odes of Wordsworth, (again,) are much inferior to the majority of the Sonnets.... The entire success of the *Ode to Duty* is exceptional, and it is connected with the fact that the poem is written in regular stanzas of a simple metrical scheme. The irregular Odes are never thus successful. Wordsworth could not command the tone of sustained rapture, and where his metrical form is irregular his ear is uncertain. The *Immortality Ode,* like *King Lear,* is its author's greatest product, but not his best piece of work" (Bradley, 117). Graham Hough says that *Intimations Ode* was nearly contemporary with *The Prelude,* and that there is a similarity between the substance of *Intimations Ode* and that of a part of *The Prelude.* Hough writes about *Intimations Ode* that "it is composed with far more literary artifice, in long strophes with varied line-lengths of the kind that were supposed, in remote imitation of Pindar, to be particularly suitable for odes. Wordsworth handles this difficult scheme magnificently, and the poem has a sustained lyric splendour of which we have hardly any other example in his works. It [*Intimations Ode*] is also notable because it is built on a piece of poetic faith that is something less than whole-hearted, near to Coleridge's 'willing suspension of disbelief, than is usual with Wordsworth" (Hough, 55). G.W. Knight praises the blending of the [subjective] style of *The Prelude* and the 'technically objective' style of Wordsworth's sonnets in *Intimations Ode*: "Two styles are, (moreover,) blended [in *Intimations Ode*]: that of *The Prelude* with that of the more technically objective sonnets [of Wordsworth]" (Knight, 42-43).

However, Cleanth Brooks has found a chain of consistent symbols in *Intimations Ode,* which, he says, "reveal so many ambiguities" (Brooks, 102) of the ode. And Brooks' overall comment on this ode is this: "The 'Ode,' for all its fine passages, is not entirely successful a poem" (Brooks, 102). Lastly, Coleridge, in his *Biographia Literaria,* made a scathing attack on stanza viii of *Intimations Ode,* particularly on lines 110-120 of that stanza which G.W. Knight calls the 'invocation' of the ode (Knight, 43). Let us quote at some length from *Biographia Literaria.* Vol. II, to show Coleridge's objections against the metaphors employed by Wordsworth in stanza viii of *Intimations Ode*: "Now here (stanza viii, lines 110-120], not to stop at the daring spirit of metaphor which connects the epithets 'deaf and silent,' with the apostrophized *eye*: or (if we are to refer it to the preceding word, philosopher) the faulty and equivocal syntax of the passage; and without examining the propriety of making a 'master *brood* o'er a slave,' or the *day* brood at all; we will merely ask, what does all this mean? In what sense is a child of that age a *philosopher*? In what sense does he *read* 'the eternal deep'? In what sense is he declared to be '*for ever haunted*' by the Supreme Being? or so inspired as to deserve the splendid titles of a *mighty prophet*, a *blessed seer*? By reflection? by knowledge? by conscious intuition? or by any form or modification of consciousness? These would be tidings indeed; but such as would presuppose an immediate revelation to the inspired communicator, and requires miracles to authenticate his inspiration. Children at this age give us no such information of themselves; and at what time were we dipped in the Lethe, which has produced such utter oblivion of a state so godlike? There are many of us that still possess some remembrances, more or less distinct, respecting themselves at six years old; pity that the worthless straws only should float, while treasures, compared with which all the mines of Golconda and Mexico were but straws, should be absorbed by some unknown gulf into some unknown abyss" (Shawcross, II, 111-112).

(VIII) ELEGIAC STANZAS
(Suggested by a Picture of Piel Castle, in a Storm, Painted by Sir George Beaumont)

This is an unusual poem of Wordsworth, in the sense that it is not inspired by any natural object or event, nor is it the result of the poet's spontaneous feelings or emotions; it is, rather, the result of the poet's deep meditation over a portrait drawn by Sir George Beaumont who was a famous painter. In that portrait one can see the renowned Piel Castle, standing in a raging storm, and a ship that seems to be tumbling in the storm-beaten seashore. In the summer of 1794, Wordsworth went to Barrow-in-Furness, near where the Piel Castle stands, and spent there about four weeks in the house of his cousin, Mr. Barket, who lived at the village of Rampside, situated opposite the Castle. Wordsworth saw the portrait inside the Castle, and was much impressed by it. Long afterwards, in 1805, the poet recalled the memory of that portrait, and the emotion and thought that were generated, in his heart and mind, by his reflection on that memory may be found in this poem.

Thematically, the poem may be divided into two parts: Part I consists of the first 8 stanzas, and Part II consists of the remaining 7 stanzas. Each stanza of the 15-stanza poem comprises four lines which follow the rhyme-scheme: a b a b.

ELEGIAC STANZAS

I was thy neighbour once, thou rugged Pile!
Four summer weeks I dwelt in sight of thee:
I saw thee every day; and all the while
Thy Form was sleeping on a glassy sea.

So pure the sky, so quiet was the air!
So like, so very like, was day to day!
Whene'er I looked, thy Image still was there;
It trembled, but it never passed away.

How perfect was the calm! it seemed no sleep;
No mood, which season takes away, or brings:
I could have fancied that the mighty Deep
Was even the gentlest of all gentle Things.

Ah! THEN, if mine had been the Painter's hand,
To express what then I saw; and add the gleam,
The light that never was, on sea or land,
The consecration, and the Poet's dream;

I would have planted thee, thou hoary Pile
Amid a world how different from this!
Beside a sea that could not cease to smile;
On tranquil land, beneath a sky of bliss.

Thou shouldst have seemed a treasure-house divine
Of peaceful years; a chronicle of heaven;—
Of all the sunbeams that did ever shine
The very sweetest had to thee been given.

A Picture had it been of lasting ease,
Elysian quiet, without toil or strife;
No motion but the moving tide, a breeze,
Or merely silent Nature's breathing life.

Such, in the fond illusion of my heart,
Such Picture would I at that time have made:
And seen the soul of truth in every part,
A steadfast peace that might not be betrayed.

So once it would have been,—'tis so no more;
I have submitted to a new control:
A power is gone, which nothing can restore;
A deep distress hath humanised my Soul

Not for a moment could I now behold
A smiling sea, and be what I have been:
The feeling of my loss will ne'er be old;
This, which I know, I speak with mind serene.

Then, Beaumont, Friend! who would have been the Friend,
If he had lived, of Him whom I deplore,
This work of thine I blame not, but commend;
This sea in anger, and that dismal shore.

O 'tis a passionate Work!—yet wise and well,
Well chosen is the spirit that is here;
That Hulk which labours in the deadly swell,
This rueful sky, this pageantry of fear!

And this huge Castle, standing here sublime,
I love to see the look with which it braves,
Cased in the unfeeling armour of old time,
The lightning, the fierce wind, and trampling waves.

Farewell, farewell the heart that lives alone,
Housed in a dream, at distance from the Kind!
Such happiness, wherever it be known,
Is to be pitied; for 'tis surely blind.

But welcome fortitude, and patient cheer,
And frequent sights of what is to be borne!
Such sights, or worse, as are before me here.—
Not without hope we suffer and we mourn.

After about eleven years, the poet recalls in imagination the portrait of Piel Castle that he saw when he was living near that Castle, and so, in the poem, he says that once he was a neighbour of that Castle which is now in a dilapidated condition ('rugged'). The poet says that for four weeks, in the summer, he lived in the neighbourhood of the castle ('dwelt in the sight of thee'), and saw the castle daily, and whenever ('all the while') he saw the castle, he saw the reflection of it in the calm or unruffled ('sleeping') and sleek ('glassy') surface of the water of the sea (*Stanza* I). During the time, when the poet was a neighbour of the castle (inside which the portrait was hung), everyday ('day to day') the sky was wonderfully clear ('pure') and the air was absolutely quiet ('so quiet')—and each day was like the other day ("So like, very like, was day to day"). Then, whenever the poet would look at the water of the sea, he would see the reflection ('Image') of the Castle of Piel on the surface of the water ('there'). There were certainly ripples in the water, and so the reflection of the castle on the water seemed to be trembling, but the reflection did never cease to be, or, in spite of the ripples, the reflection of the castle was still there on the surface of the water ('it never passed away') (*Stanza* II). Then the sea ('Deep') remained perfectly calm, and yet the sea did not seem to be sleeping ('it seemed no sleep'); and the calm of the sea did not seem to be a particular state ('mood') of the sea—the state that changes as the weather ('season') changes; *i.e.*, the sea seemed to be perpetually or naturally calm ("No mood, which season takes away, or brings"). At that time, the poet could imagine or fancy that the particular powerful ('mighty') sea ('Deep') was the most suave or calm of all things (*Stanza* III).

So far the poet has told about his actual experiences of the castle's reflection on the water of the calm sea, of the clear sky, and of the silent air. But, in the portrait, painted by Sir George Beaumont, that was hung in the Piel Castle, the castle was dilapidated, the sky was 'rueful' and the sea was 'in anger.' When the poet, eleven years ago, saw the beautiful Piel Castle and its surround, and also the beautiful reflection of the castle on the calm sea, he could not quite like the portrait, because, to him, the portrait did not agree with reality, with the real castle and with its real reflection in the sea-water. And so then he wished ('Ah!') to paint the portrait of the Piel Castle in a manner different from Sir George Beaumont's. If he had been a painter ('if mine had been the Painter's hand'), and could have painted ('express') what he actually saw then, he would have painted the castle and all that (in the picture painted by Sir Beaumont) in a different manner. Had he been a painter, he would have added brilliance ('gleam') or light to the 'sea and land,' in the portrait, which lacked in brilliance and light; and thus he could have hallowed or sanctified ('consecration') the portrait of the castle; and also he could have added imagination and fancy ('Poet's dream') to the portrait (*Stanza* IV).

The poet tells the very old ('hoary') Castle of Piel that, had he been a painter, he would situate ('plant') it (the Castle of Piel) in an environment or surround quite different from that in which it now stood in the picture ("Amid a world how different from this!"). He would then situate the castle by the shore ('Beside') of a comfortable or gentle or silent sea ('that could not cease to smile'), and on a quiet or peaceful ('tranquil') expanse of land, under a sky that would seem to be full of bliss (*Stanza* V). He says that the castle should seem to be a heavenly source of peace and happiness ('a treasure-house divine/ Of peaceful years'), and it should seem to be a place of heavenliness, or the castle should have been a story ('chronicle') of peace or heavenliness. And the sweetest or the most delightful of all sunshines should have been added to the loveliness of the castle ('had to thee been given') (*Stanza* VI). If the poet were a painter, he would draw the portrait in such wise that the painting or portrait ('Picture') would have been a source of eternal happiness ('lasting ease'); and the portrait would look like the imaginary or mythological Elysium, where peace dwells, ('Elysian quiet') and where there is no strife, and where there is no necessity of labouring too much ('toil') for one's livelihood. The portrait of the poet would appear to be a place where there would have been no violent stirrings or commotions ('No motion'), but where there would be found springs or running brooks ('moving tide') and breeze or slow-moving wind; or, alternatively, there would be found only the living nature existing in quietude ('Or merely silent Nature's breathing life') (*Stanza* VII). The poet further says that if he had been a painter, he would have made the picture of the castle with his dear and wistful imagination ('in the fond illusion of my heart'), at an earlier date (or eleven years ago when he first saw the castle) ('at that time'). And after executing that picture or portrait, he would see that in every part or portion of that portrait there was quintessence of truth ('soul of truth') and also unwavering or undisturbed ('steadfast') peace that would never be deceived ('betrayed') or obliterated by violence (*Stanza* VIII).

Here the poet deviates from his earlier discourse, as is obvious from the first line of the ninth stanza: "So once it would have been,—'tis so no more." What we were hearing from the poet, so far, was his earlier wish. Eleven years ago, had he been a painter, he would have painted the castle in a calm but glittering and lovely surround. The lapse of eleven years has changed the poet phenomenally, and during this period of time he has lost something, though he has also gained something else, instead. The poet says that now ('new') he has acquired the power of restraint, of rationality, and of forbearance ('control'), *i.e.*, he is now able to rein in his earlier uncontrollable joy in the beauty of nature. On the other hand, he has lost his capability of enjoying the delight of nature ('A power is gone'), and that capability will never come back to him ('which nothing can restore'). His distressful experiences of the world have now made him a really worldly man ('humanised my Soul'). Before, he remained so engrossed in the beauty of nature that he was not like so many other men—men who have to share the poignant sorrows of life. But now, after his experiences of the pains of the world, he is like all the other men: "A deep distress hath humanised my Soul" (*Stanza* IX). The poet's mind has now become so radically changed that he now cannot, even for a moment, see that delightful ('smiling') sea that he saw earlier, and even cannot revive his earlier state of mind, or resume ('be') his earlier state of mind, that he then experienced to be his own state of mind ("what I have seen'). Or, he cannot become as delightful as he saw nature to be ('what I have seen'). The pain (due to the loss of his delight in nature, or due to the loss of his brother John Wordsworth) ('feeling of my loss') will constantly remain with him, fresh and acute ('will ne'er be old'). The poet is saying all this, not being perturbed or excited, but very coolly ('with mind serene') (*Stanza* X). He says that (if life is really so distressful and pathetic, as he has by now experienced it, then) he now calls Beaumont (the painter of the portrait of the Castle of Piel), and none else ('who would have been the Friend'), his alter ego ('Friend') with all enthusiasm, because it was only Beaumont who could feel like with him. Had Beaumont been alive at this hour ('If he had lived')—Beaumont, whose death the poet mourns ('deplore')—, then the poet would tell him that he (the poet) does not find faults with his (Beaumont's) portrait ('This work of thine I blame not'); rather, he (the poet) now appreciates ('commend') the portrait. The poet now appreciates that the sea is turbulent ('in anger'), and that the beach of the sea looks hopeless ('dismal') (*Stanza* XI).

The poet can now realise that the portrait has been painted with the genuine passion of the artist ('a passionate Work'), *i.e.* the portrait is not a mechanically drawn picture, and that the portrait bears the impress of the real experiences of life of the artist. And, nevertheless, the portrait is wisely and realistically or skilfully drawn. The poet further says that the theme and the idea of the portrait were wisely ('Well') chosen by the artist (Beaumont). The well chosen ideas or symbols of the portrait are: the ship ('Hulk') that is trying with effort ('labours') to keep it steady in the fearful ('deadly') waves ('swell') of the sea; the pitiful or mournful ('rueful') sky; and the concatenation or train ('pageantry') of other dreaded objects ('pageantry of fear') (*Stanza* XII). The poet says that he loves to see, in the portrait, the undaunted and confident ('braves') appearance or attitude ('look') of the high-rise or majestic ('sublime') castle, which is surrounded by ('Cased in[1]) an old wall that is devoid of sensibility ('unfeeling armour'). And the castle is standing majestically against the ravages of "lightning, the fierce wind, and trampling waves" (*Stanza* XIII). The feelings and the emotions of the poet have now become sympathetic and 'humanised,' and so he is bidding farewell to his former feelings and emotions ('heart'), aroused by the previous perception of the same portrait feelings and emotions that earlier remained aloof from humanity or from human beings, other than himself, ('at a distance from the kind'), and remained only within the heart of the poet ('that lives alone'). His former feelings and emotions were, therefore, not realistic, but were illusory ('Housed in a dream'). The poet says that the happiness or joy, that he previously got, from whatever sources ('wherever it be known'), was pitiable or a matter of regret, because such happiness or joy was certainly irrational or unrealistic ('blind'), because it did not take into account the sufferings and distress of life that 'humanise' us (*Stanza* XIV). He now gladly accepts ('welcome') fortitude, and patience, cheerfully. He welcomes frequent visitations of fearful and gloomy situations or events of life ('sights'), as are reproduced in the portrait, that humanity is to bear with ('what is to be borne'). Nay, he is inviting not only such distressful situations of life as are there in the portrait ('as are before me here'), but situations or conditions that are worse than these. He does so, because he hopes that such distressful conditions of life will make us suffer and mourn, and thereby they will bestow upon us the saving fortitude and stoic patience with which we shall be able to overcome distresses, and live cheerfully and hopefully in future ("Not without hope we suffer and we mourn") (*Stanza* XV).

The poem contains, as we said earlier, Wordsworth's personal sorrow, of course among other things—sorrow due to the death of his son John Wordsworth, by drowning, in 1805, the year in which this poem was composed. F.W. Bateson writes in this regard: "In or about 1805 Wordsworth no longer wrote great poetry, and February 1805 was the date of John Wordsworth's death. John's drowning has been described by de Selincourt as 'the most terrible blow either William or Dorothy had ever suffered.' For weeks their grief was uncontrollable. William cried like a baby. The ultimate effect, he claimed, was to 'humanise his soul' ('Elegiac Stanzas suggested by a Picture of Peele Castle'):

> I have submitted to a new control;
> The power is gone, which nothing can restore;
> A deep distress hath humanised my soul.

But there is little evidence either in his poems or his letters that John's loss did make him more human. It seems on the contrary to have desiccated his soul" (Bateson, 171-172).

This poem shows, among other things, that it is misprising Wordsworth to call him the poet of childhood, because during the time of the composition of this poem, and also afterwards, he realised that childhood is only a part of human life, and that adult life necessarily constitutes another part—perhaps the most important part—of a man's life. Like most of the other great Romantic poets, Wordsworth had drunk the wine of life to the lees: he realised that life was a feast of joy, but he also realised that life has miseries, pains, fears and distresses, in its store. This new realisation of his we barely find in his poems, composed before 1805—before he wrote this poem, and in this sense, this poem deserves special notice. Wordsworth did not take the miseries, pains, fears and distresses of life to be absolutely evil, to be all negative; he rather thought that these negative elements of life have some positive effects. At the end of this poem, the poet says that all these negative elements of life have 'humanised' his soul, and have made a stoic philosopher of him. He now sees a ray of hope even in the glum of life, and so does not want to flinch away from life; rather, like the stoic philosophers, he is now all ready to face or confront the negative elements of life with all prowess, because he is hopeful that he will be able to elbow his way through those negative elements of life: "Not without hope we suffer and we mourn." The poem may dispel our wrong idea about Wordsworth that to him nature was always and without fail calm, serene and soothing. Wordsworth was not blind, particularly in his poems composed after 1805, to the other aspects of nature: violent, fearsome and distressful. In *Elegiac Stanzas Suggested by a Picture of Peele Castle, in a Storm, Painted by Sir George Beaumont,* the nature is violent, dismal and distressing: "This sea in anger, and that dismal shore." Such an attitude of nature we also find in *A Night- Piece,* composed in 1798: "—The sky is overcast/ With a continuous cloud of texture close,/ Heavy and wan." But, in *Elegiac Stanzas Suggested by.... Sir George Beaumont,* unlike in *A Night-Piece,* not only is the external world violent and distressful, but the inner world of the poet also sustains the agony the impact of the violence and distress of the external world.

(IX) ODE TO DUTY

About 1805, there occurred a sea-change in the themes of Wordsworth's poetry. Till about that year, in his poetry, Wordsworth was solely concerned with such themes as beauty, love, truth and nature, but about 1805, another theme came to occupy his consciousness—the concern for morality. Wordsworth wrote this ode in 1805, following Thomas Gray's *Hymn to Adversity,* as the two beginning lines of the two poems—*Hymn to Adversity* and *Ode to Duty*—may indicate. Gray's *Hymn to Adversity* begins with the line "Daughter of Jove, relentless power," and Wordsworth's *Ode to Duty* begins with the line "Stern Daughter of the Voice of God!" *Ode to Duty* is one of the early poems of Wordsworth that show his deep and sincere concern for morality. The poem was first published in 1807, and is included in Wordsworth's group of poems known as 'Poems of Sentiment and Reflection.' It is included in Palgrave's *Golden Treasury*. In the 1807 edition of the poem, *i.e.* when the poem was first published, it comprised an additional stanza, which was placed between stanzas V and VI of the poem, as we read it today. The particular stanza was extrapolated from the poem in its subsequent editions. In *The Golden Treasury* also that particular stanza is not included. The stanza may be cited below:

Yet not the less would I throughout
Still act according to the voice
Of my own wish; and feel past doubt
That my submissiveness was choice:
Not seeking in the school of pride
For "precepts over dignified,"
Denial and restraint I prize
No farther than they breed a second Will more wise.

Ode to Duty

Stern Daughter of the Voice of God!
O Duty! if that name thou love
Who art a light to guide, a rod
To check the erring, and reprove;
Thou, who art victory and law
When empty terrors overawe;
From vain temptations dost set free;
And calm'st the weary strife of frail humanity!

There are who ask not if thine eye
Be on them; who, in love and truth,
Where no misgiving is, rely
Upon the genial sense of youth:
Glad Hearts! Without reproach or bolt;
Who do thy work, and know it not:
Oh! if through confidence misplaced
They fail, thy saving arms, dread Power! around them cast.

Serene will be our days and bright,
And happy will our nature be,
When love is an unerring light,
And joy its own security.
And they a blissful course may hold

Even now, who, not unwisely bold,
Live in the spirit of this creed;
Yet seek thy firm support, according to their need.

I, loving freedom, and untried;
No sport of every random gust,
Yet being to myself a guide,
Too blindly have reposed my trust:
And oft, when in my heart was heard
Thy timely mandate, I deferred
The task, in smoother walks to stray;
But thee I now would serve more strictly, if I may.

Through no disturbance of my soul,
Or strong compunction in me wrought,
I supplicate for thy control;
But in the quietness of thought:
Me this unchartered freedom tires;
I feel the weight of chance-desires:
My hopes no more must change their name,
I long for a repose that ever is the same.

Stern Lawgiver! yet thou dost wear
The Godhead's most benignant grace;
Nor know we anything so fair
As is the smile upon thy face:
Flowers laugh before thee on their beds
And fragrance in thy footing treads;
Thou dost preserve the stars from wrong;
And the most ancient heavens, through Thee, are fresh and strong.

To humbler functions, awful Power!
I call thee: I myself commend
Unto thy guidance from this hour;
Oh, let my weakness have an end!
Give unto me, made lowly wise,
The spirit of self-sacrifice;
The confidence of reason give;
And in the light of truth thy Bondman let me live!

The poet would like to address Duty (personified) as the draconian ('Stern') daughter of the will or command of God ('Voice of God'), if she (Duty) would like the epithet. He says that Duty is a sort of light (in the moral darkness of the world) to conduct (men) with, and a whip to chastise ('cheek') the moral defaulters or evil-doers ('erring') for the correction of their conduct. She is a sort of light with which the moral defaulters are to be reprimanded. Duty (or responsibility) always prevails over ('victory') meaningless and inconsequential terrorism, that cows down innocents, and also imposes order ('law') in the society. Duty disentangles or holds back one from paltry ('vain') allurements, and assuages or tempers the enervating and destructive wrangles ('weary strife') of the erring and immoral ('frail') human beings. (Stanza I) There are people who do not want or recognise Duty's presence and authority over them ('who ask not if thine eye/ Be on them'); and such people are interested only in unalloyed ('Where no misgiving is') love and truth or knowledge, and are happy or dependent ('rely') on the pleasing sensualities ('genial sense') of youth (as Wordsworth himself in his youth happened to be). The poet wonders that such people are extremely glad in their sensual levity, or in their pursuit of truth or knowledge ('truth'), without ever being scolded or chastised ('reproach or bolt'), and that such people sometimes do moral acts ('Who do thy work'), without understanding that their acts are moral ('and know it not'). Such people confide in the value of their sensual and cognitive enterprises and employments; but, to the poet, such people are wrongly believing in their endeavours ('confidence misplaced'); and they, therefore, says the poet, cannot achieve what they should ('They fail'). The poet, therefore, urges Duty, the formidable might, to retrieve such (morally failing) people, by imposing full control over them, or by staving them off from their wrongs, with the help of her (Duty's) sympathetic power or might ('thy saving arms, dread Power! around them cast') (*Stanza* II).

The poet says that our lives will be peaceful ('serene') and prosperous ('bright'), and we will be happy ('happy will our nature be'), if the light of love does not lead us astray ('unerring), and if the joy that we enjoy out of love protects ('security') the love itself (protects love from such destructive forces as jealousy, hatred, doubt, etc.). Those people ('they'), who sincerely and strongly ('bold') believe ('Live') in the essence of this belief or philosophy ('the spirit of this creed')—of course not foolishly ('not unwisely')—, may lead a blissful life ('course'), even in these days when both love and joy are rare and rarely true ('now'). But even if such people may live a life of love and joy ('Yet'), they will at times have to seek the firm support of Duty or stern command of moral responsibility, whenever they will feel the need of it (*Stanza* III). The poet says that once he was a lover of freedom, and was never judged wrong, or censured, ('untried') for his free-style life, and yet he was never a sporting thing to his disordered effusions of passions ('random gust'). Nevertheless ('Yet'), he himself was his monitor, and he believed in his own guidance ('have reposed my trust'), of course not at all considering if this was justified or not ('Too blindly'). And then it frequently happened that in his heart or conscience he heard the dictates of Duty or responsibility or morality, but, instead of carrying out the commands or dictates of Duty, he kept them a side, with a view to taking those up later on ('I deferred/ The task'), and chose to lead a careless or easy ('smoother') life ('walks'). However, the poet now promises to Duty that from now on he will obey her commands ('serve') more sincerely ('strictly'), if he gets the opportunity, or if he can ('if I may") (*Stanza* IV).

The poet is saying all this, or praying ('supplicate') to Duty for her (Duty's) guidance ('control'), not because he is disturbed in his soul, or not because he is sorely ('strong') pricked by his conscience ('compunction in me wrought'), but he is doing this after serenely thinking ('quietness of thought') about the freedom or the care-free style of life he earlier enjoyed, and after understanding the necessity of acquiring the sense of duty or moral responsibility. The poet says that now he is averse to, or tired of, his uncontrolled or unrestricted ('uncharted') freedom. He now feels or understands the evil or grave consequences of his earlier inconstant desires ('the weight of chance-desires') of love and truth. Now his desires or hopes are certainly constant—now his desires or hopes will not be changed from time to time, *i.e.*, these will not be these now and those then ('My hopes no more must change their name'). He is now eager to get rest or peace of mind ('repose') for ever, and this eagerness of his will always remain the same (*Stanza* V).

The poet tells the draconian Duty ('Stern Lawgiver') that even now ('Yet')—even when disorderliness and irresponsibility prevail in the society—, the most kind favour ('benignant grace') of God envelops herself, *i.e.*, Duty ('thou dost wear/ The Godhead's most benignant grace'). He says that nothing known to us is more beautiful than the kind or compassionate look, or the smile, on her face. He says that the flowers in the trees ('beds') smile because she (Duty) is present, and that wherever she is present, or wherever she walks ('thy footing treads') there is happiness or sweet smell ('fragrance'). The poet tells Duty that it is because of her presence that the stars cannot do any wrong, and that the sense of duty and order, that are prevalent in the 'most ancient heavens,' are still unalloyed or uncorrupted ('fresh') and efficacious ('strong') because of her (Duty's) presence (*Stanza* VI).

Lastly, the poet invokes ('call') Duty ('awful Power') to do a small thing ('humbler function'): to guide him (the poet) (Duty guides the big and innumerable stars, and compared to the stars, the poet is a small thing, and so to guide him is also a small thing or a 'humbler function'). He recommends himself to her (Duty) for being guided by herself, from the present moment, so that ('let') his moral weakness or negligence may go away from him. The poet prays to Duty to make him humble or meek ('lowly') and wise, to give him the 'spirit of self-sacrifice' and to give him confidence in his own rationality ('reason'). He calls himself a slave or servant ('Bondman') of Duty ('thy'), and prays to her to help him live with the enlightened guidance of the truth of duty or moral responsibility ('in the light of truth') (*Stanza* VII).

In 1802 (or 1803), the year in which Wordsworth wrote *Ode: Intimation of Immortality*, we first noticed that there was brewing a change in the poet's mood as well as in his attitude to life. At that time the poet was around only thirty, and even at such an early stage of life he vowed to renounce the animal enjoyment of the beauty of nature, in order to delve deep into the mystry of life and its sufferings, and into the region beyond the bound of life. The poet said good-bye to his earlier frivolous and sensuous enjoyment of nature: "The radiance which was once so bright/ Be now for ever taken from my sight." Wordsworth now turned a stoic: he was now determined to utilise the rest of his life—'what remains behind'—in the participation of 'the primal sympathy' that generates 'Out of human suffering,' though—he thus qualified his statement—he would continue to verily enjoy the beauty of nature. But this change in his mood, or in his attitude to life, took a firm foothold only three years afterwards—in 1805, the year in which Wordsworth composed *Ode to Duty*, because since that date his changed mood and attitude did not flag. And, therefore, we may take the year 1805 as the dividing line between the early Wordsworth and the later Wordsworth. David Daiches writes in this regard: "One sees the transition, perhaps, in the 'Ode to Duty,' written in 1805, and first published in 1807, which both in theme and treatment shows Wordsworth moving away from his characteristic dependence on perception and its poetic consequences" (Daiches, 1996, 882).

This sea-change in Wordsworth's perception, attitude and mood assumed a more defined contour when, on 6th February, 1805, his dear brother John Wordsworth, Commander of the E.I. Company's ship, was drowned. On that sad occasion, Wordsworth wrote *Elegiac Verses*: *In Memory of My Brother, John Wordsworth*, in which poem occur the following lines that show that he now very keenly felt the ephemerality of life and the illusiveness of 'earthly hope':

> Long as these mighty rocks endure,—
> Oh do not Thou too fondly brood,
> Although deserving of all good,
> On any earthly hope, however pure!

Such lines we never hear before 1805—such lines of inwardness, of unexpressibly deep pain. In the same year (1805) Wordsworth wrote *Elegiac Stanzas in* which he speaks of his heart-felt sorrows, and says that these sorrows humanized his soul: "A deep distress hath humanized my Soul." And since this time, Wordsworth's mind was drawn inwards, and, consequently, he began to hear the call of his conscience—the call for assuming duty towards humanity, while stoically bearing all his share of human sorrows. Therefore, we may say that Wordsworth's sense of duty towards humanity originated in his distresses and pains.

The poet was now aware of the call of duty, but what is this duty? The poet does not explicitly answer the question, but only says that the duty is to sacrifice one's self ('self-sacrifice'), understandably for the cause of saving human beings from suffering and pains, or, at the least, for sympathetically and humbly sharing the sufferings and pains of humanity. From now on, instead of enjoying the sensuous beauty of nature, the poet will follow the dictates of the draconian conscience—the 'Stern Lawgiver.' The term 'Stern Lawgiver' reminds us the German philosopher Immanuel Kant's (1724-1805) moral term 'Categorical Imperative.' Kant said that the dictates of conscience are insuperable, inviolable; and if these are, nevertheless, violated, appropriately stern punishments will be awarded by conscience itself. But does Wordsworth's concept of (moral) duty bear any religious undertone? Wordsworth was never much concerned with either religion or God. Bradley informs us that Wordsworth did never show any inclination to respect religious rites, and that he did never go to church till the fag end of his life, and also that he made up this deficiency of his by writing *Ode to Duty*: "'He [Wordsworth] wrote his Ode to Duty,' said one of his friends, 'and that he had done with that matter'" (Bradley, 120).

Though in *Ode to Duty* Wordsworth lays emphasis on duty or moral obligation, he has not altogether ignored God, as is evident in the beginning line of this poem: "Stern Daughter of the Voice of God!" Further, though henceforth he showed his concern for moral obligation, he did not leave his joy in nature's beauty in the limbo, as is evident in most of his so many poems written after 1805. But, it is true that since 1805 he became stoical and began to search into his own soul. Apparently, it seems that there is a contradiction: how can a stoical person become interested in nature, particularly in its beauty? But the apparent contradiction will fizzle out when we will know that stoicism believes in the unity of man, God and nature. Gilbert Highet says that Wordsworth was influenced by Greek and Roman stoicism, and that he accepted stoicism as his motto of life (of course after he attained the age of 30 years). Highet further means to say that Wordsworth's conception of the unity of God, man and nature came from classical stoicism. He, in his *The Classical Tradition*, writes: "The second great classical influence on Wordsworth was Greek philosophy. He seems not to have read the Greek stoics (apart from Epictatus who belongs to the Roman period), but he knew a great deal of the Roman Stoics, particularly that difficult author Seneca. The effect of this was to strengthen his belief in the unity of God, man, and the external world. Man (the Stoics held) is a part of the physical world, and the world is a manifestation of God" (Highet, 410). Wordsworth was influenced not only by the metaphysical speculations of the ancient stoics, but also by their thoughts and convictions about moral obligations. Highet further writes about Wordsworth's stoicism: "In his attitude to moral obligations (also), Wordsworth was a stoic. They should be accepted as natural, not justified by external praise or endangered by external blame, but recognized as part of the universal process. Virtue for the Stoic, means living according to nature; and a good action is complete once it has been willed—whether it succeeds or not is unimportant, the essential thing being the harmony of man's will with the spirit of the universe. Two of Wordsworth's most famous poems on moral subjects express this belief: *Character of the Happy Warrior* and the *Ode to Duty*; both were written in 1805, and the latter is prefaced by a motto from Seneca to stress its Stoic inspiration" (Highet, 411).

(X) THE SOLITARY REAPER

This is one of the most famous poems of Wordsworth, like *Tintern Abbey, Nutting, Daffodils* ('I wandered lonely as a cloud'), *Lucy Gray, Michael, The Idiot Boy,* etc. In 1803, Wordsworth undertook a tour over Scotland, where he was much impressed by the pastoral scenarios there. This tour supplied him with some beautiful themes on which he wrote a number of poems; and the pastoral description of the present poem was suggested by some of the scenarios he witnessed there in Scotland. However, Alan Gardiner writes about the origin of *The Solitary Reaper;* "The idea of the poem came not from an experience of Wordsworth's but from a sentence in an account of visit to Scotland written by a friend, Thomas Wilkinson: 'Passed a female who was reaping alone: she sang in Erse as she bended over her sickle; the sweetest human voice I ever heard: her strains were tenderly melancholy, and felt delicious, long after they were heard no more'" (Gardiner, 63). Gardiner further writes: "As Wordsworth acknowledged in a note, the last line of his poem [*The Solitary Reaper*] borrows directly from Wilkinson's description" (Gardiner, 63). The poem was composed in 1805, in the rhyme-scheme a b c b d d e e, and was first published in 1807.

The Solitary Reaper

Behold her, single in the field,
Yon solitary Highland Lass!
Reaping and singing by herself;
Stop here, or gently pass!
Alone she cuts and binds the grain,
And sings a melancholy strain;
O listen! for the Vale profound
Is overflowing with the sound.

No Nightingale did ever chaunt
More welcome notes to weary bands
Of travellers in some shady haunt,
Among Arabian sands:
A voice so thrilling ne'er was heard
In spring-time from the Cuckoo-bird,
Breaking the silence of the seas
Among the farthest Hebrides.

Will no one tell me what she sings?—
Perhaps the plaintive numbers flow
For old, unhappy, far-off things,
And battles long ago:
Or is it some more humble lay,
Familiar matter of to-day?
Some natural sorrow, loss or pain,
That has been, and may be again?

Whate'er the theme, the Maiden sang
As if her song could have no ending;
I saw her singing at her work,
And o'er the sickle bending;—
I listened, motionless and still;
And, as I mounted up the hill,
The music in my heart I bore,
Long after it was heard no more.

The poet asks the reader to look at ('Behold') the single or lonely highland girl who is reaping corn, and is singing to herself, in the field. He asks the reader to stop at the spot and to listen to the song of the girl, or to go away without making any sound ('gently pass'), so that the girl is not disturbed or distracted. The girl is cutting the stalks of corn ('grain') and is binding the stalks in sheaves, while she is singing a melancholic song ('strain'), and the deep and wide valley ('Vale profound') is being flushed with that song (*Stanza* I). The poet says that no nightingale did ever sing ('chaunt') to groups of tired travellers ('weary bands/ Of travellers'), in some oft-frequented ('haunt') shady place, or in an oasis in the Arabian desert ('sands'), such a sweet song as that of the girl. The poet further says that so thrilling voice, as that of the girl, was never heard, in spring, from the cuckoo that sings from the northernmost part of the world which is called Hebrides (Hebrides or Western Islands is a group of islands in the north of Scotland, once supposed to be the northernmost part of the world), 'Breaking the silence of the seas' (*Stanza* II).

The poet wants to understand the meaning of the song of the girl, but there is nobody beside him, or nobody is able to tell him the meaning ("Will no one tell me what she sings?—)". Therefore, he probabilistically construes the song of the girl as a song of mourning or lamentation ('plaintive numbers'), that tells about ('flow/ For') some unhappy things or incidents of the past, or about battles that occurred in the long past. Alternatively, the poet asks whether the girl's song ('lay') is about some trifling ('humble') and familiar things of our contemporary generation, or of the present time ('to-day'). Or, the poet once again asks, whether her song is about some sorrow or loss, or pain which the common men are ordinarily or naturally heir to ('natural sorrow, loss or pain')—sorrow, or loss, or pain that has occurred in the life of human beings ('That has been'), or may occur, again, in the life of human beings (*Stanza* III). (So long the poet was speaking in the present tense, but from the fourth or the last stanza of the poem it is clear that he was in fact telling us about an incident that had taken place before his telling.) The poet says that whatever might be the bearing or purport of the song of the girl, she was singing in such a manner that it seemed to him that her song would never cease. The poet now says that he saw her singing, while working in the field, bending over her sickle. He listened to her song, keeping himself motionless, still, and then he 'mounted up the hill.' And he saw her no more, and, nevertheless, says the poet, the sweet cadences and modulations ('music') of the song of the girl remained within his heart ('I bore') for a long time after he ceased hearing her song with his (physical) ears ('after it was heard no more').

Wordsworth has sometimes been charged for being tendentiously moralistic, and that not very unjustly, for the poet, as a poet, professed that he wanted to be a teacher (of morality) or nothing else. Again, he has sometimes been found with the fault of dwelling too long on the narrative part of his poetry, or, which is the same thing, with the fault of expatiating too much on the narrative part of his poetry. But the present poem, as some others like this one, shows that, at times, Wordsworth can also write poetry without any moral teaching and without elaborating too much on the materials of the poem, that he can sometimes be succinct, and yet passionate. *The Solitary Reaper* is a meet instance of this kind of Wordsworthian poetry. Graham Hough writes in this regard: "Readers of Wordsworth must learn to expect a good deal of material and circumstantial detail in his poetic experience: it is sometimes obstructive, but it is also what gives us the sense that he has his feet on the ground far more firmly than any other poet of his age. When the experience is cluttered up with circumstance and explanation, it can find expression in flashes of that magical and immediate loveliness in which Wordsworth is sometimes supposed to be deficient. This is so in *The Solitary Reaper,* where there is not narrative thread and no moral—just a girl singing as she reaps a field" (Hough, 46).

As we have said, in most poems Wordsworth builds up a collocation of materials or details, and from that collocation some deep thought or painful feeling comes out very naturally. In *Tintern Abbey,* for instance, the details ultimately lead to a keen feeling of pain, in the last two lines of the poem: "To me the meanest flower that blows can give/Thoughts that do often lie too deep for tears." In *The Solitary Reaper,* there is almost no detail, and yet it produces a deep thought in our mind, and this deep thought, in turn, gives rise in our hearts some indefinable but deep feeling, and a profound emotion that seeks a vent. Of the eight lines of the poem—from line 13 to line 20—, Graham Hough writes that these "lines (which) catch the *lacrimae rerum* more memorably than those of any poet since Virgil" (Hough, 46). Further, merely the two lines of the poem—"For old, unhappy, far-off things,/And battles long ago"—

transport us to a far-off world of pensive memories, and engross us in deep meditation over those memories. It is for this reason that F.W. Bateson is highly appreciative of these two lines: "These lines from 'The Solitary Reaper' are almost alone apparently in possessing the elixir of Coleridge, Shelley and Keats—'something,' as Swinburne puts it, 'in the mere progress and resonance of the words, some secret in the very motion and cadence of the lines, inexplicable by the most sympathetic acuteness of criticism" (Bateson, 14). On the other hand, Alan Gardiner has found *The Solitary Reaper* as yet another instance, beside many others of Wordsworth's poems, of how the poet perceived man and nature in perfect harmony with each other. The girl, who is reaping and singing, is not in any way disturbed by the silent valley; rather, the beautiful valley is flushed with the cadences of her song. Again, the valley is silent, profound and meditative; and it is such an ambience in which one feels nostalgic, like the singing girl in the valley does, as is apparent from her song that tells of "old, unhappy, far-off things,/And battles long ago." Gardiner writes about the poem: "In Wordsworth's treatment of the incident, the reaper's song becomes expressive of a profound harmony between man and nature" (Gardiner, 63). Further, Alan Gardiner has found some similarity between *The Solitary Reaper* and *Resolution and Independence,* in the sense that in both the poems the poet expresses his reaction to a solitary person, in the lap of nature —in the latter poem, he really met a solitary person (the leech-gatherer), but in the former poem, he saw a solitary person (the reaping and singing girl) from a distance.

However, the poem is astonishingly simple, while its affective bearing is stunningly profound; and so it can certainly be taken to be one of Wordsworth's representative poems. The locale of the poem is a lonely (except the reaping girl) valley, but the thought that the song of the solitary reaper gives rise to transports us to the far-off Hebrides, to the 'Arabian sands,' and to the battlefields of the hoary past. The voluble and harmonious song of the girl inundates the whole of the valley. And all these are done in the poem with minimum of suggestions. David Daiches highly praises *The Solitary Reaper*. He says that in *Tintern Abbey,* the rhymings and the rhythms provide additional sympathetic strings to the poem for enhancing the emotion created, and that the thought of the poem creates a sense of *Einfuhlung* (empathy with an object, or entering into the 'soul' of an object) with the surround. Daiches further writes: "'The Solitary Reaper' does some thing similar in a more subdued and melodious manner: here the verse movement enables the emotion to rise with the contemplation" (Daiches, 1996, 887). David Daiches praises the alteration of the short and long lines of the poem: "The alteration of short and long lines in the eight-line stanza is geared to the movement of the emotion to a degree unusual in Wordsworth" (Daiches, 888). Lastly, Daiches also praises the purity of statement and the mystical undertone of the poem: "The sheer purity of statement, in a style both natural and lapidary, is related to the mystical element in Wordsworth's faith. Here [in *The Solitary Reaper*] his mystical sense of the relation between life, death, and natural objects gives the poem its quiet intensity" (Daiches, 1996, 888).

(XI) SHE WAS A PHANTOM OF DELIGHT

The 'She,' in the poem, is undoubtedly none else than Mary Hutchinson whom the poet married on 4 October, 1802, and with whom he lived a very happy married life, long and tranquil as well as simple,—an ideal married life that everyone would wish to have. The poem was written two years after their marriage, to wit, in 1804. In the poem, the poet goes backward in time, and describes the external and the internal, *i.e.*, the physical and the mental, beauty of Mary Hutchinson, before her marriage with him. The poem is a hearty compliment of the poet to her. Wordsworth was only too honest when he wrote about the poem: "It was written from my heart as is sufficiently obvious." The poem was included in the group of poems generally known as 'Poems of the Imagination' which includes such other famous poems as *A Night-Piece, Nutting, Ruth, The Thorn, Tintern Abbey, To a Skylark* and *Peter Bell.* The poem is included in Palgrave's *The Golden Treasury.* The poem is not entitled, and is known by its beginning line. The present poem may remind us of Byron's *She Walks in Beauty.*

She was a Phantom of Delight

She was a Phantom of delight
When first she gleamed upon my sight;
A lovely Apparition, sent

To be a moment's ornament;
Her eyes as stars of Twilight fair;
Like Twilight's, too, her dusky hair;
But all things else about her drawn
From May-time and the cheerful Dawn;
A dancing Shape, an Image gay,
To haunt, to startle, and waylay.

I saw her upon nearer view,
A Spirit, yet a Woman too!
Her household motions light and free,
And steps of virgin-liberty;
A countenance in which did meet
Sweet records, promises as sweet;
A Creature not too bright or good
For human nature's daily food;
For transient sorrows, simple wiles,
Praise, blame, love, kisses, tears, and smiles.

And now I see with eye serene
The very pulse of the machine;
A Being breathing thoughtful breath,
A Traveller between life and death;
The reason firm, the temperate will,
Endurance, foresight, strength, and skill;
A perfect Woman, nobly planned,
To warn, to comfort, and command;
And yet a Spirit still, and bright
With something of angelic light.

When the poet first saw Mary Hutchinson, she was so sparkling in her beauty that she appeared to the poet not as something real, but as something unreal, as a vision, or as some immaterial form that was so delightful. She seemed to be an angel ('Apparition') sent from heaven down to earth, for a moment's enjoyment ('ornament'). Her eyes were like stars, shining during a beautiful twilight, and her hair was near-black like twilight ('dusky hair'). Her other parts, besides her eyes and hair, were, as if, culled ('drawn') from spring-time ('May-time') that is full of beauty and vitality, and from the freshness or delight of the morning ('cheerful dawn'). Her physical features were rhythmic, and she was darting and lambent ('dancing shape'), and her stature and personality were full of gaiety ('Image gay'), as if she was intent upon frequently impressing her beauty and presence on others ('To haunt'), and upon surprising and capturing them by her attractive beauty ('way-lay').

When the poet saw her from a short distance ('upon nearer view'), she seemed not to be an earthly, but a heavenly, being ('Spirit'), and yet she bore all the qualities of an earthly woman. She possessed all the skills of a household woman, having swift but lambent motions and masterfulness ('free'), and she walked ('step'), like a virgin does, with independence ('virgin-liberty'). In her mien, there was a concord between the impressions of her sweet behaviour and the signs of her sweet manners in future ('promise'). But she was not an extremely beautiful or spritely girl, or an extremely good-natured girl, so that she might prove to be a caviare for a common man's ('human nature's') daily (or perpetual) enjoyment ('daily food'). She could be the source of 'transient sorrows' (*i.e.* she could hurt mildly and temporarily), of 'simple' or innocuous 'wiles,' and of "Praise, blame, love, kisses, tears, and smiles."

Previously, Mary Hutchinson was incessantly active and vibrating, so much so that she seemed to be a machine, and not a woman of flesh and blood, and then it seemed that she did not possess any feeling or passion ('pulse'). But now, as the poet has become matured, and therefore become 'serene,' he can understand ('see') that behind her machine-likeness, there is passion ('pulse'). She is now a living being ('breathing'), having the capacity to think over the fact that she is, as if, a traveller in the path of life, that begins with birth and ends with death. Now, she possesses unflagging rationality ('reason firm'), moderated or domesticated volition ('temperate will'), endurance, foresight, mental strength or conviction of beliefs, and skills of all sorts, necessary for the ways of the world. And, therefore, now she is an ideal ('perfect') and noble ('nobly planned') woman who can 'warn,' 'comfort' and 'command' somebody. And, nevertheless, she is even now ('still') spirit-like or spritely, and is resplendent, as if, with the light that radiates from angels ('angelic light').

The poem is a testimony of Wordsworth's profound love of, and fascination for, Mary Hutchinson (Mrs. Wordsworth), two years before they were married to each other. How far the description of the beauty of Mary Hutchinson, as in the poem, is true to reality, is a different thing, but the poet is, apparently, quite honest in his description of his perception of her beauty, through the prism of his love for her. Thomas de Quincey, in his *Reminiscences of the English Lake Poets,* writes about this poem and about some features of Hutchinson: "Once for all, these exquisite lines were dedicated to Mrs. Wordsworth; were understood to describe her—to have been prompted by the feminine graces of her character: hers they are, and will remain for ever.... Her figure was tolerably good. In complexion she was fair, and there was something peculiarly pleasing even in this accident of the skin, for it was accompanied by an animated expression of health, a blessing which, in fact, she possesses uninterruptedly" (De Quincey, 95).

She was a Phantom of Delight may remind one of Byron's *She Walks in Beauty,* where also the poet describes the exquisite beauty of a woman:

SHE WALKS IN BEAUTY

I

She walks in beauty, like the night
Of cloudless climes and starry skies;
And all that's best of dark and bright
Meet in her aspect and her eyes:
Thus mellow'd to that tender light
Which heaven to gaudy day denies.

II

One shade the more, one ray the less,
Had half impair'd the nameless grace
Which waves in every raven tress,
Or softly lightens o'er her face;
Where thoughts serenely sweet express
How pure, how dear their dwelling-place.

III

And on that cheek, and o'er that brow,
So soft, so calm, yet eloquent,
The smiles that win, the tints that glow,
But tell of days in goodness spent,
A mind at peace with all below,
A heart whose love is innocent!

Whereas Byron wrote this poem confessedly being persuaded by his friend, the Hon. Douglas Kinnaird, for a selection of Hebrew melodies, Wordsworth wrote *She was a Phantom of Delight* being inspired by the beauty of, and by his love for, Mrs. Wordsworth. Comparing Wordsworth's *She was a Phantom of Delight* with Byron's *She Walks in Beauty,* Jerome Beaty and William H. Matchett say that Byron's poem lacks in 'vantage point' and so it cannot create the desired effect, but in Wordsworth's *She was a Phantom of Delight* there is the 'vantage point' which endows the poem authority and conviction. Vantage point is the commanding position from which the poet may create appropriate situation and effective emotion. By the term 'vantage point,' Beaty and Matchett mean "the position of the speaker in relation to the material and the consequent implications thereof" (Beaty and Matchett, 112, f. n.). Beaty and Matchett say that without the vantage point, we cannot well appreciate a poem, and so the vantage point of a poem should be specified. They write: "Specifying vantage point can make a description comprehensible or credible. If someone were to tell you he saw the top of a card table as a parallelogram with pairs of angles of sixty and one hundred and twenty degrees, you might not know whether to doubt him or your own understanding of the nature of card table. If he told you the position from which he was viewing the table you might then understand that the distortion of the square was a matter of perspective and would then believe he was correctly reporting what he saw (and, perhaps, realize he was seeing more accurately and less conventionally than you were). So it is with the clarifying and convincing qualities of the vantage point in a poem" (Beaty and matchett, 112).

Now Beaty and Matchett go on to criticise Byron's *She Walks in Beauty* for its lack of vantage point, and to appreciate Wordsworth's *She was a Phantom of Delight* for having the same: "No speaker (or singer) is identified in the Byron poem. The description, as a result, appears objective, authoritative: her beauty is not just "one man's opinion." Though no speaker is identified, a location of sorts is implied—we see the lady only from the outside, and indeed from a distance. Though we are close enough to her to see her physical features, and even the light in her eyes, we are not close enough to touch her nor are we presented with her thoughts or feelings. There is no sense of closeness or intimacy or even of any long acquaintance. When, therefore, with line 11, the poem describes the lady's inner qualities, this close-but-not-intimate vantage point leads to difficulties. We are not told, dogmatically and authoritatively, that she is pure, good, innocent, as we are told that in every tress waves "nameless grace;" this would be to violate the external vantage point. We are told instead that her character can be ascertained from her appearance, a rather naive and dubious proposition that may well run counter to our experience. It is as if we were told that the parallelogram of the card table had pairs of angles of fifty and one hundred degrees: the evidence does not add up to what we know or think we know axiomatically or experientially (about the number of degrees in the angles of a quadrangle; about telling wine by the barrel it is in, a book by its cover, etc.). Thus what the physical description gained in objectivity by the impersonal external vantage point, the moral description loses in authority by the limitations of that vantage point.

Wordsworth, on the other hand, sacrifices the immediate authority of the objectified view by using a first-person speaker. Since the implied relationship in the first stanza is as distant and brief as that in the Byron poem, his description has, if anything, even less authority. But the second stanza offers a "nearer view" and implies somewhat longer acquaintance ("household motions"); still, at least to line 16, and perhaps a few lines beyond, the moral qualities are described externally and in physical terms. In the third stanza, the dramatic "now" of the poem, she seems to be known very well indeed and her moral or spiritual qualities judged at close range over a protracted period of time. Though there is always possibility of error in one person's judgment of another, and we have no absolute authority for the lady's spiritual qualities, the speaker has gained authority and conviction by the intimate if limited vantage point" (Beaty and Matchett, 114-115).

These two poems of Wordsworth and Byron may be compared with Coleridge's *To Asra* (written on and for his beloved Sara Hutchinson, sister-in-law of Wordsworth). But, while both Wordsworth and Byron describe, in their respective poems, the physical and mental beauties of two particular women, Coleridge, in his poem, only expresses his deep love for his beloved fiancée, saying, among other things, that her beauty beggars description: "Dear Asra, woman beyond utterance dear!"

(XII) LAODAMIA

This is an unconventional as well as rare Wordsworthian poem, in the sense that its theme is not love of nature, or spirituality of nature, but nuptial affection between two characters of Greek mythology: Protesilaus, the husband, and Laodamia, the wife. Protesilaus, the "son of Iphiclus and Astyoche, was native of Phylace in Thessaly. He is called *Phylacius* and *Phylacides,* either from that circumstance or from his being a grandson of Phylacus. He led the warriors of several Thessalian places against Troy, and was the first of all the Greeks who was killed by the Trojans, being the first who leaped from the ships upon the Trojan shore. According to the common tradition he was slain by Hector" (Smith, 341). Laodamia was the "daughter of Acastus, and wife of Protesilaus. When her husband was slain before Troy, she begged the gods to be allowed to converse with him for only 3 hours. The request was granted. Hermes (Mercury) led Protesilaus back to the upper world; and when Protesilaus died a second time, Laodamia died with him" (Smith, 233).

Laodamia was written in 1814, the year in which *The Excursion* was published, and the poem was published the next year. The poem is generally included in the group of poems commonly known as 'Poems of the Imagination.'

LAODAMIA

"With sacrifice before the rising morn
Vows have I made by fruitless hope inspired;
And from the infernal Gods, 'mid shades forlorn
Of night, my slaughtered Lord have I required:
Celestial pity I again implore;—
Restore him to my sight—great Jove, restore!"

So speaking, and by fervent love endowed
With faith, the Suppliant heavenward lifts her hands;
While, like the sun emerging from a cloud,
Her countenance brightens—and her eye expands;
Her bosom heaves and spreads, her stature grows;
And she expects the issue in repose.

O terror! What hath she perceived?—O joy!
What doth she look on? —whom doth she behold?
Her hero slain upon the beach of Troy?
His vital presence? His corporeal mould?
It is—if sense deceive her not—'tis He!
And a God leads him, winged Mercury!

Mild Hermes spake—and touched her with his wand
That calms all fear; "Such grace hath crowned thy prayer,
Laodamia! That at Jove's command
Thy Husband walks the paths of upper air:
He comes to tarry with thee three hours' space;
Accept the gift, behold him face to face!'"

Forth sprang the impassioned Queen her Lord to clasp;
Again that consummation she essayed;
But unsubstantial Form eludes her grasp
As often as that eager grasp was made.
The Phantom parts—but parts to re-unite,
And re-assume his place before her sight.

"Protesilaus, lo! thy guide is gone!
Confirm, I pray, the vision with thy voice:
This is our palace,—yonder is thy throne;
Speak, and the floor thou tread'st on will rejoice.
Not to appal me have the gods bestowed
This precious boon; and blest a sad abode."

"Great Jove, Laodamia! doth not leave
His gifts imperfect:—Spectre though I be,
I am not sent to scare thee or deceive;
But in reward of thy fidelity.
And something also did my worth obtain;
For fearless virtue bringeth boundless gain.

"Thou knowest, the Delphic oracle foretold
That the first Greek who touched the Trojan strand
Should die; but me the threat could not withhold:
A generous cause a victim did demand;
And forth I leapt upon the sandy plain;
A self-devoted chief—by Hector slain."

"Supreme of Heroes—bravest, noblest, best!
Thy matchless courage I bewail no more,
Which then, when tens of thousands were deprest

By doubt, propelled thee to the fatal shore;
Thou found'st—and I forgive thee—here thou art—
A nobler counsellor than my poor heart.

"But thou, though capable of sternest deed,
Wert kind as resolute, and good as brave;
And he, whose power restores thee, hath decreed
Thou shouldst elude the malice of the grave:
Redundant are thy locks, thy lips as fair
As when their breath enriched Thessalian air.

"No Spectre greets me, —no vain Shadow this;
Come, blooming Hero, place thee by my side!
Give, on this well-known couch, one nuptial kiss
To me, this day, a second time thy bride!"
Jove frowned in heaven: the conscious Parcae threw
Upon those roseate lips a Stygian hue.

"This visage tells thee that my doom is past:
Nor should the change be mourned, even if the joys
Of sense were able to return as fast
And surely as they vanish. Earth destroys
Those raptures duly—Erebus disdains:
Calm pleasures there abide—majestic pains.

"Be taught, O faithful Consort, to control
Rebellious passion: for the Gods approve
The depth, and not the tumult, of the soul;
A fervent, not ungovernable, love.
Thy transports moderate; and meekly mourn
When I depart, for brief is my sojourn—"

"Ah wherefore?—Did not Hercules by force
Wrest from the guardian Monster of the tomb
Alcestis, a reanimated corpse,
Given back to dwell on earth in vernal bloom?
Medea's spells dispersed the weight of years,
And Aeson stood a youth 'mid youthful peers.

"The Gods to us are merciful—and they
Yet further may relent: for mightier far
Than strength of nerve and sinew, or the sway
Of magic potent over sun and star,
Is love, though oft to agony distrest,
And though his favourite seat be feeble woman's breast.

"But if thou goest, I follow—" "Peace!" he said,—
She looked upon him and was calmed and cheered;
The ghastly colour from his lips had fled;
In his deportment, shape, and mien, appeared
Elysian beauty, melancholy grace,
Brought from a pensive though a happy place.

He spake of love, such love as Spirits feel
In worlds whose course is equable and pure;
No fears to beat away—no strife to heal—
The past unsighed for, and the future sure;
Spake of heroic arts in graver mood
Revived, with finer harmony pursued;

Of all that is most beauteous—imaged there
In happier beauty; more pellucid streams,
An ampler ether, a diviner air,
And fields invested with purpureal gleams;
Climes which the sun, who sheds the brighest day
Earth knows, is all unworthy to survey.

Yet there the Soul shall enter which hath earned
That privilege by virtue. —"Ill," said he,
"The end of man's existence I discerned,
Who from ignoble games and revelry
Could draw, when we had parted, vain delight,
While tears were thy best pastime, day and night;

"And while my youthful peers before my eyes
(Each hero following his peculiar bent)
Prepared themselves for glorious enterprise
By martial sports, —or, seated in the tent,
Chieftains and kings in council were detained;
What time the fleet at Aulis lay enchained.

"The wished-for wind was given: —I then revolved
The oracle, upon the silent sea;
And, if no worthier led the way, resolved
That, of a thousand vessels, mine should be
The foremost prow in pressing to the strand,—
Mine the first blood that tinged the Trojan sand.

"Yet bitter, oft-times bitter, was the pang
When of thy loss I thought, beloved Wife!
On thee too fondly did my memory hang,

And on the joys we shared in mortal life,—
The paths which we had trod—these fountains, flowers;
My new-planned cities, and unfinished towers.

"But should suspense permit the Foe to cry,
'Behold they tremble! —haughty their array,
Yet of their number no one dares to die?
In soul I swept the indignity away:
Old frailties then recurred: —but lofty thought,
In act embodied, my deliverance wrought.

"And Thou, though strong in love, art all too weak
In reason, in self-government too slow;
I counsel thee by fortitude to seek
Our blest re-union in the shades below.
The invisible world with thee hath sympathised;
Be thy affections raised and solemnised.

"Learn, by a mortal yearning, to ascend—.
Seeking a higher object. Love was given,
Encouraged, sanctioned, chiefly for that end;
For this the passion to excess was driven—
That self might be annulled: her bondage prove
The fetters of a dream opposed to love." —

Aloud she shrieked! for Hermes reappears!
Round the dear Shade she would have clung—'tis vain:
The hours are past—too brief had they been years;
And him no mortal effort can detain:
Swift, toward the realms that know not earthly day,
He through the portal takes his silent way,
And on the palace-floor a lifeless corpse She lay.

Thus, all in vain exhorted and reproved,
She perished; and, as for a wilful crime,
By the just Gods whom no weak pity moved,
Was doomed to wear out her appointed time,
Apart from happy Ghosts, that gather flowers
Of blissful quiet 'mid unfading bowers.

—Yet tears to human suffering are due;
And mortal hopes defeated and o'erthrown
Are mourned by man, and not by man alone,
As fondly he believes. —Upon the side
Of Hellespont (such faith was entertained)

A knot of spiry trees for ages grew
From out the tomb of him for whom she died;
And ever, when such stature they had gained
That Ilium's walls were subject to their view,
The trees' tall summits withered at the sight;
A constant interchange of growth and blight!

Laodamia's husband Protesilaus died in Troy, and so her hope of being blessed with nuptial happiness was defeated, proved vain ('fruitless hope'). But she was not depressed thereby; on the contrary, she felt the urge to meet her husband the more ('inspired'). To day, before the sun rose up in the east ('before the rising morn'), she made sacrifices to the gods, and prayed to them ('Vows have I made'), and told them that she wanted ('required') her slaughtered husband Protesilaus retrieved (for three hours, so that she could talk with him in his incarnation) from amongst the other ghosts or spirits or apparitions ('shades') of the wretched or forsaken ('forlorn') in the dark ('night') lower region or world. She was now once again reverentially urging upon the gods to show pity for her ('Celestial pity again I implore'). She was praying to great Jove to bring him back ('Restore') to her view. Praying thus ('speaking'), with warm ('fervent') love for her husband and with faith in the god, she lifted her hands toward heaven. Then the sun came out from behind a cloud, and brightened her face ('countenance'), and she wondered, with expanded eyes and jactitation of heart, though remaining still or at ease ('repose'), at the possibility of her prayer being granted, or of the possibility of her wish being born ('issue') or being materialised ('expects the issue in repose').

Soon and suddenly she saw that her husband Protesilaus, who was 'slain upon the beach of Troy,' appeared (in the upper air or vacancy overhead) in all flesh and spirit ('vital presence' and 'corporeal mould'). At the sight of the presence of her husband (incarnation), Laodamia was both afraid ('terror') and overjoyed. She saw her husband, but, at first, could not believe her sense of sight ('if sense deceive her not'), but then she wonderfully took the incarnated ghost or apparition of her husband to be really her husband (''tis He'), and she saw the winged god Mercury to have led her husband there.

Hermes, the herald of Greek gods and patron of herdsmen, arts and eloquence, who is mild by nature, with his wand touched Laodamia, who had been perturbed by her fear (at the appearance of her husband), and her fear went away, and she was thus calmed. Hermes told her that all her prayers were granted (by Jove) with grace, and that her husband had come there in the upper region of the sky, alive ('walk') to converse with her, for three hours. So saying, Hermes requested Laodamia to accept the gift or boon from Jove to her (the boon of talking with her husband), and to see her husband 'face to face.' And Laodamia, the 'impassioned Queen,' on seeing her husband, tried ('essayed') with all alacrity ('sprang') to hug the body of her husband, once again, as she did, to materialise, or to fulfil or complete, their nuptial relation ('consummation'), when Protesilaus was alive on this earth. But though Laodamia tried several times to grasp or clutch the body of her husband, she failed in her effort ('elude'), because his body had only a form or contour and no matter or mass ('unsubstantial'). And as she tried to grasp the insubstantial body of her husband Protesilaus, his body once broke into insubstantial ('Phantom') parts, but immediately afterwards the parts or fragments were reunited, so that the form or contour of the insubstantial or phantom body of Protesilaus once again became ('re-assumed') a whole body. And in this way Laodamia strived to grasp his body over and over again, and the body broke into fragments, and then the fragments were reunited over and over again, in her sight or view: "The Phantom parts—but parts to re-unite,/ And re-assume his place before her sight."

Then, addressing Protesilaus, Laodamia told him that his guide, Mercury, had left that place, and so urged upon him to confirm that he was really Protesilaus, and not a fancy or image ('vision') of himself, by speaking to her ("Confirm, I pray, the vision with thy voice"). She further told him that only they two were in the palace (of Protesilaus), and there stood his throne. She also told him that if he did speak to her, even the floor (of the palace), on which he was walking, would be gladdened, and that the god allowed ('bestowed') her this precious privilege ('boon') of accosting him not to frighten or non-plus ('appal') her, but the god (Jove) blessed the mournful palace ('sad abode') (to arrange for a real conversation between them),

Protesilaus told her that Jove did not present her with an imperfect gift (*i.e.*, Jove did not send him to her in his shape of a ghost, having no flesh and blood, but sent him incarnated) because though he was but a ghost ('Spectre'), he was not sent to frighten or deceive her, but he was sent to her as a desert or reward of her faith in Jove ('fidelity'). And also because, in addition to her faith in Jove, he (Protesilaus) had shown, in his earlier life, undaunted courage ('fearless virtue') in landing on the soil of Troy, against the prohibitory oracle that whosoever of Greece would put his feet first on the coast of Troy would be killed. And this undaunted courage of his was also rewarded when he was sent to her (incarnation) by Jove, because such acts of undaunted courage bring immense reward ('boundless gain'): "And something also did my worth obtain;/ For fearless virtue bringeth boundless gain." Protesilaus reminded ('knowest') Laodamia about the prophecy ('oracle') of Apollo at Delphi that the first Greek, who would touch the margin or coast ('strand') of the sea of Troy, would not be able to stave off, or escape, the universal ('general') doom or damnation ('curse') that he would be decapitated, killed ('victim'). And no sooner had Protesilaus came by this oracle than he immediately ('forth') landed on the sandy shore ('sandy plain') of Troy, as he was a self-willed or autocephalic ('self-devoted') chieftain, and was slain by Hector.

Laodamia then addressed Protesilaus as 'Supreme of Heros—bravest, noblest, best,' and told him that she was mourning not because his former 'matchless courage' was now not with him—the 'matchless courage' that propelled him towards the calamitous shore of Troy ('fatal shore'). She forgave him of his losing that 'matchless courage' just because she had then got him back ('Thou found'st'), and because she had found in him a 'nobler counsellor' to herself, who was a better counsellor than her own 'poor heart.' Laodamia told him that he had been 'capable of sternest deed,' and yet he was kind, resolute, good and brave. She also told him that Jove ('he'), who rehabilitated him (Protesilaus) in his incarnated mode, willed ('decreed') that he (Protesilaus) should not be subjected to, or suffer, the oppressions or pains or humiliations ('malice') in his grave ('should elude the malice of the grave'). Laodamia further told him that she now needed not his (beautiful) locks of hair (for feeling attracted or drawn to him), because his lips were still as attractive ('fair') as they had been when he went to Thessaly where the women of that country were drawn to, or the country of Thessaly itself was attracted by, those bright and sweet ('enriched') lips of his. Laodamia lastly told Protesilaus that he was no ghost or shade that greeted herself; and then addressing him as a 'blooming Hero' she invited him to sit by herself. And then (presumably, Protesilaus responded to her request and sat by Laodamia) requested him to kiss her; and then prayed to him to sit on the 'well-known couch' ('well-known'), because it was on this couch that the royal pair used to lie upon), and then requested him to kiss her for the second time, deeming herself his bride ('nuptial kiss'). At this request of Laodamia, Jove became angry ('frown') in heaven, and then Parcae, the guardian god of mortality, distempered, or marginalised, the red colour ('roseate') of the lips of Protesilaus with paleness, or grey colour, or the colour of hell ('Stygian hue'), because Parcae then became aware ('conscious') of the fact that Protesilaus was in fact dead. Parcae (Roman) (plural), who were called Moerae in Greece, "were for Homer the individual and inseparable destiny which followed every mortal being.... They were three in number, daughters of Night, and they were called: Clotho, Lachesis and Atropos. Clotho, the spinner, personified the thread of life. Lachesis was chance, the element of luck that a man had the right to expect. Atropos was inescapable fate [death]" (Hamlyn, 163).

However, on the request of Laodamia of kissing her, Protesilaus told her that his changed appearance ('visage')—changed by Parcae—insinuated that doom was decreed by Jove upon him (to return to his earlier state, *i.e.*, to once again become a spectre or ghost). But he asked her not to mourn for the change of his earlier (incarnated) state, and for the fact that the joys or pleasures of their sense organs were certainly gone before long ("even if the joys/ Of sense were able to return as fast/ And surely as they vanish"). Protesilaus told her that the earth justly ('duly') destroys the extreme pleasures ("raptures') of the senses, and the dark or gloomy Hades or hell or the lower world—the dwelling place of the dead—justly holds in contempt ('disdain') the pleasures of the senses. He, however, assured Laoamia that there were non-sensual and non-exciting ('Calm') pleasures which were, though fraught with 'pains,' majestic. And so he, addressing her as his 'faithful Consort,' asked her to control her sensual passion, because, said he, though the gods commended ('approve') man's deeper sensual pleasures ('depth'), they did not commend the tumultuous or irrational pleasures either of the senses or of the soul. The gods certainly approved deep ('fervent') love, but not the love that could not be reined in ('ungovernable'). Protesilaus asked her to want or desire from him ('transport'), anything else moderate ('Thy transport moderate'). He also asked her to mourn moderately ('meekly') when he would go back to the lower world, or vanish from her, because he had been allowed to converse with her only for a short while.

Protesilaus explained to her the reason of his going back to the lower world. He raised the question: why was he going back ('Ah wherefore?')? And he answered thus. He said that Hercules (the only mortal god) forcefully plucked or pulled his dead body or corpse ('corse') from Alcestis, the monster-guardian of graves ('tomb'), reanimated it, and brought him back to earth. He raised the question: why ('wherefore') did Hercules do so? And he answered that Hercules did this certainly not to enable him to enjoy the beauty of the floreated spring time ('vernal bloom'). He told her that only enchanters or enchantresses used their art or craft for producing sensuality, as Medea (an enchantress) reduced the old age ('dispersed the weight of years') of king Aeson and made him young among his youthful comrades (for sensual enjoyments of the king). Medea was an "Enchantress, daughter of Aeetes, king of Colchis; niece of Circe; she fell in love of Jason when he and the Argonauts came to Colchis in quest of the Golden Fleece.... Today Medea is most often associated with vengefulness, jealousy and sorcery" (Lass, 143-44). Protesilaus said that the gods were merciful to human beings, and that they could be more merciful, or could become more soft, than they are ('relent'). He said that love was far mightier than physical strength ('strength of nerve and sinew'), or than the magical or unbelievable potentiality or strength, or than the strength or power that was induced by magic, over the sun and the stars ('the sway/ Of magic potent over sun and star'), though oftentimes women may suffer the agony ('distress') (due to love), and though the love that is there in woman's breast—the favourite seat of love—be little or weak ('feeble').

Saying thus far, Protesilaus was about to go away, when Laodamia cried out, and told him that if he went away, she would follow him. Protesilaus asked her not to be hasty, and not to be anxious to go with him, but to keep her aplomb ('Peace!'). Laodamia looked at him, and became calm and cheerful. Now the disgustingly ('ghostly') pale and hellish ('Stygian') colour of his lips went away; and his shape or form, facial appearance ('mien') and demeanour ('deportment') changed completely, so that now he became a heavenly ('Elysian': Elysium was the abode of the blessed dead) beauty where there was melancholic grace, or grace tinged with a little melancholy to enhance that grace,—the melancholic grace that was brought from a thought-provoking and happy place. Protesilaus then talked of love—the sort of love that spirits or angels felt in the purer region where there was no discrepancy ('equable'); and where no one was scared by ('to beat away') fear; and where there was no wrangle ('strife') to mollify ('heal'); and, lastly, where nobody had to sigh or mourn for his past, and everybody was certain of his future (gains). Besides, somewhat digressingly, Protesilaus talked of the great or 'heroic' arts (such as epics) which recalled ('Revived') past heroic deeds, and which were composed in a meditative ('graver') mood and were wrought ('pursued') in finer melody ('harmony'). He told Laodamia that in those works ('heroic acts') are reflected ('imaged') more beautifully ('In happier beauty') the most beautiful things, such as very crystalline ('pellucid') rivulets ('streams'), very pure or spacious regions of ether ('ample ether'), very heavenly air, and fields invested with purple brilliance ('purpureal gleams'). There were also reflected, in those great or heroic works (such as epics), very beautiful climates or environments that even the sun, that sends ('sheds') days to the earth, was unworthy of being able to view or see ('survey').

However, Protesilaus told Laodamia that the virtuous soul could certainly ('shall') acquire the right to enter into such climates or environments: "Yet there the Soul shall enter which hath earned/ That privilege by virtue." He said that he would enter into such regions ('I'll'), because he had seen ('discerned') the end of man's life, *i.e.*, because he had understood that life ends in death. He said that he would be able to enter such regions because, before ('when') he parted with herself (Laodamia) at the time of his death, he could withdraw ('draw') himself from the lowly or sensuous affairs and consequent pleasures thereof ('ignoble games and revelry') (with her), and also from the meaningless ('vain') delights of the world. He said that when he had been parting with these ignoble things of the world, she (Laodamia) had been so incessantly shedding tears for him that it seemed that doing so was her 'best pastime.'

Protesilaus then narrated to her the exploits undertaken by him while he had been living on earth. He said that when ('What time') their fleet of ships remained anchored ('enchained') at Aulis, he saw ('before my eyes') that his youthful friends ('peers'), each of whom was a hero, were pursuing their individual branch of martial profession (or exercising their arts) ('bent'), and thus making themselves competent ('Prepared themselves') for the glorious battle against the Trojans ('enterprise'), by engaging themselves in martial exercises ('sports'); or saw the friends, who were 'Chieftains,' sitting in 'the tent' along with kings, for a long time ('detained'), devising military stratagems ('council'). Protesilaus then wished that favourable winds blew over the seas, and actually such a wind came ('The wished-for wind was given'). He said that there was the oracle that whosoever would first land on the coast of Troy would be killed. But he (Protesilaus) defied ('revolved') that oracle, and set sail over the noiseless or unturbulent ('silent') sea, towards the strand or landing place or coast of Troy. He resolved that, or he had the firm belief that, if there was no man worthier than himself ('if no worthier'), then of all the one thousand ships ('vessels'), that set sail for the strand of Troy, his ship would ply before all the rest ('foremost prow in pressing to the strand'), and that he would first incarnadine or redden the sand along the Trojan coast with his blood ("Wine the first blood that tinged the Trojan sand").

Then, addressing Laodamia as his 'beloved Wife,' Protesilaus told her that, in spite of all that (his gallantry in sacrificing himself on the Trojan coast), he frequently felt bitter pangs in his heart whenever he thought that he lost the company of his wife after his death (being killed on the Trojan coast by Hector) by getting separated from her. Protesilaus bore with him (even after his death, and while he was existing in the lower world) the memory of his wife, and the joy that they shared, when he was alive. He also bore the memory of the paths on which they both walked, and the memory of the fountains and the flowers that were there by the side of those paths. He further remembered the cities and the towers which he newly planned but could not finish (due to his untimely death) in his life-time. He also remembered that when he, along with his troops, approached the Trojan strand, the enemies held themselves in suspense, after seeing his (Protesilaus') troops, and then cried out in indignation: "Look, the Grecian soldiers ('they') tremble in fear though they all ('their array') are furious ('haughty'), and no one of all of them is courageous enough to land on the shore of Troy and die!" At first Protesilaus brushed off his enraged hatred ('swept the indignity away') for the Trojans, because he felt his weaknesses ('frailties') of, or because he was afraid of, dying. But afterwards the courageous thought ('lofty thought') of becoming a hero by dying on the enemy country came to him, and he materialised that thought by acting (fighting) in accordance with that thought, and thus made ('wrought') the deliverance of his soul from his body ('my deliverance wrought').

Protesilaus then told Laodamia that though she was 'strong in love,' she was very weak in her rationality, and that she was 'too slow' in controlling her own passion of love ('in self-government too slow'). He advised her to have fortitude, and seek their reunion (reunion of Protesilaus and Laodamia, after the latter's death) in the lower world ('in the shades below') which was invisible, and which was sympathetic to her. Therefore, Protesilaus wished her love purified or spiritualised ("Be thy affections raised and solemnised"). He advised her to learn to rise above the worldly or fleshy passions ('ascend'), and to strive for higher or spiritual love ('higher object') by yearning or craving for that as a mortal being. He told her that love was given to mankind, and love was "Encouraged, sanctioned' (by heaven) 'chiefly for that end.' Human beings were given the passion of love, in excess, so that they might spiritualise their passion of love ('For this'), and so that their selves, or rather the narrowness of their selves might be obliterated ('annulled'). But if the passion of love was circumscribed or polluted by physical desires, the soul would be in bondage (of the lowly things, so that the soul would not be able to enjoy the heavenly bliss) ('her bondage'), and then the soul would be bound ('fetters') only by illusive or seeming love ('dream') which was contrary to real or spiritual or heavenly love.

At this moment, Hermes once again appeared there, understandably to take Protesilaus back to the lower world, and, seeing Hermes, Laodamia cried aloud in agony ('for Hermes reappears!'). Laodamia strove to cling to the ghost or the phantom or the dead body ('Shade') of Protesilaus, but in vain, because the appointed three hours, allowed for the couple, were over. Here the poet says that instead of being only three hours, if the time allowed to the couple had been several hours, even then that long space of time would seem to them very inadequate ('too brief). He, however, says that no worldly striving ('mortal effort') was able to detain Protesilaus (from going back to the lower world) any more, and that Protesilaus then silently but swiftly went through the gateway ('portal') towards the lower world ("realms') where the sun did not shine ('know not earthly day'). The poet further says that after Protesilaus departed from the place, Laodamia ('She'), like a corpse ('corse'), lay on 'the palace floor.' Protesilaus' exhorting and reproving of Laodamia proved fruitless, because she the sooner succumbed to death ('perished'). The just gods ('Gods'), who are not moved by unjust ('weak') pity or persuasion, declared ('doomed') that Laodamia must wearily spend the rest of her life ('appointed time'), in isolation from the happy ghost of Protesilaus, which, like such other ghosts, had been enjoying the 'blissful quiet' ("gather flowers/ of blissful quiet") of the lower world, remaining among ("mid') the perennially green bowers.

The poet, lastly, says that, contrary to ('Yet') the truth of Protesilaus' wise counsel, tears roll down from human eyes when human beings suffer, or when their worldly ('mortal') hopes are frustrated ('defeated') or rejected ('o'erthrown'), and that it is not only human beings that so shed tears, as human beings wistfully believe ('As fondly he believes') (but also non-human beings, or other beings, so shed tears). The poet says that in ancient Greece ('Hellespont'), it was believed that ('such faith was entertained') a knot of high-rise ('spiry') trees used to grow, for a long time or for a certain period of time, on the grave of Protesilaus, for whom Laodamia died ('out of the tomb of him for whom she died'). When the trees grew to a certain height ('such stature they had gained') from where those trees could see the walls of Troy ('Illium'), the higher parts of those trees withered or got seared when those trees actually saw the walls of Troy ('at the sight'); but, afterwards, those trees again began to grow to that same height. Here the poet philosophically wonders at the perpetual ('constant') alternations ('interchange') of the growth of those trees to that particular height and the succeeding searing ('blight') of their upper parts.

Laodamia is a fine classical poem. It has got special importance on at least two counts: firstly, in it Wordsworth has referred to maximum number of Greek mythological figures or characters, as in none else of his poems; and secondly, and more importantly, in this poem Wordsworth has rejected his own theory of poetic diction that the language of poetry must be the language of the common man, and that poetry does not require what is generally called 'poetic diction' or elevated diction. *Laodamia* is packed up with Greek mythological characters, place names and notions, such as Jove, Parcae, Erebus, Hercules, Medea, Aeson, Hellespont, 'Trojan sand', 'Elysian beauty' and 'Illium's walls.' Protesilaus and Laodamia are also Greek mythological characters. The myth of the trees that grow to a certain height and then get blighted in their upper parts also belong to Greece. Again, in this poem, Wordsworth, in disregard of his own theory of poetic diction, has used some traditionally accepted 'poetic dictions,' such as 'spake,' 'lo,' 'yonder,' 'thou,' 'blest' and 'deprest.'

In *Laodamia,* Wordsworth has emphasised the belief that the gods certainly favourably respond to human beings' sincere prayers and sacrifices, and fulfil their desires. Laodamia desired to meet her husband's ghost's incarnation (or her husband's dead body in living condition) and so sincerely prayed to the 'infernal Gods,' and made sacrifices to them. She very earnestly prayed to Jove for celestial pity:

> Celestial pity I again implore:—
> Restore him to my sight—great Jove, restore!

And her prayer was granted: she met Protesilaus in flesh and blood. By this Wordsworth means to prove that the heavens are not—at least not always—deaf and blind to human sufferings and desires.

Wordsworth had a sort of nausea for carnality: everything fleshy and sensual was abominable to him. He believed that everything was essentially spiritual, and wanted to see this spirituality revealed in everything: in every object of nature and in all human beings, and also in the relationships among human beings. We know that Wordsworth, throughout the rest of his life, suffered from the pangs of his own conscience, due to his impetuous carnal relationship with Anette Vallon, since the occurrence of that relationship. The spiritual bent of his mind could not accommodate even the idea of carnality even in wedlock. Wordsworth's morality, like that of his poetic mentor Milton, was absolutely pure and far from all shades of carnality. This is quite evident in *Laodamia.* After Jove granted her prayer of meeting with her dead husband in his living condition and Protesilaus accordingly appeared before her, Laodamia, out of her sheer carnal desire, requested her husband to kiss her: "Give, on this well-known couch, one nuptial kiss/ To me." And immediately Jove became angry, and Parcae drew off the blood from the roseate lips of her husband: "Jove frawned in heaven: the conscious Parcae threw/ Upon those roseate lips a Stygian hue." Parcae are conscious, *i.e.* conscious about the breach of the spiritual nature of nuptial relationship in the act of kissing carnally. The poem *Laodamia,* therefore, presents Wordsworth's concept of morality, though partially.

Wordsworth of course approves of love, but then, as told earlier, his love is spiritual in nature (like his love of Dorothy). But, according to Wordsworth, love may be as deep as possible, but in no case should it be uncontrollable or wild. This is evident in Protesilaus' persuasion of Laodamia not to be violent in her love for him:

> the Gods approve
> The depth, and not the tumult, of the soul;
> A fervent, not ungovernable, love.

Wordsworth pleads that, though initially nuptial love may have a tinge of carnality, for unavoidable reasons, with passage of time, that modicum of carnality should also be avoided, and thus the nuptial love should be elevated to the plane of spirituality. It was for this reason that Protesilaus advises Laodamia thus:

Learn, by a mortal yearning, to ascend—
Seeking a higher object.

Love was given to human beings, says Wordsworth, to help them transcend the narrow sphere of their self-love. Protesilaus told Laodamia that love was given to man, and that in excess, so that man might transcend his self-love. In love we forget ourselves, in favour of our beloved objects, and thus transcend our love of our own selves. When we shall be able to love others, forgetting ourselves, our love will be spiritualised. This was the objective of God in investing us with the passion of love, in excess. On the other hand, if we love only ourselves, we will be but thralls of our own self-love—self-love that is illusory: "her bondage prove/ The fetters of a dream opposed to love."

In *Laodamia*, Wordsworth does not only forbid excesses of love, self-love, and carnality, but also advocates forbearance, control or measure, and capability of undergoing sufferance. In short, he pleads for stoicism in all aspects of human life. Geoffrey Durrant writes: "In 'Laodamia' (1814), Wordsworth expresses with classical elegance and firmness a Stoic view of human passion. Here Virgil seems to speak again in English verse:

—Yet tears to human suffering are due;
And mortal hopes defeated and o'erthrown
Are mourned by man, and not by man alone,
As fondly he believes."

(Durrant, 13)

In *Laodamia*, Wordsworth has amply demonstrated his power of imagination, particularly where, in the poem, he describes the beauty of the lower region—the dwelling place of the spirits or souls of the good or ideal human beings. The souls of the bad ones go to Hades, but those of the good ones go to the lower region or world. Wordsworth, in this poem, very beautifully describes the lush environment of the lower world:

Of all that is most beauteous—imaged there
In happier beauty; more pellucid streams,
And ampler ether, diviner air,
And fields invested with purpureal gleams;

Climes which the sun, who sheds the brightest day
Earth knows, is all unworthy to survey.

In *Laodamia*, Wordsworth has very skilfully utilised the myth, prevalent in Greece ('Hellespont'), that certain 'spiry trees' grow there, on the grave of Protesilaus, to a certain height from which those trees can view 'Illium's walls,' and then those trees begin to wither away from the top, and then once again they begin to grow to that particular height, and this process continues *ad infinitum*. The poet construes this mythical phenomenon as a symbol of the 'constant interchange of growth and blight' of the phenomena of the creation. This 'constant interchange of growth and blight'—of the interchange of hope and despair, we may say—is also a property of life, according to Wordsworthian philosophy. The poem also presents an instance of the medieval knightly chivalry, in the character of Protesilaus:

'Supreme of Heroes—bravest, noblest, best!
Thy matchless courage I bewail no more,
Which then, when tens of thousands were deprest
By doubt, propelled thee to the fatal shore;....

Lastly, the poem bears an effective undertone of pathos, when the poet sympathises with the pitiful state of Laodamia:

—Yet tears to human suffering are due;
And mortal hopes defeated and o'erthrown
Are mourned by man,....

The pathetic lot of Laodamia is also the lot of all of us, and this suggestion of the poem arouses tragic pity and fear in us, and so the poem may be taken to be a graphic delineation of the universal pathos of human life.

PART 3

3

The Five 'Lucy' Poems of Wordsworth

There are, in all, five so-called Lucy poems: *She dwelt among the untrodden ways, Strange fits of passion have I known, Three years she grew in sun and shower, A slumber did my spirit seal,* and *I travelled among unknown me.* The first four were composed in 1799, when William and Dorothy Wordsworth were at Goslar in Germany, and the fifth was composed in 1801, when they were in England. *Lucy Gray* (or *Solitude*), which was also composed in 1799, at Goslar in Germany, is not a 'Lucy' poem. The Lucy poems are 'so apparently simple,' but 'are Wordsworth's most enigmatic statements.' In the autumn of 1798, Wordsworth and Dorothy, along with Coleridge, went to Germany—Coleridge to have a first-hand knowledge of German idealist philosophy, and Wordsworth and Dorothy to refresh their knowledge of German. Soon, there in Germany, Coleridge went to the University of Gottingen, while Wordsworth and Dorothy hired winter quarters "in the remote little town of Goslar." Wordsworth wrote the first four (stated above) Lucy poems while living in this winter quarters. He also began *The Prelude* while in this quarters. Those four Lucy poems first appeared (were first published) in the 1800 edition (second edition) of *Lyrical Ballads*, and all the five Lucy poems first appeared in the third edition of *Lyrical Ballads.*

All the Lucy poems do not belong to the same category, regarding their tenor or general run of purpose. *Strange fits of passion have I known,* for instance, belongs to the poems 'founded on the Affections,' while *Three years she grew in sun and shower* is a poem of the imagination. Nevertheless, says F.W. Bateson, there is a connecting thread running through the first four of them: "One thing of the Goslar poems have in common is that they are almost all connected, directly or indirectly with Wordsworth's Childhood or boyhood" (Bateson, 150). The group of five Lucy poems are written centering on the imaginary girl Lucy, like Wordsworth's three 'Mathew poems' are written in gratitude to William Taylor, the headmaster of Hawkshead school where he studied, who died when Wordsworth was a schoolboy.

The winter of 1798-99 was 'the coldest of the century,' and yet Molly Lefebure writes, "Wordsworth's mind was opened at Goslar; there returned the glimmering lake; the smooth green turf where the woodcocks ran; the little boat tied to the willow tree. Out of the mists came the girl with the pitcher on her head, not, as yet, to take her place in *The Prelude,* but to inspire verses written in commemoration and celebration of a child of Nature the Lucy poems and Ruth" (Lefebure, 276). However, there is a common problem among all the Lucy poems: who was Lucy? Geoffrey Durrant answers the question thus: "Who was Lucy? There is no answer to this question except to say that it is irrelevant. Lucy may or may not have been inspired by Dorothy Wordsworth, by Annette Vallon, or by another young woman. There is no reason to suppose that Wordsworth had any particular person in mind; and whatever the nature of the personal experience behind them, these [the Lucy poems] are not personal confessions. They are 'lyrical ballads', each of which tells a verse story and presents it dramatically" (Durrant, 60-61). Coleridge thought that the Lucy poems were at least inspired by Dorothy, but Alan Gardiner does not agree with Coleridge, and says that the image of Lucy may be a composite image. Gardiner writes: "There has been much speculation over the girl's (Lucy's) identity. There is no evidence that at the time of writing the poems Wordsworth had loved a girl who died, and many commentators have been guided by Coleridge's interpretation of 'A slumber did my spirit seal' and have concluded that they (the Lucy poems) were inspired by his love of Dorothy (Coleridge said of the poem, 'Most probably, in some gloomier moment he (Wordsworth) had fancied the moment in which his sister might die.') A difficulty here is that the Lucy of 'Three years she grew in sun and shower' is of 'stately height,' which does not correspond to descriptions and portraits of Dorothy. Lucy may therefore have been a composite figure made up from several girls Wordsworth knew" (Gardiner, 41). Molly Lefebure, on the other hand, says that Lucy was a common name of a lovely girl to the Romantic poets, and that Wordsworth perhaps chose this common name for his ideal beloved imaginary girl: "This was a name much favoured by English Romantic poets for their rustic heroines. Wordsworth, on occasion, referred to Dorothy as 'Lucy'; this was when he wished to present her in the guise of natural simplicity. Emma (another Romantic name) was also his sobriquet for Dorothy" (Lefebure, 277). Lefebure presumes that Lucy represents or symbolises Wordsworth's notion of the spirit in nature: "The girl haunting the poet in the Lucy poems is a spirit of wild places and dream-love, a vagrant wraith of Romantic imagination. What little tangibility she possesses seems to stem from that first love whom Wordsworth discovered in the fell-country landscape of

> ...bare common
> A maked naked pool that lay beneath the hills,
> The beacon on the summit."
>
> (Lefebure, 276)

Nevertheless Molly Lefebure says that "Although Dorothy herself was not the actual Lucy of these poems [the Lucy poems], she was in some measure the inspiration behind them, for it was surely her intimate presence which inspired Wordsworth in Goslar" (Lefebure, 277).

(I) Strange Fits of Passion Have I Known

This is the first of the five Lucy poems. It is a 'lyrical bailad,' 'a story in verse and in dramatic form.' It is included in the collection of poems that Wordsworth called 'Poems Founded on the Affections,' which collection consists of 38 poems in all. The theme of the poem is mutability of nature, though, on the surface of the poem, it appears that it is a poem about the love of a lover for his beloved. As told earlier, the poem was composed at Goslar in Germany, in 1799, and was first published in the 1800 edition (2nd edition) of *Lyrical Ballads*. In the poem, the poet has fallen in love of one lovely girl, Lucy. Some commentators have identified Lucy with Dorothy Wordsworth, as we have said earlier, but such a conjecture seems to be very wide. The poem was not given any title by Wordsworth, and is known by its beginning line, like many other poems included in the collection *Poems Founded on the Affections.*

Strange Fits of Passion Have I known

Strange Fits of Passion Have I known:
And I will dare to tell,
But in the Lover's car alone,
What once to me befell.

When she I loved looked every day
Fresh as a rose in June,
I to her cottage bent my way,
Beneath an evening-moon.

Upon the moon I fixed my eye,
All over the wide lea;
With quickening pace my horse drew nigh
Those paths so dear to me.

And now we reached the orchard-plot;
And, as we climbed the hill,
The sinking moon to Lucy's cot
Came near, and nearer still.

In one of those sweet dreams I slept,
Kind Nature's gentlest boon!
And all the while my eyes I kept
On the descending moon.

My horse moved on; hoof after hoof
He raised, and never stopped:
When down behind the cottage roof,
At once, the bright moon dropped.

What fond and wayward thoughts will slide
Into a Lover's head!
"O mercy!" to myself I cried,
"If Lucy should be dead!"

The poet felt ('known') exceedingly great ('Strange') bouts of the passion of love. He was bold enough to confess of course only to lovers ('Lover's ear') what once in the past happened in his life ('befell'). When his beloved Lucy seemed to be growing in freshness day after day, as a rose does seem in the month of June, he rode post-haste ('bent my way') towards her cottage, in the evening, when the moon shone in the sky ('Beneath an evening-moon').

While he rode towards her cottage, across the wide and open country or pasture or dale ('lea'), he kept his eyes fixed on the moon, and his horse galloped fast, and almost ('nigh') approached the paths ('drew nigh') (near the cottage of Lucy) which were very dear to him. When he and his horse ('we') reached the orchard ('orchard-plot') and climbed the hill (both near the cottage of Lucy), he saw that the moon, which earlier was high up in the sky, was gradually ('near, and nearer still') declining ('sinking') towards the cottage of Lucy, *i.e.* the moon was gradually setting in the western horizon, behind the cottage of Lucy.

All these whiles, the poet was so much engrossed in the beauty of the moon, and the surround, and in his love of Lucy, that he felt to be dreaming a sweet dream that is the softest or the most sympathetic blessing ('gentlest boon') of the sympathetic nature, to man. And he was enjoying his dream-like ride, keeping his eyes on the 'descending moon': (The poet here means to say that while he was enjoying his riding, he remained quite unconscious about what might have happened in the immediate future in the life of Lucy, *i.e.*, as he was then in a dream-like state, or he was dreaming that life was all full of dreams or of love and happiness, he was absolutely oblivious of the fact that life was all chancy-chancy, and was not full of love and happiness.)

However, the horse of the poet continued to run, raising its two pairs of legs, one pair after another ("hoof after hoof/ He raised"), and the horse never stopped running. While the horse was so running, the poet saw that the bright moon suddenly ('at once') quite set in the western horizon, 'behind the cottage roof', of Lucy. And then the poet wondered that (sometimes) foolish or credulous or loving ('fond') and whimsical or irrational or obstinate ('wayward') thoughts surreptitiously enter ('slide') into the consciousness or mind of a lover, and that (at that moment) such a credulous and foolish and obstinate thought entered into his head. And the thought was this: he thought that (as the moon set in the western horizon, or the moon 'died'), Lucy might have died. And then he cried out (in agony): 'O mercy,' *i.e.*, might God wish to show mercy to Lucy, so that she had not to die.

The poem is, as we have said, in the ballad form, like the other four Lucy poems, but its ballad quality is more poignant and striking than that of the other four Lucy poems. The poem, as presented here, contains 28 lines. But the original manuscript version of it contained the following four additional lines at the end of it:

> I told her this; her laughter light
> Is ringing in my ears:
> And when I think upon that night
> My eyes are dim with tears.

When the poem was first published, in the 1800 edition of *Lyrical Ballads*, the foregoing four lines were dropped, and this has, to an extent, obscured the intended meaning of the poem.

Apparently, the meaning of the poem is quite simple: the poem describes the irrational or illogical and unaccounted for fear of the lover of the death of his beloved Lucy. The lover (the poet) was riding towards Lucy's cottage, perhaps for a dating, keeping his eyes glued to the moon in the western half of the sky. As he neared Lucy's cottage, he suddenly saw that the moon had sunk down beneath the western horizon behind Lucy's cottage, and then his heart began to palpitate in the apprehension that like the sudden disappearance of the moon, it might have occurred that Lucy also disappeared from the earth, *i.e.* Lucy died. In this situation, the fire of the poet's love or passion naturally rose fitfully high. Wordsworth's thought-process here worked on Hartley's psychology of association: the disappearance of the moon, by association, gave rise to the thought of the disappearance or death of Lucy, because somehow the moon was associated with Lucy, in the mind of the poet (may be due to the poet's frequently visiting Lucy's cottage in moonlit nights). But the fear of the death of Lucy is illogical and unfounded, because Lucy cannot normally be associated with the moon, let alone her death or disappearance with the disappearance of the moon.

But the meaning of the poem is not so simple, because under the surface meaning of the poem, there is a deeper meaning. To show the deeper meaning of the poem underlying the surface meaning of it, we cannot do better than quoting at some length from what Geoffrey Durrant has to say about the meaning of the poem. Durrant writes: "On a first reading it seems that this poem is concerned merely to show that lovers have foolish thoughts on very slight provocation. However, Wordsworth originally meant something rather different, for in the manuscript version there is an additional stanza which makes it clear that the lover's fear was later justified:

> I told her this; her laughter light
> Is ringing in my ears:
> And when I think upon that night
> My eyes are dim with tears.

Although this stanza was delected from the final version, we must suppose that Wordsworth's intention was to give some validity to the apparently 'fond and foolish thought' by which the lover fears that Lucy may be dead.

If we now look more carefully at the poem, we shall see that it suggests two different ways of thinking about our lives in time. Usually we think of time as divisible into weeks, days, hours, minutes, and seconds; and we can therefore project into an indefinite future our own lives and the lives of others.

The lover sees Lucy as existing from day to day, and does not normally think that sooner or later she must die:

> When she I loved looked every day
> Fresh as a rose in June,
> I to her cottage bent my way,
> Beneath an evening-moon.

The comparison with the rose, which blossoms in June only to fade soon after, offers an ironic comment on the complacency of the lover's view of Lucy, whom he sees 'every day' blossoming like a rose, but of whom he does not usually allow himself to think that she must sooner or later fade. The hint is made more strongly with the introduction of an 'evening-moon'—in other words a moon that is about to set. When the lover says that 'all the while' he kept his eyes upon the descending moon he is ironically unaware of what he is saying. He sees the moon sinking, but at the same time he thinks of Lucy as a rose that will go on blooming 'every day.'

The lover continues his story, and as he does so he illustrates the way in which we eagerly move forward through clock-time, without realizing that every step forward through time brings us nearer to an end:

Upon the moon I fixed my eye,
All over the wide lea;
With quickening pace my horse drew nigh
Those paths so dear to me.

Here the lover, though watching the moon descending, is not aware that it is doing so. For him time is represented by the 'quickening pace' of his horse towards the object of his desire. In the next stanza the drama is heightened:

And now we reached the orchard-plot;
And, as we climbed the hill,
The sinking moon to Lucy's cot
Came near, and nearer still.

The slow descent of the moon—'near, and nearer still'—towards Lucy's cot suggests the approach of a threat. But still the lover has not consciously learned the lesson that the moon is about to convey to him. The reason for this, as the poet now suggests, is that we find it intolerably painful to think of time as a process by which all living things move through decay to their deaths. We prefer the clock-time with which we are familiar, and which we can imagine as being extended indefinitely into the future:

In one of those sweet dreams I slept,
Kind Nature's gentlest boon!
And all the while my eyes I kept
On the descending moon.

The repetition of the 'evening-moon', the 'sinking moon', and now the 'descending moon', creates an insistent pattern of suggestion which, because of his natural resistance to such awareness, the lover ignores. He continues his journey in unconsciousness of moment that the moon disappears entirely, and thus forces to the lover's mind the consciousness of what has been enacted:

My horse moved on; hoof after hoof
He raised, and never stopped:
When down behind the cottage roof
At once, the bright moon dropped.

With this sudden disappearance of the moon the curve of its motion across the sky—imperceptible until it cuts the horizon and disappears—is dramatically revealed. The speed with which it vanishes is not in itself mysterious; Wordsworth is always careful with such details. The rotation of the earth, causing the moon to set, and the lover's closer approach to the cottage on the hill, which cuts the moon from his view as it sets, account sufficiently for the sudden vanishing. When this happens, the lover suddenly fears that Lucy may be dead, because in a flash of intuition, he realizes that the 'rose in June' is fated to die as surely as the moon is fated to set. We do not think of the moon as it shines in the sky as 'setting' or of a rose in full bloom as 'dying', but if we remember that life is a process, and not the movement of an unchanging object through clock-time, we realize that the moon's setting is implied in its shining, and that death is implied in life. This notion of the curve of life is stated more directly in the 'Mutability' sonnet:

> From low to high doth dissolution climb,
> And sink from high to low, along a scale
> Of awful notes, whose concord shall not fail;
> A musical but melancholy chime.

The lover's fear, although it is not immediately shown to be well founded, is no 'fond and foolish thought', in spite of his desire to believe this. In the original version Wordsworth made this plain in the additional stanza telling us of the lover's 'tears' when he looks back on that night. What the lover experiences is a moment of shocking realization of a truth that can be faced only briefly—that all life, including Lucy's, is a pattern in which growth and decay form a single process, the end of which is certain. Lucy, like the rose and the moon, is, after all, subject to the 'touch of earthly years'" (Durrant, 61-64).

Alan Gardiner agrees with Durrant's interpretation of the poem. Gardinar believes that in all the Lucy poems, there is a closeness between Lucy and nature, such that she herself is reflected in nature, and such that the poet's thought about her is also reflected in nature. In this regard, this poem is not very different from the other four Lucy poems. However, Gardiner writes about this poem (let us again quote at some length):

"Here the comparison with the rose serves (also) to evoke her [Lucy's] beauty, and, more significantly, the inevitability that this beauty will fade. The lover, however, did not think of this possibility; to him Lucy was everlasting and she looked like a rose in June 'every day.' His illusion prevented recognition of what happens to the rose once June is over. The use of the past tense is itself evidence of Lucy's mortality: '*When* she I loved looked every day'—the clear implication is that she looks like this no longer. The 'evening moon' similarly suggests changeability, a significance that is reinforced by the emphasis on its descent. Ironically the poet gazes fixedly at the sinking moon but (until the final stanza) remains ignorant of the transitoriness it symbolizes. As he eagerly approaches his lover's cottage ("With quickening pace my horse drew nigh/ Those paths so near to me") the description of the descending moon begins to carry the suggestion of a threat:

> *The sinking moon to Lucy's cot*
> *Come near, and nearer still.*

As in other Lucy poems, the girl lives surrounded by nature. The poet passes an orchard-plot and then ascends a hill to reach her cottage. As he nears his destination he is in a trance-like state similar to that described in the opening stanza of the final Lucy poem, 'A slumber did my spirit seal':

> *In one of those sweet dreams I slept.*
> *Kind Nature's gentlest boon*!
> *And all the while my eyes I kept*
> *On the descending moon.*
>
> *My horse moved on; hoof after hoof*
> *He raised, and never stopped....*

The repetition of 'hoof after hoof' and the assonance of 'hoof,' 'moved' and 'moon' create a strange, hypnotic effect; Geoffrey Hartman calls it a feeling of 'motion approaching yet never quite attaining its end.' It is as if the lover is blissfully unaware of time and therefore of mortality, even though the sinking moon, on which his eyes continue to be fixed and which ironically helps to induce his reverie, is an insistent reminder of both. Appropriately, it is the sudden disappearance of the moon which breaks the trance and shocks the poet into consciousness of the inescapability of death:

> *'O mercy!' to myself I cried,*
> *'If Lucy should be dead!'*

The poet had watched the moon's descent but had not foreseen that this process must end with the moon dropping out of sight behind the horizon. When it does, its unexpected disappearance impresses upon him the inevitability of change and, by a convincing process of association, reminds him of Lucy's mortality. In the original manuscript version of the poem there is an additional stanza in which the episode becomes a foreshadowing of Lucy's actual death, reinforcing the validity of the poet's fear:

> *I told her this; her laughter light*
> *Is ringing in my ears*
> *And when I think upon that night*
> *My eyes are dim with tears.*

In 'She dwelt among the untrodden ways' reference to Lucy's death becomes explicit" (Gardiner, 42-43).

So we find that Wordsworth has, in this poem, presented us with a deeper experience and truth of life, and in this his endeavour, he has been quite successful. F.R. Leavis writes in this regard: "His [Wordsworth's] success [in *Strange fits of passion have I known*] depends upon his conveying the peculiarly private value, the intensely personal significance, of the concrete incident—of the experience in immediacy. Yet, without resorting to analysis or reflection, he adopts the habitual mode of 'recollection in tranquillity.' Through a medium of glassy serenity we see the emotional episode enacted, the medium, with its suggestion both of quiet intentness and of the contemplation of the placed and familiar, assuring us implicitly of the weighed importance of what is presented" (Leavis, 200-201). Leavis further writes about this poem: "It is a poem such as only Wordsworth could have written, and it belongs peculiarly to its [Romantic] period. It seems to come close to its characteristic faults, but it has his characteristic virtues. It is of the essence to be in a mode remote from any form of 'wit'. It is completely successful, yet we feel that its poise is an extremely delicate, almost a precarious one, and our sense of its success is bound up with its feeling" (Leavis, 202). However, Wordsworth is generally supposed to be lacking in the genuine passion of love, and, consequently, to have written no love-poems, in the true sense of the term, but at least in this poem and in the four other Lucy poems, he has demonstrated that he can, if he wills, create the genuine passion of love and write genuine love poems. A.C. Bradley writes in this regard: "The poems about Lucy are not poems of passion, in the usual sense, but they surely are love-poems" (Bradley, 112).

(II) Three Years She Grew in Sun and Shower (or The Education of Nature)

This poem is one in the bouquet of poems called 'Lucy poems.' The theme of this present 'Lucy poem' is the educative value of nature, as according to Wordsworth, as that of the previous 'Lucy poem' was mutability of life. The present poem consists of 7 stanzas, each stanza consisting of six lines in the rhyme-scheme a a b c c b. This poem is also untitled and is known by the beginning line of it. According to Graham Hough, the poem tells us about the "influence of Nature on the formation of human life" (Hough, 47). The 'purely lyrical strain' of this poem, as that of the other 'Lucy poems,' is unforgetable.

Three Years She Grew in Sun and Shower

Three years she grew in sun and shower,
Then Nature said, "A lovelier flower
On earth was never sown;
This Child I to myself will take;
She shall be mine, and I will make
A Lady of my own.

"Myself will to my darling be
Both law and impulse; and with me
The Girl, in rock and plain,
In earth and heaven, in glade and bower,
Shall feel an overseeing power
To kindle or restrain.

"She shall be sportive as the fawn
That wild with glee across the lawn
Or up the mountain springs;
And hers shall be the breathing balm,
And hers the silence and the calm
Of mute insensate things.

"The floating clouds their state shall lend
To her; for her the willow bend;
Nor shall she fail to see
Even in the motions of the Storm
Grace that shall mould the Maiden's form
By silent sympathy.

"The stars of midnight shall be dear
To her; and she shall lean her ear
In many a secret place
Where rivulets dance their wayward round,
And beauty born of murmuring sound
Shall pass into her face.

"And vital feelings of delight
Shall rear her form to stately height,
Her virgin bosom swell;
Such thoughts to Lucy I will give
While she and I together live
Here in this happy dell."

Thus Nature spake—The work was done—
How soon my Lucy's race was run!
She died, and left to me
This heath, this calm, and quiet scene;
The memory of what has been,
And never more will be.

For three years Lucy ('she') grew up in a natural environment where there were abundant sun shine and rain. Then nature said about Lucy that no girl, more sweet and beautiful than she, was born on earth ("On earth was never sown"). Nature said that she would adopt ('take') this girl Lucy, and that Lucy would be her own child, and also that she (nature) would nurse her (Lucy) to grow up into a lady who would belong to her (nature) (*Stanza* I). Nature said that she would teach Lucy, her 'darling', discipline or order ('law'), and also sensibility ('impulse'). Nature said that Lucy would roam or wander about over the hills and plains, in open spaces in woods ('glade'), and in shady places in gardens, along with herself ('earth'), across the transcendentally beautiful places ('heaven'). After roaming over those different places, she (Lucy) would realise the existence of the superior and controlling ('overseeing') power that generates 'kindle') sensibilities within our hearts as well as control our sensibilities (*Stanza* II).

Nature said that Lucy would be as sportive as a young deer ('fawn') that, with its overmuch or uncontrollable ('wild') mirth, boundingly runs 'across the lawn' or 'up the mountain.' Then Lucy would enliven or quicken the dumb and insensate things by infusing into them her sweet breath ('balm'), and then they would get silence or quietude from her (*Stanza* III). The slow-moving clouds of the sky would teach Lucy how to move blithely or liltingly and elegantly ('state shall lend'), and the (soft) willow would make her pliant and flexible. Lucy would not fail to notice that even in the violent motions of the storm, there is a sort of grace or elegance, and that grace or elegance would unnoticeably ('silent') be sympathetic towards her, and would, therefore, bestow upon her the grace ('form') in violence, *i.e.*, even when Lucy would be in a violent passion, she would remain graceful (*Stanza* IV). Lucy would love the midnight stars, and she would intently listen ('to lean her ear'), keeping herself at many secluded ('secret') places, the sweet murmuring sound of the waters of narrow rivers or streams running uncontrollably ('wayward') its course ('round'), while her face would be glowing in beauty—the beauty that would originate ('born') in the 'murmuring sound' of the streams ("And beauty born of murmuring sound/Shall pass into her face.") (*Stanza* V). The lively or energizing feelings of delight that Lucy would derive from all these things, would uphold her elegant personal beauty, or her beautiful stature ('rear her form to stately height')—her beautiful stature that would be crowned by the swelling of her young breast. Nature said that she would tell Lucy all these things ('Such thoughts') when Lucy and she would be living together in this small valley ('dell') (*Stanza* VI).

The poet says that nature told him all these ('Thus Nature spake'), and that nature actually nurtured and brought up Lucy to be a lady of her choice ('The work was done'). But the poet is remorsefully astonished to see Lucy die very soon ("How soon my Lucy's race was run!") Lucy died leaving behind her, for the poet, this calm and quiet heath, and the memory of herself and her activities ("The memory of what has been") that will never come back to him in reality ("And never more will be") (*Stanza* VII).

As told earlier, the poem speaks, in fundamentals, of the healthy bond between man and nature ("she and I live/ Here in this happy dell"). The poem belongs to the category 'Poems of the Imagination,' like such other poems as *She was a Phantom of Delight, The Simplon Pass, I Wandered Lonely as a Cloud, A Slumber did My Spirit Seal, The Reverie of Poor Susan,* and *A*

Night-Piece. Excepting the last stanza, and the beginning stanza and a half line, the whole poem *Three Years She Grew in Sun and Shower* is spoken by nature, the narrator of the poem: 'Then Nature said' (line 2) and 'Thus Nature spake' (line 37). In the poem, Lucy is compared with a flower: she is the ever most beautiful flower. Nature said, she would be Lucy's adopting mother (or nurse) and Lucy would be nature's adopted daughter "This Child I to myself will take;/ She will be mine"). Perhaps in no other poem of Wordsworth does nature so strikingly and sympathetically play the role of a nurse or surrogate mother to a human being.

Alan Gardiner says that in the fourth line of the poem, there is a suggestion of death ("This Child I to myself will take"), which, in turn, may suggest that "Lucy died when she was three years old," but Gardiner hastens to add that if nature adopts Lucy as her daughter, Lucy will forfeit her 'human-ness,' and so her human limitations, such as her mortality. Nature is immortal, and so if Lucy is adopted by nature—*i.e.*, if Lucy becomes a part of nature—Lucy will become immortal, and she cannot be a part of nature if she does not forsake her 'human-ness.' Gardiner writes: "The impression is given that a close relationship with nature is a kind of death because it entails an existence which is close to the eternal source of life and therefore free of the limitations of human mortality. Death itself is the ultimate consummation of this relationship" (Gardiner, 45). Further Alan Gardiner has noticed an antithetical pattern in the poem. Gardiner writes: "There is an antithetical pattern in the poem that begins with the reference to 'sun and shower' in the opening line and is most noticeable in this verse: 'law and impulse', 'rock and plain', 'earth and heaven', 'glade and bower', 'Kindle and restrain.' Geoffrey Durrant says that "These opposing principles are the loom in which the elaborate fabric of life is woven" (Durrant, 65). Durrant believes that the philosophy, or rather the metaphysic, behind the poem is that these opposing forces churn out the complex life from the matrix of the simple earth. Durrant writes about this metaphysic of the poem: "The poem deals with one of Nature's favourites, a young woman upon whom she showers her greatest benefits of grace and beauty. The promise that Nature makes is to produce an almost perfect woman, and in doing so she reveals the methods by which she works to create the complex unity of a living being. Wordsworth shows a recurrent interest in the emergence of organic forms of life from the brute matter and the simple forces of the physical universe. In the poem the process is one of opposing polarities, of a dialectic from which the living complexity arises" (Durrant, 65). This idea is also suggested in *The Prelude* (Bk I, lines 301-306).

> Fair seed-time had my soul, and I grew up
> Fostered alike by beauty and by fear:
> Much favoured in my birthplace, and no less
> In that beloved Vale to which erelong
> We were transplanted—there were we let loose
> For sports of wider range.

Lucy's fast-coming death ("The work was done—/How soon my Lucy's race was run!") was but an inelactable property of her existence, as a part of nature.In nature there is the unending process of birth, growth and decay, and so, as a part of nature, Lucy's death is an irretrievable conclusion of the process of her existence. In the poem, this process of nature has been skilfully described, that Lucy's death is a very natural occurrence, but, nevertheless, the grief for the death has not in any way been attenuated. Alan Gardiner writes: "It is the achievement of the poem to give full recognition to the aptness of Lucy's death without minimizing in any way the poet's feeling of loss" (Gardiner, 47).

Geoffrey Durrant says that in the last stanza of the poem, there is a dramatic inversion. Lucy was expected, in the earlier part of the poem, to grow into a beautiful lady, but in the last stanza of it we find her metamorphosed into a part of nature (as a consequence of her death). Durrant comments upon the last stanza of the poem: "The final stanza with its reversal of expectation and its sudden intrusion of Lucy's death gives a poignant ending to the poem. The joyful creation of life has as its inevitable result the creating of death. This again is not merely a lament over the death of a particular young woman called Lucy. It is a statement of the condition of all human life, in which all the powers of nature combine in complex ways to create a human being, which is doomed by nature's law of death" (Durrant, 67).

The sub-title of the poem, 'The Education of Nature,' should be taken notice of. The sub-title refers to one of Wordsworth's most fundamental tenets of philosophy of life. Wordsworth believed, almost like Jean-Jacques Rousseau, that the poetically and ethically attuned normal human can grow up only in the lap of nature, or it is only nature that teaches man how to be human. The sub-title of this poem is perhaps taken from the sub-title of Rousseau's famous book *Emile or The Education of Nature.*

(III) I Travelled Among Unknown Men

This poem reveals Wordsworth's intense partiotism, particularly because of the fact that Lucy belongs to England, *i.e.*, the poet's love of England is reinforced by his love of Lucy. When, in 1799, Wordsworth was in Germany, he felt his love of England more intensely than when he had been in England, which was only natural. During the time of the composition of this poem, Wordsworth's enthusiasm for republicanism, ignited by the French Revolution, fizzled out ("'Tis past, that melancholy dream!"), and he turned into a sincere conservative. While in Germany, a country far away from England, the poet's memory of the ideal girl Lucy, engrossed him, and this prompted him to write this poem. But, it must be pointed out that the poem was not actually composed in Germany, but in England. In 1801, when the poet was in England, he revivified his feeling of being away from Lucy and England while he had earlier been in Germany, and this revivified feeling or recalled memory of his feeling, while in Germany, prompted him to write this poem (while in England). Though the poem was written in 1801, it was published six years afterwards—in 1807.

I Travelled Among Unknown Men

I Travelled among unknown men,
In lands beyond the sea;
Nor, England! did I know till then
What love I bore to thee.

'Tis past, that melancholy dream!
Nor will I quit thy shore
A second time; for still I seem
To love thee more and more.

Among thy mountains did I feel
The joy of my desire;

And she I cherished turned her wheel
Beside an English fire.

Thy mornings showed, thy nights concealed,
The bowers where Lucy played;
And thine too is the last green field
That Lucy's eyes surveyed.

Coming back from Germany to his fatherland, England, the poet recalls that, while in Germany, he had been wandering among alien and unknown people ('travelled among unknown men'). Then he had been in Germany ('in lands') which was far away from England ('beyond the sea'). The poet tells England that before going away from her ('till then') he could not realise how intense was his love for her (England) ("What love I bore to thee"). While in Germany, he had gloomily been wishing ('melancholy dream') to return to England. But now, as he has already returned to England, that gloomful wish is no more with him (''Tis past'). He says he will never ('A second time') leave England ('quit thy shore'), to go to a foreign country, because he now feels his love of England more intensely ('more and more').

The poet tells England that he desired joy and got ('did I feel") that joy among her mountains ('Among thy mountains'). He says that he loved Lucy ('she I cherished') who worked at the spinning wheel ('wheel') sitting beside fire, in England. The poet says that when he was in England, he saw in the mornings the hut or cottage ('bowers') of Lucy, where she used to play, as if those mornings revealed ('showed') her cottage; and when nights came, her hut remained invisible ('concealed'), as if enveloped by the darkness of those nights. The poet says that, before she died ('last'), Lucy saw ('Lucy's eyes surveyed') the 'green field' of England, as her last object of perception.

The poem is divided into four stanzas, the first two of which are, according to Geoffrey Durrant, a sort of preface "in which the narrator describes his return after foreign travel to the scenes he associates with Lucy" (Durrant, 73). Durrant says that the narrator's love of England "is a love of imaginative order" (Durrant, 74). Durrant further writes about the poem: "The narrator's return to the scene of his earlier love is a return to the order of a pattern which, although it involves loss and pain, is yet familiar and therefore to some degree reassuring. The history of Lucy as it is told here is firmly cyclical; the spinning-wheel that Lucy turns beside 'an English fire', dominates the last part of the poem, in which she is shown as moving through a cycle of childhood, maturity and death. The sense of return to a known and familiar pattern is so strong in this poem that it makes the story of Lucy seem predetermined and yet not painful. The turning of the wheel of day and night, youth and age, beside the hearth and within the security of the mountains, speaks of a protective, encircling order. The love of Lucy has been fostered in England, among the mountains, and Lucy herself has lived through the recurring days and nights by the encircling 'bowers' in which she played as a child. Her death is not mentioned, but only implied, as though she has completed the turning of the wheel; moreover, it is implied in an image of rest and peace, and in a suggestion of the Psalmist's words: 'He maketh me to lie down in green pastures':

> And thine too is the last green field,
> That Lucy's eyes surveyed,"

(Durrant, 74)

The images of the poem belong to the pastoral, particularly the last two stanzas of it: the 'mountains,' the 'wheel,' the 'mornings,' the 'nights,' the 'bowers,' and the 'green field.' However let us conclude our discussion on this poem with Geoffrey Durrant's comment on it: "This is of course in one sense a love story, but it is also an account of the natural piety by which Wordsworth increasingly believed it necessary to live. The restlessness of foreign travel led him to value familiar places, familiar patterns, and a natural inter connection of all the various parts of experience. This poem marks a distinct decline from the tragic perception and intellectual energy of the other 'Lucy' poems. It shows the beginning of the tendency to seek for 'a repose that ever is the same' that slowly led Wordsworth's poetic powers to decline. This is not to say that the poem is without value. On the contrary, it expresses with quiet assurance the value of a life lived within the protective circle of a national and social tradition" (Durrant, 75).

(IV) She Dwelt Among the Untrodden Ways

This is a very sweetly lyrical poem of lost love, that innuendoes to the deep spring of love in the heart of Wordsworth, contrary to the general impression that the poet lacked in the genuine passion of love. But in the case of Wordsworth's love, the only exceptional thing is that we are not certain if the object of love is real or imaginary. This is true not only about this present poem, but about all the other four Lucy poems. The central idea of the poem is that fame is not a part of the property or essential quality of the beloved, but her beauty certainly is. The poem was composed at Goslar in Germany, in 1799 and was first published in the 1800 edition of *Lyrical Ballads*.

She Dwelt Among the Untrodden Ways

She dwelt among the untrodden ways
Beside the springs of Dove,
A Maid whom there were none to praise
And very few to love:

A violet by a mossy stone
Half hidden from the eye!
Fair as a star, when only one
Is shining in the sky.

She lived unknown, and few could know
When Lucy ceased to be;
But she is in her grave, and, oh,
The difference to me!

In the foregoing three Lucy poems, Lucy's death was only suggested or implied, but in the present poem, her death is explicit ("few could know/When Lucy ceased to be"). Again, in no other Lucy poem has Wordsworth given so detailed a description of Lucy's beauty, and that in clear terms. In the second stanza, the poet compares Lucy with a violet against a 'mossy stone'. The colour of the flower and that of the 'mossy stone' are contrasting colours, and this has enhanced the beauty of the violet, and so, by inference, of Lucy. Lucy is as beautiful as the single bright star in the sky. From her comparisons with the violet and the lonely star, it may be assumed that Lucy's beauty was not admired by all, by the public—nobody so much cares the violet, that blooms in an unfrequented place, or the single star in the sky.

Some critics are of the opinion that Lucy is, in this poem, loveless, because she does not make any response to the urgent love of the poet; and that she is sexless, because, though she is called a woman, she never shows any womanly qualities. But, in this poem, she certainly reveals herself as a woman with the passion of love. Lucy is like the single star in the sky, *i.e.*, she is like Venus, the goddess of love. Geoffrey Durrant writes: "Some critics comment on the sexlessness of Lucy in this poem. But she is compared here with the star which is usually seen shining when 'only one' is visible, the planet Venus, star of the goddess of love. And it is urgent to note that Wordsworth's original version suggests some interest in Lucy's physical attractions:

> My hope was one, from cities far,
> Nursed on a lonesome heath;
> Her lips were red as roses are,
> Her hair a woodbine wreath.

(Durrant, 71)

The last stanza of the poem summarises the whole argument of the poem: Lucy is most beautiful, but few people but the poet cares her beauty, and so when she is dead, her absence quite changes the state of the poet. Geoffrey Durrant says that the last two lines of the poem have a great dramatic effect: "No direct statement is made of this [of the death of Lucy, and of the feeling of great loss, of the poet] in the last two lines; but its very phrasing, the exclamation at the end of the line—as though wrenched out of the speaker by pain—and the lack of any attempt to find an exact equivalent for the speaker's grief, all combine to give a strictly dramatic sense of the speaker's loss" (Durrant, 71). Geoffrey Durrant has found a 'cyclical structure' in this poem also. Durrant writes: "The 'springs of Dove' suggest the origins of life, the 'violet by a mossy stone' its emergence from brute matter.... Lucy, we are told, 'lived unknown' the story of her life completed in two words—and has 'ceased to be.' Now 'she is in her grave,' and the circle is closed" (Durrant, 71-72). And the last comment of Durrant on this poem is: "This apparently simple poem contains within itself a part of the revolution in thought that was taking place in Wordsworth's time. The poet Gray in his 'Elegy in a Country Churchyard' considers that there are many humble and obscure persons who, with better opportunities, might have become famous and highly valued. What this poem [*She Dwelt Among the Untrodden Ways*] asserts, however, is that value has nothing to do with public judgment. The individual mind may create its own value, and Lucy is no less fair, and no less loved, although she is valued by one person only. This is a firm assertion of the validity of subjective judgments of value—a belief held at no time with more assurance and firmness than in Wordsworth's day" (Durrant, 72-73).

(V) A Slumber Did My Spirit Seal

According to Alan Gardiner, this poem is the "greatest of the Lucy poems. It is the shortest poem in the group and exemplifies Wordsworth's language at the most spare and simple. Nevertheless it is a poem of extraordinary ambiguity and suggestiveness and one that repays repeated scrutiny. John Bear describes it as 'a gnomic and reverberant statement, over which one might puzzle for ever, like a riddle of the Sphinx' (Gardiner, 47). The poem was written at Goslar, in Germany, in 1799, and was first published in the 1800 edition of *Lyrical Ballads*. It is included in the group of poems generally called 'Poems of the Imagination.' Only two Lucy poems are included in Palgrave's *The Golden Treasury: Three Years She Grew in Sun and Shower* (Or, *The Education of Nature*) and *A Slumber Did My Spirit Seal.*

A Slumber Did My Spirit Seal

A Slumber did my spirit seal;
I had no human fears:
She seemed a thing that could not feel
The touch of earthly years.

No motion has she now, no force;
She neither hears nor sees;
Rolled round in earth's diurnal course,
With rocks, and stones, and trees.

A simple paraphrasing of the poem will not do, because each one of the expressions of it is fraught with a reference to the imaginative and enigmatic, but the central character of the Lucy poems—Lucy. Here, in the poem, the poet says that when Lucy died, he was so much aggrieved and afraid that his consciousness ('spirit') of the surrounding objects, or of the world at large, was obliterated ('sealed'), like one's awareness goes away from him when he falls into sleep ('Slumber'). The poet was so deeply unconscious that he had even no fear about human beings' inevitable doom—death. However, after her death, Lucy has been reduced to an inanimate object ('a thing')—inanimate object that is not aware of the continual transmogrification of all the objects (including itself) of the world under the influence of the passage of time. And, as Lucy is now a dead thing, she is also not aware ('feel') of the decaying or the transmogrification of the objects of the world, under the influence of the passage of time ('touch of earthly years')—the passage of time that is there only on this earth (and not in heaven, or in any other place transcendental to this earth).

In the second stanza, the poet says that, as Lucy is now a dead thing, she has no automotion or the power ('force') of moving from one place to another ('No motion has she now'), like living beings. And for the indentical reason (she is dead, and is an inanimate object), she cannot hear any sound whatsoever and cannot perceive any object. (Wordsworth believed that it was the soul that actually gives us motion, and perceives through sense-organs. And as, after her death, Lucy is devoid of her soul, she, or rather her corpse, cannot move, of itself, and cannot perceive.) Being reduced to an inanimate object, Lucy is now no different from other inanimate objects of the earth, such as rocks, stones, and trees, and now she is moving round and round ('Rolled round') as the earth is moving round and round on its axis day after day ('diurnal'), along with such inanimate objects as rocks, stones, and trees.

The poem is very short, but subtle and difficult. It presents, Wordsworth's philosophy or perception of the difference, and relation, between life and death. The word 'Slumber,' in the poem, refers to the poet's stupefaction due to his feeling of utter desolation, at the sudden demise of Lucy. He was so stupefied, and his awareness was so much obliterated, at the death of Lucy, that he was unaware even of the surrounding objects. The expression 'earth's diurnal course' of the poem is of great significance. Astronomically, when we say that the earth has its diurnal revolution on its axis, we understand by the earth an immense lump of inanimate, and therefore passionless, matter. In the second or the last stanza of the poem, the poet means to say that, after her death, Lucy (or, rather, her body) has been absorbed into, and unified with, the inanimate and passionless earth. From this, it may be deduced that while living, *i.e.*, while Lucy possessed a soul, she was a passionate girl or woman. This means that, according to Wordsworth, human beings are composed of two elements: inanimate and passionless brute matter and soul or spirit. So long as the soul is within us, we are conscious of our surrounding, and we can hear and see, but as soon as the soul leaves our body, we are no different from the lifeless and passionless earth. Such is Wordsworth's simple and common-sense philosophy of the relation between soul and body, or between life and death. Simplistic though this philosophy may seem, it has a great moment, particularly when considered against the 18th century conception of man. In the 18th century, it was held that human beings are a tribe of highly cultured and sophisticated beings, who are quite different from other creatures, but Wordsworth found no difference between man and other creatures, because he believed that all the creatures, including human beings, are merely compounds of two things: lumps of earth (matter) and souls. In this sense, Wordsworth's philosophy of man was scientifically far advanced than the 18th century philosophy of man, according to which man was far superior to other living creatures. Whether Wordsworth was a pantheist or not we cannot be certain about, but we may at least hazard the opinion that he tended to be a pantheist, in that he seemed to believe that soul or spirit is present in all living creatures—men, beasts, and trees—and also inanimate objects. Wordsworth believed that the soul or spirit could exist in two different modes or states: conscious and unconscious. In the living creature, the soul exists in the conscious state, while in the inanimate object or in a dead creature it exists in the unconscious state. Lucy, being dead, simply lost her soul in the conscious mode or state, and so behaved like inanimate objects. This philosophy of Wordsworth may be found in this Lucy poem. Coleridge thought that Lucy's death, in this poem, may have been a symbolic apprehension of Wordsworth that Dorothy might one day suddenly die, and thereby lose her sprightliness and get reduced to inanimate and brute matter. Coleridge said about this poem: "'Most probably, in some gloomy moment he [Wordsworth] had fancied the moment in which his sister might die'" (Gardiner, 41).

The poem is really very difficult to understand—so much so that even Alan Gardiner perfers to cite, in his *The Poetry of Wordsworth*, the analysis of the poem by A.P. Rossiter, before giving his own interpretation of the poem. Let us quote at some length from Gardiner's book *The Poetry of Wordsworth*: "In a stimulating analysis of this poem A.P. Rossiter drew attention to the possibility of two opposite and apparently irreconcilable interpretations. In one reading (and this is the interpretation broadly followed by most critics) the two stanzas contrast the poet's state of mind before and after his loved one's death. The first stanza tells of the deluded belief he once had that she was immortal. 'Slumber' implies a dream-like state from which he would eventually awake, recalling the poet's reverie as he approached Lucy's cottage in 'Strange fits of passion'. 'Seal' similarly suggests that he was enveloped in a false security from which reality was excluded, the recurrent sibilants of the line reinforcing the serenity. As he now recognizes, he was foolish to have no 'human fears' because the woman was a human being and therefore subject to mortality. He blindly thought of her not as human but as a 'thing' to which the normal conditions of earthly human existence did not apply ('seemed' expresses the illusory nature of this perception). The second stanza then registers the shock of her death, which has destroyed the poet's delusion and forced him to acknowledge reality. She is now utterly devoid of life, unable to hear, move or see. Burried in the earth, she is as dead as rocks or stones (ironically, she has now become the 'thing' he took her to be in the first stanza). The poet's cruel loss has given him a new awareness of the impersonal forces which govern the universe. The unfeeling inexorability of these forces is reflected in the use of the coldly scientific word 'diurnal.'

"In the second interpretation the entire poem, not just the final stanza, describes the poet's reaction to the woman's death. The first stanza is in the past tense because it recollects a moment of visionary insight experienced after his loved one had died; the second stanza elaborates on what he sensed during this experience and is in the present tense because he believes that his vision revealed to him a still pertaining truth. Viewed in this light the tone of the poem becomes much more positive. Although the woman was dead, the poet had a blissful sense of her essential immortality; he knew that she was free of human constraints and had become part of a larger transcendent reality. She was now 'a thing that could not feel/The touch of earthly years.' In the second stanza the poet reflects that although the woman is now humanly inert ('No motion has she now, no force') she is at one with the vital generating forces of the universe ('Rolled round in earth's diurnal course'). Seen from this perspective, the last two lines have a majestic sweep which suggests that her death was an ennobling experience."

"These two readings of the poem are not incompatible but mutually illuminating. In fact it is possible to take something from each of the interpretations and produce a third reading, in which the poet's delusion about Lucy's immortality is destroyed by her death but the pain caused by the shattering of this delusion is offset by the recognition that the loved one has, by dying, attained another kind of immortality. The important point, however, is that none of these readings is more 'true' than the others; an intelligent response to the poem must accept its essential ambivalence. The ambiguity of the poem confirms what the other Lucy poems suggest: Wordsworth's acceptance of death was threatened by this acute sense of the grief and distress it causes to the bereaved" (Gardiner, 47-49).

PART 4

4

Six Select Sonnets of Wordsworth

Wordsworth has to his credit in all 523 sonnets. No other English Romantic poet could produce so astonishingly great number of sonnets. Wordsworth's sonnets are generally divided into several groups, depending on their themes or occasions or some central objects, and the different groups of sonnets appear under various rubrics, such as 'Sonnets Dedicated to Liberty and Order,' 'Sonnets Upon the Punishment of Death,' 'Ecclesiastical Sonnets,' and 'Miscellaneous Sonnets.' In the genre of sonnet (as well as elsewhere), Wordsworth's model was not the obvious Shakespeare, but Milton: out of his 523 sonnets, only one is composed in the Shakespearean form, the others mostly being Miltonic in form. Regarding his number of sonnets, Wordsworth can be compared with Milton who also wrote more than 500 sonnets (Preminger-783). After Milton, the sonnet was virtually an extinct literary species, but with the advent of the Romantic period, and with the continuous pouring out of sonnets by Keats, Shelley and Wordsworth, interest in this genre of poetry quickly returned. According to J.A. Cuddon, of all the sonnets, produced in the Romantic period, "Wordsworth's are generally thought to be the best, especially his *Composed upon Westminster Bridge. September 3. 1802, To Toussaint L'Ouverture.* and *On the Extinction of the Venetian Republic*" (Cuddon, 645).

The Shakespearean, or the English, sonnet generally follows the rhyme-scheme: a b a b, c d c d, e f e f g g. Milton, on the other hand, "always used the same rhyme-scheme for the octave: a b b a, a b b a. But he used different rhyme-schemes for the sestet: c d e c d e, c d c d c d, etc. with variations even in these" (Sarker, 1998, 33). Following Milton, Wordsworth also did not vary the rhyme-scheme of the octave of his sonnets, and stuck to the rhyme scheme: a b b a, a b b a, but he varied, again following Milton, the rhyme-scheme of the sestet, of course his preferred rhyme-schemes of the sestet were: c d c d c d, or c d e c d e, or c d c d c d. Wordsworth's admiration of the sonnets of Milton and his inspiration of writing sonnets, received from Milton, have an interesting story behind them: "One day in 1801 he [Wordsworth] took fire on hearing his sister read the sonnets of Milton, and produced three of his own the same afternoon" (Elton, 79). Most of Wordsworth's were sonnets dealing with 'public affairs,' and the greatest number of sonnets that the poet produced in a single year was in 1802. But, though Wordsworth was undoubtedly great in sonnet, he could never reach near his model Milton. Graham Hough writes: "His [Wordsworth's] model was Milton rather than the earlier Ranaissance sonneteers.... But Milton has always a secure and unshakeable sense of style. This Wordsworth has not. When he is writing from the more superficial layers of his mind he is capable of horrid flatness which he apparently does not notice" (Hough, 54). Hough further writes about Wordsworth's sonnets: "Gerard Manley Hopkins once complained that there was too much white neckcloth about him—meaning too much sententious moralizing; a view with which I cannot help agreeing" (Hough, 54). Though Wordsworth wrote a great number of sonnets, to-day he is not remembered for his sonnets, but for his other short poems and two epical poems, because he excelled in them, and not in the sonnets, barring only a handful of them. Geoffrey Durrant's comment is quite correct: "Most of Wordsworth's sonnets, (then) must be regarded as inferior to his best work. However, there are a small number that amply repay a close and careful reading" (Durrant, 150).

(I) Composed Upon Westminster Bridge, September 3, 1802

In 1802, Wordsworth married Mary Hutchinson. Before the marriage, Wordsworth paid the second visit to France with the principal objective of settling issues with Annette Vallon. This sonnet was composed on his way to France. In the morning of July 31, 1802, Wordsworth, along with Dorothy, crossed the Westminster Bridge, on his way back to London. This sonnet records the poet's impression of that morning. The date of composition of this poem, as per its title is September 3, 1802.

But, the morning, referred to in the poem, is not, in all probability, that of September 3, but of July 31. Dorothy, in her Journal, recorded her own impression of the neighbourhood of the Westminster Bridge in the morning of July 31. This record dovetails with the description of the Bridge as we find in this sonnet. This sonnet is included in Palgrave's *The Golden Treasury*.

Composed Upon Westminster Bridge, September 3, 1802

Earth has not anything to show more fair:
Dull would he be of soul who could pass by
A sight so touching in its majesty:
This City now doth, like a garment, wear
The beauty of the morning; silent, bare,
Ships, towers, domee, theatres, and temples lie
Open unto the fields, and to the sky;
All bright and glittering in the smokeless air.
Never did sun more beautifully steep
In his first splendour, valley, rock, or hill;
Ne'er saw I, never felt, a calm so deep!
The river glideth at his own sweet will:
Dear God! the very houses seem asleep;
And all that mighty heart is lying still!

In the sonnet, the poet says that there is nothing on earth that is more beautiful than the sight of the Westminster Bridge, in that particular morning. The man who can pass across the Bridge without noticing the majestic and touching beauty of the scenario hanging around the Bridge has an insensible ('Dull') soul. The city of London is now, as if, wearing the beautiful morning, as one wears a garment. There is a parallel phrase to lines 4 and 5 of this sonnet, in Psalms chapter IV, 2: "Who coverest thyself with light as a garment." However, the poet says that the ships, towers (one of the towers may be the Tower of London), domes (one of the domes may be the dome of St. Paul's), theatre houses and temples—all are silent, and are not covered or shadowed by clouds ('bare'). And all these are standing ('lie') openly in a row, horizontally up to the fields, and vertically up to the sky. And these are standing brightly and glisteningly in the 'smokeless air.' The poet says that never before did the sun so beautifully imbue or tinge ('steep') the valley, the rocks of the hill, or the hill itself, with its first splendourous glow, and never has the poet seen or felt so heavy or impressive quietude, as there is, in this morning, around him. And the river is running lambently, blithely and smoothly ('glideth'), as accords its will. The poet is stunningly overjoyed ('Dear God!') to see that even ('very') the houses (around him, at a distance: in London) seem to be asleep, and that the whole ('all') of the great ('mighty') city of London ('heart') (London is, as if, the heart in the body that is England) is sprawlingly sleeping ('lying') quietly ('still').

This sonnet is just a beautiful and memorable pen-picture of an attractively serene morning scenario around the Westminster Bridge, and is nothing more or nothing less than that. We know that Wordsworth was a devoted poet of nature, of natural beauty, and here in this sonnet, though he is not describing a part of nature—nature in the Wordsworthian sense of the term 'nature'—what he is describing is also an aspect of nature, albeit there is no wood, no stream, and no hill. In this sonnet, therefore, we come across the wider meaning of the term nature. We also know that Wordsworth was utterly averse to the busy and boisterous city, and this is evident in most of his poems. In the beginning or invocatory lines of *The Prelude*, for instance, the poet expresses his feeling of being relieved of the pent-house that is the city (of London), and his feeling of being soothed and revivified by the 'gentle breeze' of the rural openness: "Oh there is blessing in this gentle breeze". Apparently, this sonnet reveals a different, nay, a contrary liking of Wordsworth—here he is drawn by the beauty of the city of London: "Earth has not anything to show more fair." But we should not lose sight of the fact that here the poet is attracted not by the waking city—the hustling and cacophonous city—when it is violently throbbing ('mighty heart'), when it is spread over with rolling black smoke, but by the quiet and sleeping city, in the calm of the morning. The beauty of the city that is now showing itself does not actually belong to the city itself, but the beauty is endowed to the city, by the generosity of the beautiful morning ('beauty of morning"): the beauty is not intrinsic to the city, but extrinsic. Behind the attraction of the city, there lies the rattlings and huddlings of the busy city. The city, at this moment of the morning, looks attractively beautiful only because the monster that is the city ('mighty heart') is asleep. Alan Gardiner writes in this regard: "Dislike of the urban life is a recurring theme in Wordsworth's poetry. In 'Tintern Abbey' the act of remembering the tranquil beauty of the Wye valley brings welcome relief from 'the din of towns and cities,' and in 'Michael' the shepherd's son is corrupted by 'the dissolute city.' It may therefore appear surprising that Wordsworth should have written a sonnet in praise of London. In fact, however, a close study of the poem reveals that his approval of the city landscape is far from unqualified. Admiration of the city as seen at this particular moment is subtly balanced by an implied aversion to its usual character" (Gardiner, 68). The present beauty of London, says Gardiner, is not integral to the city, but is adventitious as well as 'transitory and deceptive': "London is said to 'wear' the beauty of the morning like a 'garment,' an image which implies that this beauty is both transitory and deceptive. Wordsworth is captivated by the loveliness of the morning scene but also thinks of it as a glittering veneer concealing a much less pleasant reality beneath" (Gardiner, 69).

Geoffrey Durrant says that in this sonnet Wordsworth has personified the city of London, and that if this personification is not understood, the diverse items of the city, mentioned in the poem, will remain *outre*. Durrant writes: "The city which wears the beauty of the morning 'like a garment' is of course a personification; but it is a personification quite different from those of Gray and Collins. Wordsworth carefully checks the suggestion of the city as a person before it emerges into too percise a picture. The idea of the city as 'wearing' the morning as a garment is allowed to develop only to the point at which we feel the presence of a unifying life. Without this suggestion the list of things which follows would be merely a mechanical catalogue. The 'Ships, towers, domes, theatres, and temples' are seen as individual things, 'All bright and glittering in the smokeless air,' and at the same time they are given a profound unity, because they form the garment worn by the city as an organic living thing" (Durrant, 154).

However, David Parkins, among many others, in his essay 'The Isolation of the Human Mind,' highly appreciates this sonnet: "Wordsworth's celebrated sonnet on Westminster Bridge is a marvelous illustration of the sort of poem which has a satisfactory meaning with relation to a fixed time and place and an equally wonderful, quite different meaning when understood 'under the aspect of eternity'" (Abrams, 42). Parkins further writes about this sonnet: "The poem is justly famous. It is a kind of dramatic monologue, in the present tense, and it seems very directly to express immediate pleasure in the eye and ear and to celebrate qualities of a particular, immediate, and personal experience, and to leave it at that, without moralizing or in any way shaking its finger at us. It is solemn without being heavy, and we are at once enchanted by the picture of London in the early morning, with its 'ships, towers, domes, theatres, and temples glittering in the smokeless air'" (Abrams, 43). However, the rhyme-scheme of the sonnet is the most favoured rhyme-scheme of Wordsworth for the sonnet: a b b a, a b b a, c d c d c d.

(II) The World is Too Much with Us

This sonnet belongs to the collection of sonnets generally called 'Miscellaneous Sonnets,' and is in the same rhyme-scheme as in the foregoing one: a b b a, a b b a, c d c d c d. We do not know the date of composition of this sonnet, but know that it was first published in 1807. One distinguishing feature of this sonnet is that in it Wordsworth has referred to Greek mythology, like in *Laodamia,* and unlike, perhaps, in any other sonnet of his. This sonnet also is included in Palgrave's *The Golden Treasury.*

The World is Too Much With Us

The world is too much with us; late and soon,
Getting and spending, we lay waste our powers:
Little we see in Nature that is ours;
We have given our hearts away, a sordid boon!
This Sea that bares her bosom to the moon;
The winds that will be howling at all hours,
And are up-gathered now like sleeping flowers;
For this, for everything, we are out of tune;
It moves us not.—Great God! I'd rather be
A Pagan suckled in a creed outworn;
So might I, standing on this pleasant lea,
Have glimpses that would make me less forlorn;
Have sight of Proteus rising from the sea;
Or hear old Triton blow his wreathed horn.

In this sonnet, the poet expresses his disenchantment with, nay, his disgust at, the artifical and dry-as-dust material civilization—in which he is living—devoid of spirituality and sweet affections—a civilization of hurriedness, and earnings and spendings—for what we do not know. He says that we are bored with, and we are tired of ('too much'), our life, in such a civilization. We are always concerned with, and apprehensive of, our 'being late,' and we are always concerned with our desire of being prompt ('soon'); or we are always concerned with the means of earning money or resources ('Getting'); or we are always concerned with the problem of spending the accumulated money or resources ('spending'); and in all these our endeavours, we exhaust our energy in trivial things ('lay waste our powers'). We are so much busy in worthless trifles that we look the least ('Little') at the beautiful, pleasant, joyful, and spiritual aspects of nature—the aspects that are there in nature ready for our enjoyments ('that are ours'). The poet says that we have dedicated ('have given away') our vitality or our life ('hearts'), for this busy, material, and valueless civilization. The poet, in despair, says that such is our life—a despicable and lowly ('sordid') life that we have received as a reward or presentation ('boon') from God, or from our parents.

In the next movement of the sonnet, the poet says that we are not in sympathy with, or, rather, we keep ourselves at bay from ('out of tune'), this sea that is in love, or in sympathy, with the moon ('bares her bosom to the moon'), or the winds that will soon begin to blow continually ('at all hours'), making a burking ('howling') sound—the winds that are now so furled or concentrated ('up-gathered') that they seem to be sleeping flowers. The poet says that we are aloof not only from these two things, but also from all the other cognate things ('everything') of nature.

In the third movement of the poem, the poet says that our material civilization ('It') does not evoke any sympathy or affection within us ('moves us not'). He is dejectedly astonished at the state of our lives ('Great God!') (compare 'Dear God!' at line 13 of *Composed Upon Westminster Bridge*). Instead of continuing to live in such a sordid civilization, the poet wishes to be ('I'd rather be') rather an uncivilized person, or one of the rustic men ('Pagan'), and wishes to have imbibed ('sucked') the villagers' tradition ('creed') of feeling oneness with nature—a tradition that has now been obliterated ('outworn'). Had he been in that tradition, then he ('So might I') could have the glimpses of the beauty of the pleasant nature, standing on this enjoyable open country or field ('bea'), and then due to the quiet and pleasant beauty of nature, he would not feel as dejected as he is feeling now (in this civilized and materialist world). And, had he been in that tradition, he could have noticed the mythological sea-god Proteus (who assumes different shapes 'to evade having to foretell the future') rising up from under the sea, or he could have seen the minor sea-god Triton ('son of Poseidon and Amphitrite, represented with a dolphin's tail, sometimes horse's forelegs, blowing a conch') blow his garlanded conch or shell ('wreathed horn').

This sonnet shows the poet's utter concern about the wreckless de-naturalization (de-forestation) that had been wrought due to the rapid industrialization of England, and about the people of England who remained engrossed in trifling things of the material world, and in worthless mundane affairs, neglecting nature that was so eager to extend its benefits to the people ("Little we see in Nature that is ours"). In the poem, the poet says that we are now so oblivious of the beautiful nature that nature no more does attract and move us ('It moves us not'). Wordsworth, the poet of nature, is very much revealed in this sonnet. He is so much exasperated at the preposterous change in the world that he is reviling the material world, and is dreaming of a mythological world of yore where he wishes to escape into to enjoy the pleasure of nature ('pleasant lea') in the ambience of mythological beings. Douglas Bush writes about the mythological allusions of this sonnet: "The finest and most familiar of Wordsworth's mythological allusions is the impassioned outburst in The World is too much with us" (Bush, 58). Regarding the mythological figures of this sonnet, Bush further writes: "In this sonnet we may find the keynote of a mass of mythological poetry of the nineteenth and twentieth centuries; the old antagonism between Pan and Christ has become a contrast between the ugly materialism of our commercial and industrial civilization and the natural religion, the ideal beauty and harmony of Hellenic life" (Bush, 59).

True, in this sonnet, Wordsworth has expressed his liking for some pagan gods, for Proteus and Triton, but from this it should not be construed that here he voices his preference for paganism over Christianity, because, in fact, he has no loyalty to show to either of the two: he is virtually a secular poet. Douglas Bush writes in this regard: "'True poetry has ever a substratum of Religion in it,' and Greek poetry owed its high character to the elements of truth in Greek religion, philosophy, and myth. But the modern world and its poetry are secular, not Christian. When Wordsworth would rather be an old pagan than a modern Englishman, he is only affirming 'that Triton is better than Plutus'" (Bush, 273-74).

(III) It is a Beautious Evening, Calm and Free

This sonnet was composed when Wordsworth, along with Annette Vallon, and his little daughter by Annette, Caroline, was spending an evening, on the beach, of Calais in the autumn of 1802. In the poem Wordsworth addresses a girl as 'Dear Child! dear Girl,' and this girl is, beyond doubt, Caroline. This sonnet shows the poet's sincere love of the tranquillity of nature, which we have already seen in the previous sonnet, as against the cacophony of the city. It was composed in August, 1802, but was published, five years later, in 1807. The rhyme-scheme of this sonnet is complex, and is quite different from that of the two foregoing sonnets—its rhyme-scheme being a b b a, a c c a, d e f d f e.

It is a Beauteous Evening, Calm and Free

It is a beauteous evening, calm and free,
The holy time is quiet as a Nun
Breathless with adoration; the broad sun
Is sinking down in its tranquillity;
The gentleness of heaven broods o'er the Sea:
Listen! the mighty Being is awake,
And doth with his eternal motion make
A sound like thunder—everlastingly.
Dear Child! dear Girl! that walkest with me here,
If thou appear untouched by solemn thought,
Thy nature is not therefore less divine:
Thou liest in Abraham's bosom all the year;
And worshipp'st at the Temple's inner shrine.
God being with thee when we know it not.

In the sonnet, the poet says that the evening is exquisite with its quietude, and freedom from usual natural encumbrances, such as cloud, rain, storm, noise, etc. ('free'). And so the present time is serene and sombre, and has a religious ('holy') overtone. The time is as quiet as a nun, who is breathelessly engaged in workship ('adoration') of God. The sun, now waxed larger, is quietly ('in its tranquillity') sinking into the celestial softness ('broods') of the sea. The poet is calling all ('Listen!') to notice that the most powerful Spirit, that pervades the whole of the creation ('mighty Being') is waking up from its unconscious state or sleep, and that the mighty ocean ('Being') is also waking up, and is in a ceaseless ('eternal' commotion, making a sound like that of a thunder in such a manner that it seems that it (the sound) will continue to be till the last point of eternity ('everlastingly'). He tells Caroline ('Dear Child ! dear Girl'), who is walking with him, that if even at this present moment she is not affected ('untouched') by her own serious or sombre ('solemn') thoughts (she is not thus affected due to her young age), yet she is no less heavenly in her being or essence ('nature'). He says that she is perpetually ('all the year') blessed ('liest in Abraham's bosom'), and that God, whom she worships, is constantly present with herself—in the inmost circle of her ('Temple's inner shrine')—and this is a fact we are not always aware of.

This is a special sonnet, in the sense that it is imbued with divinity throughout, as very few sonnets of Wordsworth are. As we have elsewhere said, Wordsworth saw nature not as a conglomeration of inanimate things, but as a sort of living being, with some sort of personality, and of course with spirituality, and this is obvious when we hear the poet say: 'the mighty Being is awake'. In this sonnet, the poet assumes that the spirituality or divinity is present not only in nature, but also in the 'dear Girl'—in Caroline. And this is obvious when, at the last line of the sonnet, the poet tells Caroline: "God being with thee when we know it not." It may be mentioned here that Mr. Harper, who has written the authoritative biography of Wordsworth, *William Wordsworth: His Life, Works, and Influence* (1916), has added a supplement to that biography, *Wordsworth's French Daughler* (1921), in which supplement it has been confirmed that the girl of this sonnet is none else than Caroline.

(IV) Milton! Thou Shouldst be Living at This Hour

This sonnet shows Wordsworth's great admiration for Milton. Wordsworth was poetically much influenced by Milton, but the impress of Milton on Wordsworth is the most noticeable in Wordsworth's sonnets, and not so much in his other genres of poetry. Milton's poetry is declamatory, and so is Wordsworth's sonnets. In this present sonnet, Wordsworth has poured forth, on the one hand, his utter disgust at the prevailing witless accumulation of wealth in the hands of a few and the maldistribution of wealth, in England; and, on the other, his praise for Milton, the only person who, Wordsworth believed, could raise a stentorian voice against the evil state-of-affairs in England.

This sonnet was actually entitled by the poet as simply 'London, 1802'. This famous sonnet belongs to the group of sonnets generally called "Sonnets on Independence and Liberty'. Two other sonnets, that belong to the same group of sonnets, and where Milton is remembered, are: 'Great men have been among us; hands that penned' and 'It is not to be thought of that the Flood'—both written in the same year, 1802. In the former sonnet Wordsworth writes:

> Great men have been among us; hands that penned
> And tongues that uttered wisdom—better none:
> The later Sidney, Marvel, Harrington,
> Young Vane, and others who called Milton friend,
> These moralists could act and comprehend...

And in the latter sonnet, he writes:

> We must be free or die, who speak the tongue
> That Shakespeare spake; the faith and morals hold
> Which Milton held.

However, this present sonnet was composed in September, 1802, and was first published in 1807.

Milton! Thou Shouldst be Living at This Hour

> Milton! thou shouldst be living at this hour:
> England hath need of thee: she is a fen
> Of stagnant waters: altar, sword, and pen,
> Fireside, the heroic wealth of hall and bower,
> Have forfeited their ancient English dower
> Of inward happiness. We are selfish men;
> Oh! raise us up, return to us again;
> And give us manners, virtue, freedom, power.

The soul was like a Star, and dwelt apart;
Thou hadst a voice whose sound was like the sea:
Pure as the naked heavens, majestic, free,
So didst thou travel on life's common way,
In cheerful godliness; and yet thy heart
The lowliest duties on herself did lay.

The poet wishes that Milton were present or were living at the time of the composition of this sonnet ('hour'), when England is in need of him (Milton: for England now needs Milton's crusade against immorality). England ('she') is now, as if, a bog or marsh where water is standing without current, or where the water is foul-smelling, *i.e.*, England is now a place where immorality predominates. The poet says that here in England, the church ('altar'), blood-shed ('sword'), malefactory writings ('pen'), fireside accusatory and counter-accusatory chats ('Fireside'), and bacchanalian entertainments in precious halls, built with the wealth seized in battles heroically won ('the heroic wealth of hall') and in gatherings of amorous persons 'bower') have taken away the place of ('Have forfeited') the people's peace ('happiness' that they received ('dower') from their tradition or their forbears ('ancient'). Now, the people of England ('We') have become selfish. Therefore, the poet urges upon the deceased poet Milton to come back to earth, to wit, to England, from his grave or from the world of the dead, and to teach the Englanders right manners, virtues, freedom, strength of mind, and morality.

The poet says that Milton's soul ('Thy soul') was as sublime as a star ('like a star'), and that Milton's soul (while he was alive) remained above, or far away from, the souls of common men ('swelt apart'). He says that Milton ('Thou') had an impressive voice, which resembled the sound of the sea, *i.e.*, the power of Milton's poetry was as great as that of the motions or currents or waves of the sea. The poet says that Milton's poetry was not only powerful, but was also as pure and unpolluted by worldly evils as the cloudless sky ('naked heavens'), and that his poetry was majestic as well as free from fear. (The phrase 'naked heavens' may remind one of Shelley's lines: "The moon doth with delight/Look round her when the heavens are bare"). However, it was due to the especial and uncommon strength of his poetry that Milton could live among the common folk ('travel on life's common way') gleefully, and like a god. And, yet, Milton ('thy heart') performed even chores or most ordinary ('lowliest') works ('duties'), taking upon himself the responsibility of performing those duties ('on herself did lay'). (We know that Milton was never loth to do even so lowly works as refurbishing or shining his own shoes. The expression 'thy heart/ The lowliest duties on herself did lay' probably refers to Milton's doing such lowly works, in actuality.)

In this sonnet, Wordsworth does not speak much about Milton, and does not produce much of informative biographical data about Milton, and yet Milton's greatness as a man and as a poet is quite obvious here, particularly when he calls Milton 'a Star'. Geoffrey Durrant writes about the image of Milton as a star: "This image tells us very little about Milton, but draws its force from the cosmic setting, which Wordsworth handles with usual sureness" (Durrant, 149). Durrant further says that the emotion created in this sonnet is related with the particular despairing condition of the England of Wordsworth's time. Therefore the created emotion is limited by the passage of time—the created emotion may not affect people of other times, and so it is not universal. Referring to this sonnet, Durrant writes: "Poems of this kind are valued in the degree to which the reader shares the sentiments expressed, and this in itself will change with the times" (Durrant, 149). Nevertheless, we may say that the sonnet is really passionate and dignified. However, the octave of the sonnet is not in Wordsworth's preferred rhyme-scheme: a b b a, a b b a; but in a different rhyme-scheme: a b a b, a b a b. The sestet is also in quite uncommon rhyme-scheme: c d d e c e.

(V) Nuns Fret Not at Their Convent's Narrow Room (or, Nuns Fret Not)

This sonnet and the next sonnet, *Scorn Not The Sonnet; Critic, You Have Frowned,* may be treated as companion sonnets, in the sense that in both the sonnets, the themes are the same: Wordsworth's love of the sonnet form. The present sonnet belongs to the collection of sonnets by Wordsworth entitled 'Miscellaneous Sonnets.' 'Miscellaneous Sonnets' were dedicated by Wordsworth to 'somebody,' but who that 'somebody' is we do not know. We only know that Wordsworth addressed that 'somebody' as 'chief of Friends'. Maybe, that 'somebody' is S.T. Coleridge. However, we do not know when this present sonnet was written, but know that it was first published in 1807.

Nuns Fret Not at Their Convent's Narrow Room

Nuns fret not at their convent's narrow room;
And hermits are contented with their cells;
And students with their pensive citadels;
Maids at the wheel, the weaver at his loom,
Sit blithe and happy; bees that soar for bloom,
High as the highest Peak of Furness-fells,
Will murmur by the hour in foxglove bells:
In truth the prison, unto which we doom
Ourselves, no prison is: and hence for me,
In sundry moods, 'twas pastime to be bound
Within the Sonnet's scanty plot of ground;
Pleased if some Souls (for such there needs must be)
Who have felt the weight of too much liberty,
Should find brief solace there, as I have found.

In the sonnet, the poet does not desire, or pine for, spaciousness in a poem, or for elaboration of a poem, and says that he is coutented with the brief confine of the sonnet. He wants to say that, in not desiring spaciousness, he is not a unique or peculiar person, for there are other persons who also do not want spaciousness, but are satisfied with their narrow confines. He cites some examples of such persons. Firstly, he says that nuns, or secluded women of religious houses, under a vow, do not grumble ('fret') because they have to remain within narrow spaces (' room') of the convents. Secondly, hermits are contented with their narrow spaces of cribs in which they dwell. Thirdly, students are satisfied with the narrow confinements of their unencroachable school-rooms ('citadels') in which they meditatively ('pensive') pursue their studies. Fourthly, spinning women sit contentedly besides their spinning wheel, as the weaving men ('weaver') sit beside their looms (in narrow confines), and all of them pass their times cheerfully or sprightly ('blithe') and happily. And fifthly, bees, which fly up, ('soar') and rush towards flowers ('bloom') that remain suspended at such a great height as that of the highest peak of the mountain ranges, called Furness-fells, are contented being confined within the small spaces of the flowers called foxglove bells—humming ('murmur') continually ('by the hour'). After saying all these, the poet presents us with a psychological truism ('In truth'). He says that the narrow spaces or confines ('prison') into which we are forced to remain ('doom') are actually no narrow confines or spaces (provided we are happy there). And so ('hence'), for the poet ('for me'), it was rather a pastime or happy engagement to remain engaged ('sundry') in poetic moods—in the composition of sonnets whose poetic spaces are very narrow or brief ('scanty plot of ground'). The poet would be pleased if there would have been such persons ('Souls')—and he knows that there are certainly such persons ('for such there needs must be')—who would have become disgusted or apathic ('felt the weight of') towards the extremely liberal form of (expatiated or long) poems, rather than towards the sonnet which is in very routinized and measured or controlled form, and if these people would find ('Should find') comfort for short whiles ('brief solace') in the sonnet, in the brief space of the sonnet ('there'), as the poet himself has found ('as I have found") comforts for short whiles.

The purpose or objective of the poet in this sonnet, as we have already said, was to the peculiar and superior beauty of the sonnet form, as well as his liking and preference for the sonnet form. The outstanding feature of the sonnet is its brevity, and its utmost poetic or, rather, prosodic restraints. But, in spite of its very narrow space, the poet says, the sonnet is like the foxglove bell that is full to the brim with the manna of honey. So, concludes the poet, space is not the point: the space may be narrow, and yet we may be contented with that narrow space, provided we may enjoy the beauty of that narrow space, to wit, the narrow space of the sonnet. This sonnet shows Wordsworth's attraction towards the sonnet form. And, that he is not pretending here is confirmed by the fact that he himself turned out as many as 525 sonnets. The present sonnet, and the sonnet that we are soon going to discuss, are unique, in the sense that perhaps no other poet has composed sonnets in praise of the sonnet form. However, in this sonnet the poet has followed yet another new rhyme-scheme that is different from the rhyme-schemes of the foregoing four sonnets: a b b a, a b b a, c d c d c d.

(VI) Scorn Not the Sonnet; Critic. you have Frowned (or Sonnet on Sonnet)

As we know, Wordsworth wrote a great number of sonnets (523 in all), and this demonstrates his keen interest in the sonnet form. We do not know if this present sonnet was prompted by some derogatory remark on the sonnet form by any witless critic, or not. But, perhaps, Wordsworth felt the need of writing this sonnet for a different reason. In the Romantic age—Wordsworth's own age—the liking for the sonnet precariously declined, which was a cause of much grief for Wordsworth who could not reluctantly accept this decline, and, perhaps, with a view to exerting some influence for resuscitating the sonnet, the poet composed this sonnet. When this sonnet was written we do not know, but we know that it was first published in 1827. This is a very peculiar sonnet, regarding its rhyme-scheme, in the sense that while its octave is Petrarchan, its sestet is Shakespearean, the whole rhyme-scheme of the sonnet being: a b b a a b b a, c d c d e e.

Scorn Not the Sonnet; Critic, You Have Frowned

Scorn not the Sonnet; Critic, you have frowned,
Mindless of its just honours; with this key
Shakespeare unlocked his heart; the melody
Of this small lute gave ease to Petrarch's wound;
A thousand times this pipe did Tasso sound;
With it Camoens soothed an exile's grief;
The Sonnet glittered a gay myrtle leaf
Amid the cypress with which Dante crowned
His visionary brow: a glow-worm lamp,
It cheered mild Sponsor, called from Faery-land
To struggle through dark ways; and when a damp
Fell round the path of Milton, in his hand
The Thing became a trumpet; whence he blew
Soul-animating strains—alas, too few!

The poet exhorts the critics not to loath the sonnet form ('sonnet'). The critics (or a particular critic) have been irrationally ('Mindless') angry ('frowned') against the recognition and praise that have justly been bestowed upon the sonnet form. To justify his stance or contention, the poet produces some instances where great poets have employed this form of poetry very successfully. Firstly, he says, Shakespeare opened ('unlocked') to the wide world his pains and sorrows, hopes and helplessness, and the "slings and arrows' that his heart received, with the help of this form of poetry. Secondly, the sweet and rhythmic sound ('melody') of the brief poem, *i.e.*, the sonnet, which is like a flute ('this small lute'), worked as a balm or soothing nostrum ('gave ease) to the Italian poet Francesco Petrarch's (1304-74) sorely sorrow ('wound'), *i.e.*, Petrarch gave vent to the agony of his heart which was lascerated by his not-yet-consummated love of his beloved Laura, by composing a century of sonnets for her, and thus got relief from his pain. Thirdly, the Italian poet Torquoto Tasso (1544-95) wrote a thousand sonnets that produced very sweet sounds, like those of a musical lute ('A thousand times this pipe'). Fourthly, the Portuguese poet, Luis vaz de Camoens (1524?-80), consoled himself in his sorrows, while serving, under duress, the Portuguese army in India, for 17 years ('exile's grief), by writing sonnets. Fifthly, the sonnet delighted the heart of another Italian poet, Dante Alighieri (1265-1321). Dante was honoured as a poet, at a place which was covered with cypresses, with mirthfully dancing ('gay') myrtle leaves that were, as if, brightened ('glittered') with the light of his sonnets. (At line 7, the expression 'myrtle leaf' refers to Dante's being honoured, because in ancient times poets used to be honoured with myrtle leaves. Again, at line 8, the expression 'Amid the cypress' refers to the time when ['Amid'] Dante's beloved Beatrice died, because the cyress is a symbol of death, and because, as we know, Dante wrote most of his famous sonnets after the death of Beatrice. Dante was a vatic or prophetic or visionary poet, and so the expression 'His visionary brow.') Sixthly, Edmund Spenser (1552?-99), while he had been suffering from pangs of his hearts, due to his unrequited love of Elizabeth Boyle ('To struggle through dark days'), wrote *Amoretti*, which contains 88 sonnets, for her. The sonnet ('It') worked as a source of bright light ('a glow-worm lamp') to the gentle ('mild') Spenser who, as if, brought those 88 sonnets from a dream-land ('called from Faery-land'), and those 88 sonnets showed him the path in his desolate state ('dark ways'). And seventhly or lastly, when John Milton's (1608-74) anti-royalist party of the Roundheads was defeated and suppressed by the royalists, Milton became evervated and dispirited ("when damp/Fell round the path of Milton"), and so he composed a number of sonnets ('The thing') of vigour, that sound like a trumpet, and with these sonnets he produced ('blew') such organic tune or music ('strain') that resuscitated and invigorated the deflated and moribund souls of the people of England. Lastly, the poet, Wordsworth, is sorry, and is repining, for the fact that Milton wrote only a few such invigorating sonnets ('alas, too few!').

As we have said, like in the immediately preceding sonnet, in this sonnet also Wordsworth wanted to vindicate the beauty, and the necessity, of the sonnet. By citing several outstanding sonneteers of the world, and by referring to the pleasures of their sonnets, he has, in this sonnet, reinforced his argument in the immediately preceding sonnet.

To have a general opinion about the quality of Wordsworth's sonnets, critics are not unanimous on the point of the worth of his sonnets. Helen Darbishire, for one, says that "he [Wordsworth] excelled in the sonnet" (Darbishire, 175). But Arthur Hugh Clough is of the opinion that "Wordsworth only wrote four really good sonnets" (Bateson, 4). However, according to Reuben Arthur Brower, Wordsworth's sonnets, whatever else they may or may not be, are pure poetry: "Wordsworth's sonnet, as he himself says, carries us so quickly into the heart of passion that in discussing it we may forget that we have been reading a poem. Which is another way of saying that it is the purest poetry" (Brower, 75).

PART 5

5

Wordsworth as a Romantic Poet

I

What Romanticism actually is we cannot clearly state, for the concept of Romanticism is too nebulous. F.L. Lucas "counted 11, 396 definitions of 'romanticism'" (Cuddon, 186), and the American scholar A.O. Lovejoy once observed that the term 'romanticism' means so many things that it was better to say that it meant nothing. J.A. Cuddon also says that the word "Romanticism means so many things—to pluck at random some of the meanings: 'attractive,' 'bombastic,' 'conservative,' 'emotional,' 'exuberant,' 'fanciful,' 'formless,' 'futile,' 'heroic,' 'irrational,' 'materialistic,' 'mysterious,' 'Nordic,' 'ornamental,' 'realistic,' 'stupid,' 'unreal,' and 'unselfish'" (Cuddon, 186). The word 'romantic' derived proximately from the French word *'romantique'* and distantly from the Old French word *'romant'*. But the meaning of the word 'romantic' or the word 'romanticism, has undergone changes—sometimes phenomenal changes, through its history. J.A. Cuddon writes: "The word *romantic (ism)* has a complex and interesting history. In the Middle Ages 'romance' denoted the new vernacular languages derived from Latin—in contradistinction to Latin itself, which was the language of learning. *Enromancier, romancer, romanz* meant to compose or translate books in the vernacular. The work produced was then called *romanz, roman, romanzo* and romance.... A *roman* or *romant* came to be known as an imaginative work and a 'courtly romance.' By the 17th c., in England and France, 'romance had acquired the derogatory connotations of fanciful, bizzare, exaggerated, chimerical. In France a distinction was made between *romanesque* (also derogatory) and *romantique* (which meant 'tender,' 'gentle,' 'sentimental' and 'sad'). It was used in the English form in these latter senses in the 18th c." (Cuddon, 587). However, it was Friedrich Schlegel, in Germany, who first stabilised the meaning of the word 'romantic,' according to whom "That which is romantic depicts emotional matter in an imaginative form" (Cuddon, 587), and it is in this sense in which the term 'romantic' is now generally being used.

René Wellek and Austin Warren say that the term 'Romanticism' is rather of recent origin, like such terms as 'humanism,' 'Elizabethanism and 'Augustanism,' and that it was somewhat arbitrarily applied to those whom we now know as Romantics: "In English, the term 'Humanism' occurs first in 1832, 'Renaissance' in 1840, 'Elizabethan' in 1817, 'Augustan' in 1819 and 'Romanticism' in 1844. These dates, derived from the *Oxford Dictionary*, are probably not quite reliable, for the term 'Augustan' appears sporadically, as early as 1690; Carlyle uses 'Romanticism' in 1831.... The Romanticists, as we know, did not call themselves Romanticists, at least in England. Apparently only about 1849 were Coleridge and Wordsworth connected with the Romantic movement and grouped with Shelley, Keats and Byron" (Wellek and Warren, 264). Wellek and Warren are not in favour of using such terms as 'humanism', 'Elizabethanism' and 'Romanticism' for the obvious reason that there has been no consensus about the definitions of such terms: "The terms 'Renaissance,' 'Classicism,' 'Romanticism,' 'Symbolism,' and recently 'Baroque' have been defined, re-defined, controverted. It is unlikely that any kind of agreement can be reached so long as the theoretical issues we have tried to clarify remain confused, so long as the men engaged in the discussions insist on definitions by class concepts, confuse 'period' terms with 'type' terms, confuse the semantic history of the terms with the actual changes of style. Quite understandably, A.O. Lovejoy and others have recommended the abandonment of such terras as 'Romanticism' (Wellek and Warren, 267).

Further, some critics refuse to admit of Romanticism as a theory of literature. They believe that the so-called Romantic period was just an evanescent phase in the history of English literature, or, rather, it was simply a movement, or more properly, a protest against the just preceding neo-classical period. Such critics so believe because, they say, Romanticism lacks in universally identifiable marks or features: Coleridge is a Romantic poet, but not in the sense in which Wordsworth is; or, Byron is a Romantic poet, but not in the sense in which Keats is; and so on. Further, Romanticism was not autochthonous, or endemic, in a particular nation or country, but, at different times swept over all the countries of Europe, showing variant features in various nations, during the 18th and the 19th centuries. Also, the Romantic movement was not confined only within the bound of literature, but the wind of Romanticism blew over other areas of thoughts and creations: pholosophy, religion, music, paintings, etc., where also Romanticism expressed itself in divergent modes. Therefore, instead of taking Romanticism as a well-defined concept, it is perhaps better to take it as a particular movement in the thought-processes of the peoples.

However, in England, the Romantic movement may be said to have been touched off, early in the 18th century, by such writers as James Thomson (1700-1748), poet; John Dyer (1700-1758), poet; and painter; and Anthony Ashley Cooper Shaftsbury (1671-1713), philosopher and admirer of the beauty of nature (grandson of Achitophel—who was caricatured in Dryden's *Absalom and Achitophel*)—but principally by Thomson, the author of *The Seasons* and *The Castle of Indolence* (an allegory in Spenserian stanzas, admired by Gray). In England, the Romantic movement gathered momentum, in the middle of the 18th century, from the works of such writers as Thomas Gray (1716-71), Oliver Goldsmith (1730-74), Laurence Sterne (1713-68), Horace Walpole (1717-97) and Samuel Richardson (1689-1761). And in the early part of the 19th century, the movement was given a fillip by such poets as Wordsworth, Coleridge, Byron, Keats, Shelley and Southey. Sir Walter Scott (1771-1832), poet, novelist, critic and man of letters, also played a great part in the Romantic movement.

The English Romantic movement had two contrary directions: negative and positive. Negatively, the Romantics raised their voice of protest against the extreme formalism, overbalance of rationalism, restraint, and insistence on universalism in poetry and other art media. And positively, they showed their ebulient enthusiasm for sentimentalism, love of nature as against urbanity, medievalism and individualism. The Romantics suspected the authenticity of reason or rationality, and relied on intuition born out of sense-perceptions. In this regard, many of the Romantics were, directly or indirectly, influenced by the critical philosophy of the Prussian philosopher Immanuel Kant (1724-1804) who, in his *Critique of Pure Reason*, demonstrated the limitations of reason or rationality, and in his *Critique of Practical Reason*, established the authenticity of intuition. The Romantics' immediate object of vilification was the neo-classical age of Pope and Dryden, which insisted that art must have balance, restraints, universality, and formality, and must shun individualism and sentimentalism. But, as we have said, all the Romantics did not betray the same Romantic elements in their works; or, if they infused many of those elements in their works, their emphases on those elements differed from one another. For instance, Oliver Goldsmith idealised nature and, particularly, rural life; Burns and Byron were interested in liberty and natural rights of the individual; and Gray emphasised sentimental melancholy.

The beginnings of the Romantic movements in Germany, France and England were almost simultaneous, though the Romantic wind began to blow westwards from Germany to England. The works of Goethe, Schiller, Heine, Huller and Wagner first fanned the fire of Romanticism in Germany. In the works of these writers we find the new German literary movement known as '*Sturm and Drang*' ('Storm and Stress'), and also *stimmung* (mood or temper) and *schwarmerei* (sentimentality). The German Romantic writers got their proclivity toward idealism and spirituality from the philosophical works of Kant, Schelling and Fichte. In France, the Romantic movement originated principally in the writings of the *philosophes*, such as Voltaire (1694-1778) and Diderot (1713-84). Voltaire's *Letters Philosophiques* and Diderot's *Encyclopédie* preached rationalist humanism, and thereby went a long way toward the obliteration of the hangover of the medieval consciousness, and toward paving the way of the Romantic movement in France. Rousseau's belief in the natural goodness of human beings in the ambience of nature; his belief in individual virtues or morality, because of that; his love of nature; his justifying the authenticity and necessity of passion; and his ideal of the 'noble savage' contributed much to the Romantic movement, not only of France, but also of England. In England, no particular writer generated so much fuel for the fire of the Romantic movement as Rousseau did in France. Nevertheless, we may say that, besides the works of the Romantic poets, Richardson's *Pamela* (1740), *Clarissa Harlowe* (l747) and *Sir Charles' Grandson* (1754); Goldsmith's *The Vicar of Wakefield* (1766); Sterne's *Sentimental Journey* (1768); Henry Mackenzie's *The Man of Feeling* (1771); and Henry Brooke's *Juliet Grenville* (1774); and such other works went a long way in ushering in the Romantic movement in England.

The Romantics liked to view this world as a make-belief world, a phenomenal world, an illusion, and conceived of an ideal world behind this work-a-day phenomenal world. They were, therefore, dreamers of sorts. The Romantic movements of all the three major countries—England, France and Germany—had some connection with the French Revolution (1789-99) whose three high ideals—liberty, equality, and fraternity—were also the common ideals of the Romantics. And these three high ideals were first floated by the high priest of individualism and natural rights: Jean-Jacques Rousseau (1712-78). "The second paragraph of his [Rousseau's] last and most influential book, *The Confessions* (published 1781-88), contains a statement which might well serve as the battle-cry of the entire Romantic Movement [not only of France, but also of all other countries]: 'I am not made like anyone I have seen; I dare believe that I am not made like anyone in existence. If I am not better, at least I am different'" (Brown, 390). However, the Romantic movements in Germany, France and England show at least one common and fundamental feature: the Romantics' reactionary attitude against the traditions. Of course the reactions in the different countries had chosen different arenas of human thoughts and activities: in Germany, the reaction was directed primarily against the predominating idealist Hegelian philosophy; in France, against the tradition of bourgeois politics; and in England, against the establishment of the neo-classical literature.

The Romantic movements of Germany, France and England got appui from two not-easily-recognisable sources: one, the medieval romantic love-story of Abelard and Heloise (or Heloisa); and two, the reactionary and anti-traditional writings of Marquis de Sada. Peter Abelard (1079-1142) was a brilliant scholastic philosopher of France, who fell head long in love with his pupil Heloise, and was condemned for that, and banished, Heloise soon after becoming a nun. But even though they could not meet with each other ever after, the fires of their loves burnt high till their deaths. In his *Historia calamitatum*, Abelard had frankly, candidly and unabashedly told, in polished Latin, of his love of Heloise. This story for long remained dormant, but just before the wind of the Romantic movement was gathering, Abelard's *Historia calamitatum* was translated into various languages, and thus the 'apostatic' love-story of Abelard and Heloise spread over the whole of Europe and England, like wildfire. Their love was illegitimate but profoundly deep, and this profound love influenced the peoples so much so that they began to question the point of the illegitimacy of such pure and profound love. They began to question, moreover, whether reason or tradition should be predominant over the desire of the heart, or the other way round. And they chose the verdict of the heart over that of the head, and this is what the Romantics wanted to say. In this way, the love of Abelard and Heloise created a ripple in the torpid and prejudice-ridden medieval hangover in the consciousness of the peoples, and prepared it for the reception of the wind of the Romantic movement.

Marquis de Sade (1740-1814) was a homosexual and cruel aristocratic novelist of France. His novels, such as *Justine ou les malheurs de la Vertu* (1791), *La philosophie dans le boudoir* (1795) and *La Nouvells Justine* (1797) preached hedonistic moral nihilism, which hit hard at the roots of the prevalent religious dogma of the pre-Romantic era. Geoffrey Gorer writes about the influence of Marquis de Sade on some great Romantic writers: "De Sade's influence on the literature of Europe since his death has bean considerable. Sainte Beuve, who was a canny critic, bracketed him with Byron as one of the twin inspirations of 'modern' writers. His influence was obvious and openly confessed in the cases of Flaubert, Baudlaire, Swinburne, Dostoevski, and Lautreamont. Today his most open disciples (though they completely caricature him) are French surrealists, with their rather impotent desire for violence, both intellectual and physical" (Gorer, 81). Sade's main thesis in all his writings was that evil was constitutional in human nature, and this opinion we also find in some of the poets of the Romantic period. Coleridge, for instance, did not differentiate between good and evil, and thought that evil was just a distortion of good. "Coleridge 'had evolved a system of good and evil by which evil was the basis of good, which had become separated from its true functioning and now existed autonomously'(...). With such a philosophy of good and evil Coleridge once supported the violence of the people of France against the monarchical tyranny during the French Revolution" (Sarker, 2001, 379-80).

The Romantics were attracted by two divergent things, all at the same time; or, rather, they were attracted the more by that beauty which was fearful. Now, if the equation between beauty and goodness, and that between fear and evil are admitted of, then Coleridge was justified in saying that there was no divide between good and evil. Further, Coleridge said that evil was more fundamental in human nature than good (in recent times, Golding, in his novel *The Flies*, wanted to prove the same thing), and in this regard his philosophy is no different from Sade's. However, as we have said, the Romantics were attracted by fearful beauty, like that of Medusa. Shelley and Goethe were particularly drawn by the fearful beauty or 'tainted beauty,' like that of Medusa. In her book *The Romantic Agony*, Mario Praz writes about Shelley's attraction towards Medusa: "No picture made a deeper impression on the mind of Shelley than the Medusa, at one time attributed to Leonardo (and now to an unknown Flemish artist), which he saw in the Uffizi Gallery towards the end of 1819" (Praz, 25). Shelley composed a poem, *On the Medusa of Leonardo da Vinci,* which, according to Mario Praz, may be considered as "a manifesto of the conception of Beauty peculiar to the Romantics" (Praz, 25). The first eight lines of the poem may be quoted below, to show Shelley's attraction towards the 'tainted beauty':

> It lieth, gazing on the midnight sky,
> Upon the cloudy mountain peak supine;
> Below, far lands are seen tremblingly;
> Its horror and its beauty are divine.
> Upon its lips and eyelids seems to lie
> Loveliness like a shadow, from which shine,
> Fiery and lurid, struggling underneath,
> The agonies of anguish and of death.

The attraction of the 'tainted beauty' is discernible in Keats' poem *La Belle Dame Sans Merci* (in stanzas IV and X):

IV

I met a lady in the meads
        Full beautiful, a faery's child;
Her hair was long, her foot was light,
        And her eyes were wild.

X

I saw pale kings, and princes too,
        Pale warriors, death-pale were they all;
Who cry'd—"La belle Dame sans merci"
        Hath thee in thrall.

In Blake's tiger also there are both beauty and fear. In *The Tyger,* Blake writes: "Tyger! Tyger! burning bright /In the forests of the night. /What immortal hand or eye /Could frame thy fearful symmetry?" The 'fearful symmetry' is Blake's 'tainted beauty.'

In Wordsworth also—howsoever spiritualist and moralist he may have been—we find the same pull towards the 'tainted beauty'. In BK III (lines 129-37) of *The Prelude,* Wordsworth tells us that he saw both beauty and terror in nature:

                                I saw them feel,
Or linked them to some feeling: the great mass
Lay bedded in a quickening soul, and all
That I beheld respired with inward meaning.
Add that whate'er of Terror or of Love
Or Beauty, Nature's daily face put on
From transitory passion, unto this
I was as sensitive as waters are
To the sky's influence;...

In *Laodamia* also Wordsworth speaks of terror (or fear) and joy (because of beauty). When Laodamia's prayer was granted by Jove, her dead husband Protesilaus appeared before her, in carnation. Seeing her husband, Laodamia became both joyous and terrified. The poet, while narrating the incident, ejaculates: "O terror! What hath she perceived?—O joy!"

Why the Romantics were inordinately drawn towards the grotesque 'tainted beauty' we do not know, but the depth-psychoanalist Carl Gustav Jung may shed some light on the issue. In his essay '"Ulysses": A Monologue,' Jung writes: "The distortion of beauty and meaning by grotesque objectivity or equally grotesque irreality is, in the insane, a consequence of the destruction of the personality; in the artist it has a creative purpose. Far from his work being an expression of the destruction of his personality, the modern artist finds the unity of his artistic personality in destructiveness" (Jung, 117-18). From what we have just now heard from Jung, it is not clear why the Romantics, particularly, were attracted by the 'tainted beauty,' but from this at least it is understandable that sometimes artists may be attracted by grotesqueness for just artistic reasons, and that propensity towards grotesqueness, histrionic passions, etc. is not quite incongruent to sanity. Michel Foucault, in his *Madness and Civilization*, writes: "The madness of desire, insane murders, the most unreasonable passions—all are wisdom and reason, since they are part of the order of nature" (Foucault, 226).

Secondly, the Romantics showed an overbalance of passion over against reason. This was perhaps due to their reaction against the neo-classicists' overbalance of reason over against passion. The Romantic poets protested against the predominance of control, restraint and measure of the neo-classical poetry. They spurned away Dryden's dictum of 'propriety of thoughts and words,' or Pope's insistence that "Good nature and good sense must ever join" (*An Essay on Criticism*) as something too much. In his *An Essay on Criticism*, Pope advised the budding writers to always remain vigilant about restraint on passions in poetry:

> 'Tis more to guide, than spur the Muse's steed;
> Restrain his fury, than provoke his speeds:
> The winged courser, like a generous horse,
> Shows most true mettle when you check his course.
> Those rules of old discover'd, not devised,
> Are Nature still, but Nature methodised:
> Nature, like liberty, is but restrain'd
> By the same laws which first herself ordain'd.

Contrarily, the Romantic poets believed in the necessity of giving full vent to passion and emotion, and so they jettisoned the neo-classicists' advice on restraint.

Thirdly, the Romantics, generally, were devoted lovers of nature. They got their poetic inspiration or revivifying energy from nature, or they got their lacerated hearts soothed under the shade of nature. It was, as if, the Anglo-Saxons' love of nature came back to the Romantics. The Romantics were fond of describing the beauty of nature. Take, for instance, the following lines from Keats' *Sleep and Nature*:

> Of a swan's neck that stirs unseen among the rushes:
> A linnet starting all about the bushes:
> A butterfly, with golden wings broad parted,
> Nestling a rose, convuls'd as though it smarted
> With over pleasure—

Or, else, take another instance from Wordsworth's *Tintern Abbey*:

> Here, under this sycamore, and view
> These plots of cottage-ground, these orchard-tufts,
> Which at this season, with their unripe fruits,
> Are clad in one green hue, and lose themselves
> 'Mid grooves and copses. Once again I see
> These hedge-rows, hardy hedge-rows, little lines
> Of sportive wood run wild: these pastoral farms,
> Green to the very door; and wreaths of smoke
> Sent up, in silence, from among the trees!

Among the Romantics, it was Wordsworth who was the most attracted by the beauty of nature. Wordsworth did see not only beauty in nature, but also a 'presence,' which was some sort of spiritual being. Or, to him the whole of nature was spiritual, and also personal. On occasions, he also treated nature as a sort of teacher—moral teacher. It was the Romantics' fascination for the beauty and quietude of nature that they nursed a hatred in their hearts for the busy, materialistic, and cacophonous city. They believed that man had become artificial and corrupted to the extent to which they removed themselves from the ambience of nature. Wordsworth was the foremost lover of, nay worshipper of, nature, to whom nature was his teacher and source of inspiration and wisdom. He confessed that he grew up to be a poet, being informed by the beauty and terror of nature, and that he received moral teaching from nature. In *The Tables Turned*, he tells his studious friend that he (his friend) can learn from nature more about human character and morality than he can from his books:

> One impulse from vernal wood

May teach you more of man,
Of moral, evil and of good,
Than all the sages can.

The Romantics did not see nature like ordinary grown-ups do, but they saw nature with the eyes of a child—with eyes full of wonder and imagination, with eyes that can perceive not only what is presented before them, but also what the mind 'half creates'. It was for this reason that the child occupied a place of prominence in the Romantic age. René Wellek and Austin Warren write: "The Romantic movement exalted the child for his unjaded, fresh perception. Matisse laboured to learn to paint as a five-year-old sees" (Wellek and Warren, 242). But, we repeat, to the Romantics, nature was not only beautiful and soothing, and wise and sympathetic, she was also harsh and terrifying, or, in other words, nature was a 'tainted beauty.'

Fourthly, the Romantics felt nostalgic for the bygone medieval age, or felt an urge to return to the past—to some unidentified and unidentifiable time in the past—or to some distant country, or to some imaginary utopia—away, far away, from this hard and insensate world, obviously because they could not adjust themselves with the world in which they walked. In some cases of the Romantics, Greece or Italy was their model habitation, not the modern Greece or Italy, but those of yore, and yet they deemed even the modern Greece or Italy as their surrogate mecca, and zealously visited those countries. The Romantics, we may therefore conclude, sufferred from some sort of mental regression. Keats' *The Eve of St. Agnes*, for instance, brings us back to the spirit as well as to the condition of the medieval age:

A casement high and triple-arch'd there was,
All garlanded with carven imag'ries
Of fruits, and flowers, and bunches of knot-grass,
And diamonded with panes of quaint device,
Innumerable of stains and splendid dyes,
As are the tiger-moth's deep-damask'd wings;
And in the midst, 'mong thousand heraldries,
And twilight saints, and dim emblazonings,
A shielded scutcheon blush'd with blood of queens and kings.

In Coleridge's *Christabel,* Sir Leoline and Lord Roland remind us of the knights of the medieval age. The Romantic poets did not only use medieval themes, prejudices and images, but also used arcane words and phrases, with a view to conjuring up the medieval atmosphere in their poems. In Coleridge's *The Rime of the Ancient Mariner,* for instance, we find such arcane or obsolete words as 'kirk' (lines 23, 605), 'wist' (lines 152, 153), 'clomb' (line 209), 'countree' (line 518), 'trowl' (line 524), etc.

Fifthly, the Romantics protested against the artificiality and mechanicalness of the life of the nascent industrialized city. They, as we have said, failed to adjust themselves with the changed condition of life. Due to rapid industrialisation, which was a sequel to the spurt of scientific discoveries, cities grew up in England like mushroom, and the people of villages deserted their traditional family moorings and made a bee line to the cities, with a view to improving their lots. Consequently, the big family clusters broke into splinter skeleton families, scattered all around, as a result of which the traditional ties of affection of the big families, mores and manners, and ethos fizzled out in a short course of time. In the next phase of the societal change, even the skeleton families broke down, to some extent and in many cases, when the father and the mother had to attend duties at different work places, depositing their children in crechés. Thus the concepts of the sweet home and family affection as well as public sympathies went into the limbo. Men became work forces, and money became the only object of human endeavour. People forgot to love nature and to be affected by passion. This was the fall-out of the rapid industrialization of the country, which is reflected in the protesting attitude of the Romantic poetry. The Romantics pined for the lost pastoral life, and for the verdure and breeze and running rivulets, and for the life of the abandon. They could not bear with the din and bustle of the life of the city, and with the hurry and palpitation of the heart—of the life of the city about which Matthew Arnold in *The Scholar Gypsy* writes:

this strange disease of modern life,
With its sick hurry, its divided aims,
Its heads o'ertax'd, its palsied hearts,....

The Romantics deemed the city to be a pent-house which they wanted to escape from. In the beginning lines of *The Prelude,*

Wordsworth expresses relief from the crucible of the city, and his maddening joy in breezy openness of the country when he writes:

> Oh there is blessing in this gentle breeze,
> A visitant that while it fans my cheek
> Doth seem half-conscious of the joy it brings
> From the green fields, and from yon azure sky.

Nevertheless what the Romantics actually pined for we do not know, nor did they; that is, we do not know what might have soothed them of their agony, but we know what aggravated their agony, their heart burning. They did not like anything existing and contemporary, or anything proximate: they had been gazing at the farthest points of time and space, albeit not knowing the nature of those two points. Coleridge felt to be insulated from the world: "Alone, alone, all, all alone,/Alone on a wide wide sea!/And 0newer a saint took pity on/My soul in agony" (*The Rime of the Ancient Mariner*). Keats found this world as man's doomed place for groanings:

> Here, where men sit and hear each other groan;
> Where palsy shakes a few, sad, last gray hairs,
> Where youth grows pale, and spectre-thin, and dies;
> Where but to think is to be full of sorrow
> And leaden-eyed despairs.
> Where Beauty cannot keep her lustrous eyes,
> Or new Love pine at them beyond tomorrow.
>
> (*Ode to a Nightingale*)

To Keats, life was so unbearable that he wished to die: "To cease upon the midnight with no pains" (*Ode to a Nightingale*). Shelley sufferred much, like Keats, but he did not wish to die like him, but only to be transported elsewhere far, far away from this earth: "Oh! lift me as a wave, a leaf, a cloud!/ I fall upon the thorns of life! I bleed!" (*Ode to the West Wind*). Byron was not morose like them, and yet he was averse to his contemporary social and political systems: "I have simplified my politics to an utter detestation of all existing governments." In Wordsworth also we find this uneasiness, dissatisfaction, despair, and even agony. He despairs that man, in the true sense of the word 'man,' is to be found only one in ten thousands: "Why is this glorious creature to be found/ Only one in ten thousand?" (*The*

Prelude, XIII. 87-88). And he remonstrates that in the city of London, nobody knows anybody: "'The face of every one/ That passes by me is a mystery!" (*The Prelude*, VII. 628-29). And he is depressed because to him the people of London, are, as if, beings of another world, full of hatred for him:

> And, on the shape of that unmoving man,
> His steadfast face and sightless eyes, I gazed,
> As if admonished from another world.
>
> (*The Prelude*, VII. 647-49)

Sixthly, the Romantics were individualists. As we have said, due to the rapid industrialization, the traditional bond between man and man, and that between man and society, broke down, as a natural consequence of which the individual found himself virtually as an insulated being, found himself lonely in a huge crowd. And man, willy-nilly, accepted this his forlorn state as a *fait accompli*. And this alternative state of his gave birth to man's new *Weltanschauung* and new attitude toward life, both of which are reflected in Romantic poetry. The individual, who was so long a part of the society, who so long leaned against the rock of the society, now stood straight on his feet—the individual man became individualist. He began to perceive and feel and think according to his own idiosyncrasies. He over-compensated his loss of the society by declaring himself free, independent, and by subordinating the society under himself. This is obvious in Rousseau's contract theory of society, according to which a number of free and independent individuals formed the society or the state by voluntarily parting with a portion of their natural rights. The Romantics were averse to the institution of society, and to the institution of state, particularly of monarchical state, and also to the sanctions of society and state, thinking that both society and state were *outre*, without having any right to curb the freedom of individuals. It was due to this that they were ardent supporters of the French Revolution, and of the Revolution's three cardinal demands: liberty, equality and fraternity. However, in any case, they could not accept the society and the state in which they lived. And they wanted either to destroy the society and the state, or to escape from them. Thus Byron was an extreme individualist, Shelley was an anarchist, Blake and Coleridge ensconced themselves in the regions of imagination, Keats lonely heard the music of the other world, and Wordsworth soothed his heart, lacerated by the 'slings and arrows' of the society with the balm of nature.

Seventhly, as the Romantics could not find in their contemporary society the human community of their hearts' desire, they escaped into the world of imagination. Imagination has always been a force or energy behind any creative work, but in the Romantic period it was the most predominant in the poets. When they rejected the real world, they had no other alternative but to create another world with the help of their imagination. A very concrete instance of this is Coleridge's plan of building a Utopian communist society, the Pantisocracy, on the strand of Sesquihanna in America, but this was only an instance of how their imagination worked in the political sphere. In the sphere of imagination, they wanted to build an halcyonic castle in the air, and pined for such a castle. Imagination is galore in Romantic poetry—imagination coloured with passion, violence and self-torture.

Eighthly, and lastly, the Romantics had almost a pathologic inwardness. In spite of their ebulient emotion, in spite of their frettings against the world, they were not bold enough to bully their objects of hatred. They rather directed their ire inwards to sizzle their own selves. In this regard they were all, so to say, masochistic, with the perhaps the single exception of Byron. The Browningian objectivity or other-directedness, and optimism were conspicuously absent in them. They could never say like Browning, having beside him, for the last moment, his beloved who is doomed to be lost to him: "So, one day more am I defied./Who knows but the world may end to-night?" They rather moaned, like Shelley: "I fall upon the thorns of life! I bleed!" Among all these cardinal characteristics of Romanticism, we also must include an overbalance of the passion of love, against the control of reason, and this love is not always cribbed within a couple, but is so large that it sometimes encompasses the whole of the creation.

II

Now the question is: in which sense of the Romantic poet is Wordsworth one; or for which particular features of a Romantic poet, should we identify him as a Romantic poet? It is not to be expected that all the features of the Romantic poetry, collectively, will be found in each one of the Romantic poets—and so in Wordsworth. But it is not actually or essentially the features of the Romantic poetry that determine if a poet is to be called a Romantic poet or no; it is rather a poet's attitude that identifies him as a Romantic poet, or otherwise. But what is that essential attitude of the Romantic poet? It is the attitude of revolting against the prevailing poetic tradition, as well as to the prevailing conceptions of man, life, nature and the world. T.S. Eliot himself raises the question, though implicitly: why was Wordsworth's verse novel an anti-tradition? And Eliot answers the question thus: "It is Wordsworth's social interest that inspires his own novelty of form in verse, and backs up his explicit remarks upon poetic diction" (Eliot, 74). To see the truth of Eliot's comment we may turn to *The Prelude* where Wordsworth has given vent to his despair at the prevailing inequality and corruptions and immorality of the society, and expresses his wish to see a republican society where all men will be equal, and nobody will be a master over others. In Bk IX (Residence in France) of *The Prelude* (lines 344-54), Wordsworth writes:

> the miseries
> Of royal courts, and that voluptuous life
> Unfeeling, where the man who is of soul
> The meanest thrives the most; where dignity,
> The personal dignity, abideth not;
> A light, a cruel, and vain world cut off
> From the natural inlets of just sentiment,
> From lowly sympathy and chastening truth:
> Where good and evil interchange their names,
> And thirst for bloody spoils abroad is paired
> With vice at home.

Wordsworth wanted to get out of this rubbish, and so he imagined an ideal Republican society where all will be equal. In the same book of *The Prelude* (lines 226-32) he speaks of such a Republican society or state:

> Of a Republic, where all stood thus far
> Upon equal ground; that we were brothers all
> In honour, as in one community,
> Scholars and gentlemen; where, furthermore,
> Distinction open lay to all that came,

And wealth and titles were in less esteem
Than talents, worth, and prosperous industry.

This egalitarian view influenced his verse in many of its aspects or contents: diction of the common man, common themes, moralising, etc. And thus his egalitarian view gave novelty to his verse.

Early in his life, Wordsworth was passionately attracted by the three crying demands of the French revolutionists: liberty, equality and fraternity. He thought that the traditional conservative philosophy and its practice destroyed the humaneness of humanity, and so he protested against it, and also against the literary form and style through which the neo-classicists wanted to preserve that sort of philosophy. Wordsworth despised the artificial and passionless poetry of the neo-classical age, particularly the poetry of Pope and Dryden, In his *Essay Supplementary to the Preface* (1815), Wordsworth writes about Pope's and Dryden's poetry: "Dryden's lines are vague, bombastic and senseless; those of Pope, though he had Homer to guide him, are throughout false and contradictory." But the strongest objection of Wordsworth against Dryden's and Pope's poetry is that it is not suffused with passion, and Wordsworth raises this objection because "Poetry is the breath and finer spirit of all knowledge; it is the impassioned expression which is in the countenance of all Science" (*Preface to the Lyrical Ballads*, 1802). Wordsworth's poetry is passionate and emotional, based on strong feelings. He says that "Poetry is the spontaneous overflow of powerful feelings: it takes its origin from emotion recollected in tranquillity" (*Preface to the Lyrical Ballads*, 1802). Again, he says that "The end of Poetry is to produce excitement" (*Preface to the Lyrical Ballads*; 1802). Now, these things—feeling, emotion, passion and excitement—or, rather, an overbalance of all these, in poetry, is not to be found in the neo-classical era; and, further, all these things, in overdoses, have made Wordsworth's poetry romantic. And coupled with all these, to make his poetry more romantically coloured, was his revolutionary zeal: his violent sympathy with the disfavourably unequal; his cry for liberty; and his love of fraternity, of fellow-feeling—all that he learnt from the French Revolution.

This revolutionary zeal of his he directed towards divers things of poetry. First the medium—the language, or the diction.

In the neo-classical age, and even in the ages preceding that, poets, particularly thought that poetry, whose principal objective is to artificially create emotion, needed a special language or diction, and not that of the everyday commerce. According to them, the language of the common man (or the natural man of the country side, as Wordsworth would like to say) was not the appropriate language of poetry, whose business was to deal with elevated things. Dryden, for instance, strived throughout his poetic life to improve the language of poetry, its diction, syntax, and style, so that, as he thought, the improved language could work appropriately to help express the elevated thoughts of the poet. Wordsworth revolted. He said that any sort of elevated thoughts could be expressed—and that with all appropriateness and efficiency—through the language of the common or natural men in the natural environment. In fact, Wordsworth's whole poetic life was dedicated mostly to the endeavour of demonstrating the veracity of this assertion of his. The so-called theory of poetic diction went even farther than saying that the language of poetry must be an elevated language, and held that there was an unbridgeable divide between the language of poetry and that of prose. But Wordsworth rejected the theory of poetic diction, and believed that there was no difference between the language of poetry and that of prose, and that we employ metre in poetry, adventiously, only to enhance the pleasure of reciting poetry. Here we find Wordsworth as a revolutionary in the field of language.

The Romantics showed a great love of nature: Keats, Shelley, Byron and even the philosophical Coleridge were enchanted by the beauty of nature, and stuffed their poetry, whenever they found the opportunity, with keen, close and vivid descriptions of the beauty of nature. But Wordsworth superseded them all in his enthusiasm for the beauty of nature. Keats was more attracted by mild moonlight or the darkness of the thick forest; Shelley was more attracted by fast-moving clouds and violent winds; Byron admired the vastness of nature; and Coleridge peculiarly loved the bizarre beauty that nature sometimes wears. But Wordsworth loved the most the beauty of the mountains—so much so that sometimes he is awarded the appellation 'mountain poet.' No poet, before him, or even after him has showed so much of love for, and devotion to, nature. He was so much in love with nature that there is hardly any poem of his where he tells of something without a mention of the beauty of nature, or of nature's soothing comfort, or of nature's wisdom. In his two longest poems, *The Prelude* and *The Excursion,* though the former is an autobiographical poem and the latter a philosophical poem, Wordsworth has expatiated so much on nature that, on the count of the fingertips, we may say that about half of the verses of the two poems deals with descriptions of nature. His nature did not comprise only the flora, but also a spiritual being; or, rather, to him nature was the manifestation of a spiritual being. Nature was to him the nurse, the teacher, and the only deity. Even since his young days, Wordsworth was very much attracted by the beauty of nature, as may be apparent in his two early compositions: *An Evening* Walk (composed 1787-9) and *Descriptive Sketches* (composed 1791-2). The 446 lines of *An Evening Walk* are, in effect, nothing but a filigree of divers beautiful facets of nature. It begins with a description of nature and ends with another, the middle of it being no different from the beginning or the ending. Wordsworth dedicated *Descriptive Sketches* to the Rev. Robert Jones, Fellow of St. John's College, Cambridge. In the Dedication what he writes for Jones may give us an insinuation to the content of the whole poem: "You will meet with few images without recollecting the spot where we observed them together,...."

In his love of nature, Wordsworth was, as we have told, immensely influenced by Rousseau. Rousseau believed in the authenticity of the ideal of the 'noble savage', and Wordsworth accepted the language of the common man in the natural environment—*i.e.* the language of Rousseau's 'noble savage'—as the medium of his poetry. True, Rousseau did not believe in the presence of some spiritual being in nature, but he believed that man's learning should begin with nature as his first teacher; and Wordsworth held that nature is the principal instructor in guiding man in his moral learning. In America, Wordsworth had two contemporaries—Ralph Waldo Emerson (1803-82) and Henry David Thoreau (1817-62)—who were also naturalists like him. But while Emerson believed in 'transcendental unity of man and nature,' Wordsworth believed in the affinity between man and nature, but not in transcendentalism. Thoreau was no different from Emerson—due to his taking the latter as his model—and so was different from Wordsworth. Of course all the three were ardent lovers of nature, yet Wordsworth was quite different from the other two, particularly because, unlike the other two, he was romantically attracted to nature. Nevertheless, some core images are common between Emerson and Wordsworth. F.O. Matthiessen writes that Emerson "saw himself, in a recurrent image, standing on the bank of a river watching the endless current upon which floated past him objects of all shapes and colours. He did not know whence they came and where they went, and he could not detain them as they passed, except by running beside them a little way along the bank. Similar images were the special signatures of nineteenth-century poets. Wordsworth felt that he escaped from uncertainty and understood the purpose of his own life by thus watching a river flow to the sea" (Matthiessen, 69). And it was for this reason that Wordsworth held nature to be his philosophical guide.

Wordsworth's claim to be counted as a Romantic poet (of course he never made such a claim) lies in his laying the most emphasis on the faculty of imagination. In fact, all the Romantics were highly imaginative persons, and believed that poetry depended not so much on anything as on imagination, but no other Romantics was as emphatic, in this their belief, as Wordsworth and Shelley. "Shelley wrote: 'The distinction between poets and prose-writers is a vulgar error,' and for him Plato, Bacon, and Rousseau are poets, for their appeal primarily is to the imagination" (Allen, 224). This we learn from Shelley's essay *A Defence of Poetry*. In the same essay, Shelley further writes: "Poetry, in a general sense, may be defined to be 'the expression of the imagination'." But Wordsworth went further than Shelley in emphasizing the importance of imagination. In his *Essay Supplementary to the Preface* (1815), he says that imagination "is perhaps the noblest of our nature." In poetry, Wordsworth has found the corporate functions of two most potent properties of the human soul: imagination and sentiment. But what role will imagination play in the creation of poetry? In the same essay of his, Wordsworth says that imagination will transform our surrounding objects as to enhance our pleasures and enjoyments of those objects, because those objects are less pleasurable and enjoyable than when they are coloured by our imagination. In the essay, he writes: "*The appropriate business of poetry* (which, nevertheless, is as permanent as pure science), *her appropriate employment, her privilege and her duty, is to treat of things not as they are, but as they appear, not as they exist in themselves, but as they seem to exist to the senses, and to the passions."* Things must *'seem', i.e.* they must be transformed or coloured by imagination, and only then they may be poetic. To demonstrate the immense power of imagination in transforming or colouring common objects and making them look poetic was the main objective of the poems of *Lyrical Ballads*. Objects may be transformed in a twofold way: the unfamiliar (rather, bizarre or fantastic) objects may be so transformed that they will seem to be familiar; and the familiar objects may be so transformed that they will seem to be unfamiliar. In his poems in *Lyrical Ballads,* Coleridge demonstrated the power of imagination in colouring the unfamiliar so that it looks familiar, as in his poems in the same volume Wordsworth demonstrated the power of imagination in colouring the familiar so that it looks unfamiliar. The plan of demonstrating this twofold power of imagination was all Wordsworth's. Subjectivism is yet another cardinal feature of Romantic poetry, and Wordsworth's poetry is unadulteratedly subjective. Subjectivism points to inwardness; escape from reality and into imagination, and in some cases into mysticism; and also lyricism; and all these are, as if, patented components of Wordsworth's poetry. When Wordsworth describes a particular spot of nature, he does so only to express his wish or his internal passion or feeling. It is not so much the external world that influences his mind as his mental state influences the external world: the poet, as if, looks at the external world through the prism of his own soul. Coleridge, in *Dejection: An Ode,* says that the beauty that we find in nature is but the projection of our imagination upon the aesthetically neutral nature: "O Lady! we receive but what we give,/And in our life alone does Nature live:/Ours is her wedding garment, ours her shroud!" Here we find Coleridge's realization of the inwardness of aesthetic experience. Whether Wordsworth too realized this we do not know, but his poetry amply demonstrates that he saw in nature or in the world only what he wanted to see. And he himself said that in poetry we do not wish to see things as they are but as they are transmogrified by our imagination.

Extreme subjectivism has led Wordsworth to a mystic attitude to life. Mysticism results out of the logical irreconcilability of the inner world of the soul and the outer world. It is for this reason that most of the Romantic poets tended towards mysticism. Keats and Shelley were other-worldly: they wanted to fly away from this every day world. But Wordsworth hesitated, wavered, vacillated. In *To a Skylark*, he is attracted by the skylark's "privacy of glorious light", but, as Keats wants to fly away on the mysterious nightingale, he does not wish to fly away with the skylark: instead, he wants to remain within the mysterious circle of imagination and reality, of subjectivity and objectivity within the overlapping circles of "Heaven and Home." This mysticism had convinced him of the presence in nature, or in the whole of the creation, of some spiritual berng. The subjectivism of Wordsworth's poetry has naturally made his verses lyrical. All his poems, except a very few, are but outpourings of his inner experiences, feelings and passions; and this is why his poetic statements, in most of his poems, are rolling, ceaseless, elaborate and periodic. He begins a statement and then goes on qualifying it, tirelessly, rhetorically. His verses are also musically delightful, like the verses of the other Romantic poets, and this love of the musicality in the verse he got from Edmund Spenser (1552?-99). However, all these are the principal characteristics of Wordsworth, as a poet, for which he is bracketed with the other great Romantic poets.

Nevertheless, as the meaning of the term 'Romantic' is admittedly nebulous, we may, after we have thus far considered Wordsworth as a romantic poet, once again raise the question: is Wordsworth a Romantic poet, and if he is, in which sense of the word 'Romantic,' is he exactly a Romantic poet? Herbert Read, in his *The True Voice of Feeling*, answers this question in a tricky and sly manner: "If to steal away and mingle with the Universe is a romantic proceeding, then Byron is the Romantic, and Wordsworth and Coleridge, who were always careful to keep logical distinctions between man and nature, were classical. But if to write a verse of (this) ease and suavity is to be classical, then Byron was classical, and the poets of *Kubla Khan* and *Michael* were romantic experimentalists, obsessed with some notion of a correspondency between form and feeling. There is more essential discipline in one of Wordsworth's sonnets [...]

than in the whole of Byron's work" (Read, 310). Now, in any case, even if we say that Wordsworth is really a Romantic poet, even then we should get this our opinion qualified with a rider. Wordsworth wrote two distinct types or classes of poems, which J.K. Stephen calls the two voices of the poet—the first voice and the second voice. The first voice can be heard in his subjective, sublime and escapist poems, such as *Intimations Ode, Tintern Abbey, The Simplon Pass* and *Ode to Duty;* and the second voice is audible in his naive, matter-of-fact, and almost crude poems, such as *The Daffodils* (or 'I wandered lonely as a cloud'), *The Tables Turned* and *Peter Bell.* The poems of the first voice are certainly Romantic in inspiration, and the poems of the second voice are Augustan in quality. F.W. Bateson calls the second voice bad voice, and the first voice good voice. Bateson writes: "The Two Voices, then, would seem to be Wordsworth's earlier manner [of writing poetry] and his later manner. The bad Voice is the poetry written up to July, 1798 (the date of 'Tintern Abbey'), the good Voice is the poetry written after that date." (Bateson, 8). This also means that, according to F.W. Bateson, if Wordsworth is a Romantic poet, he is so since July, 1798, before which date, he had been an Augustan poet. Such a change in a poet's sensibilities and feelings and emotions as in his manner of writing poetry is not outlandish and eerie, for we know, for instance, that the early W.B. Yeats was a Romantic poet (cf. his *The Stolan Child*) while the later Yeats was verily a modern poet par excellence.

6

Wordsworth's Theory of Poetry

In this chapter we will, very briefly, discuss what Wordsworth's thoughts about the poet and about poetry, and also about some subsidiary but relevant matters. We will discuss about the poet's opinion about poetry, keeping ourselves mostly confined within the limits of three principal questions about poetry: the subject-matter of poetry, the diction of verse, and the function of imagination in the creation of poetry. Wordsworth has indicated his opinions about these three matters of poetry in his three great essays: *Preface to Lyrical Ballads* (1802), *Appendix on Poetic Diction* (1802), and *Essay Supplementary to the Preface* (to *Lyrical Ballads* of 1802) (1815). We will first give a patient hearing to what Wordworth has to say about the above-mentioned three critical questions about poetry, in his three above-mentioned essays, and then we will enter into a general consideration of Wordsworth's opinions regarding them.

I

(*Preface to Lyrical Ballads*)

Let us begin with the *Preface* of 1802 which Wordsworth felt to be necessary to justify the new genre of poetry that he and Coleridge were going to float through *Lyrical Ballads*. In the *Preface*, Wordsworth says that the prime objective of the poet should be to gratify some of our habits of association. According to him, poetry deals with incidents and situations, that are pleasurable, and that are connected with one another by "the primary laws of our nature: Chiefly, as far as regards the manner in which we associate ideas in a state of excitement." (*Preface*) This is how poetry works upon our consciousness. But what is poetry, and how does it originate in the consciousness of the poet? Wordsworth answers: "I have said that poetry is the spontaneous overflow of powerful feelings: it takes its origin from emotion recollected in tranquillity: the emotion is contemplated till, by a species of reaction, the tranquillity gradually disappears and an emotion, kindred to that which was before the subject of contemplation, is gradually produced, and does itself actually exist in the mind. In this mood successful composition generally begins..." (*Preface*). (We may, incidentally, note here that Wordsworth does not seem to distinguish between the connotations of the two words, 'feeling' and 'emotion,' and uses the two terms interchangeably.) This point of argument of Wordsworth is psychologically admissible. The rose is attractive, because somehow we have been habituated to associate the rose with love. This habit of associating one sensation or feeling with another sensation or feeling, or with more than one sensations or feelings is the ground on which, according to Wordsworth, the spray of poetry blossoms. We know that in his early life, Wordsworth, like Coleridge, was immensely influenced by David Hartley's (and also by David Hume's) theory of association that if two stimuli are contiguous as to space or time, they tend to be so associated in our consciousness that if one of them is aroused at a later time, the other will also be automatically aroused thereby. However, Wordsworth further says that as our habit of associating sensations or feelings changes from age to age, the elements of our poetry will also concomitantly vary from one age to another.

Wordsworth, next, moves on to the point of the subject-matter of poetry. He tells us that in *Lyrical Ballads*, the subject-matters of the poems have been chosen from the humble and rustic life, and not from the too busy and artificial life of the city. The reasons he produces in favour of his novel selection are the following four (the *Preface*):

(i) "because in that condition, the essential passions of the heart find a better soil in which they can attain their maturity, are less under restraint, and speak a plainer and more emphatic language."

(ii) "because in that situation our elementary feelings exist in a state of greater simplicity and consequently may be more accurately contemplated and more forcibly communicated."

(iii) "because the manners of rural life germinate from those elementary feelings; and from the necessary character of rural occupations are more easily comprehended, and more durable;"

(iv) and, lastly, "because in that situation the passions of men are incorporated with the beautiful and permanent forms of nature."

Wordsworth wrote the *Preface* in 1798, and so the question necessarily arises: did he stick to his theory after that date? Barring the subject-matters of *The Prelude* (which is autobiographical; and *The Excursion* (which is philosophical), and also barring one or two rare poems of his—such as *Laodamia*—we may say that, as regards his theory of poetry, Wordsworth was parennially quite honest.

Regarding the medium (or language) of his poetry, Wordsworth says in the *Preface* that he chose the language of the rustic folk "because such men hourly communicate with the best objects from which the best part of language is originally derived; and because, from their rank in society and the sameness and narrow circle of their intercourse, being less under action of social vanity, they convey their feelings and notions in simple and unelaborated expressions." He says that the language of the rustic folk "arising out of repeated experience and regular feelings, is a more permanent, and for more philosophical language" (*Preface*) than the artificial language of the city, and so far more suitable for poetry, and for this reason throughout the whole of his poetic career, he employed the language of the rustic folk in his poetry.

Wordsworth says that poetry must have a 'purpose' (a purpose other than that of giving pleasure), though, he confesses, he never wrote poetry with "a distinct purpose formally conveived," because "all good poetry is the spontaneous overflow of powerful feelings." He came to realise this nature of poetry from his "habit of meditation" over the nature of poetry. But, then, poetry must have a purpose. What that purpose is Wordsworth has not expressed in the *Preface*, but since we know that he (as a poet) wanted to be a 'teacher, or nothing else,' and since he always urges us, through his poetry, to learn morality from nature, we may assume that, according to him, the purpose of poetry should be teaching morality—in the widest sense of the term. And, for the same reason, he says that poetry should give "importance to the action and situation, and not action and situation to the feeling" (*Preface*). It may be mentioned here that when Wordsworth speaks of purpose in poetry, he contradicts the concept of 'pure poetry.' "Pure poetry is a prescriptive rather than a descriptive term in that it designates, not an actual body of verse, but a theoratical ideal to which poetry may aspire. Any theory of poetry which seeks to isolate one or more properties as essential and proceeds to exclude materials considered to be non-essential may be classed as a doctrine of pure poetry. Interpreted in the widest sense, it could be applied to divergent points of view occurring within a broad historical range, such as Sidey's strictures on tragi-comedy and the 18th-c. idea of 'sublimity.' 'Most specifically, the term refers to 'La Poesie pure,' a doctrine derived from Edgar Allan Poe by the French symbolist poets, Baudlaire, Mallarme, and Yalery, and widely discussed in the late 19th and early 20th centuries. In this context, 'pure' is equivalent to absolute, on the analogy of absolute music. The analogy is significant in that both the theory and practice of the symbolists were influenced by the relations of poetry and music." (Preminger, 682). In his essay 'The Poetic Principle,' Poe writes: "But the simple fact is, that, would we but permit ourselves to look into our own souls, we should immediately there discover that under the sun there neither exists nor can exist any work more thoroughly dignified—more supremely noble than this very poem—this poem *per se*—this poem which is a poem and nothing more—this poem written for the poem's sake" (Poe, 890-91). In the same essay, Poe further writes: "... I would define, in brief, the Poetry of words as *The Rhythmical Creation of Beauty*. Its sole arbiter is Taste. With the Intellect or with Conscience, it has only collateral relations. Unless incidentally, it has no concern whatever either with Duty or with Truth" (Poe, 892).

However, according to Wordsworth, the poet must possess "more than usual organic sensibility," and must have "thought long and deeply" over the subject-matter of his poetry. He may perceive an object through more than one sense-organs, and may thus receive a variety of sensations, but those sensations must be integrated—they must not remain isolated from one another—and the integrated sensations must lead to a unitary feeling. When the unitary feeling will be achieved, only then shall we say that the sensations, out of which the unitary feeling will originate, are organic. Wordsworth says that the feelings of the poet must be "modified and directed by our thoughts which are indeed the representatives of all our past feelings," that is, the present feelings of the poet must be modified by his memory. Wordsworth says that our mind is not absolutely dependent on sensations, *i.e.*, the degree of the excitation of our mind does not always depend upon the degree of the strength or force of the sensations; rather, the mind is semi-independent of the sensations "For human mind is capable of being excited without the application of gross or violent stimulants," requiring sometimes only faint stimulations.

Wordsworth's theory of diction of poetic compositions is very novel. He says that in poetic compositions he prefers "to adopt the very language of men"—the language of the common or rustic folk—, because he wants "to keep the Reader in the company of flesh and blood" and "to bring my language near to the language of men," and also because "the pleasure which I have proposed to myself to impart, is of a kind very different from that which is supposed by many persons to be the proper object of poetry." Before going on any further to listen to what Wordsworth has to say about poetic diction, let us stop here to fully understand what Wordsworth implies by the above-mentioned phrases of his. Wordsworth wants, in poetry, "to adopt the very language of men." Here, by 'men', as we have already said, he means the common folk, the rustic people. He wants to do so because he wants "to keep the Reader in the company of flesh and blood." To him, the people of the city are mechanised, artificial, and so are devoid of "flesh and blood". On the contrary, he means to say, the rustic people are natural, have primal instincts uncorrupted and unmodified by the artificially created culture of the city, and so they are in "flesh and blood." Wordsworth prefers to employ, in his poetry, as far as possible, the ordinary and the supposedly unpoetic language of the common folk, *i.e.*, he wants "to bring my language near to the language of men"—men who are rustic or common. Thus far we have understood him perhaps quietly rightly. But why should the pleasure of Wordsworth's poetry, as he himself says, be very different from that of the poetry of other poets? Because, says Wordsworth, he is a poet of nature, and absolutely such, and because he wants to impart to the reader the knowledge of the spirituality of nature—the knowledge that will elevate and strengthen his being, and will enable him to enjoy the special kind of pleasure in the beauty of nature—and also because he will arouse the moral sense of the reader, through his poetry.

In the *Preface,* next, Wordsworth expresses his view about the supposed difference between the language of poetry and that of prose. He says that "There neither is, nor can be, any essential difference between the language of prose and metrical composition." He further writes about the fundamental link between poetry and prose: "We are fond of tracing the semblance between Poetry and Painting, and, accordingly, we call them Sisters: but where shall we find bond of connection sufficiently strict to typify the affinity betwixt metrical and prose composition? They both speak by and to the same organs; the bodies in which both of them are clothed may be said to be of the same substance, their affections are kindred, and almost identical, not necessarily differing even in degree; Poetry sheds no tears 'such as Angels weep,' but natural and human tears; she can boast of no celestial ichor that distinguishes her vital juices from those of prose; the same human blood circulates through the veins of them both." Wordsworth reinforces this statement of his by saying that some of the most excellent metrical compositions of such great poets as Milton "in no respect differ from that of good prose."

But, all the same, Wordsworth is of course well aware of the minimal difference between the language of poetry and that of prose, and it is for this reason that he has qualified his statement that there is no difference between the language of poetry and that of prose by incorporating in the statement the vital term 'essential'. There may be some difference between the language of poetry and that of prose, but the difference is not essential, and basic, but superficial, and minimal, and admitting the existence of this non-essential and superficial difference between the two sorts of languages, Wordsworth has this to say that though the poet should employ the language of the common folk, he should be selective, *i.e.*, he should utilise only the selected parts of the language of the common folk in metrical compositions. Wordsworth recommends "selection of the language really spoken by men."

But though Wordsworth does not notice any essential difference between the language of poetry and that of prose, and though he recommends to the poet the "language really spoken by men," curiously enough, he admits of the necessity of metre in poetry. The selectivity of the language of the common folk and the employment of metre, according to Wordsworth, will make the language of poetry a little bit different from that of prose. Only this much allowance did Wordsworth make in the supposed similitude between the language of poetry and that of prose. Though he recommends the use of metre in poetry, he says metre is not an essential element of poetry. But, then, if metre is not an essential element of poetry, why has wordsworth himself used it in his poetry? To this question he answers "that a very small part of the pleasure given by Poetry depends upon metre, and that it is injudicious to write in metre, unless it is accompained with the other artificial distinctions of style with which metre is usually accompanied, and that, by such deviation, more will be lost from the shock which will thereby be given to the Reader's associations than will be counterbalanced by any pleasure which he can derive from the general power of numbers." In the *Preface,* Wordsworth further writes that seriousness of subject-matters, delicacy of style, and regularity of metre, of poetry, are also not essential elements of it. To justify this opinion of his, he informs us that "poems are extant, written upon more humble subjects, and in a still more naked and simple style, which have continued to give pleasure from generation to generation." However, it should be noticed in the *Preface* that Wordsworth has not absolutely rejected the salubrious function of metre in poetry. He says that metre, in conjuction with rhyme, is congenial particularly to relatively more pathetic themes: "There can be little doubt but that more pathetic situations and sentiments, that is, those which have a greater proportion of pain connected with them, may be endured in metrical composition, especially in rhyme, than in prose." Wordsworth further admits that metre gives pleasure by showing "similitude in dissimilitude," as in "sexual appetite" that is so fundamental in human nature. Metre, Wordsworth confesses, certainly adds to the pleasure of poetry, and it is especially for the reason of the pleasure due to metre, says he, that "the verse will be read a hundred times where the prose is read once." But, Wordsworth cautions us, even if one writes poetry according as has been told above, the poetry may not be interesting to one and all, for, he writes in the *Preface*, "an *accurate* taste in poetry, and in all other arts, as Sir Joshua Reynolds has observed, is an *acquired* talent, which can only be produced by thought and long-continued intercourse with the best models of composition." We may, here, mention that Ralph Waldo Emerson also, like Wordsworth, did not give metre a place of prominence in poetry. According to him, "It is not metres, but a metre-making argument that makes a poem" (Emerson, 178). On the other hand, Edgar Allan Poe thinks that metre is certainly one of the constituent element of poetry in verse: "Verse originates in human enjoyment of equality, fitness. To this enjoyment, also, all the moods of verse—rhythm, metre, stanza, rhyme, alliteration, the *refrain*, and other analogous effects—are to be referred" (Poe, 911).

II

(*Appendix on Poetic Diction*)

In *Appendix on Poetic Diction*, Wordsworth expatiates on his views about the so-called poetic diction. He writes: "I am to give an exact notion of the sense in which the phrase poetic diction has been used." Earlier, in his *Preface* (to *Lyrical Ballads* of 1802), he expressed his views about poetic diction, but in *Appendix on Poetic Diction* he elaborates on, and clarifies his views on, poetic diction. In *Appendix*, he says that "The earliest poets of all nations generally wrote from passion excited by real events; they wrote naturally, and as men: feeling powerfully as they did; their language was daring, and figurative. In succeeding times, Poets, and men ambitious of the fame of Poets, perceiving the influence of such language, and desirous of producing the same effect without being animated by the same passion, set themselves to a mechanical adoption of these figures of speech, and made use of them, sometimes with propriety, but much more frequently applied them to feelings and thoughts with which they had no natural connection whatsoever. A language was thus insensibly produced, differing materially from the real language of men in any situation." According to Wordsworth, this is the reason of the birth of the so-called 'poetic diction.'

In the *Appendix*, Wordsworth repeats what earlier he said in the *Preface* that there is no essential difference between the language of poetry and that of prose, and that the poet should employ the language of the common man. But in the *Appendix* he admits that the language of poetry of the 'earliest poets' was 'felt' to be different because "it was the language of extraordinary occasions;" or, in other words, it was the language of poetry—poetry, that always deals with extraordinary occasions. Nevertheless, in the *Appendix*, he says that even the language that the earliest poets used "was really spoken by men." He further says that the earliest poets employed some sort of metre to the language of the earliest men, for the language was being used by the earliest poets for extraordinary occasions, and that this employment of metre to some extent distanced the language of poetry from the language of the common man. Wordsworth calls this distancing some sort of corruption, and, yet, he says that the 'first poets' spoke "the language of men" (the common men). But, says Wordsworth, the succeeding poets, following the lead of the 'first poets', aggravated this corruption to please the readers "by easier means"—*i.e.*, by introducing more artificialities of metre, in their poetic compositions. Thus, in course of time, metre came to be supposed to be a symbol of poetry, and consequently, the taste of men gradually became perverted, as they slowly but steadily began to equate metrical compositions with poetry, and as "with the progress of refinement this diction [the language of the common men as already to an extent corrupted by the 'earliest poets,' and by the introduction of metre became daily more and more corrupted, thrusting out of sight the plain humanities of nature by a motely masquerade of tricks, quaintness, hieroglyphics, and enigmas." But why does such an artificial language, that is fully of "tricks, quaintness, hieroglyphics, and enigmas" interest the reader? Wordsworth says that this is due to two reasons: firstly, the reader prides himself for being able to understand that not-easy-to-understand language; and secondly, that artificial (corrupted, Wordsworth would like to say) language gives him a novel sensation by "unsettling [his] ordinary habit of thinking," and by "assisting the Reader to approach that perturbed and dizzy state of mind in which if he does not find himself, he imagines that he is balked by a peculiar enjoyment which poetry can and ought to bestow."

So far, as we have seen by now, both in the *Preface* and in the *Appendix*, Wordsworth has rejected all 'decorations' of the language of poetry—metre, rhyme (which Milton earlier rejected as barbarism), and 'poetic diction'—and also the other points of prose. Where, then, we may raise the question, does the beauty and pleasure of poetry lie? Wordsworth answers: in the imagination, and in the created emotion or sentiment of the poetic composition. He says that where there are imagination and sentiment, the diction, in fundamentals, is the same—the diction of the common men—be it in poetry or in prose. Wordsworth confesses that this understanding of his "has been my chief guide in all I have said,—namely, that in works of *imagination and sentiment*, for those only have I been treating, in proportion as ideas and feelings are valuable, whether the composition be in prose or in verse, they require and exact one and the same language."

III

(*Essay Supplementary to the 'Preface'*)

In this essay, Wordsworth defines the business of poetry, and thereby further clarifies his conception of poetry. He writes: "*The appropriate business of poetry* (which, nevertheless, is as permanent as pure science), *her appropriate employment, her privilege and her duty, is to treat of things not as they are, but as they appear, not as they exist in themselves, but as they seem to exist to the senses, and to the passions.*" Poetry, Wordsworth means to say, colours things with imagination, and quickens them to our sensations and sentiments. It is for this reason, says Wordsworth, that youths, who are naturally prone to, and delight in, delusion, very wrongly take up poetry; and, again, it is for this reason that the anxiety-ridden and business-burdened old people take up poetry—again, very wrongly—to escape into delusion and to "forget the world." Wordsworth says that in 'higher poetry' (where there is no delusion to be supplied to the reader for his skin-deep and evanescent pleasures), where there is the "wisdom of the heart and the grandeur of the imagination," there is simplicity of language, and "the glaring hues of diction" is absent there. Wordsworth says that poetry is of "divine origin", and that there is sort of religious mood, or sacredness, in poetry. Poetry is of passionate nature, and so the mature person, whose "passion is contracted" by the "weight of life"—the mature person who has religious and moral inclinations—develops a mistaken conception of poetry, due to his inquiring mind, which is always after truth (not, of course, poetic truth), and consequently he values only those authors whose poetry reveals truths, not caring for the pure enjoyment of poetry.

Wordsworth, next, speaks about the affinity between poetry and religion—"between religion making up the deficiencies of reason by faith; and poetry—passionate for the instruction of reason; between religion—whose element is infinitude, and whose ultimate trust is the supreme of things, submitting herself to circumscription, and reconciled to substitutions; and poetry—ethereal and transcendent, yet incapable to sustain her existence without sensuous incarnation." The faith of religion is dependent on the infinite which we fail to quite comprehend if we cannot find an instantiation of the infinite in some finite object; and poetry, through *einfuhlung* and passion, can comprehend the infinite through its finite subject-matter. And so there is a sort of bridge, or complementarily, between religion and poetry.

Wordsworth says that public taste of poetry changes from age to age, and even from time to time within an age. He writes about this: "Who is there that now reads the *Creations* of Dubratas? Yet all Europe once resounded with his praise; he was caressed by kings, and when his poem was translated into our language, *The Faery Queene* faded before it. The name of Spenser, whose genius is of a higher order than even that of Ariosto, is at this day scarcely known beyond the limits of the British Isles." Wordsworth further writes: "The early editions of the *Paradise Lost* were printed in a shape which allowed them to be sold at a low price, yet only three thousand copies of the Work were sold in eleven years; and the Nation, says Dr. Johnson, had been satisfied from 1623 to 1664, that is forty-one years, with only two editions of the Works of Shakespeare, which probably did not together make one thousand copies; facts adduced by the critic to prove the 'paucity of Readers'." Therefore, public taste continuously undergoes changes; and, therefore, authors sometimes have to keep in their minds the quality of the public taste, while writing for them. But, then, says Wordsworth, a new poet, if he is powerful enough, need not submit to the prevailing public taste, or need not wait for a new public taste to originate; rather he should create his own taste for the public to relish. Wordsworth writes: *"Every author has had the task of creating the taste by which he is to be enjoyed; so has it been, so will it continue to be."*

Wordsworth says that creating a new taste is not an easy task, because it needs overcoming a number of hurdles, which are real difficulties. Wordsworth denotes these difficulties, by implication, through putting some questions about those difficulties: "Is it in breaking the bond of custom, in overcoming the prejudices of false refinement, and displacing the aversions of inexperience? Or, if he labours for an object which here and elsewhere I have proposed to himself, does it consist in divesting the reader of the pride that induces him to dwell upon those points wherein men differ from each other, to the exclusion of those in which all men are alike, or the same: and in making him ashamed of the vanity which renders him sensible of the appropriate excellence which civil arrangements, less unjust than might appear, and Nature illimitable in her bounty, have conferred on men who may stand below him in the scale of society? Finally, does it lie in establishing that dominion over the spirits of readers by which they are to be humbled and humanised, in order that they may be purified and exalted?"

IV

(*Discussion on Poetic Diction*)

There has perhaps never been so fierce debates on, and criticisms about, Wordsworth's views about poetry as the debates on, and the criticisms about, his views about 'poetic diction', or, to be precise, about his rejection of the theory of poetic diction. William K.Wimsatt and Ceanth Brooks write about the origin of the terms 'diction' and 'poetic diction': "The precise terms 'diction' and 'poetic diction' seem to have arisen..., in the Augustan era. Dryden uses 'diction' with an apology for Latinism, in the preface to *Sylvae*, 1685. The first person to use the term 'poetic diction' is apparently Dennis, in his *Advancement and*

Reformation of Modern Poetry (ch. V), 1701" (Wimsatt and Brooks, 343). John Dennis (1657-1734) wrote eight unsuccessful dramas, and is to-day remembered only as a critic of some standing. He noticed that poetry uses certain exclusive words which are not usable in prose, and that is a parameter of poetry. The classical poets wrote what they did without being aware of the supposed difference between 'poetic diction' and the common language. But in the Augustan era, this dichotomy of language surfaced. Alexander Pope (1688-1744) believed that the language of poetry was gradually distancing itself from the language of the common people since the time of Homer, and that the distinction between the language of poetry and that of the common folk was reasonable, necessary and justified. Pope writes: " 'It must also be allowed that there is a majesty and harmony in the Greek language, which greatly contribute to elevate and support the narration. But we must also observe, that this is an advantage grown upon the language since Homer's time: for things are removed from vulgarity by being out of use; and if the words we could find in any present language were equally sonorous or musical in themselves, they would still appear less poetical and uncommon than those of a dead one, from this only circumstance, of being in every man's mouth'" (Wimsatt and Brooks, 342). Alexander Pope believed that words become vulgar being frequently used, and that particularly by vulgar persons; and that as this is so, and as the office of poetry is an elevated one, poets should shun the vulgar diction. Pope was not alone in this siding with the theory of poetic diction, but there were notable others, including Thomas Gray (1716-71) who wrote in clear and emphatic terms about the distinction between the poetic and the popular diction: "The language of the age is never the language of poetry; except among the French, whose verse, where the thought and image does not support it, differs in nothing from prose. Our poetry, on the contrary, has a language peculiar to itself, to which almost everyone that has written has added something by enriching it with foreign idioms and derivations: nay, sometimes words of their own composition or invention. Shakespeare and Milton have been great creators this way; and no more licentious than Pope and Dryden, who perpetually borrow expressions from the former" (Wimsatt and Brooks, 343). However, to go back to our earlier question—since when actually did the poetic diction come up? Among others, Dr. Johnson and Pope differ very much from one another, on this question. According to Dr. Johnson, "'There was... before the time of Dryden no poetic diction'" (Wimsatt and Brooks, 343). But Pope believed that poetic diction originated long back in the history of poetry—at the hands of Homer: "'We acknowledge him [Homer] the father of poetic diction'" (*Ibid*).

The cry for poetic diction was not echoed by every poet or critic: there were a good number of protesters against the theory of poetic diction. Wimsatt and Brooks write that "Two kinds of protest against poetic diction have occurred: that of the classicist, hostile to pedantry and affectation, appealing to polite idiom, the educated spoken word; and that of the romantic, hostile to the same things, but appealing to the primitive, the naive, the directly passionate, the natural spoken word" (*Ibid*). Wordsworth's protesting voice against the theory of poetic diction joined the denouncing voice of the second group of protesters. "The first of these protests [referred to above] occurs intermittently throughout the classical and Renaissance era. It is the voice of Horace (...), of Ben Jonson ("Pure and neat Language I love, yet plain and customary"), of Dryden in his preface to *Annus Mirabilis* ("'Tis not the jerk or sting of an epigram...nor the jingle of a more poor paronomasia"), of Pope in his *Essay* (II, lines 311-314):

> False eloquence, like the prismatic glass,
> Its gaudy colours spreads on every place;
> The face of Mature we no more survey,
> All glares alike, without distinction gay."

(Wimsatt and Brooks, 343-44)

"The final and successful revolt against classical 'poetic diction' was more violent—a protest of the second type, primitive, naive, 'vegetally' radical, the first of its kind, at least in English literature, and a thing distinctive of a new social and philosphic era" (Wimsatt and Brooks, 344-45). Wordsworth participated in the "final and successful revolt against classical 'poetic diction,'" and his revolt was more prurient than others. But his protest was directed "not so much against Spenser, Milton, and Pope, the poets who had created English poetic diction, as against his own now anonymous contemporaries who wrote the melange of dictions which was than poetic sample" (*Ibid*).

V

(*Coleridge's Arguments Against Wordsworth's Opinion About Poetic Diction*)

However vociferous may have been the protest against poetic diction—Wordsworth being in the front phalanx of the protesters—those supporting the intrinsic value of poetic diction did not yield, and the use of poetic diction did not go out of vogue, any time in the history of English poetry. Rather, counter-protest was voiced principally by Coleridge. Coleridge's arguments against Wordsworth's opinion about poetic diction may be summarised as follows:

(a) Wordsworth did not notice any essential difference between the language of poetry and that of prose, because, according to him, both poetry and prose use the same vocabulary—the same store of terms. Thus far, Coleridge admits, Wordsworth is quite right. But, from the foregoing statement of Wordsworth "Coleridge concluded that Wordsworth really meant that the manner of combining words of poetry was no different from that of prose. And this, he retorted, was patently false" (Wimsatt and Brooks, 348). Here, we may suffer doubt as to whether Wordsworth really meant what Coleridge deduced from the former's statement.

(b) Wordsworth said that if even a good word or phrase or a figure of speech is too frequently repeated, it loses its poetic value (if it has any), and becomes hackneyed: it becomes degraded into a bad word, phrase or figure. But Coleridge says that "the reason for the badness is not that the figure is a repetition of what other poets have done, but that it is in some way a violation of 'grammar, logic, psychology,' 'good sense,' or 'taste'—the 'rules of the imagination'" (*Ibid.*) Wordsworth, further, meant that a line of verse is bad in so far as it distances itself from the conversational language of the common man—from prose—and to the corresponding degree makes itself into an artificiality. But in *Biographia Literaria* (II. 58), Coleridge writes: "It is a bad line, not because the language is distinct from that of prose; but because it coveys incongruous images, because it confounds the cause and effect, the real thing with the personified *representative* of the thing; in short, because it differs with the language of Good Sense! That the 'Phoebus' is hackneyed and a school-boy image, is an *accidental* fault, dependent on the age in which the author wrote."

(c) Wordsworth believed that urban manners and instructions and customs vitiate the inherent purity of the soul and of thought, and vitiate the naturalness of the language of the common man, and that this is insalubrious to the poetic faculty. "Coleridge argued that education, and not the lack of it, tends to make a poet. Uneducated men are disorderly in their writing; they lack 'surview'. If the peasantry of Wordsworth's Westmoreland and Cumberland spoke a pure and vigorous language, this came not from uninstructed communion with nature, but from a spirit of independence and from a solid religious education and acquaintance with the Bible and hymn book" (Wimsatt and Brooks, 349).

Further, Coleridge discovered that Wordsworth himself could not altogether avoid poetic diction, and that he sometime used a melange diction—a queer combination of poetic and prosaic diction. "In his appreciation of Wordsworth's poetic performance, Coleridge noted that Wordsworth suffered the difficulties of a ventriloquist in his undue liking for the dramatic form. Either a rustic speaker was invested with a Wordsworthian authority of utterance, or an opposite fault appeared, matter-of-factness, circumstantiality, and a downright prosaism. 'I've measured it from side to side; 'Tis three feet long, and two feet wide.' It is not possible for a poet, urged Coleridge, especially not for a lyric poet, "to imitate truly a dull and garrulous discourser, without repeating the effects of dullness and garrulity" (*Ibid.*).

Though Wordsworth was against poetic diction, some critics are of the opinion that Wordsworth himself has introduced a new kind of poetic diction: ('Before many years had passed, a reviewer of Wordsworth's poems would raise his voice to accuse even Wordsworth of having fostered his own kind of poetic diction, more dangerous than the old, because more 'covert and surreptitious,' more 'insidous.' A new set of 'stock words' seemed to this reviewer to be sprinkled through the 'fugitive' poetry of the day 'with a sort of feeling senselessness'—words, for instance, like *wild, bright. dark, lonely, light, dream*. The principle of their use was sentimental association lending colour to a 'pretext of conveying sense'—'in a manner which Mr. Wordsworth's prefaces will be found to explain'" (*Ibid.*).

According to Wimsatt and Brooks, the controversy between Wordsworth and Coleridge on the point of poetic diction is amiss, because the two poets understand and term 'poetic diction' in two different ways. "The theoretical issue of poetic diction seemed to Wordsworth an issue between artifice and nature. To Coleridge it seemed more like an issue between propriety and impropriety, congruity and incongruity" (Wimsatt and Brooks, 354). Wordsworth is vexed about frequently repeated, that is hackneyed, phrases—about cliches. But cliches as such are not always *passe* or jejune; a skilled hand can certainly employ them profitably or effectively. "The usual rule of thumb is that a poet should avoid cliches. But a higher rule is that he should be a master of cliches—at all levels. The mastery of the cliches may be illustrated sharply, if simply, in a kind of twisted echo phrase which has been called the 'cliche extended.'

At the top of a brass hat.
To guild the lily with radiator point

A penny saved is a penny to squander.
A man is known by the company he organizes."

(Wimsatt and Brooks, 357)

T.S. Eliot says that Wordsworth's view of poetic diction is actually not new. Eliot says that even Dryden himself has said what Wordsworth said about poetic diction, or almost the same thing; and that the thing is that we could not quite understand what Dryden said, and that is why we think that it was Wordsworth who first raised his voice against poetic diction. Eliot writes: "Wordsworth, when he said that his purpose was 'to imitate, and as far as possible, to adopt, the very language of men,' was only saying in other words what Dryden had said, and fighting the battle which Dryden had fought" (Eliot, 1933, 71). What did Wordsworth actually mean by 'The very language of men?' Eliot says that by the phrase Wordsorth did not actually mean the language of the very common men or lowly people, but the "'language of the middle and lower classes of society'" (*Ibid.*).

He says that the language of the 'middle and lower classes of society' is of course appropriate for matters that belong to the said two strata of the society. He writes that when the poet is "representing dramatically the *speech* of these classes ['the middle and lower classes of society'], then no other language is proper" (*Ibid.*). So far Eliot admits of Wordsworth's view of poetic diction. But, says he, when the poet is dealing a matter belonging to the upper class of society, he should not confine within the bound of "the very language of men." He writes: "But on other occasions, it is not the business of the poet to talk like any class of society, but like himself—rather better, we hope, than any actual class" (Eliot, 1933, 71-72).

VI

(*Wordsworth's View of the Poet and of Poetry*)

Regarding Wordsworth's view of the poet, here, we shall raise only one question. We know that to be a poet, only having keen sensibilities and powerful imagination will not do; acquiring the technicalities is as well necessary as having those two desiderata—one has to learn how to be poet. That is, in brief, poets are made. But our question to Wordsworth is: are there born poets, that is, are some men born with all the essential faculties of a poet, albeit even being born with all the essential qualities of a poet one may not, at any time throughout his life-time, reveal himself as a poet? The answer to the question, according to Wordsworth, is: yes. Wordsworth believed that there are two categories of poets: poets by training and born poets. In *The Excursion* (Bk I, lines 77-91), Wordsworth says that there are born poets who live and die in oblivion, *incognito*:

> Oh! many are the Poets that are sown
> By Nature; men endowed with highest gifts,
> The vision and the faculty divine;
> Yet wanting the accomplishment of verse,
> (Which, in the docile season of their youth,
> It was denied them to acquire, through lack
> Of culture and the inspiring aid of books,
> Or haply by a temper too severe,
> Or a nice backwardness afraid of shame)
> Nor having e'er, as life advanced, been led
> By circumstance to take unto the height

The measure of themselves, these favoured Beings,
All but a scattered few, live out their time,
Husbanding that which they possess within,
And go to the grave, unthought of.

However, Wordsworth had great respect for poetry. In his *Preface* to *Lyrical Ballads*, he is very fluent in his praise of poetry. There he writes: "Poetry is the breath and finer spirit of all knowledge; it is the impassioned expression which is in the countenance of all Science" and "Poetry is the first and last of all knowledge—it is as immoral as the heart of man." What more do we need to know of Wordsworth to understand his great respect for poetry? However, in the same *Preface,* Wordsworth says about the poet: "He is the rock of defence for human nature; and an upholder and preserver, carrying every where with him relationship and love. In spite of difference of soil and climate, of language and manners, of laws and customs: in spite of things silently gone out of mind, and things violently destroyed; the poet binds together by passion and knowledge the vast empire of human society, as it is spread over the whole earth, and over all time." Such was the eulogy of the poet for the poet.

However, Coleridge could not accept Wordsworth's theory of the origination, or of the process of creation, of poetry. Wordsworth, earlier, emphasised spontaneity in the creation of poetry—spontaneity of the expression of powerful feeling. He said that poetry was the "spontaneous overflow of powerful feeling." But later he changed his definition of poetry, and that quite phenomenally, and said that poetry is "emotion recollected in tranquillity." Wordsworth emphasised the emotive element of poetry, but he was not alone in this regard; Hazlitt, Mill and other contemporaries of his also did the same. But while they all were emphasing the emotive element of poetry, they were thinking only of lyric poetry, and did not take into account epic poetry (where emotion plays a subdued role). "But Wordsworth, Hazlitt, Mill, and many of their contemporaries, conceiving poetry as the language of feeling, thought of the lyrical poem, instead of epic or tragedy, as the exemplary form, and replaced history as the logical opposite of poetry by what Wordsworth called 'matter of fact or science'" (Preminger, 644). In this regard, Wimsatt and Brooks write about Wordsworth's emotion theory of poetry: "If the Wordsworthian formula 'emotion recollected in tranquillity' be taken in an approximately hylomorphic way, one may suppose that 'emotion' refers to a kind of poetic content, and tranquil 'recollection' to the control or shaping this content—the formal poetic principle. In the Coleridgean formula of the creation of poetry, on the other hand, the emphasis is reversed: here emotion is not the content but the organizing principle, and so here, unlike in the Wordsworthian formula, the emphasis is on emotion."

VII

(*The Function of Imagination in the Creation of Poetry*)

Imagination, like fancy, is an important agent in the creation of art, and so of poetry, and there is no disagreement among artists or poets regarding the importance of imagination and fancy in the birth of art objects. But throughout the history of thoughts about art, there has been a long-drawn battle over the nature of imagination, and contribution of imagination in creative works, and also over the relation between imagination and fancy. The great power of imagination was not unknown to Shakespeare. Theseus, in *A Midsummer Night's Dream*, clubs together the lunatic, the lover, and the poet, because all of them are so and so under the influence of imagination:

> The lunatic, the lover, and the poet,
> Are of imagination all compact;....

Theseus, in the same play, speaks about how far imagination informs the poet at work:

> The poet's eye, in a frenzy rolling,
> Doth glance from heaven to earth, from earth to heaven;
> And as imagination bodies forth
> The forms of things unknown, the poet's pen
> Turns them to shapes, and gives to airy nothing
> A local habitation and a name.

The immense importance of imagination in creative works was noticed by Coleridge, may be under the guidance of Shakespeare, and under the influence of the German idealist philosophers. Coleridge conceived of another faculty of mind, besides the faculty of imagination—the faculty of fancy—and took pains to differentiate between these two faculties. But, Wimsatt and Brooks say that before Coleridge, Wordsworth could faintly perceive the distinction between imagination and fancy: "An early and somewhat haphazard attempt on the part of Wordsworth to discriminate between imagination ('Impressive effects out of simple elements') and fancy ('Pleasure and surprise... excited by sudden varieties of situation and accumulated energy') appears in a note to 'The Thorn' in the 1800 edition of '*Lyrical Ballads*' (Wimsatt and Brooks, 386)." In 1813, one William Taylor wrongly conceived of the functions of imagination and fancy: "'A man has imagination in proportion as he can distinctly copy in idea the impressions of sense: it is the faculty which *images* within the mind the phenomena of sensation. A man has fancy in proportion as he can call up, connect, or associate, at pleasure, those internal images (*phantazein* is to cause to appear) so as to complete ideal representations of absent objects'" (*Ibid.*). Wordsworth objected to the lopsided view of Taylor: "Wordsworth's objection was in part simply that the terms, as an antithetic pair, were turned upside down" (*Ibid.*). Wordsworth thought that imagination was a faculty of a higher order than fancy, and that it was a higher creative power than fancy. According to Wordsworth, "Imagination was a 'conferring,' an 'abstracting,' a 'modifying,' an 'endowing' power. The imagination 'unites' and 'coalesces.' It 'shapes and creates'" (Wimsatt and Brooks, 387). But, says Wordsworth, fancy does not coalesce or unite or shape or create new things: in fancy things exist independently of each other. Wordsworth writes about fancy: "'Fancy does not require that the materials which she makes use of should be susceptible of change in their constitution, from her touch; and where they admit of modification, it is enough for her purpose if it be slight, limited, and evanescent'" (Wimsatt and Brooks, 386-87). To Wordsworth, both fancy and imagination are inventive, creative. The only difference between the two is that "one [fancy] was frolicksome, and inferior, the other [imagination] was totally serious, and superior" (Wimsatt and Brooks, 388).

At this stage, let us get our notions of fancy and imagination more clarified with the help of two examples—one each for fancy and imagination (with which examples perhaps both Wordsworth and Coleridge would agree). An example of fancy is the 'Queen Mab speech' in Shakespeare's *Romeo and Juliet* (I. iv):

O, then I see Queen Mab hath been with you.
She is the fairies' midwife, and she comes
In shape no bigger than an agate stone
On the fore finger of an alderman,
Drawn with a team of little atomies
Athwart men's noses as they lie asleep;
....
This is she—.

Here the images are in a cluster; they are joined each to each; but they do not coalesce and make image—they do not form a unit, but remain somewhat independent of each other. They are like the petals of a flower, arranged in a beautiful order, and that is all. On the other hand, in imagination (or creative imagination, which Coleridge calls 'secondary imagination'), images merge into one another, *i.e.,* they coalesce, in such a way that the images lose their independent existence, and create a new whole, a new unity, as in the following four lines (lines 67-68 and 815-16) of Shakespeare's *Venus and Adonis*:

Look how a bird lies tangled in a net,
So fast'ned in her arms Adonis lies;...
and
Look how a bright star shooteth from the sky,
So glides he in the night from Venus' eye;...

B.L .K. Henderson has very clearly shown the difference between fancy and imagination: "...Fancy differs from Imagination, in that it consists in finding an outward resemblance between two things not, at first sight, closely alike. The great majority of Similes are the result of Fancy; whereas Metaphors are rather the product of Imagination. Fancy usually stops short at stating a material resemblance; Imagination requires some touch of suggestiveness. Thus Fancy might compare the blossom of an orchard to 'white or rosy clouds of flowers,' but Imagination is called into play if we speak of them as the 'bridal veils' of the trees. For this reason Fancy is inferior to Imagination—it lacks suggestiveness" (Henderson, 316).

Coleridge did not agree with Wordsworth that both fancy and imagination are creative. Wordsworth said that both fancy and imagination are creative, in the sense that both have evoking and elevating power. And so he did not notice much difference between the two in their functions in the creation of art. But Coleridge very forcefully objected to the view of Wordsworth. In Chapter XII of his *Biographia Literaria,* Coleridge comes down heavily on Wordsworth's view: "If, by the power of evoking and elevating, Mr. Wordsworth means the same as, and no more than, I meant by the aggregative and assertive, I continue to deny, that it belongs at all to the imagination; and I am disposed to conjecture, that he has mistaken the co-presence of fancy with imagination for the operation of the latter singly'"(Wimsatt and Brooks, 388). But then, how does Coleridge distinguish between imagination and fancy? In Chapter XIII of his *Biographia Literaria,* Coleridge explains the two notions in very clear terms: "The IMAGINATION then, I consider either as primary, or secondary. The primary IMAGINATION I hold to be the living power and prime Agent of all human Perception, and as a repetition in the finite mind of the eternal act of creation in the infinite I AM. The secondary Imagination I consider as an echo of the former, co-existing with the conscious will, yet still as identical with the primary in the *kind* of its agency, and differing only in *degree,* and in the *mode* of its operation. It dissolves, diffuses, dissipates, in order to recreate; or where this process is rendered impossible, yet still at all events it struggles to idealize and unify. It is essentially *vital,* even as all objects (as objects) are essentially fixed and dead. "Fancy, on the contrary, has no other counters to play with, but fixities and definites. The fancy is indeed no other than a mode of Memory emancipated from the order of time and space; while it is blended with, and modified by the empirical phenomenon of the will, which we express by the word CHOICE. But equally with the ordinary memory the Fancy must receive all its materials ready made from law of association." From what has been said so far about Wordsworth's and Coleridge's individual views on imagination, it appears that they greatly differed from one another, but Wimsatt and Brooks say that they did certainly differ from each other, but not greatly: "It is our view that Coleridge did not differ vitally from Wordsworth about 'imagination,' and that the two may well be considered together, although Coleridge no doubt may be conveniently accepted as the more articulate and more theoretical spokesman of the two" (Wimsatt and Brooks, 388-89). However, whatever Wordsworth may have said or written about poetry, and whatever alterations or modifications, he may have made in his views about poetry, one thing is clear and confirmed about him that it was his conviction that "Poetry is passion: it is the history or science of feelings" (Wordsworth and Coleridge, 283).

The element of passion in poetry cannot be ignored. It is not only the Romantics that demanded this vital element in poetry, but even such great philosophical poets as Milton could not reject the element of passion in poetry. Milton said that poetry must be 'simple, sensuous and passionate', and Wordsworth's poetry shows these three things in the most articulate forms—simplicity, sensuality and passion. Another very important utterance of Wordsworth about poetry is that 'the appropriate business of poetry...is to treat of things not as they *are*, but as they *appear*; not as they exist in themselves, but as they *seem* to exist to the *senses*. and to the *passions*.' Wordsworth saw things not as such, but as coloured, modified, and transformed by imagination. In doing so, he was representing the poetic vogue of the Romantic age, if not that of the whole history of poetry down to our own day. Wordsworth went even farther than this: he treated things, or saw things as symbols—sometimes as separate symbols and sometimes the collectivity of things as a unitary symbol. For instance, he saw nature as a whole as a vast symbol of the infinite spirit. And in seeing nature as a symbol, he was not a queer fellow, for may others also saw nature as a symbol. For instance, Herman Melville and Emerson also treated nature as a symbol: "Melville came to believe no less than Emerson that 'Nature is the symbol of Spirit'. He made Ahab exlaim in his soliloquy on the whale's skull: 'O Nature, and O soul of man! how far beyond all utterance are your linked analogies! not the smallest atom stirs or lives on matter, but has its cunning duplicate in mind'" (Matthiessen, 43). These and some other views of Wordsworth about poetry will continue to have great bearings on anyone's considerations of what poetry really is, and how it comes into being.

7

Wordsworth as a Poet of Nature

P.B. Shelley, in his poem *To Wordsworth*, calls Wordsworth 'Poet of Nature,' as William Hazlitt calls him poet of the mountains, and both these appellations are very appropriate for Wordsworth, because Wordsworth both got his poetic inspiration and materials for his poems from nature. Right from the poems which he wrote in his early years, when he was neither aware of the spirituality of nature nor got any moral instructions from her, down to the poems of his advanced years, we find that his poems are suffused with the beauty and descriptions of nature, as if nature followed him like a shadow. As early as in 1786, when he was around 16, Wordsworth wrote the following lines which are imbued with the softness of nature (we repeat):

> Thus, while the Sun sinks down to rest
> Far in the regions of the west,
> Though to the vale no parting beam
> Be given, not one memorial gleam,
> A lingering light he fondly throws
> On the dear hills where first he rose.

And the following verses (we, again, repeat):

> Calm is all nature as a resting wheel.
> The kine are couched upon the dewy grass;
> The horse alone, seen dimly as I pass
> Is cropping audibly his later meal:
> Dark is the ground; a slumber seems to steal
> O'er vale, and mountain, and the starless sky.

These two extracts from his perhaps earliest poems might show the future 'Poet of Nature' that Wordsworth was. Whatever may be the themes of his poems—short or long—his verses are always redolent of the beauty, or, in rare cases, the horror, of nature. Helen Darbishire writes: "Wordsworth's creed may be said in three words: God, Man, Nature. These three were [to Wordsworth] divine: it might be said that they were one divinity. God was necessarily greatest, Man comes next, and Nature, which had taught him to know the divinity in man, was last yet first, the source of his inspiration and first step in all his vital knowledge" (Darbishire, 133). So much valuable was nature to Wordsworth.

But what actually does the word 'nature' denote when we say that Wordsworth was a poet of nature? The word has signified many things at different times of the history of literature, and also to different persons of the same period of history. Joseph Warren Beach writes: "There was, to begin with, the widespread view of nature as signifying the natural way of living, associated with residence in the country. There was the view of nature as constituting a cosmic order, of which the visible world is one expression and the moral world another, the whole being characterized by design and purposiveness and operating according to universal laws. This view had been greatly reinforced in the seventeenth and eighteenth centuries by the brilliant speculation of Newton particularly in regard to the all-embracing principle of gravitation; and the scientific concept of natural law had been made a bulwark of religion in many popular works of 'natural theology,' as well as being given an anti-religious turn in the writings of free thinkers" (Beach, 26). However, Wordsworth used the word 'nature' in two different senses: in the abstract sense of human behaviour; for instance, when, in his *Preface* to *Lyrical Ballads* (1802), he speaks of "primary laws of nature;" and in the sense of the arboreal parts of the world. Wordsworth used the word in both the meanings, of course laying emphasis on, and frequently referring to, the latter meaning.

Nature, in the second or latter sense, was not, to Wordsworth, simply a collocation of trees, bushes, hills, streams and such other things; it was something more than the mathematical summation of all these dumb and insensate objects of the world. To him nature was almost as good as a personality, with wisdom, moral sense, capability of showing sympathy to human kind in their crying need of affection and soothing balm for hurt hearts, and the power to poetically inspire those who love her. Joseph Warren Beach writes about Wordsworth's view of nature: "Nature is for Wordsworth a world of wide and lofty significance. In his view the world of eye and ear is somehow the embodiment, the symbol, or the shrine of all that is most inspiring and fortifying in the moral life. It is possible for man to hold communion with this visible world as with a spiritual being and to receive from it an essential and rewarding education of the spirit. It is difficult at this day to conceive how much a sober mind as Wordsworth's could have read so much significance into the mere external nature—'fountains, meadows, hills, groves'" (Beach, 26). Wordsworth's such view of nature was behind the particular quality of his poetry that he produced, and was behind the sustained poetic inspiration of his. Beach writes about how the objects of nature influenced Wordsworth's poetry: "We must suppose that these objects of aesthetic delight [in nature], or the nature they stood for in his mind, constituted the focal point for a number of ideas associated with the word 'nature' that taken together would be amply sufficient to account for the power and importance assigned to it in his poetry" (Beach, 26).

All poets generally have shown their affinity with, and love of, nature; and no poet has ever shown hatred towards nature; and this may confirm our belief that poets tend to be attracted by nature, or that there is some connection between poetry and nature. The cool breeze, the dancing of flowers on branches of trees, the gushing spring, the fog-screened lonely valley, the undulating paths over the hills and dales, the flower-bedecked meadows, the silent, mirror-like water of the pond camouflaged within a wood, the ponderous serpentine village path, etc.—all have ever attracted and delighted poets. But no other poet was so much drawn to all these delightful things of nature as Wordsworth was. And no other poet but Wordsworth did ever treat nature not as a collocation of dumb and insensate things—such as trees and bushes, ponds and hills—but as a veritable person: as a friend, teacher and guide, having sympathies, like humans, and having the power of communications sans human languages. And, far more than all that, no poet, excepting Wordsworth, could feel the presence of spirituality in nature.

Oliver Elton writes in this regard: "Other poets had lain in the lap of nature now and then, but Wordsworth would espouse her. He did so; he wrote the story of the courtship and nuptials at length. What if he sometimes portrays her as a kind of severe governess, and poses about her power to moralise the young? Oftener she is young herself, incarnate in some joyful figure, a Highland girl or a Lucy, who is moulded by the rhythm of waves or the lines of the flowers, and is thus in some sort their explanation; a creature bred anew 'in every age,' as Blake would have said, for the refreshment of humanity" (Elton, 57-58). This view of nature as a spiritual being came to Wordsworth at a later date, and slowly, but since the dawn of his wakeful life, he was passionately in love of the changing, shifting, chamaleon-like beauty of nature, and took nature to be his only close and fast friend. At a very early age, he could faintly realise that he was going to be a poet, and even at that tender age he, being imbibed with the unearthly beauty of nature, resolved that as a poet it would be his sacred vocation to open the eyes of the human kind to the beauty of nature—he resolved to be a committed poet. Oliver Elton writes: "Wordsworth is one of the poets, like Milton, Pope, and Shelley, who has made, recorded, and kept a definite vow: he says that he was not more than fourteen when he first became aware 'of that infinite variety of natural appearances which had been unnoticed by the poets of any age or country, so far as I was acquainted with them; and I made a resolution to supply, in some degree, the deficiency'" (Elton, 57).

It was certainly a bold step for Wordsworth to undertake to literally personify and spiritualise nature, particularly at a time when the *zeitgeist* of England was contrary. The eighteenth century English philosophy was out and out materialistic, especially under the influences of Newton's (1642-1727) physics and Hume's (1711-76) association psychology. Newton's theories of gravitation and of motion gave fillip to the general belief that the creation could be explained absolutely in terms of the material laws of physics, *i.e.*, with the principles of matter and motion, and so the concept of God, or of any prime mover, or of any other spiritual being, was only redundant. In the sphere of the psychological phenomena, it was the general belief that all mental phenomena whatsoever could be explained only with the help of the principles of association as laid down by Hume. Hume denied the ontological existence of mind or spirituality, and claimed that what we call mental phenomena are but the products of the sense-impressions that we receive from the non-mental, non-spiritual, but material, world,—the sense-impressions that obey the physical laws of association. Hume therefore granted furlough to the concepts of mind and soul. Ironically, in spite of their materialistic interpretations of the phenomena—both physical and mental—both Newton and Hume held to the belief in God, while the people, their contemporary people, in general, remained unconcerned, insouciant, about the ontological status of God, or of spirituality. In this hard materialistic *zeitgeist*, Wordsworth brought in the air of spirituality. To him, nature, or rather the whole of the creation, was not devoid of spirituality. Nature, to him, was not insensate, impersonal, incommunicable, and dead, but was beautiful, compassionate, wise, moral and spiritual. Wordsworth believed that man can communicate with nature, and nature can poetically mould the soul of man, and can guide him in his path of moral upliftment. It may be mentioned here that in all these beliefs of his, Wordsworth might have been influenced by Erasmus Darwin (1731-1802)—the grandfather of the celebrated evolutionary theorist Charles Darwin (1809-82)—who was a botanist and a poet. In his *The Botanical Garden*, written in heroic couplets, Erasmus Darwin treated with nature in such a manner that as if nature was a person, and showed his deep love of, and respect for, nature. It was perhaps from Erasmus Darwin's *The Botanical Garden* that Wordsworth took the lesson that nature was not unrelated to man—that there was a sort of physical and mental symbiosis between the two. Particularly, Erasmus Darwin's love of, and devotion to, nature, perhaps, influenced Wordsworth's attitude to nature.

But the greatest influence on Wordsworth's attitude to nature certainly came from Jean-Jacques Rousseau (1712-78). It was Rousseau's writings that clarified, enriched, and fortified Wordsworth's conceptions of, and attitude to, nature and man, although Wordsworth has not admitted this in clear terms, nor has he, while meditating on nature and man, in his verses, the oftener alluded to the French naturalist. Rousseau was indeed a great lover of nature. In the twelfth or the last book of his

Confessions, he writes: "Botany—as I had always considered it and as I still did when it began to become a passion with me—was exactly the kind of idle pursuit to fill the void of my leisure, leaving no room for the mildness of the imagination or for the boredom of total inaction. To wander carelessly through the woods and fields, and mechanically to pluck here and there, sometimes a flower and sometimes a branch, to munch my fodder almost haphazard, to observe the same things thousands and thousands of times and always with the same interest, because I always forgot them each time: that was the way to pass eternity without the possibility of a moment's boredom." Such was Rousseau's love of nature, his affinity with nature, and in numerous places of his writings, he has referred to his love of nature. Rousseau was not only a lover of nature, but also of man—the 'natural man,' unadulterated by the artificialities of the civilized world. He also believed in a sort of symbiosis between nature and man. On a particular occasion he forced himself to meditate over the relation between nature and man. On that occasion he came across, in an issue of *Mercure de France*, an announcement that the Dijon Academy "would bestow a prize for the best essay on whether manners had been improved and purified by the arts and sciences in France" (Brown, 396). The vagabond Rousseau was delighted, and started very deeply to think over the matter of the condition of human beings in the artificial civilization. "He said that he sat down under a tree to collect himself, so great had been the force of the emotion and the surge of ideas about the human state. When calm returned he discovered the front of his waistcoat was wet with tears he couldn't remember having shed. 'Ah, if I could ever have written the quarter of what I saw and felt under that tree, with what clearness should I have brought out all the contradictions of our social system...'" (Brown, 397). But what vision of man and nature did he get at that moment? The vision that he had laboured all through the rest of his life to express in so many thousand words of his works—the vision that showed him that man had been absolutely perfect, in the sense of being sensible, sympathetic and imaginative, in his original condition of his existence, before he was corrupted by civilization. The vision of the 'noble savage'—the man in the lap of nature with a maximally developed heart, and with a highly imaginative mind like that of a poet. And Wordsworth's conception of the 'natural man' is virtually no different from Rousseau's 'noble savage.'

From his meditations on the 'natural man' or the 'noble savage,' or rather on the relation between man and nature, Rousseau came to the conclusion that nature and man are 'organically' related to each other, and that the introduction of civilization (the artificiality of manners coupled with the artifacts invented by science) has only corrupted the innocent natural man so much so that he has now become a quite different being, his transformation being the worst for himself (almost the same idea may be found in Sigmund Freud's *Civilization and Its Discontents*). This organicity of the relation between man and nature, which is the main thesis in all of Rousseau's writings, we find also in all of Wordsworth's works. According to Wordsworth, man's sufferings are ultimately due to the dissociation or disconnectedness between man and nature; and in so far as man is disconnected from nature, he is also away from his original or fundamental nature; and in so far, again, as he is away from his original nature, he is denied the benefit of happiness. This disconnectedness of man from nature has corrupted him—his body as well as his mind. However, H.W. Garrod writes about Wordsworth's position regarding the relation between man and nature, and regarding the primordial condition of the 'natural man': "Wordsworth starts, then, from the position not only that Nature is good, but that it is from the natural goodness of the senses, operating simply and directly, that we derive ' the fountain-light of all our day.' We get farthest from the source of things the near we draw to all that in life is complex and artificial. Wherever we have things and persons whom chance, or the order of the world, has kept free from the bond of custom, has left simple and not complex, there we may look for illumination upon the things that really matter—the things that matter to the soul. It is thus that the child and the peasant become to Wordsworth the types of a wisdom higher than that of the world. He even goes further. He is prepared to find insight and inspiration in the mad, the crazed, and the idiotic. We are apt to attribute this penchant in him for Bedlamites, imbeciles, and 'simples' to mere childish whim. Yet, however perverse it may be, it is in fact a most solid part of his theory of life and of the mind and of truth" (Garrod, 99-100). What we have just now heard from H.W. Garrod about Wordsworth may lead us, if we are not chary, to believe that Wordsworth was crazy, irrational, in his belief or in his system of philosophy about man and nature, in so far as he gave a higher status even to 'the mad and the crazy and the idiotic' over the custom-oriented man of the civilized world. But we should in no case hold Wordsworth's philosophy to be puerile, because it was deduced from his keen observations and deep meditations. He may seem to be crazy to us, because we are ourselves a part of the civilized world. What Wordsworth wanted to say is simply this that 'the mad, the crazed, and the idiotic' are such and such only to the eyes of those who belong to the civilized society, and not to the eyes of those who are nursed by, and live in the ambience of, nature. However, as we have said, Wordsworth was, as if, imbibed with the spirit of nature. A.N. Whitehead, the great physicist, mathematician, and philosopher, is quite right when he writes (in a Lecture of his book *Science and the Modern World*: Cambridge University Press: 1926) about Wordsworth: "Wordsworth was passionately absorbed in nature. It has been said of Spinoza, that he was drunk with God. It is equally true that Wordsworth was drunk with nature" (Abrams, 22).

This inordinate enthusiasm for, and almost constitutional belief in, the truth of nature, of Wordsworth drove him to reject the authenticity of science. Wordsworth has called science 'props for our infirmities,' and philosophy an 'ape' (*The Prelude*). He rejects science because science is ineffectual in explaining the mystery of life; because science, in its effort to understand the organism, actually kills it, destroys it ("dissect to analyse"); because science may supply us with informative data, but cannot give us knowledge of the value of our existence or of the things of the creation; and because science denigrates the spirit of organisms. But Wordsworth is the most irate against science particularly because science is absorbed merely in the speculations of the abstractions, as against of the concrete objects, and because science never takes cognizance of the imposing influence of nature on our feelings and emotions. A.N. Whitehead, in the Lecture cited above, writes in this regard: "He [Wordsworth] alleges against science its absorption in abstractions. His consistent theme is that the important facts of nature elude the scientific method. It is important, therefore, to ask, what Wordsworth found in nature that failed to receive expression in science. I ask this question in the interest of science itself; for one main position in these lectures is a protest against the idea that the abstractions of science are irreformable and unalterable. Now it is emphatically not the case that Wordsworth hands over organic matter to the mercy of science, and concentrates on the faith that in the living organism there is some element that science cannot analyse. Of course he recognises, what no one doubts, that in some sense living things are different from lifeless things. But that is not his main point. It is the brooding presence of the hills which haunts him. His theme is nature *in solido*, that is to say, he dwells on that mysterious presence of surrounding things, which imposes itself on any separate element that we set up as an individual for its own sake. He always grasps the whole of nature as involved in the tonality of the particular instance. That is why he laughs with the daffodils, and finds in the primrose 'thoughts too deep for tears'" (Abrams, 22-23).

But even if we say that Wordsworth was anti-science, we must not take it as a blanket generalization, for he was against all the branches of science, but geometry. His reason was that geometry, unlike the other branches of science is concerned with eternity and unchangeability. His love of geometry we find in a dream of his that he has narrated in Bk V of *The Prelude*, where he saw an Arab with a stone and a shell, the stone symbolizing Euclid's geometry, and the shell symbolizing harmony, and both the stone and the shell being objects of great attraction to him. Secondly, Wordsworth rejected science only because science generally does not see beyond the bound of matter—science does not see the spirituality behind matter, due to its cataract, but science does not always fail to see the spirituality. For instance, Newton (1642-1727), in his *Principia Mathematica*, has admitted of the existence of some 'ethereal spirit' that 'interpenetrates both the material world and the human mind.' Newton writes: "'And now we might add something concerning a certain most subtle spirit which pervades and lies hid in all gross bodies; by the force and attraction of which spirit the particles of bodies attract one another at near distances, and cohere, if contiguous;... and light is emitted, reflected, refracted, inflected, and heats bodies; and all sensation is excited, and the members of animal bodies move at the command of the will, namely by vibrations propagated along the solid filaments of the nerves, from the outward organs of sense to the brain, and from the brain to the muscles. But these are things that cannot be explained in a few words, nor are we furnished with that sufficiency of experiments which is required to an accurate determination and demonstration of the laws by which this electric and elastic spirit operates'" (Durrant, 42). Here we may hazard the conjecture that Newton was influenced by Réne Descartes (1596-1650) in his conception of the 'spirit,' for Descartes accepted the ontological existence of mind, in addition to that of matter, and tried to reconcile the two divergent things with the introduction of a third 'thing'—the 'vital energy' which is not very different from Newton's 'spirit.' We should notice here that both Newton's 'spirit' and Descartes' 'vital energy' are non-material. Wordsworth may have been influenced by this seventeenth-century conception of the existence of some non-material being or 'thing', but we are not certain. However, he believed in the ontological existence of some non-material being in nature or in the whole of the creation, which he could not, or did not, name, and only expressed and indicated by the simple word 'presence.' This 'presence' is nothing but spirit or a spiritual being, of which he has spoken at several places in his works—the 'presence' with which nature is invested, the 'presence' which pervades the whole of nature. For instance, in *Tintern Abbey* (lines 93-102) he writes:

And I have felt
A presence that disturbs me with the joy
Of elevated thoughts; a sense sublime
Of something far more deeply interfused,
Whose dwelling is the light of setting suns,
And the round ocean and the living air,
And the blue sky, and in the mind of man:
A motion and a spirit, that impels
All thinking things, all objects of thought,
And roll through all things.

Wordsworth again speaks of the 'presence' or spirit of nature in *The Prelude* (Bk I. 464-66), as in some other places:

Ye Presences of Nature in the sky

And on the earth! Ye Visions of the hills!
And Souls of the lonely places!

This 'presence' is, says Wordsworth, beyond rational comprehension (*verstehand*), because it is mysterious, and so it can be realised only through empathy or *einfuhlung* (being on someone's wavelength, or to insert one's consciousness into that of another or into some other being). Here Wordsworth is beyond doubt a genuine mystic. As an *obiter dictum*, here we may say that Coleridge also betrayed a mystical turn of mind. Somewhere in his works he once said, referring to a piece of stone on a table that if one ever thought about why and how that piece of stone was there, he would be engulfed by an overpowering mysticism. But Wordsworth's mysticism is of course different from that of Coleridge, for while Coleridge's mysticism originated in the failure of his rationalist approach to the understanding of the phenomena, Wordsworth's mysticism was born in his sensual experiences of nature—it was intuitively drawn.

Wordsworth's belief in the 'presence' or spirit of nature obliterated his conception of God, though not always, because though throughout the most part of his life he did not show any interest in God, yet at the fag end of his life he sometimes tended to believe in God. This does not mean that Wordsworth did never feel the necessity of believing in some supernatural being or in spirituality: his 'presence' was his surrogate God. But, in fact, we are not certain about his position vis-a-vis God. Coleridge believed that he was an atheist, others said that he was insouciant about God, and only a few thought that, to him, nature was the incarnation of God. But why so? Perhaps because he got everything that we pray to God for—love, sympathy, solace, moral guidance and wisdom—from the spirit or the 'presence' of nature. If Wordsworth did not recognise God, can he be taken to be a religious man? F.R. Leavis says that Wordsworth believed in some sort of pantheism—which was of course limited within the province of nature—and that his devotion to the spiritualized nature can be called religion. Leavis writes about Wordsworth's religion: "What he had for presentment was a type and a standard of human normality, a way of life; his preoccupation with sanity and spontaneity working at a level and in a spirit that it seems appropriate to call religion" (Leavis, 164). And, we should add that human normality and sanity and spontaneity are, according to Wordsworth, to be expected only in the ambience of nature. To Wordsworth, nature is divine and nature is truth. In *The Excursion* (Bk IV), the Wanderer tells the Solitary:

> My heart a daily sacrifice to Truth,
> I now affirm of Nature and of Truth,
> Whom I have served, that their DIVINITY
> Revolts, offended at the waves of men...
>
> (lines 982-85)

What is God if not truth and divinity, the one coupled with the other? And Wordsworth discovered both truth and divinity in nature.

Even if we call Wordsworth's devotion to nature his religion, we should not equate his religion with what we generally mean by the term 'religion,' because the essence of his religion did not require surrendering one's self to the mercy of the Almighty, but in seeking purity of heart, normalcy or naturalness of behaviour, and moral consciousness—all that can grow and develop only in the lap of nature. Among these three objects to be sought by a religious man, Wordsworth laid emphasis on the last one: moral consciousness. Morality, Wordsworth believed, was to be sought in nature, where there is (genuine and pure) love and self-abnegation, and beauty, because moral sense originates in the complex relationship of these three elements, and because these three elements are available only in nature. We may perhaps better understand why Wordsworth urges upon us to learn morality from the great teacher that is nature if we recall what Shelley has written about the "great secret of morals' in his *A Defence of Poetry:* "The great secret of morals is love; or a going out of our own nature, and an identification of ourselves with the beautiful which exists in thought, action, or person, not our own. A man, to be greatly good, must imagine intensely and comprehensively; he must put himself in the place of another and of many others; the pains and pleasures of his species must become his own. The great instrument of moral good is the imagination; and poetry administers to the effect by acting upon the cause.... Poetry strengthens the faculty which is the organ of the moral nature of man, in the same manner as exercise strengthens a limb" Now, all the prerequisites of the moral sense, enumerated by Shelley in the above extract, can be met with, according to Wordsworth, in the ambience of nature, and not in the hurried, selfish, ugly, and matter-of-fact life of the city. Poetry, Shelley says, enhances and fortifies our moral sense, as also does our sense of beauty, and Wordsworth says that both our sense of poetry and our sense of beauty we may derive only from our love of nature and from our affinity with her. Such an explanation of how nature can instruct us regarding moral sense may not fully satisfy us, and so let us turn to *Tintern Abbey* where Wordsworth has a clearer explanation. Graham Hough has very succinctly expressed Wordsworth's arguments for the belief that nature has the power of instructing us in the sense of morality. Referring to *Tintern Abbey*, Hough writes: "Wordsworth first relates his moral doctrine: the memory of this beautiful scene has been not only calming and restorative, but has aroused almost unnoticed sensations of pleasure, which have had their results in impulses of kindness and love. This seems truer and more adequate than saying that a wood in spring can teach you all about ethics" (Hough, 50).

Wordsworth said that he wanted to be a teacher, or nothing else: he wanted to be a teacher of morality. What he did exactly meant by morality is perhaps not very clear to us, but he probably meant by morality purity of mind, fellow-feeling, sympathy for all objects of the creation, and realization of the spirit of nature, which is the foundation of all other elements of morality. He saw the prevalence of morality in the whole of the creation. In Bk III of *The Prelude* (lines 127-32), he writes:

> To every natural form, rock, fruit, or flower,
> Even the loose stones that cover the high-way,
> I gave a moral life: I saw them feel,
> Or linked them to some feeling: the great mass
> Lay bedded in a quickening soul, and all
> That I beheld respired with inward meaning.

Here it is clear that Wordsworth's conception of morality is at variance with our general conception of it, and also far more wider in scope than it, and also it is clear that Wordsworth is always at pains to link morality with nature, in the widest sense of the term 'nature.' A.C. Bradley says that Wordsworth's conception of morality may be equated with the goodness that the poet finds in nature: "Wordsworth's morality is of one piece with his optimism and with his determination to seize and exhibit in everything the element of good." Nature is good, to Wordsworth, and, therefore, nature is moral. It is for this reason that some critics hold that Wordsworth's conception of morality is narrow and extremely puritanical. But A.C. Bradley exonerates Wordsworth of this accusation and rather extols his moral theory: "Nor is his [Wordsworth's] morality narrow. It is serious, but it is human and kindly and not in the least ascetic.... There is no want of sympathy in Wordsworth's own picture of the 'convivial exaltation' of his Waggoner...and that his treatment of sexual passion is always grave and, in a true sense moral, but it is plain and manly and perfectly free from timidity or monkishness" (Bradley, 121-22). H.W., Garrod says that Wordsworth's morality has a twofold implication: inspiration (for an elevated sense of value, and poetic view of life and the world) that is to be got from our childhood experiences in the lap of nature, and a sense of obligation to fellow beings. Garrod writes: "I doubt whether Wordsworth, in his best period, ever abandoned the doctrine that the highest moral achievement is that which presents itself as an inspiration, that which is part of our natural life, that which is bound up with the childhood and its unthinking 'vision.' Duty is a second-best; we seek support from that power when higher and free powers fail us. The purer moral life is that which binds together our days that the vision of childhood suffices to later years" (Garrod, 124). In any case, therefore, according to Wordsworth, childhood experiences are the fountain head of our moral perceptions; but not only childhood experiences, but the childhood experiences must be donated by nature—nature, the supreme source of morality, and the best instructor in the science or philosophy of morality.

The question of an object's having the sense of morality can arise only when we must admit that that object is a living being, and that that object has got consciousness. How then in Wordsworth's system of philosophy are we going to believe that the rocks, the spring in the 'ghyll,' the trees, etc. have moral sense, or a conglomeration of them all? To answer this question we must first take into account the fact that Wordsworth believed in some sort of hylozoism, the philosophical theory according to which even material objects have life (*hyle*, meaning matter;

and *zoe*, meaning life). Nay, he went even further than this, and said that all the objects of the creation are in fundamentals spiritual, that the different objects of nature are but different forms or manifestations of the all-pervading primal and irreducible spirit, which he sometimes designates as 'presences' or as 'active Principle.' This belief of his Wordsworth has graphically described in Bk IX (lines 1-15) of *The Excursion*:

> 'To every Form of being is assigned,'
> Thus calmly spake the venerable Sage,
> 'An *active* Principle—however removed
> From sense and observation, it subsists
> In all things, in all natures: in the stars
> Of azure heaven, the unending clouds,
> In flowers and tree, in every pebble stone
> That paves the brooks, the stationary rocks,
> The moving waters, and the visible air.
> Whatever exists hath properties that spread
> Beyond itself, communicating good,
> A simple blessing, or with evil mixed;
> Spirit that knows no insulated spot,
> No chasm, no solitude; from link to link,
> It circulates, the Soul of all the worlds.

All this is Spinozistic. Benedictus or Baruch Spinoza (1632-77) believed that God comprised everything of the creation, and manifests Himself through them. If we replace the concept of God from Spinoza's system of philosophy by Wordsworth's concept of the all-pervading spirit (the spirit is, Wordsworth says, in nature, but he also says that it is everywhere), Wordsworth becomes an alter ego of Spinoza. But Wordsworth differs from Spinoza on the question of the status of the sensible world as against the spirituality expressed through it; and also on the question of the comprehensibility of the ultimate reality of which the whole creation is the manifestation. Spinoza believed that the ultimate reality can be grasped only with the help of rationality, and that if we could comprehend it, we could realize that spirituality (or mind, or consciousness) existed parallely with the sensible world. He said that none of the two—the sensible world and the spiritual world—is superior to, or predominant over, the other, and that the two together constitute the whole that is God. To Wordsworth, on the other hand, the thing is otherwise. He says that as the spiritual world manifests itself through the sensible world, the more appropriate means (or, rather, the only means) of comprehending the spiritual world will not be ratiocination, but feeling or sensation. Wordsworth further says that even when we have realised the spirituality behind the material world, the latter will remain the same to our ordinary perception. The hill, for instance, will remain, to our ordinary perception, the same hill after we have comprehended, through our sensation and feeling (or, rather, through intuition), that the hill is in reality a limited manifestation of the all-pervading spirit or 'Presence.' Therefore, to Wordsworth, there is actually no difference between the sensible world and the spiritual world. But when we have comprehended the spirituality behind the materiality of the object, we have certainly more fully comprehended the object. This is clear from what A.C. Bradley writes about Wordsworth's conception of the spiritual world as enveloped by the material world: "This 'spiritual world' is itself the sensible world more fully apprehended: the daffodils do not change or lose their colour in disclosing their glee" (Bradley, 131). Wordsworth's all-pervading spirit may also be compared with the existentialist philosopher Karl Jasper's ultimate, primordial and all-pervading spiritual being whom he calls the Encompassing.

As according to Wordsworth each and every form of the beings of the creation is invested with spirituality, he should have been equally interested in, and attracted by, all forms of the beings of the creation, but, in fact, he was especially attracted by certain special forms of beings, or things. For instance, he was especially attracted by the beauty of hills, dales, flowers, birds, clouds and stars. Wordsworth was inordinately drawn to the beauty of flowers and plants, and has stuffed his verses with praises for them, so much so that some critics have even expressed their resentment at this. Helen Darbishire writes that Wordsworth "had a fondness for flowers and plants which has enraged some of his critics, from Clough onwards" (Darbishire, 167). Wordsworth was also delighted by some particular sounds. W.L. Renwick writes about his sensitivity to some sounds, especially those that are available in nature: "He was indeed extremely sensitive to sound, delighted in 'the sounding cataract,' in echoes, and bird-song and the noises of the wind and water, and—the ultimate test—in silence and the delicate indefinable sounds that thread the silences" (Renwick, 166). His delight in sounds continued to remain with him till very advanced age of his, if not till his last. This is evidenced by the fact that at the age of fifty-eight, he wrote his poem *The Power of Sound.* In *Power of Music* (1806), he describes how people from all walks of life gather to listen to the music produced by a young blind musician, and praises him:

> O blest are the hearers, and proud be the hand
> Of the pleasure it spreads through so thankful a band;
> I am glad for him, blind as he is!—all the while
> If they speak 'tis to praise, and they praise with a smile.

Herbert J.C. Grierson and J.C. Smith say that Wordsworth certainly loved beasts, birds, winds, and their sounds, but he could not enjoy instrumental music, and that Wordsworth's three sense-organs—those of smell, taste, and touch—were weak: "He had a keen ear (too) for all natural sounds, the calls of beasts and birds, and the sounds of winds and waters: the 'soughing' of boughs in a high wind set his mind working, and he composed thousands of lines wandering by the side of a stream. On the other hand he had no ear for music, at least for instrumental music; he had practically no sense of smell at all; and compared with a poet like Keats he was poorly endowed in the intellectual sense of touch, taste, and temperature. 'Fragrant,' 'smooth,' 'luscious,' 'warm'—these are no epithets for Wordsworth's world. It is an austere world; it is almost bleak—

> The bare trees and mountain bare."

(Grierson and Smith, 322)

Therefore, we may conclude, Wordsworth's perception of the beauty of nature was—how much so ever he may have been delighted by her beauty—partial, limited. Wordsworth, nevertheless, loved so many objects of nature, but, according to Gilbert Highet, he was the most attracted by the spectacles of mountains. Highet says that Wordsworth loved mountains so much, and wrote about them so much that he should rather be called the poet of mountains, or the mountain poet: "We think of William Wordsworth as an observer of nature and of natural man. The mountains which ennobled his boyhood and strengthened his manhood (it is inadequate to call him a 'Lake poet': he was a Mountain poet; there have been very few, and he was the greatest), the mountains which in physical nature were the counterpart of the lofty spiritual ideals by which he lived; the lakes in which he swam and on which he skated and rowed (always surrounded by the dominating mountains), the lakes which symbolized the soft gracious influence of his sister and his wife; the trees and flowers, the fields, the men and women who worked the land and wandered over it, that visible proof of the world's divinity,

> the infinite magnificence of heavens;

his own enraptured soul that saw the best and truest in all these; and the great spirit which pervades them and is their life—these made his poetry" (Highet, 408).

Herbert J.C. Grierson and J.C. Smith, as we have heard from them, have pointed out the deficiency in Wordsworth's three sense-organs: those of smell, taste and touch. But the deficiency was well made up with two other sense-organs—the eye and the ear, which are more important than the other three, in enjoying almost all that are in store in nature. The same Grierson and Smith, who complained of the deficiency of the three sense-organs in Wordsworth, themselves describe how Wordsworth's eye could make up most of that deficiency: "His eye, though not exceptionally quick, was at once far-seeing and penetrating; he looked through the visible scene to what he calls its 'ideal truth,' pouring over objects till he fastened their images on his brain, and brooding on these in memory till they acquired the liveliness of dreams; dwelling especially on the larger features of the scene, the mountain and the deep and gloomy wood, the clouds, the sky; enraptured above all by sunrise and sunset—it was in the sweetness of a summer dawn that he first knew himself a dedicated spirit, and his last glimpse of the celestial light that had once apparelled the earth came to him on an evening of extraordinary splendour and beauty" (Grierson and Smith, 322). Wordsworth's ear also made up some of the deficiency in the three other sense-organs of his. The chirping of birds, the music of the eddying spring, the shooing of the wind, and such other sounds of nature delighted him. He was more attracted by solo sounds than by choric; more drawn by a sound against the backdrop of a profound silence, than by a sound in a cacophony. In *To the Cuckoo*, he is delighted by the warbling of a single cuckoo 'captive' mid damp vaults unsunned':

Not the whole warbling grove in concert heard
When sunshine follows shower, the breast can thrill
Like the first summons, Cuckoo! of thy bill,
With its twin notes inseparably paired.

Again in *The Solitary Reaper*, he is infatuated by the solo song of a single girl:

Behold her, single in the field,
Yon solitary Highland Lass!
Reaping and singing by herself;
....
O listen! for the Vale profound
Is overflowing with the sound.

Wordsworth is generally known as the poet of nature, but this appellation is partial, for he had two other principal themes (or concerns) for his poetry—man and God. He was very much concerned about the original nature of man, about the ideal man on the one hand, and about the decadence of man, on the other. His concern about man is clear to us when we hear him mourn for the decadence of man in *The Prelude* (Bk XIII, lines 87-89):

Why is this glorious creature to be found
Only one in ten thousand? What one is,
Why not millions be?

But Wordsworth was not so much interested in man, in his very early years, as he was in nature. He confesses that his love for, and reverence of, man grew in him, early in his life, only when he saw man against the backdrop of nature, or in the ambience of nature. Therefore, he was first a lover of nature, and then, through his love of nature, he became a lover of man as well. In *The Prelude* (Bk VIII lines 256-81), Wordsworth graphically describes this mental development of his:

A rambling schoolboy, thus
I felt his presence in his own domain,
As of a lord and master, or a power,
Or genius, under Nature, under God,
Presiding; and severest solitude
Had more commanding looks when he was there

> When up the lonely brooks on rainy days
> Angling I went, or trod the trackless hills
> By mists bewildered, suddenly mine eyes
> Have glanced upon him distant a few steps,
> In size a giant, stalking through thick fog,
> His sheep like Greenland bears; or as he stepped
> Beyond the boundary line of some hill-shadow,
> His form hath flashed upon me, glorified
> By the deep radiance of the setting sun:
> Or him have I descried in distant sky,
> A solitary object and sublime,
> Above all height! like an aerial cross
> Stationed alone upon a spiry rock
> Of the Chartreuse, for worship. Thus was man
> Ennobled outwardly before my sight,
> And thus my heart was early introduced
> To an unconscious love and reverence
> Of human nature; hence the human form
> To me became an index of delight,
> Of grace and honour, power and worthiness.

Herbert J.C. Grierson and J.C. Smith say the same thing—that Wordsworth came to love, revere, wonder at, and delight in, man only when he saw man as a part of nature: "We think of Wordsworth first as a poet of Nature, and rightly; for though the Concordance shows that Nature was less often his theme than Man, it is by his poetry of Nature that he is unique, and it was the love of Nature, he tells us, that led him to the love of Man. Indeed what he loved and revered in men were the things most akin to great natural forces, their primitive unreasoned instincts" (Grierson and Smith, 322).

Wordsworth's preference for, and love of, nature over against everything else, is connected with his childhood, or, rather, with the memories of his childhood, when with his primal instincts he imbibed the beauty, mixed with fear, of nature, and was surfeited. He believed that the purest experience of nature is possible only during our childhood when our perception is not yet adulterated with our rationality; when, also, our passion is pure, and not controlled, or, rather, hampered with our reason—reason, that diverts us from our enjoyment of natural passions towards our sense of duty or obligation to our fellow beings.

Reason, Wordsworth believed, is pragmatic, worldly; but our childhood perception and sensibilities are spiritual, heavenly, visionary. It is for this reason that he called the child a 'prophet.' In our childhood experiences of nature, we 'half-unconsciously come across the truth of life, through the beauty and terror that nature presents before us, and this truth of life is the authenticity of morality and goodness. But as we grow up, we are adulterated by the corruptions of the society, and are overburdened with the artificial sanctions and compulsions of the society, and thus we lose the joy and elevated existence of our childhood. H.W. Garrod writes: "On the side, then, of Nature, Wordsworth finds the highest and deepest truth in the pure report of the senses, unspoiled by reason; on the side of morality, he finds the highest virtue in a natural goodness unspoiled by the calculations of Duty" (Garrod, 125). As we grow up, our natural goodness, natural virtue, and natural morality or piety is replaced by our artificial sense of duty (perhaps born out of artificial social sanctions). It is for this reason that Wordsworth so much extols our childhood. He says that we can comprehend truth and goodness in nature, in our childhood, as we then see the pure and passionate beauty of nature, and that only those adults, whose childhood memories are not yet blurred by the 'eternal whirls of trivial things' of the 'busy world,' can appropriately appreciate the beauty of nature (and can sustain his inborn poetic faculty), and can understand the truth and goodness of life.

Wordsworth said, more than once, that he wanted to be a teacher, or nothing else. But what sort of teacher did he want to be, and what actually did he want to teach people? He wanted to teach men the truth that our soul can have its normal growth, without being tainted by the adulterations of the adult life, only in the ambience of nature. He wanted to teach people that it is civilization, the life of the busy city, that imposes upon us the concern about our duties—pressing obligations—and thereby rob us of our childhood pure, delightful, and heavenly sensibiliies; and that in the course of our growing up as adults, we are doomed to get corrupted; and also that if, even in our adult life, we can keep alive our childhood memories—our experiences of nature—we can continue to live with our pure sensibilities, and with our sense of morality, of goodness, and of beauty; in short, we can be wise and visionary, as we had been in our childhood. He wanted to teach men that nature is the greatest teacher of mankind, and this he says in the following four lines of his poem *The Tables Turned* (lines 21-24):

> One impulse from the vernal wood
> May teach you more of man,
> Of moral evil and of good,
> Than all the sages can.

Is there any psychological etiology behind Wordsworth's almost fanatic, frantic love of nature? Many guesses may be made, but we can never be sure of any. One guess-work is that losing his mother at a very early age, Wordsworth, since his early age and throughout his old age, had been suffering from a sense of isolation and dejection, and so always strived to seek solace in the soothing refuge of nature. William Hazlitt has another way of explaining why, relinquishing every other thing behind, Wordsworth sought the refuge of nature: "Prevented by native pride and indolence from climbing the ascent of learning or greatness, taught by political opinions to say to the vain pomp and glory of the world 'I hate you,' seeing the path of classical artificial poetry blocked up by cumbrous ornaments of style and turgid *commonplaces*, so that nothing more could be achieved in that direction but by the most ridiculous bombast or the tamest servility; he has turned back partly from the bias of his mind, partly perhaps from a judicious policy—has struck into the sequestered vale of humble life, sought out the Muse among sheep-cots and hamlets and the peasant's mountain-haunts, has discarded all the tinsel pageantry of verse, and endeavoured (not in vain) to aggrandise the trivial and add the charm of novelty to the familiar" (Hazlitt, 254). Wordsworth took refuge in nature, never to come out of it, and he thought he got what he wanted to get from life, from nature, and so he was so much indebted to nature. He said that he owed everything to nature—his moral sense, his philosophy, his joy, and even his poetry. But Oscar Wilde would not so much agree with Wordsworth: according to Wilde, Wordsworth was too much adulatory towards nature, at the least when he says that he owes his poetry to nature. Wilde writes: "'One touch of Nature may make the whole world kin, but two touches of Nature will destroy any work of art. If, on the other hand, we regard Nature as the collection of phenomena external to man, people only discover in her what they bring to her. She has no suggestions of her own. Wordsworth went to the lakes, but he was never a lake poet. He found in stones the sermons he had already hidden there. He went moralising about the district, but his good work was produced when he returned, not to Nature but to poetry. Poetry gave him 'Laodamia,' and his fine sonnets, and the great Ode, such as it is. Nature gave him 'Martha Ray' and 'Peter Bell,' and the address to Mr. Wilkinson's spade" (Wimsatt and Brooks, 361).

Wordsworth's deep love of nature, interestingly, may be seen in some of his rare instances where in deep deference to nature he even stood against the propagation of science. F.W. Bateson writes: "When it was proposed to extend the railway line from Kendal to Winderemere he resisted the proposal with all the eloquence he could then command (1844) in both verse and prose. But to the advocates of the extension who pointed out that the new railway would now enable the poor to enjoy the scenary of the Lake District he could only reply (in a letter to the *Morning Post*); 'Rocks and mountains, torrents and wide spread waters, and all those features of nature which go to the composition of such scenes as this part of England is distinguished for, cannot, in their finer relations to the human mind, be comprehended, or even very imperfectly conceived, without processes of culture or opportunities of observation in some degree habitual. The admission, however, is fatal to a central thesis of *The Prelude*—that the basis of the good life is *unconscious* intercourse with natural beauty'" (Bateson, 177). Wordsworth loved nature to an extent blindly, for the terrifying and violent aspect of nature was not as obvious to him as its beautiful and soothing aspect. His view of nature was partial. Nature is generally beautiful, calm and soothing, but sometimes she is also violent, ugly, insensate, and unsympathetic to us. But in Wordsworth's poetry we rarely come across the negative aspects of nature, for instances, in *Eliziac Stanzas, suggested by a Picture of Peele Castle, in a Storm, painted by Sir George Beaumont,* and in *Ruth*. In the former poem, the poet sees "This sea in anger, and that dismal shore," and also—

> That Hulk which labours in the deadly swell,
> This rueful sky, this pageantry of fear!

And this huge Castle, standing here sublime,
I love to see the look with which it braves,
Cased in the unfeeling armour of old time,
The lightning, the fierce wind, and trampling waves.

And in *Ruth* we find these two lines:

The wind, the tempest roaring high,
The tumult of a tropic sky,....

But, according to Wordsworth, these are only uncommon and unnatural aspects or manifestations of nature. Nature is basically mild, soothing, and sympathetic to man. Nature acts as a balm to our hurt hearts, and is salubrious to our body and mind. This is why, in *The Excursion* (Bk VI. lines 167-75), the Pastor or Vicar advises the moribund Solitary thus:

'Go to the hills,' said one, 'remit a while
This baneful diligence:—at early morn
Court the fresh air, explore the heaths and woods;
And, leaving it to others to foretell,
By calculatious sage, the ebb and flow
Of tides, and when the moon will be eclipsed,
Do you, for your own benefit, construct
A calendar of flowers, plucked as they blow
Where heath abides, and cheerfulness, and peace.

But, Wordsworth is dejected because man's love for nature is gone, gone for ever, and so he feels nostalgic for the bygone bucolic surrounds of human kind. He expresses his nostalgia, in *The Excursion* (Bk VIII. lines 82-87), through the following words of the Wanderer:

'Happy,' rejoined the Wanderer, 'they who gain
A panegyric from your generous tongue!
But, if to these Wayfarers once pertained
Aught of romantic interest, it is gone
Their purer service, in this realm at least,
Is past for ever....

The bucolic and pastoral romanticism of nature 'Is past for ever' because of the intrusion of science, because of the dawning of 'An inventive Age.' To Wordsworth, science may be necessary, 'as props for our infirmities' but it is, nevertheless evil, because it is only practical, and mundane. Man cannot be happy with mundanity, for he always aspires after some sort of sublimity, consciously or unconsciously,—the sublimity that manifests itself through beauty, truth, and goodness, all of which only nature can show us, in their celestial purity. But as the sublimity that is there in nature is not mundane, and so beyond the ken of science or rationality, it is mysterious, and so it can be comprehended only intuitively, only, as Wordsworth tells us, through our unadulterated sense-organs that continue to keep up the childhood freshness, though we may be advanced in years.

To conclude this chapter, both Wordsworth and Emerson loved and revered nature more than anything else, in spite of the fact that their views of nature were not identical. Both of them, we repeat, revered nature: we have for long seen Wordsworth worshipping nature, and now let us hear how Emerson urges upon us to worship nature: "Let us not longer omit our homage to the Efficient Nature, *natura naturans*, the quick cause before which all forms flee as the driven snows" (Emerson, 247). However, at some point, the two sages are so similar that if the following lines, that Emerson wrote in his essay 'Nature', were written by Wordsworth, we would not be astonished: "Nature is loved by what is best in us. It is loved as the city of God, although, or rather because there is no citizen. The sunset is unlike anything that is underneath it: it wants men. And the beauty of nature must always seem unreal and mocking, until the landscape has human figures that are as good as itself. If there were good men, there would never be this rapture in nature" (Emerson, 247).